C-371
G
27
G

TEACHER'S MANUAL

EXPLORING CAREERS

THIRD EDITION

Joan Kelly-Plate
Career Educator
Lake Suzy, Florida

Ruth Volz-Patton
Career Consultant
Springfield, Illinois

Glencoe
McGraw-Hill

New York, New York   Columbus,   Peoria, Illinois

Glencoe/McGraw-Hill

A Division of The **McGraw·Hill** *Companies*

Printed in the United States of America

Send all inquiries to:
Glencoe/McGraw-Hill
21600 Oxnard Street, Suite 500
Woodland Hills, CA 91367

ISBN 0-02-643183-1 (Student Text)
ISBN 0-02-642593-9 (Teacher's Annotated Edition)

1 2 3 4 5 6 7 8 9   027   05 04 03 02 01 00 99 98

Table of Contents

Welcome to *Exploring Careers!*

Can you remember being asked when you were a student, "What do you want to do with your life? What do you dream of becoming?" Did you know? Did you always want to be a teacher? For most students these are challenging questions. However, the reality is, almost every student will have to choose a career someday. No matter what kind of career a student chooses, he or she must be prepared for the world of work.

Exploring Careers introduces students to the world of work. It gives students the opportunity to explore the various career areas that exist and introduces them to the realities involved with the workplace.

The text prepares students for the rapidly changing nature of the workplace. It emphasizes the skills outlined in SCANS (the Secretary's Commission on Achieving Necessary Skills) as being those necessary for workplace success.

A bright design with attractive visuals, clear type, and an easy-to-read style invites students of all backgrounds and abilities to explore the content.

Exploring Each Chapter

Exploring Careers is divided into three units. Each unit focuses student attention on three specific areas: Career Exploration, Employment Skills, and Lifelong Learning. Within each unit there are four to six chapters.

A Friends and Family Activity provides an opportunity for students to extend their investigation of the chapter topic at home and with friends.

The opening pages of each chapter tell students what they will learn.

Bright photographs, clear organization, and easy-to-read type draw students into the content of each chapter.

Exploring Each Lesson

Each chapter of Exploring Careers is divided into two or three lessons. Each lesson introduces chapter material in manageable segments.

> Discover lists the objectives students will cover in the lesson.

> Key Terms are listed in the side column at the beginning of the lesson. They are also in boldface type as they are introduced with the text and are accompanied by clear, in-context definitions.

LESSON ● 2-1

What Is Work All About?

Discover . . .
- why people work.
- how work affects people's lives.

Why Explore the World of Work?
You'll probably spend part of your life working. You'll want to choose work that is right for you. That will be easier to do if you understand why people work and how work can affect your life.

Key Terms . . .
- job
- career
- full-time
- lifestyle

Think about your world—your everyday world. Where do you go? What do you do? Who are the people in your life? You probably spend a lot of time at home and in school. The people around you are mostly family and friends. Your days are full. You have classes and homework. Maybe you take part in after-school activities.

This is the world you know—today. One day, though, your world will be different. Work will be part of your life.

What Is Work?

That's a good question. A quick, easy answer is that work is what people do to earn money. **Figure 2-1** shows that people need money to pay for their needs and wants. Money is not the whole story, though.

➤ You're with all kinds of people at school each day. Where do you think you'll meet people when you've finished school?

24   Chapter 2 Thinking About Work

> Full-color photographs, illustrations, charts, and graphs bring chapter concepts to life. Each illustration is accompanied by a teaching caption that reinforces lesson content.

LESSON 2-2 ● REVIEW AND ACTIVITIES

LESSON REVIEW AND ACTIVITIES. See the *Teacher's Manual* for answers.

Vocabulary Review
Write a speech about the changing world of work, using all the key terms for this lesson. Read your speech to the class.

economy   global economy
goods   job market
services   workplace

Check Your Understanding
Choose the correct answer for each item below. Write your answers on a separate sheet of paper.
1. Three changes that will affect future careers include _____.
   a. legal, technological, and ethical changes
   b. technological, global, mentor, and social changes
   c. global, technological, and social changes

2. The global economy is _____.
   a. the way the world environment changes the economy
   b. the way the world's economies are linked and managed
   c. the way we manage our world currency

Critical Thinking
On a separate sheet of paper, answer the following questions.
1. What careers interest you? How do you think technology has changed work in one of those careers?
2. In what ways do you think people of different backgrounds are changing the workplace?
3. Which of the following do you think has changed work the most: teams, outsourcing, or telecommuting? Explain your answer.

Connecting to the Workplace
Technology in the Workplace
- In a newspaper, look at the classified ads for jobs. Focus on jobs that interest you.
- Find ads for five jobs that call for knowledge of or experience with technology.
- Look for mention of computers, software, lasers, or robotics, for example.
- Clip, photocopy, or hand copy the ads.
- With the rest of the class, make a bulletin board display of jobs using technology.

Teamwork
What to Do   ● In a small group, select a career from the agribusiness and natural resources cluster. Look at "Investigating Career Clusters" on page 37 for ideas.
- Use library resources or the Internet to find out how work in that career is changing.
- Prepare a documentary or factual presentation about the career. Tell about the career and how change will affect it. Make visuals such as charts and graphs to show information.

36   Lesson 2-2 Review

> The Lesson Review and Activities page provides review questions and activities to guide students in reviewing the major concepts developed in the lesson.

Have Fun with Feature Activities

High-interest features in each chapter engage students, enhance their understanding, and expand their involvement with real-world situations.

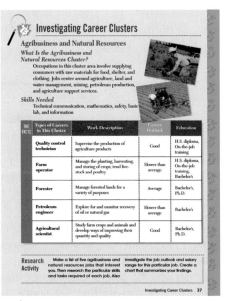

Investigating Career Clusters

Agribusiness and Natural Resources

What Is the Agribusiness and Natural Resources Cluster?
Occupations in this cluster area involve supplying consumers with raw materials for food, shelter, and clothing. Jobs center around agriculture, land and water management, mining, petroleum production, and agriculture support services.

Skills Needed
Technical communication, mathematics, safety, basic lab, and information

THE FACTS	Types of Careers in This Cluster	Work Description	Career Outlook	Education
	Quality control technician	Supervise the production of agriculture products	Good	H.S. diploma, On-the-job training
	Farm operator	Manage the planting, harvesting, and storing of crops; tend livestock and poultry	Slower than average	H.S. diploma, On-the-job training, Bachelor's
	Forester	Manage forested lands for a variety of purposes	Average	Bachelor's, Ph.D.
	Petroleum engineer	Explore for and monitor recovery of oil or natural gas	Slower than average	Bachelor's
	Agricultural scientist	Study farm crops and animals and develop ways of improving their quantity and quality	Good	Bachelor's, Ph.D.

Research Activity
Make a list of five agribusiness and natural resources jobs that interest you. Then research the particular skills and tasks required of each job. Also investigate the job outlook and salary range for this particular job. Create a chart that summarizes your findings.

Investigating Career Clusters 37

The Right Attitude provides tips for building a positive attitude.

The RIGHT Attitude!

Attitude Counts

Success depends on more than hard work. In the recipe for success, in both career and life, attitude is an essential ingredient. You can start cultivating a positive attitude today. What are some positive attitude skills? Enthusiasm, asserting yourself, managing stressful situations, flexibility, self-esteem, and treating people with respect all play a part.

Apply Your Skills!
    Brainstorm with a partner, a list of qualities that show a positive attitude. Come up with five or six qualities and share your list with the class. Make a list on the board of all the qualities chosen and pick 10. Write them out on a large sheet of construction paper, and post them in your classroom.

Career Q & A answers questions about exploring careers that might come to mind as students read the text.

CAREER Q&A

Finding Out More About a Job

Q: What if I have the skills and aptitudes for a job, but I'm still not sure that I'll like it?

A: Talk to people who work in the job that interests you. Find out what they like about their job. What are the working conditions like? The people who actually work in the jobs that interest you can give you the best idea as to whether you might like the job yourself.

Investigating Career Clusters offers information on one of the fifteen career clusters, or areas. The research activity at the end of the feature will help students think about how the career cluster relates to them.

The Global Workplace identifies work-related cultural differences to prepare students for the global workplace they will enter one day.

The Global Workplace

Business Cards Are An Essential Tool
    Common business practice requires the exchange of business cards. With a card, an associate can remember your company's name and your job title and can contact you. In most of Southeast Asia, Africa, and the Middle East, it is considered rude to present a card with your left hand. In Japan, present cards with both hands. Make sure the words face the recipient and are right side up.

Exploration Activity!
    Research business cards. What kind of information is listed on business cards? What do they look like? Make up a business card for a job you would like to have.

Career Opportunities gives a short newspaper-ad description of a job in a particular career cluster, or area. It concludes with a critical thinking question to challenge students' minds.

CAREER OPPORTUNITIES

Communications and Media
    If you love working with computers and surfing the 'net, check out this job in communications.

Critical Thinking
    Why would communication skills be important for this job?

CLASSIFIED

THURSDAY

Webmaster
Clothing store needs a webmaster to build a Web site and create an online catalog of its merchandise. Requirements: fluency in HTML, a working knowledge of Photoshop and Java, and excellent communication skills. Ability to play a leadership role essential.

Reinforcing Chapter Concepts

Each chapter ends with a two-page review designed to help students recall, use, and expand on the concepts presented in the chapter.

Chapter Highlights lists the main points discussed within the chapter.

Thinking Critically asks students to use their higher-level thinking skills as they consider the basic concepts of the text.

Recalling Key Concepts helps students review and recall the main topics in the chapter.

Applying Academic Skills encourages students to connect academic skills to real-life work scenarios.

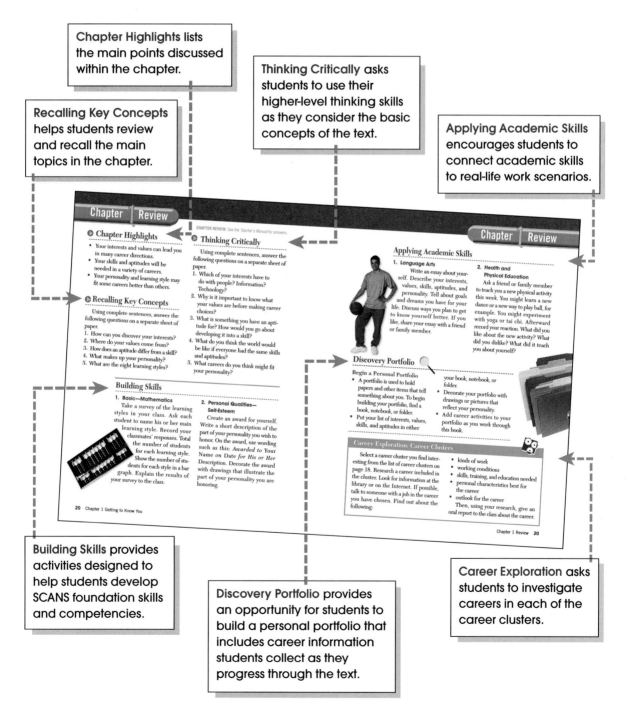

Building Skills provides activities designed to help students develop SCANS foundation skills and competencies.

Discovery Portfolio provides an opportunity for students to build a personal portfolio that includes career information students collect as they progress through the text.

Career Exploration asks students to investigate careers in each of the career clusters.

Teaching Strategies Designed to Meet Your Classroom Needs

The *Teacher's Annotated Edition* of *Exploring Careers* helps you motivate and involve your students in career exploration. Teaching suggestions and ideas within the *Teacher's Annotated Edition* will assist you in reaching students of all levels of ability and backgrounds and will make the course more rewarding for you—and for your students.

Using the Four-Step Teaching Plan

Exploring Careers and its *Teacher's Annotated Edition* makes full and effective use of a mastery approach in four steps: focus, teach, assess, and close. This widely accepted instructional method develops students' understanding of subject matter while providing a consistent framework that makes it easy for you to teach the material.

Step 1: Focus

As a teacher, you know that the first step in presenting new material is to capture students' interest. The *Teacher's Annotated Edition* suggests a variety of interesting motivational activities to focus students' interest.

Step 2: Teach

The second step in the instructional process contains the presentation and exploration of new material. The *Teacher's Annotated Edition* of *Exploring Careers* presents a teaching plan designed to give you maximum flexibility in meeting the needs of your class. The variety of approaches, strategies, and activities allows you to help all students assimilate the content of each chapter.

Step 3: Assess

This third step involves an assessment of students' learning. The Assess lesson of the *Teacher's Annotated Edition* provides a variety of evaluation and reteaching activities designed to accommodate a wide range of learning abilities.

Step 4: Close

The final step of the instructional process provides an opportunity for students to look back over the new material presented in the lesson. Students summarize what they have learned, evaluate their own learning processes, and view the relevance of the new material to their own lives.

Using the Chapter Planning Guide

To help you select activities that will best meet the needs of your students, the *Teacher's Annotated Edition* includes a two-page Planning Guide at the beginning of each chapter's lesson activities in the Teacher's Manual.

Lesson Objectives lists the performance-based objectives for each lesson of the chapter.

Lesson and Chapter Resources provides information on the various support materials available to you and your students.

SCANS Correlation Chart shows the specific SCANS foundation skills and workplace competencies that students develop as they work in that chapter.

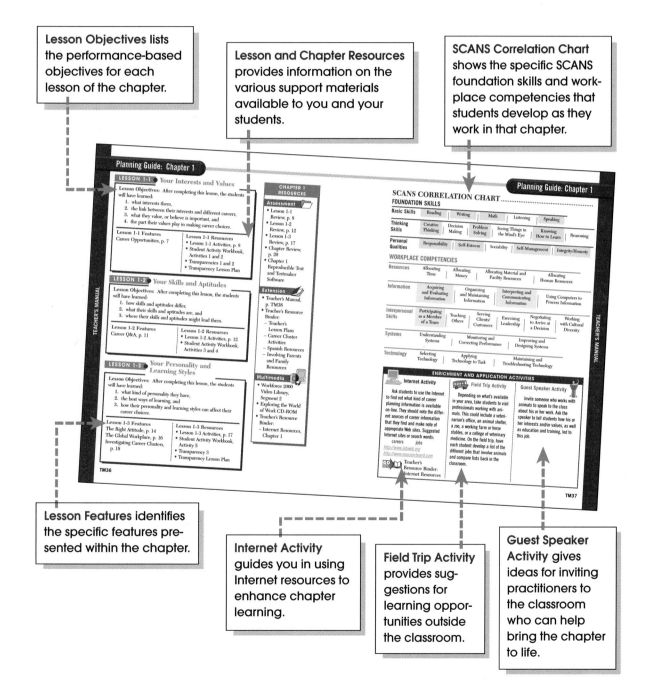

Lesson Features identifies the specific features presented within the chapter.

Internet Activity guides you in using Internet resources to enhance chapter learning.

Field Trip Activity provides suggestions for learning opportunities outside the classroom.

Guest Speaker Activity gives ideas for inviting practitioners to the classroom who can help bring the chapter to life.

Teaching Each Chapter

The *Teacher's Annotated Edition* provides teaching suggestions both at the beginning of the text and within each chapter. These suggestions guide you in introducing and reviewing the chapter in ways suited to your students' needs.

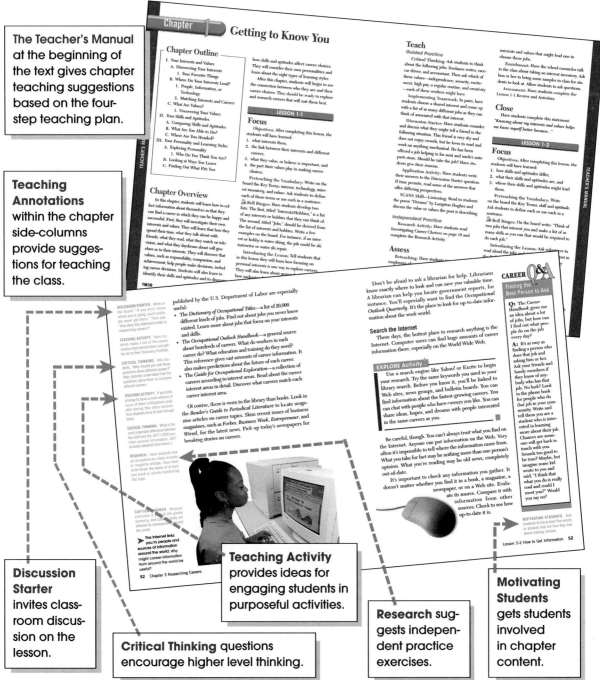

The Teacher's Manual at the beginning of the text gives chapter teaching suggestions based on the four-step teaching plan.

Teaching Annotations within the chapter side-columns provide suggestions for teaching the class.

Discussion Starter invites classroom discussion on the lesson.

Critical Thinking questions encourage higher level thinking.

Teaching Activity provides ideas for engaging students in purposeful activities.

Research suggests independent practice exercises.

Motivating Students gets students involved in chapter content.

Classroom Resources Help You Meet Every Teaching Challenge

The Exploring Careers program offers a complete selection of teacher support materials. Used in conjunction with the Teacher's Annotated Edition, these materials will enable you to tailor the program to meet the specific needs of your classes. The program resources are specially developed to support you in meeting your course objectives and in maximizing student learning.

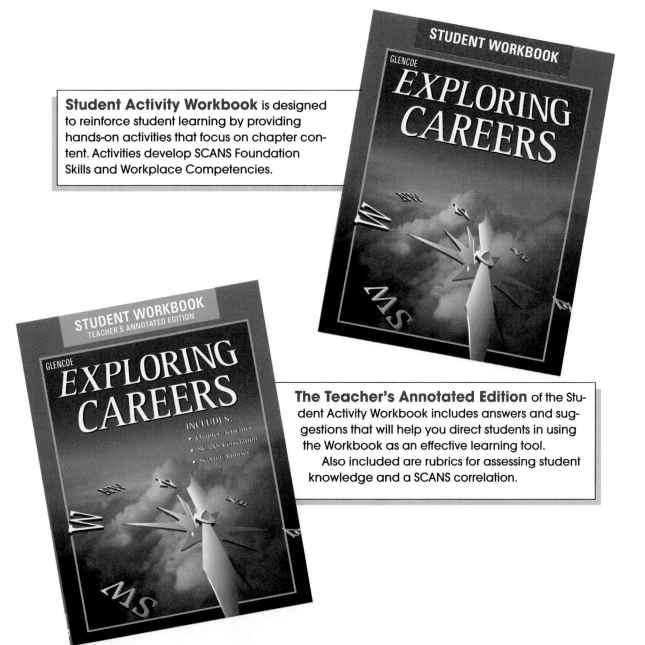

Student Activity Workbook is designed to reinforce student learning by providing hands-on activities that focus on chapter content. Activities develop SCANS Foundation Skills and Workplace Competencies.

The Teacher's Annotated Edition of the Student Activity Workbook includes answers and suggestions that will help you direct students in using the Workbook as an effective learning tool.

Also included are rubrics for assessing student knowledge and a SCANS correlation.

The Assessment Software Binder is a complete assessment resource that will help you evaluate students' progress. This testing program includes a printed testbank of all test questions, the Testmaker User Guide, and Windows and Macintosh software disks with a complete selection of test questions. Reproducible Tests, located in the *Teacher's Resource Binder,* are also available.

ASSESSMENT SOFTWARE

GLENCOE

EXPLORING CAREERS

INCLUDES:
- Printed Testbank
- Testmaker User Guide (Windows and Mac)
- Testmaker Software (Windows and Mac)

Glencoe McGraw-Hill

Exploring the World of Work
An Interactive Career Planner

Glencoe McGraw-Hill

Exploring the World of Work—An Interactive CD-ROM delivers the latest career-planning information in an exciting yet easy-to-use CD-ROM format. This CD-ROM is designed to assist students in every aspect of career planning and research. Included on this CD-ROM are articles and videos on the career clusters, career success tips, career planning and assessment activities, a résumé builder, and a tic-tac-pros game.

Workforce 2000 Video Library provides an exciting career exploration video and teaching activities to accompany each video segment. Video segments in English and Spanish are specifically designed to be used with each chapter of *Exploring Careers.* The video program is available as either a set of six videotapes or two level one videodiscs.

The Teacher's Resource Binder provides the following resources for your use:

- **Teacher's Lesson Plans** outlines the lesson objectives and teaching resources available for teaching every lesson in the student text. This valuable resource simplifies lesson planning and saves you time.

- **Full-Color Transparencies and Transparency Teaching Suggestions** enable you to visually expand on chapter content.

- **Reproducible Tests** includes blackline masters of Chapter, Unit, and Final Tests to assess students' knowledge.

- **Career Cluster Activities** provides blackline master activities that expand upon students' knowledge of the career clusters. Also included is a resource list of careers within each career cluster.

- **Internet Resources** presents a detailed overview of the Internet and ideas for incorporating the Internet into your classroom. Includes blackline masters of chapter Internet activities for students and Teaching Suggestions for each activity.

- **Involving Parents and Family in Career Education** provides information on the importance of involving parents and family in the classroom and chapter blackline masters that detail for parents the objectives of each chapter and suggestions for becoming involved in student learning.

- **Spanish Resources** offers a complete Spanish glossary of the key terms found in the student text.

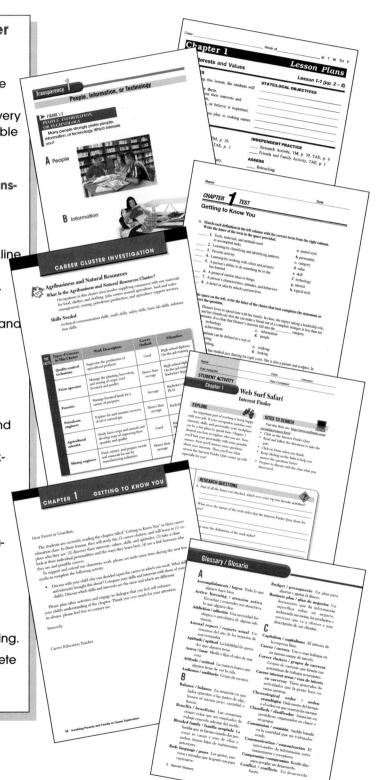

Developing a School-to-Work Program

School-to-work programs have been one of the most important developments in recent educational reform. These programs assume many different forms in order to meet the particular needs of different communities, schools, and students; all forms offer the following benefits for students:

- An improved understanding of self,
- A clearer vision of a productive future and how to make that vision a reality,
- Familiarity with a wide range of career options,
- An appreciation of the relevance of school learning to "real life," and
- Increased motivation to stay in and to succeed in school.

An effective school-to-work program involves a close relationship between schools and local businesses. This relationship, when thoughtfully developed and carefully tended, can result in benefits to schools and to businesses alike, as well as to parents and the community at large.

School-to-Work Opportunities Act of 1994

Much of the impetus for growth in school-to-work programs has been provided by the School-to-Work Opportunities Act of 1994. This legislation encourages states to create systems to implement school-to-work programs. The stated purposes of the Act help clarify the intent, as well as the benefits, of school-to-work programs.

PURPOSES OF THE SCHOOL-TO-WORK OPPORTUNITIES ACT

- To facilitate the creation of a universal, high-quality school-to-work transition system that enables youths in the United States to identify and pursue paths to progressively more rewarding roles in the workplace;
- To utilize workplaces as learning environments in the educational process by making employers and educators joint partners in providing opportunities for students to participate in high-quality, work-based learning;
- To promote the formation of partnerships dedicated to linking the worlds of school and work among secondary schools and private and public employers, labor organizations, government, community-based organizations, parents, students, state and local educational agencies, and training and human service agencies;
- To increase knowledge and improve skills of students by integrating academic and occupational learning and building links between junior high or middle school, secondary, and post-secondary educational institutions;
- To motivate all students, including low-achievers, dropouts, and those with disabilities, to stay in or return to school or an alternative classroom setting and strive to continue their education in postsecondary institutions;
- To expose students to a broad array of career opportunities and facilitate the selection of major areas of study, based on individual interests, goals, and abilities.

Components of a School-to-Work Program

A school-to-work program has three essential elements:

- **School-Based Learning:** career exploration and counseling, choice of a career major or cluster, and a planned program of study that is based on high academic skills and standards. The student text focuses on career exploration. Students study the career clusters and research career alternatives. Each chapter focuses on a specific career cluster.
- **Work-Based Learning:** a program of job training that makes use of business and work-sites as part of a school's curriculum. A **Community Involvement** chapter activity provides ideas for students to investigate workplaces in their communities.
- **Connecting Activities:** the involvement of employers, schools, and students in such activities as matching students with appropriate work-based learning opportunities; providing in-service training for counselors, teachers, and mentors; helping with the placement of students in jobs; further education and/or training; and follow-up on students' progress after graduation.

Each chapter of the student text includes **Connecting to the Workplace** activities that encourage students to relate chapter learning to the workplace.

Each of these aspects of a school-to-work program must be carefully developed, and all three aspects must support each other.

Making Choices

There is no single answer to the question, "What kind of school-to-work program do we need?" Rather, each school community must consider its own particular assets and needs in selecting a school-to-work learning model. Involving teachers, counselors, administrators, parents, students, business people, and labor organizers at every step of the decision-making process can, in itself, be a unifying activity, and it will help you develop the school-to-work program best suited to your community and students.

Integrating Career Education Across the Curriculum

In a recent survey of high school graduates—many of whom had gone directly to work rather than into post-secondary education—more than half the respondents said their high schools should have placed more emphasis on the following academic skills:

- Communication
- Mathematics
- Reading
- Science

These students—like so many others—failed to recognize the relevance and value of much of their course work while they were in school. Integrating students' academic and career/technical learning can make students more aware of the connections between school work and the real world—before it's too late to take advantage of those connections.

In addition, a program that integrates career and academic learning is best able to foster students' development of the SCANS Foundation Skills and Workplace Competencies. Integrated learning offers the following additional benefits to students:

- It provides examples of real-world learning and thus establishes patterns of lifelong learning.
- It improves the academic achievement of all students—including those who will begin their careers directly after high school, those who will go on to post-secondary education or training, and those who will obtain four-year college degrees.
- It supports students in making realistic plans for their own careers and education.

Team Planning and Team Teaching

In many cases, integrated learning is developed through team planning. You might begin with the simplest possible team: just you and one teacher from another discipline—math or English, for example. Together, you can discuss your routine lesson plans and agree on simple changes that will connect the two disciplines. Eventually, teachers of career classes may meet with teachers from traditional academic areas—English, math, science, and social studies—to develop integrated curriculum plans for an entire semester.

Another approach to integrated learning is team teaching, in which you work with one other teacher—or even several others—to plan a presentation of interrelated materials from two or more fields. Then you work together in both classrooms, presenting and developing the materials in each area and integrating it with the materials your co-teacher presents.

Addressing Cultural Diversity

Your students are preparing to enter a workforce noted for its cultural diversity. For students to become productive workers and responsible citizens, they must be open to cultural differences.

The following chart shows major ethnic groups as percentages of the total population in 1995 and, as projected, in 2025.

Major Ethnic Groups in the United States		
Percentage of the Total Population	**1995**	**2025**
African Americans	12.6	14.2
Asian Americans	3.7	7.5
European Americans (Non-Hispanic)	72.7	60.5
Hispanic Americans	10.2	16.8
Native Americans	0.8	1.0

As students learn about skills and attitudes in the workplace, they should keep in mind the diversity of the people they are likely to encounter in every aspect of their working lives. In class and in one-on-one conferences, you can help students consider the diversity of the U.S. population and the worldwide population, not only in terms of ethnicity, but also in terms of customs, attitudes, religious beliefs, language backgrounds, and physical capabilities. High school students should come to understand that ability and success do not come packaged in one skin color or one gender.

Each chapter of the text includes a feature entitled, **The Global Workplace**. This feature addresses the cultural diversity of the international workplace. You can use this feature as the basis of class discussion on cultural diversity.

During class activities, you may also find it appropriate to integrate questions related to cultural diversity.

- Would your response change if the customer were not a native speaker of English? If so, how?
- Would your decision change if your coworker were a male (female)? From your own ethnic background? From a different background? Why?

The Global Workplace

Business Cards Are An Essential Tool

Common business practice requires the exchange of business cards. With a card, an associate can remember your company's name and your job title and can contact you. In most of Southeast Asia, Africa, and the Middle East, it is considered rude to present a card with your left hand. In Japan, present cards with both hands. Make sure the words face the recipient and are right side up.

Exploration Activity!

Research business cards. What kind of information is listed on business cards? What do they look like? Make up a business card for a job you would like to have.

The Importance of Involving Parents and Family

Family involvement is a vital link to student success. When parents and families are effectively engaged in the education of their children, many positive successes take place. Research studies prove that family involvement equates to student success. Students whose families are involved tend to

- achieve more, regardless of socioeconomic status, ethnic/racial background, or the parents' educational level.
- have better grades and higher test scores.
- have better school attendance.
- complete homework more consistently.
- exhibit more positive attitudes and behavior.
- have higher graduation rates and greater enrollment rates in post-secondary institutions.

We hope your desire is to get more parents and family members actively involved in the day-to-day educational activities of your students. This is a mission that all educators should adopt.

Educators and schools must design and develop activities that challenge parents/guardians to become more involved, encourage parents/guardians to visit the schools more often, and engage parents/guardians in assisting student activities.

One way to encourage and motivate parent involvement is to communicate with them on a regular basis. A second way to encourage parent involvement is to design activities that reach all families.

Within the *Teacher's Resource Binder* you'll find a **Parent and Family Involvement** section. This section provides a list of guidelines for involving parents and families. It also includes newsletters and activities that you can use to help families get more involved in their child's education. There is no one approach to making this happen. You must develop a strategy that works for your program and school. It is vital that your plan focuses on student success while encouraging and motivating parent involvement.

Integrating Technology into Your Career Education Program

Technology—particularly computers and all types of computer-related technology—is changing the way people work, play, and live. Telecommuting allows people to work from home and spend more time with their families. Interactive educational software allows people to learn about the world around them as they "play" at exploring or designing. Access to the Internet allows people to do research and exchange ideas with others from all over the world.

Teaching students about technology is especially important in a career education program because it helps them to compete and succeed in the world of work.

Technology Resources

Exploring Careers gives you a platform for teaching and integrating technology into your career education program.

- **Chapter content** emphasizes technological changes affecting the workforce.
- The *Teacher's Manual* includes chapter **Internet Activities** for integrating the Internet into your classroom.
- The *Teacher's Resource Binder* includes **Internet Activities** and teaching suggestions for each activity.
- **The Workforce 2000 Video Library** contains video segments related to each chapter in *Exploring Careers*. A detailed *Teacher's Manual* provides instructions for incorporating the video into your career education program and activities for expanding and reinforcing the video content.

- **Exploring the World of Work, An Interactive CD-ROM** provides career-planning information in a dynamic CD-ROM format.

Other Resources

Several outside resources may also be available to help you bring technology to your students. Among these resources are on-line services and school resources.

- **Online Services.** If your school or local library has access to an on-line service, schedule time to have the service demonstrated to students.
- **School Resources.** Introduce students to technology by planning activities with other teachers and students responsible for computer and audiovisual equipment. For example, have students role-play job interviews with each other and videotape them. Or, use a computer to create a résumé.

SCANS and *Exploring Careers*

In 1991, the U.S. Department of Labor released a report entitled, "What Work Requires of Schools: A SCANS Report for America 2000." The SCANS report identified five competencies that, in conjunction with a three-part foundation of skills and personal qualities, lie at the heart of job performance and are needed by all workers in order to prosper in the emerging workplace. These skills and competencies have been integrated into the *Exploring Careers* program.

THE FOUNDATION	CHAPTER CORRELATION	ACTIVITY CORRELATION
Basic Skills—reading, writing, math, listening, and speaking.	Chapters 1–11, 13–16	• **Building Skills** *Reading*—Chapter 2 *Writing*—Chapters 3, 16 *Math*—Chapter 1 *Listening*—Chapter 5 *Speaking*—Chapter 6 • **Applying Academic Skills** *Math*—Chapters 2, 4, 5, 6, 7, 8, 12, 13, 14 *Social Studies*—Chapters 2, 7, 9, 10, 13, 14, 15 *Science*—Chapters 5, 11 *Language Arts*—Chapters 1, 6, 12, 15, 16 *The Arts*—Chapters 3, 8, 9
Thinking Skills—creative thinking, decision making, problem solving, seeing things in the mind's eye, knowing how to learn, and reasoning.	Chapters 1–16	• **Thinking Critically**—Chapters 1–16 • **Building Skills** *Creative Thinking*—Chapter 13 *Decision Making*—Chapter 4 *Problem Solving*—Chapter 9 *Seeing Things in the Mind's Eye*—Chapter 16 *Knowing How to Learn*—Chapter 8 *Reasoning*—Chapter 12
Personal Qualities—responsibility, self-esteem, sociability, self-management, and integrity and honesty.	Chapters 1, 2, 7, 8, 11	• **Building Skills** *Responsibility*—Chapter 2 *Self-Esteem*—Chapter 1 *Sociability*—Chapter 8 *Self-Management*—Chapter 11 *Integrity/Honesty*—Chapter 7

WORKPLACE COMPETENCIES	CHAPTER CORRELATION	ACTIVITY CORRELATION
Resources—allocating material and facility resources, and allocating human resources.	Chapter 15	• **Building Skills** *Allocating Material and Facility Resources*—Chapter 15 *Allocating Human Resources*—Chapter 15
Interpersonal Skills—participating as a member of a team, teaching others, serving clients and customers, exercising leadership, and working with cultural diversity.	Chapters 1–16	• **Building Skills** *Participating as a Member of a Team*—Chapters 5, 9 *Teaching Others*—Chapter 16 *Serving Clients/Customers*—Chapter 4 *Exercising Leadership*—Chapter 12 *Working with Cultural Diversity*—Chapter 8 • **Applying Academic Skills** *Foreign Language*—Chapter 3 *Health and Physical Education*—Chapters 1, 11 • **Teamwork**—Chapters 1–16
Information—acquiring and evaluating information, organizing and maintaining information, interpreting and communicating information, and using computers to process information.	Chapters 1–16	• **Building Skills** *Acquiring and Evaluating Information*—Chapter 3 *Organizing and Maintaining Information*—Chapters 11, 14 *Interpretating and Communicating Information*—Chapter 10 *Using Computers to Process Information*—Chapter 6 • **Connecting to the Workplace**—Chapters 1–16 • **Discovery Portfolio**—Chapters 1–16 • **Career Exploration**—Chapters 1–16
Systems—understanding systems, and monitoring and correcting performance.	Chapters 1–16	• **Building Skills** *Understanding Systems*—Chapter 13 *Monitoring and Correcting Performance*—Chapter 14 • **Connecting to the Workplace**—Chapters 1–16
Technology—selecting technology, and applying technology to task.	Chapters 4, 7, 10	• **Building Skills** *Selecting Technology*—Chapter 10 *Applying Technology to Task*—Chapter 7 • **Applying Academic Skills** *Computer Science*—Chapters 4, 10

Implementing Cooperative Learning

Both in the workplace and the classroom, emphasis on teamwork is growing. Working in teams is so much a part of the workplace today that many employers give prospective employees inventories and assessments to determine their ability to function within a team framework.

In the classroom, teachers are moving away from the lecture format to more student involvement via learning teams. It makes sense for students to practice teamwork at school, so they can carry that skill to the workplace and to other areas of life.

Cooperative learning offers the classroom teacher a structured method of teaching team-building, collaborative social skills, and team decision making while teaching basic concepts.

Benefits of Cooperative Learning

Cooperative learning offers many benefits, including the following:

- Through higher-level thinking, students are drawn into learning situations that require them to be directly involved. Each student must make a contribution as well as process input from others.
- Students discover how to work with people of all types. Schools with racially or ethnically mixed populations often improve interracial and multicultural relationships among students.
- The pressures of competition, common in many teaching situations, are diminished as students learn to work in a cooperative atmosphere.

- Empathy grows as students are compelled to consider the feelings of others when they work closely together.
- Communication and social skills are strengthened.
- Students learn to work through conflicts.
- Students develop self-esteem as they support and encourage each other in the pursuit of successful outcomes. Attitudes become more positive toward self and others.

Methods of Implementation

A variety of structures can be used to implement cooperative learning. The following are some of the most widely used learning modes in cooperative learning. You can adapt these structures to fit course content and your own teaching style.

- *Student Teams Achievement*. Students are assigned to teams. The teacher presents the lesson to the class as a whole. Then teams

work together to make sure all members understand the information. Weekly quizzes assess achievement.

- *Team-Games Tournament.* The weekly quizzes of the Student Teams Achievement mode are replaced with weekly tournaments (or competitions).
- *Jigsaw I.* Divide an assignment into separate parts (one for each team member). Each team member works independently to gather the necessary information. Through the cooperation of everyone on the team, the information is collected, organized, and reported back to the class.
- *Jigsaw II.* This learning mode is more demanding than Jigsaw I because the team is given the entire assignment and team members determine how the tasks and responsibilities will be divided.
- *Learning Together.* Students work together to complete an activity and produce a finished product.
- *Group Investigation.* Students accept greater responsibility because they decide what they will learn, how they will organize their group to accomplish the task, and how they will share what they learn with the rest of the class.

Teaching Cooperative Learning

The following will help you establish an effective cooperative learning environment:

- Assign students to heterogeneous groups of four to six. Mix the group in ability, sex, and ethnicity.
- Coordinate the efforts of all participants in the group.
- Arrange the classroom so students can face each other as they work.
- Set the task and goal structure and make sure the team goal is well defined and understood.
- Provide the appropriate materials.
- Discuss cooperation and social skills, encour-

age all students to participate, and express the need to support team members.
- Monitor student interaction. Intervene when necessary to mediate or solve problems and teach skills. Evaluate student outcomes.

Cooperative Learning in This Text

Exploring Careers provides many opportunities for cooperative learning. Lesson Review and Activities pages include **Teamwork** activities that are designed as group activities.

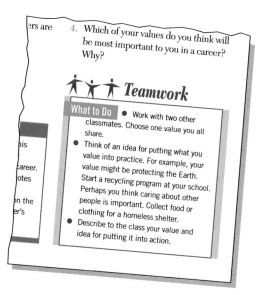

The **Building Skills** section of the Chapter Review includes *Interpersonal Skills*, building activities in which students focus on solving problems that involve teamwork. You can easily adapt others. For example, assign students to work in pairs to discuss and complete the activities **Reviewing Key Terms, Recalling Key Concepts,** and **Thinking Critically**.

Cooperative learning is especially effective for more difficult learning tasks such as problem solving and critical thinking. Divide students into groups of four to complete the **Thinking Critically** activities or activities that require research, and have them present their findings to the class.

Assessment Strategies

As a teacher, you will need a variety of ways to assess what your students have learned.

One traditional method of measuring student progress is a written test that evaluates recall of subject content. This program contains an **Assessment Software Binder** and **Reproducible Tests** as traditional methods of assessment. It is also necessary to assess far more than students' rote learning skills. New curriculum objectives focus on the acquisition of knowledge and skills that will help students function in the work world, such as critical thinking, problem solving, communication, and human relations skills. The acquisition of those skills is not so easily evaluated using the traditional paper-and-pencil test.

Performance Assessment

Performance assessment carries out a specific task, often through role-playing. For example, how does the student perform in an interview? Or, how does the student handle a work-related conflict with a coworker? A paper-and-pencil test will not demonstrate your students' skills in these areas.

Exploring Careers provides you with many activities, projects, and situations that create opportunities for alternative assessment. Within the end-of-chapter are **Building Skills** activities. Any of the skills and competencies, such as decision making and participating as a team member, are scenario-based. Students must write or demonstrate responses to real-life situations. **Applying Academic Skills** links various academic areas to work scenarios that students might actually encounter. In the **Teamwork** activity, students work in teams to complete a project. **Discovery Portfolio** allows students to develop career portfolios.

Determining Assessment Strategies

The chart shown on the opposite page can help you determine which assessment strategies will work best for you and your students. By comparing the advantages and disadvantages of different strategies, you will be able to make this text's variety of assessment strategies work to your advantage.

Evaluation of student performance is fundamental to the teaching and learning process.

ASSESSMENT STRATEGIES	ADVANTAGES	DISADVANTAGES
Objective measures Multiple choice Matching Item sets True/False	Reliable, easy to validate Objective, if designed effectively Low cost, efficient Automated administration Lends to equating	Measures cognitive knowledge effectively Limited on other measures Not a good measure of overall performance
Written measures Essays Restricted response Written simulations Case analysis Problem-solving exercises	Face validity (real life) In-depth assessment Measures writing skills and higher level skills Reasonable developmental costs and time	Subjective scoring Time consuming and expensive to score Limited breadth Difficult to equate Moderate reliability
Oral measures Oral examinations Interviews	Measures communications and interpersonal skills In-depth assessment with varied stimulus materials Learner involvement	Costly and time consuming Limited reliability Narrow sample of content Scoring difficult, need multiple raters
Simulated activities In-basket Computer simulations	Moderate reliability Performance-based measure	Costly and time consuming Difficult to score, administer, and develop
Portfolio and product analysis Work samples Projects Work diaries and logs Achievement records	Provides information not normally available Learner involvement Face validity (real life) Easy to collect information	Costly to administer Labor and paper intensive Difficult to validate or equate Biased toward best samples or outstanding qualities
Performance measures Demonstrations Presentations Performances Production work Observation	Job-related Relatively easy to administer In-depth assessment Face validity	Rater training required Hard to equate Subjective scoring Time consuming if breadth is needed
Performance records References Performance rating forms Parental rating	Efficient Low cost Easy to administer	Low reliability Subjective Hard to equate Rater judgment
Self-evaluation	Learner involvement and empowerment Learner responsibility Measures dimensions not available otherwise	May be biased or unrealistic

Teaching Critical-Thinking Skills

The teaching of critical-thinking skills is a goal of all educational disciplines. Today's business environment—be it a corporate setting, self-employment, or a small business—is highly competitive and demands skilled employees. One of the factors in achieving success in the workforce is an individual's ability to deal with the varied demands of the fast-paced world of business, which requires insightful decision making, creative problem solving, and interacting with diverse groups, be it employees, management, investors, customers, or clients. By teaching students critical thinking, you are equipping them with essential skills necessary for achieving success in today's workforce.

Critical thinking, the process of reasonably or logically deciding what to do or believe, involves the ability to

- compare and contrast,
- solve problems,
- make decisions,
- analyze and evaluate,
- synthesize and transfer knowledge, and
- conduct metacognitive exercises.

Critical-thinking skills are important for the following reasons:

- Critical-thinking skills help students to investigate their own ways of solving problems and finding creative resolutions.
- Critical-thinking skills lead students to investigations that compare and contrast what they know with unknowns.
- Critical-thinking skills allow students to make

decisions about their own learning and also make them aware of the processes they use.

Emphasizing Critical Thinking

The wealth of activities and guidance that is provided both in the student text and this *Teacher's Annotated Edition* will help you integrate critical-thinking skills into your daily plans. Each chapter includes the case study **Career Opportunities** with critical-thinking questions relevant to the career cluster presented. Each lesson concludes with a review page that includes critical-thinking questions; and as part of the end-of-chapter activities, there is a series of critical-thinking questions. In the *Teacher's Annotated Edition*, the **Guided Practice** activities provide critical-thinking questions for every lesson of the chapter.

Meeting Individual Needs and Learning Styles

One of your greatest challenges as a teacher is to provide a positive learning environment for *all* students in your classroom. Because each student has his or her own unique set of abilities, perceptions, and needs, the learning styles and the physical abilities of your students may vary widely.

Assisting Students with Individual Needs

In order to help you provide all your students with a positive learning experience, this text provides a variety of activities. This diversity will stimulate student interest, motivate learning, and facilitate understanding.

The *Teacher's Annotated Edition* provides **Independent Practice** activities. These activities reinforce chapter learning by allowing students to progress at their own pace.

Teaching Students with Special Needs

Students in your classroom may be physically challenged. They may have impaired hearing or vision, learning disabilities, or behavior disorders (all of which may interfere with their ability to learn). The learning styles of your students can also vary. Some students may be visual learners; others may learn more effectively through hands-on activities. Some students may work well independently while others need the interaction of others. Students may come from a variety of cultural backgrounds, and some students may have limited English proficiency.

Once you determine the special needs of your students, you can identify the areas in the

curriculum that may present barriers to them. In order to remove those barriers, you may need to modify your teaching methods.

On the following pages are two charts. The first chart, **Meeting Special Needs**, describes some of the special needs you may encounter with students in your classroom and identifies sources of information. Also provided are tips for modifying your teaching style to accommodate the special needs of your students.

The second chart, **Eight Ways of Learning**, will help you identify your students' learning styles. The chart gives a description of each type of learner; describes the likes of each type, what each type is good at, and how each learns best; and names some famous learners. Once you have identified each student's learning style, you can modify your teaching strategies to best suit his or her needs.

Meeting Special Needs

SUBJECT	DESCRIPTION	SOURCES OF INFORMATION
Limited Proficiency in English	Certain students often speak English as a second language, or not at all. Customs and behavior of people in the majority culture may be confusing for some of these students. Cultural values may inhibit some of these students from full participation in the classroom.	• *Teaching English as a Second Language* • *Mainstreaming and the Minority Child*
Behaviorally Disordered	Children with behavior disorders deviate from standards or expectations of behavior and impair the functioning of others and themselves. These children may also be gifted or learning disabled.	• *Exceptional Children* • *Journal of Special Education*
Visually Impaired	Children who are visually disabled have partial or total loss of sight. Individuals with visual impairments are not significantly different from their sighted peers in ability range or personality. However, blindness may affect cognitive, motor, and social development.	• *Journal of Visual Impairment and Blindness* • *Education of Visually Handicapped* • *American Foundation for the Blind*
Hearing Impaired	Children who are hearing impaired have partial or total loss of hearing. Individuals with hearing impairments are not significantly different from their peers in ability range or personality. However, the chronic condition of deafness may affect cognitive, motor, social, and speech development.	• *American Annals of the Deaf* • *Journal of Speech and Hearing Research* • *Sign Language Studies*
Physically Challenged	Children who are physically disabled fall into two categories—those with orthopedic impairments (use of one or more limbs severely restricted) and those with other health impairments.	• *The Source Book for the Disabled* • *Teaching Exceptional Children*
Gifted	Although no formal definition exists, these students can be described as having above average ability, task commitment, and creativity. They rank in the top 5 percent of their classes. They usually finish work more quickly than other students and are capable of divergent thinking.	• *Journal for the Education of the Gifted* • *Gifted Child Quarterly* • *Gifted Creative/Talented*
Learning Disabled	All learning disabled students have a problem in one or more areas, such as academic learning, language, perception, social-emotional adjustment, memory, or ability to pay attention.	• *Journal of Learning Disabilities* • *Learning Disability Quarterly*

TIPS FOR INSTRUCTION

- Remember that students' ability to speak English does not reflect their academic ability.
- Try to incorporate students' cultural experiences into your instruction. The help of a bilingual aide may be effective.
- Include information about different cultures in your curriculum to help build students' self-image.
- Avoid cultural stereotypes.
- Encourage students to share their cultures in the classroom.

- Work for long-term improvement; do not expect immediate success.
- Talk with students about their strengths and weaknesses, and clearly outline objectives.
- Structure schedules, rules, room arrangement, and safety for a conducive learning environment.
- Model appropriate behavior for students and reinforce proper behavior.

- Modify assignments as needed to help students become independent.
- Teach classmates how to serve as guides for the visually impaired.
- Tape lectures and reading assignments for the visually impaired.
- Encourage students to use their sense of touch; provide tactile models whenever possible.
- Verbally describe people and events as they occur in the classroom for the visually impaired.

- Limit unnecessary noise in the classroom.
- Provide favorable seating arrangement so hearing-impaired students can see speakers and read their lips (or interpreters can assist); avoid visual distractions.
- Write out all instructions on paper or on the board; overhead projectors enable you to maintain eye contact while writing.
- Avoid standing with your back to the window or light source.

- With the student, determine when you should offer aid.
- Help other students and adults understand physically disabled students.
- Learn about special devices or procedures and if any special safety precautions are needed.
- Allow students to participate in all activities including field trips, special events, and projects.

- Emphasize concepts, theories, relationships, ideas, and generalizations.
- Let students express themselves in a variety of ways including drawing, creative writing, or acting.
- Make arrangements for students to work on independent projects.
- Make arrangements for students to take selected subjects early.

- Provide assistance and direction; clearly define rules, assignments, and duties.
- Allow for pair interaction during class time; utilize peer helpers.
- Practice skills frequently. Distribute outlines of material presented in class.
- Allow extra time to complete tests and assignments.

Eight Ways of Learning

TYPE	DESCRIPTION	LIKES TO...
Verbal/Linguistic Learner	Intelligence is related to words and language, written and spoken.	read, write, tell stories, play word games, and tell jokes and riddles.
Logical/Mathematical Learner	Intelligence deals with inductive and deductive thinking and reasoning, numbers, and abstractions.	perform experiments, solve puzzles, work with numbers, ask questions, and explore patterns and relationships.
Visual/Spatial Learner	Intelligence relies on the sense of sight and being able to visualize an object, including the ability to create mental images.	draw, build, design, and create things, daydream, do jigsaw puzzles and mazes, watch videos, look at photos, and draw maps and charts.
Naturalistic Learner	Intelligence has to do with observing, understanding, and organizing patterns in the natural environment.	spend time outdoors and work with plants, animals, and other parts of the natural envionrment; good at identifying plants and animals and at hearing and seeing connections to nature.
Musical/Rhythmic Learner	Intelligence is based on recognition of tonal patterns, including various environmental sounds, and on a sensitivity to rhythm and beats.	sing and hum, listen to music, play an instrument, move body when music is playing, and make up songs.
Bodily/Kinesthetic Learner	Intelligence is related to physical movement and the brain's motor cortex, which controls bodily motion.	learn by hands-on methods, demonstrate skill in crafts, tinker, perform, display physical endurance, and challenge self physically.
Interpersonal Learner	Intelligence operates primarily through person-to-person relationships and communication.	have lots of friends, talk to people, join groups, play cooperative games, solve problems as part of a group, and volunteer help when others need it.
Intrapersonal Learner	Intelligence is related to inner states of being, self-reflection, metacognition, and awareness of spiritual realities.	work alone, pursue own interests, daydream, keep a personal diary or journal, and think about starting own business.

IS GOOD AT...	LEARNS BEST BY...	FAMOUS LEARNERS
memorizing names, dates, places, and trivia; spelling; using descriptive language; and creating imaginary worlds.	saying, hearing, and seeing words.	Maya Angelou—poet Abraham Lincoln—U.S. President and statesman Jerry Seinfeld—comedian Mary Hatwood Futrell—international teacher, leader, orator
math, reasoning, logic, problem solving, computing numbers, moving from concrete to abstract, thinking conceptually.	categorizing, classifying, and working with abstract patterns and relationships.	Stephen Hawking—physicist Albert Einstein—theoretical physicist Marilyn Burns—math educator Alexa Canady—neurosurgeon
understanding the use of space and how to get around in it, thinking in three-dimensional terms, and imagining things in clear visual images.	visualizing, dreaming, using the mind's eye, and working with colors and pictures.	Pablo Picasso—artist Maria Martinez—Pueblo Indian famous for black pottery Faith Ringgold—painter, quilter, and writer I. M. Pei—architect
measuring, charting, mapping, observing plants and animals, keeping journals, collecting, classifying, participating in outdoor activities.	visualizing, hands-on activities, bringing outdoors into the classroom, relating home/classroom to the natural world.	George Washington Carver—agricultural chemist Rachael Carson—scientific writer Charles Darwin—evolutionist John James Audobon—conservationist
remembering melodies; keeping time; mimicking beat and rhythm; noticing pitches, rhythms, and background and environmental sounds.	rhythm, melody, and music.	Henry Mancini—composer Marian Anderson—contralto Midori—violinist Paul McCartney—singer, song writer, musician
physical activities such as sports, dancing, acting, and crafts.	touching, moving, interacting with space, and processing knowledge through bodily sensations.	Marcel Marceau—mime Jackie Joyner-Kersey—Olympic gold medalist in track and field Katherine Dunham—modern dancer Dr. Christian Bernard—cardiac surgeon
understanding people and their feelings, leading others, organizing, communicating, manipulating, mediating conflicts.	sharing, comparing, relating, cooperating, and interviewing.	Jimmy Carter—U.S. President and statesman Eleanor Roosevelt—former first Lady Lee Iacocca—president of Chrysler Corporation Mother Teresa—winner of Nobel Peace Prize
understanding self, focusing inward on feelings/dreams, following instincts, pursuing interests, and being original.	working alone, doing individualized projects, engaging in self-paced instruction.	Marva Collins—educator Maria Montessori—educator and physician Sigmund Freud—psychotherapist Anne Sexton—poet

Course Planning Guide

Full-Year Course (Six-Week Grading System)

Grading Period	Chapter	Chapter Title
■ FIRST	Unit 1	Career Exploration
	Chapter 1	Getting to Know You
	Chapter 2	Thinking About Work
	Chapter 3	Researching Careers
■ SECOND	Chapter 4	Making Career Decisions
	Chapter 5	Your Career Plan
■ THIRD	Chapter 6	Finding a Job
	Chapter 7	Applying for a Job
	Unit 2	Employment Skills
	Chapter 8	On the Job
■ FOURTH	Chapter 9	Working with Others
	Chapter 10	Basic Skills Count
	Chapter 11	Staying Healthy and Safe
■ FIFTH	Chapter 12	Moving Toward Your Goals
	Unit 3	Lifelong Learning
	Chapter 13	Our Economic System
	Chapter 14	Managing Your Money
■ SIXTH	Chapter 15	Living a Balanced Life
	Chapter 16	Looking Beyond Today

Full-Year Course (Nine-Week Grading System)

Grading Period	Chapter	Title
■ FIRST	Unit 1	Career Exploration
	Chapter 1	Getting to Know You
	Chapter 2	Thinking About Work
	Chapter 3	Researching Careers
	Chapter 4	Making Career Decisions
■ SECOND	Chapter 5	Your Career Plan
	Chapter 6	Finding a Job
	Chapter 7	Applying for a Job
	Unit 2	Employment Skills
	Chapter 8	On the Job
■ THIRD	Chapter 9	Working with Others
	Chapter 10	Basic Skills Count
	Chapter 11	Staying Healthy and Safe
	Chapter 12	Moving Toward Your Goals
■ FOURTH	Unit 3	Lifelong Learning
	Chapter 13	Our Economic System
	Chapter 14	Managing Your Money
	Chapter 15	Living a Balanced Life
	Chapter 16	Looking Beyond Today

Semester Course (Six-Week Grading System)

Grading Period	Chapter	Chapter Title
■ FIRST	Unit 1	Career Exploration
	Chapter 1	Getting to Know You
	Chapter 2	Thinking About Work
	Chapter 3	Researching Careers
	Chapter 4	Making Career Decisions
	Chapter 5	Your Career Plan
■ SECOND	Chapter 6	Finding a Job
	Chapter 7	Applying for a Job
	Unit 2	Employment Skills
	Chapter 8	On the Job
	Chapter 9	Working with Others
	Chapter 10	Basic Skills Count
	Chapter 11	Staying Healthy and Safe
■ THIRD	Chapter 12	Moving Toward Your Goals
	Unit 3	Lifelong Learning
	Chapter 13	Our Economic System
	Chapter 14	Managing Your Money
	Chapter 15	Living a Balanced Life
	Chapter 16	Looking Beyond Today

Semester Course (Nine-Week Grading System)

Grading Period	Chapter	Chapter Title
■ FIRST	Unit 1	Career Exploration
	Chapter 1	Getting to Know You
	Chapter 2	Thinking About Work
	Chapter 3	Researching Careers
	Chapter 4	Making Career Decisions
	Chapter 5	Your Career Plan
	Chapter 6	Finding a Job
	Chapter 7	Applying for a Job
■ SECOND	Unit 2	Employment Skills
	Chapter 8	On the Job
	Chapter 9	Working with Others
	Chapter 10	Basic Skills Count
	Chapter 11	Staying Healthy and Safe
	Chapter 12	Moving Toward Your Goals
	Unit 3	Lifelong Learning
	Chapter 13	Our Economic System
	Chapter 14	Managing Your Money
	Chapter 15	Living a Balanced Life
	Chapter 16	Looking Beyond Today

Block Scheduling

In most high schools in the United States, the typical school day is made up of six, seven, or eight class periods of 40 to 50 minutes that meet 180 days a year. In "block scheduling," class sessions are scheduled for longer periods of time over fewer days. For example, a school day of block scheduling might consist of four blocks of 90-minute sessions that run for 90 days, or half a school year.

In the following planning guide for *Exploring Careers*, to the right of each unit title is the suggested total number of days for that unit, based on a 90-minute class period; this number is the sum of the days suggested to teach each chapter in that unit. This schedule includes the presentation of the features and end-of-chapter activities, as well as **Unit** and **Chapter Tests, Transparencies**, and activities in the **Student Activity Workbook**.

Optional activities, which enhance that particular chapter, are not listed but include the **Internet Resources, Career Cluster Resources, Spanish Resources, Workforce 2000 Video Library,** and the **Exploring the World of Work Software.** These optional activities, of course, will require more time than given here for each chapter. Typically, optional activities take from one-third to one-half a day each. You may wish to include these optional activities if you find you have some extra time. Or, if you want your students to do one of the optional activities, you could do less of something else, say, fewer end-of-chapter activities.

UNIT/CHAPTER		DAYS
Unit 1 Career Exploration		42
Chapter 1	Getting to Know You	6
Chapter 2	Thinking About Work	6
Chapter 3	Researching Careers	6
Chapter 4	Making Career Decisions	6
Chapter 5	Your Career Plan	6
Chapter 6	Finding a Job	6
Chapter 7	Applying for a Job	6
Unit 2 Employment Skills		28
Chapter 8	On the Job	6
Chapter 9	Working with Others	6
Chapter 10	Basic Skills Count	6
Chapter 11	Staying Healthy and Safe	5
Chapter 12	Moving Toward Your Goals	5
Unit 3 Lifelong Learning		20
Chapter 13	Our Economic System	5
Chapter 14	Managing Your Money	5
Chapter 15	Living a Balanced Life	5
Chapter 16	Looking Beyond Today	5

Career Exploration

Overview

In Unit 1, students will think about who they are and assess their values, interests, skills, and aptitudes. They will think about the world of work and will begin to see a link between who they are and possible careers. Students will learn how to conduct career research and develop a career plan. They will also explore how to find and apply for a job.

Unit Introduction

Lead a discussion on career exploration by asking students the following questions:

1. Why is it important to know yourself as well as you can before you make important career decisions?
2. What might happen to a person who decides to take "whatever job comes along"?
3. If you are going to find a job, what would you do first?
4. Have you ever had a job?
5. What types of careers interest you? What do you think of when you think of careers?

Discuss students' answers and explain to them that they will learn more about these areas in this unit of the text.

Unit Closure

Have students create a chart with art and text depicting the steps they will take to research and plan their careers.

Evaluation

Administer the reproducible Unit 1 Test found in the *Teacher's Resource Binder.*

Chapters within the Unit

Chapter 1
Getting to Know You

Chapter 2
Thinking About Work

Chapter 3
Researching Careers

Chapter 4
Making Career Decisions

Chapter 5
Your Career Plan

Chapter 6
Finding a Job

Chapter 7
Applying for a Job

TEACHER'S MANUAL

LESSON 1-1 ● Your Interests and Values

Lesson Objectives: After completing this lesson, the students will have learned:

1. what interests them,
2. the link between their interests and different careers,
3. what they value, or believe is important, and
4. the part their values play in making career choices.

Lesson 1-1 Features	**Lesson 1-1 Resources**
Career Opportunities, p. 7	• Lesson 1-1 Activities, p. 8
	• Student Activity Workbook, Activities 1 and 2
	• Transparencies 1 and 2
	• Transparency Lesson Plan

LESSON 1-2 ● Your Skills and Aptitudes

Lesson Objectives: After completing this lesson, the students will have learned:

1. how skills and aptitudes differ,
2. what their skills and aptitudes are, and
3. 'where their skills and aptitudes might lead them.

Lesson 1-2 Features	**Lesson 1-2 Resources**
Career Q&A, p. 11	• Lesson 1-2 Activities, p. 12
	• Student Activity Workbook, Activities 3 and 4

LESSON 1-3 ● Your Personality and Learning Styles

Lesson Objectives: After completing this lesson, the students will have learned:

1. what kind of personality they have,
2. the best ways of learning, and
3. how their personality and learning styles can affect their career choices.

Lesson 1-3 Features	**Lesson 1-3 Resources**
The Right Attitude, p. 14	• Lesson 1-3 Activities, p. 17
The Global Workplace, p. 16	• Student Activity Workbook, Activity 5
Investigating Career Clusters, p. 18	• Transparency 3
	• Transparency Lesson Plan

CHAPTER 1 RESOURCES

Assessment

- Lesson 1-1 Review, p. 8
- Lesson 1-2 Review, p. 12
- Lesson 1-3 Review, p. 17
- Chapter Review, p. 20
- Chapter 1 Reproducible Test and Testmaker Software

Extension

- Teacher's Manual, p. TM38
- Teacher's Resource Binder:
  - Teacher's Lesson Plans
  - Career Cluster Activities
  - Spanish Resources
  - Involving Parents and Family Resources

Multimedia

- Workforce 2000 Video Library, Segment 2
- Exploring the World of Work CD-ROM
- Teacher's Resource Binder:
  - Internet Resources, Chapter 1

SCANS CORRELATION CHART ....

FOUNDATION SKILLS

Basic Skills	Reading	Writing	Math	Listening	Speaking

Thinking Skills	Creative Thinking	Decision Making	Problem Solving	Seeing Things in the Mind's Eye	Knowing How to Learn	Reasoning

Personal Qualities	Responsibility	Self-Esteem	Sociability	Self-Management	Integrity/Honesty

WORKPLACE COMPETENCIES

Resources	Allocating Time	Allocating Money	Allocating Material and Facility Resources	Allocating Human Resources

Information	Acquiring and Evaluating Information	Organizing and Maintaining Information	Interpreting and Communicating Information	Using Computers to Process Information

Interpersonal Skills	Participating as a Member of a Team	Teaching Others	Serving Clients/ Customers	Exercising Leadership	Negotiating to Arrive at a Decision	Working with Cultural Diversity

Systems	Understanding Systems	Monitoring and Correcting Performance	Improving and Designing Systems

Technology	Selecting Technology	Applying Technology to Task	Maintaining and Troubleshooting Technology

---

ENRICHMENT AND APPLICATION ACTIVITIES

Internet Activity

Ask students to use the Internet to find out what kind of career planning information is available on-line. They should note the different sources of career information that they find and make note of appropriate Web sites. Suggested Internet sites or search words:

careers   jobs

http://www.jobweb.org
http://www.monsterboard.com

GO TO Teacher's Resource Binder: Internet Resources

Field Trip Activity

Depending on what's available in your area, take students to visit professionals working with animals. This could include a veterinarian's office, an animal shelter, a zoo, a working farm or horse stables, or a college of veterinary medicine. On the field trip, have each student develop a list of the different jobs that involve animals and compare lists back in the classroom.

Guest Speaker Activity

Invite someone who works with animals to speak to the class about his or her work. Ask the speaker to tell students how his or her interests and/or values, as well as education and training, led to this job.

Chapter **1** Getting to Know You

Chapter Outline

Chapter Overview

In this chapter, students will learn how to collect information about themselves so that they can find a career in which they can be happy and successful. First, they will investigate their own interests and values. They will learn that how they spend their time, what they talk about with friends, what they read, what they watch on television, and what they daydream about will give clues as to their interests. They will discover that values, such as responsibility, compassion, and achievement, help people make decisions, including career decisions. Students will also learn to identify their skills and aptitudes and to discover

how skills and aptitudes affect career choices. They will consider their own personalities and learn about the eight types of learning styles.

After this chapter, students will begin to see the connection between who they are and their career choices. They should be ready to explore and research careers that will suit them best.

LESSON 1-1

Focus

Objectives: After completing this lesson, the students will have learned:
1. what interests them,
2. the link between their interests and different careers,
3. what they value, or believe is important, and
4. the part their values play in making career choices.

Preteaching the Vocabulary: Write on the board the Key Terms: *interest, technology, interest inventory,* and *values.* Ask students to define each of these terms or use each in a sentence.

Bell Ringer: Have students develop two lists. The first, titled "Interests/Hobbies," is a list of any interests or hobbies that they can think of. The second, titled "Jobs," should be derived from the list of interests and hobbies. Write a few examples on the board. For instance, if an interest or hobby is water skiing, the job could be ski instructor or water ski repair.

Introducing the Lesson: Tell students that in this lesson they will learn how focusing on personal interests is one way to explore careers. They will also learn about personal values and how understanding their own personal values will help them to make career choices.

Teach

Guided Practice

Critical Thinking: Ask students to think about the following jobs: freelance writer, race-car driver, and accountant. Then ask which of these values—independence, security, excitement, high pay, a regular routine, and creativity—each of these workers might have.

Implementing Teamwork: In pairs, have students choose a shared interest and come up with a list of as many different jobs as they can think of associated with that interest.

Discussion Starter: Have students consider and discuss what they might tell a friend in the following situation. This friend is very shy and does not enjoy crowds, but he loves to read and work on anything mechanical. He has been offered a job helping in his aunt and uncle's auto parts store. Should he take the job? Have students give their reasons.

Application Activity: Have students write their answers to the Discussion Starter question. If time permits, read some of the answers that offer differing perspectives.

SCANS Skill—Listening: Read to students the poem "Dreams" by Langston Hughes and discuss the value or values the poet is describing.

Independent Practice

Research Activity: Have students read Investigating Career Clusters on page 18 and complete the Research Activity.

Assess

Reteaching: Have students imagine they are employees of a small business, such as a computer consultant, catering, or greenhouse supply business. Choose one or think of one of your own. Ask students to think of three jobs associated with one of these businesses and write down the name of each job and the interests and values that might lead one to choose these jobs.

Enrichment: Have the school counselor talk to the class about taking an interest inventory. Ask him or her to bring some samples to class for students to look at. Allow students to ask questions.

Assessment: Have students complete the Lesson 1-1 Review and Activities.

Close

Have students complete this statement: *"Knowing about my interests and values helps me know myself better because..."*

LESSON 1-2

Focus

Objectives: After completing this lesson, the students will have learned:
1. how skills and aptitudes differ,
2. what their skills and aptitudes are, and
3. where their skills and aptitudes might lead them.

Preteaching the Vocabulary: Write on the board the Key Terms: *skill* and *aptitude*. Ask students to define each or use each in a sentence.

Bell Ringer: On the board write: "Think of two jobs that interest you and make a list of as many skills as you can that would be required to do each job."

Introducing the Lesson: Ask volunteers to read aloud the jobs and skills they wrote about in the Bell Ringer activity and discuss what they wrote.

Teach

Guided Practice

Critical Thinking: Have students compare their interests (from Lesson 1-1) to their skills and aptitudes. Have them write a brief paragraph about the connections they find.

Discussion Starter: Discuss as a class the connections between *interests* and *skills* and *aptitudes* that students found in the Critical Thinking activity above.

Implementing Teamwork: In small groups, have students list three or four jobs (for example, astronaut, greenskeeper, plumber). Have each group identify how required courses such as English, math, and history might help someone become a better worker in the specific jobs. Have each group discuss other school courses that would be helpful in each job.

Application Activity: Have students write a one-page summary of their skills and aptitudes and the kinds of jobs that might require them. Do these jobs interest them? Why or why not?

SCANS Skills—Speaking: Have students present their findings from the Application activity above to the class. They can use charts, pictures, or collages as visuals for their presentations.

Independent Practice

Research Activity: Have students research the skills they will need in the future for a job or career they are interested in. They can use the Internet, a CD-ROM database, the on-line catalog at the library, or the *Reader's Guide to Periodical Literature* to look for books or articles on the topic of *work skills*.

Assess

Reteaching: Have students review the jobs they wrote about in the Reteaching activity from Lesson 1-1. (The jobs were associated with computer consultant, catering, or garden and greenhouse supply businesses). Have them write down the name of each job again and add the skills and aptitudes that might lead one to choose these jobs.

Enrichment: Ask the school counselor to talk to the class about *aptitude* and find out if he

or she has access to aptitude tests. Ask him or her to discuss what aptitude tests do and don't find out about a person.

Assessment: Have students complete the Lesson 1-2 Review and Activities.

Close

Have students complete this statement: *"Knowing about my skills and aptitudes helps me know myself better because..."*

Focus

Objectives: After completing this lesson, the students will have learned:

1. what kind of personality they have,
2. their best ways of learning, and
3. how their personality and learning styles can affect their career choices.

Preteaching the Vocabulary: Write on the board the Key Terms: *personality* and *learning styles*. Ask students to define each of these terms or use each in a sentence.

🔔 **Bell Ringer:** Have students answer this question in one or two paragraphs: "How might the way you learn affect your career choices?"

Introducing the Lesson: Ask volunteers to tell how they answered the Bell Ringer question. Discuss their answers.

Teach
Guided Practice

Discussion Starter: Ask students: "How are personality and learning style connected to interests, values, skills, and aptitudes?"

Implementing Teamwork: In small groups, have students draw diagrams or make collages that show the relationship between personality, learning style, interests, values, skills, and aptitudes. Have them display and discuss their work.

Critical Thinking: Have students recall from Lesson 1-2 that they will not necessarily have an aptitude for everything they want to learn, but that shouldn't stop them from learning whatever they wish to learn. While you can't change your aptitudes, you can change your skills. Can the same be said for personalities and learning styles? Can you change your personality? Can you change your learning styles? Have them give reasons for their answers.

Application Activity: Have students draw self-portraits. Ask them to write a paragraph that tells how the portrait reflects their personality.

SCANS Skills—Writing: Have students write a 250-word essay describing the work they think they will be doing 10 years from now. Be sure they describe in as much detail as possible what they will be doing during the course of a typical day.

Independent Practice

Research Activity: Have students research the topic of personalities and write a one-page report on their findings. Ask them to cite their sources.

Assess

Reteaching: Have students identify a favorite activity or hobby. Then have them write answers to these questions: What *values* do you express through this hobby? What *interests* help you enjoy it? What *skills* with *people, information,* and *technology* does it demand? What *aptitudes* or *abilities* do you bring to it? How does it fit your *personality*?

Enrichment: Ask students to interview a working adult whom the students know well. Guide the students in their choice of interviewees to be sure that the people selected are successful in their positions, regardless of the positions they hold. The primary purpose of the interview should be to find out what that person's responsibilities are and how his or her interests, abilities, and personality traits are helpful on the job. Have each student prepare a two-minute oral report to share his or her interview findings with the rest of the class.

Assessment:
1. Have students complete the Lesson 1-3 Review and Activities.
2. Have students complete the Chapter 1 Review.
3. Assign the Chapter 1 Test for students to complete.

Close

Have students complete this statement: *"By knowing myself better I will be better able to choose a career because..."*

LESSON 1-1 REVIEW ANSWERS

Vocabulary Review

Students' sentences should reflect an understanding of the definitions of the lesson key terms. Have student partners correct each other as necessary.

Check Your Understanding
1. c   2. a

Critical Thinking
1. through subjects you study in school, through activities, through experiences you have, by talking with others
2. so that you can enjoy what you do in your career and stay interested in it
3. a family member, teacher, or other person in your life who has helped shape your values or whom you respect and trust
4. Students should name a value they've identified and explain its significance for them.

Connecting to the Workplace

Students should prepare a list of initial questions and follow-up ideas for the interview. Urge students to contact their teacher after the interview if they have additional questions or need to clarify ideas.

Teamwork

Make sure students focus on a value rather than an interest. Assist groups that are having difficulty coming to a consensus about a value. Students should identify a way to put their value into practice at school or in the community.

LESSON 1-2 REVIEW ANSWERS

Vocabulary Review

Students should explain in their own words that a skill is the ability to do something you've learned and an aptitude is the ability to learn something.

Check Your Understanding

1. F; it becomes a skill.
2. T
3. F; an aptitude is the ability to learn something.
4. T

Critical Thinking

1. by taking lessons or training, by practicing
2. Students should describe skills that they have had to work hard to learn because they did not have any natural ability in that area.
3. Students should demonstrate an understanding of the difference between a skill and an aptitude and should name skills and aptitudes appropriate to the dream career they identify.
4. More job opportunities will be open to those with more skills.

Connecting to the Workplace

Careers named by students may include the following: working with special tools: carpenter, plumber, electrician; operating machines: pilot,

utility worker, postal clerk, truck driver; drawing: architect, graphic artist, fashion designer; speaking in front of an audience: actor, member of clergy, manager of a company; writing: screenwriter, journalist, technical writer; working with numbers: insurance agent, loan officer, accountant, investment broker; typing rapidly: administrative assistant, keyboard operator, clerk-typist, newspaper reporter; solving problems: doctor, physicist, mechanical engineer, social service worker, computer programmer; organizing schedules: travel agent, air traffic controller, event planner, administrative assistant; entertaining others: recreation worker, professional athlete, child-care worker, tour conductor.

Community Involvement

Students may need help identifying appropriate people in their community and finding their addresses. Discuss the format of a business letter with students. Students' letters should be courteous, clear, and to the point. Allow time for students to share the responses they receive.

LESSON 1-3 REVIEW ANSWERS

Vocabulary Review

Clues students devise should reflect the definitions of the lesson key terms.

Check Your Understanding

1. a   2. c   3. b   4. a

Critical Thinking

1. by trying out different kinds of activities, putting yourself in different kinds of situations, spending time with different kinds of people
2. linguistic: writer; logical/mathematical: scientist; spatial: city planner; musical: musician; bodily/kinesthetic: dancer; interpersonal: politician; intrapersonal: medical researcher; naturalist: park ranger.
3. because your work will be connected to the special way you think and learn, because your

work will seem like part of you, because you will be comfortable with your work and will be able to do your best at it

Connecting to the Workplace

Students should identify aspects of their partner's personality and make correlations between those personality traits and specific careers.

Teamwork

Remind students to keep their skits short. Skits should not name the learning styles they portray. Encourage students to help other members in their group put on their skits.

CHAPTER 1 REVIEW ANSWERS

▶ Recalling Key Concepts

1. You can discover your interests by thinking about how you spend your time, what you like to talk about with friends, and what you daydream about. Your favorite school subjects, activities, books, magazines, TV shows, and movies are also signs of your interests.
2. You learn your values from important people in your life, such as family members, teachers, and religious leaders.
3. A skill is your ability to do something you've learned, and an aptitude is your ability to learn something.
4. Your personality is made up of your characteristics, or qualities; your attitudes, or ways of thinking; and your behavior, or ways of acting.
5. The eight learning styles are linguistic, logical/mathematical, spatial, bodily/kinesthetic, musical, interpersonal, intrapersonal, and naturalist.

▶ Thinking Critically

1. Students should correctly classify their interests as having to do with people, information, or technology.
2. Some careers do not fit some values. You want to find a career that goes with your

values. That way you will be able to enjoy what you do and do your best at it.
3. Students should identify one of their aptitudes and outline steps they would take to develop it.
4. The world would not be the interesting place it is, because everyone would have the same strengths and would be doing the same things as everyone else.
5. Students should name careers that fit their characteristics, attitudes, and behaviors. To clarify their career choices, ask students to describe aspects of their personality.

▶ Building Skills

1. Direct students to follow the instructions for the activity carefully. Students should accurately represent the results of their survey in a bar graph.
2. Students' awards should focus on a specific aspect of their personality and should illustrate that feature.

▶ Applying Academic Skills

1. Students' essays should demonstrate self-awareness and describe aspects of themselves they have discovered in the course of study of this chapter. Their essays should be well organized, with clear topic sentences and supporting details.
2. Make sure students choose an activity that is completely new to them. Students may share their reaction to the activity with classmates.

▶ Discovery Portfolio

As necessary, further clarify the concept of a portfolio. Remind students to continue adding items to their portfolios.

▶ Career Exploration

Students' reports should cover the points outlined in the activity and should be based on the designated sources.

LESSON 2-1 ● What Work Is All About

Lesson Objectives: After completing this lesson, the students will have learned:

1. why people work and
2. how work affects people's lives.

Lesson 2-1 Features
Career Opportunities, p. 28

Lesson 2-1 Resources
- Lesson 2-1 Activities, p. 29
- Student Activity Workbook, Activities 1, 2, 3, and 4
- Transparencies 4 and 5
- Transparency Lesson Plan

LESSON 2-2 ● How Work Is Changing

Lesson Objectives: After completing this lesson, the students will have learned:

1. how the global economy affects jobs,
2. how technology is changing the way people work,
3. how the working population is changing, and
4. other recent changes in the workplace.

Lesson 2-2 Features
The Global Workplace, p. 31
Career Q & A, p. 33
The Right Attitude, p. 35
Investigating Career Clusters, p. 37

Lesson 2-2 Resources
- Lesson 2-2 Activities, p. 36
- Student Activity Workbook, Activities 5, 6, 7, and 8
- Transparency 6
- Transparency Lesson Plan

CHAPTER 2 RESOURCES

Assessment
- Lesson 2-1 Review, p. 29
- Lesson 2-2 Review, p. 36
- Chapter Review, p. 38
- Chapter 2 Reproducible Test and Testmaker Software

Extension
- Teacher's Manual, p. TM46
- Teacher's Resource Binder:
  - Teacher's Lesson Plans
  - Career Cluster Activities
  - Spanish Resources
  - Involving Parents and Family Resources

Multimedia
- Workforce 2000 Video Library, Segment 1
- Exploring the World of Work CD-ROM
- Teacher's Resource Binder:
  - Internet Resources, Chapter 2

TEACHER'S MANUAL

SCANS CORRELATION CHART ....

FOUNDATION SKILLS

Basic Skills	Reading	Writing	Math	Listening	Speaking

Thinking Skills	Creative Thinking	Decision Making	Problem Solving	Seeing Things in the Mind's Eye	Knowing How to Learn	Reasoning

Personal Qualities	Responsibility	Self-Esteem	Sociability	Self-Management	Integrity/Honesty

WORKPLACE COMPETENCIES

Resources	Allocating Time	Allocating Money	Allocating Material and Facility Resources	Allocating Human Resources

Information	Acquiring and Evaluating Information	Organizing and Maintaining Information	Interpreting and Communicating Information	Using Computers to Process Information

Interpersonal Skills	Participating as a Member of a Team	Teaching Others	Serving Clients/ Customers	Exercising Leadership	Negotiating to Arrive at a Decision	Working with Cultural Diversity

Systems	Understanding Systems	Monitoring and Correcting Performance	Improving and Designing Systems

Technology	Selecting Technology	Applying Technology to Task	Maintaining and Troubleshooting Technology

ENRICHMENT AND APPLICATION ACTIVITIES

Internet Activity

Ask students to use the Internet to find out about jobs available in national parks and other outdoor places. They should write about two specific jobs found on the Internet. Suggested Internet sites or search words:

national parks   jobs

http://www.gorp.com
http://www.coolworks.com

Teacher's Resource Binder: Internet Resources

Field Trip Activity

Identify a business in your area that manufactures or uses state-of-the-art technology in their business. Contact their human resources or public relations department to arrange a field trip to show students how changing technology has affected the way the business works.

Guest Speaker Activity

Ask a career counselor from a local college, university, or technical school to talk to your class about various job opportunities. He or she should discuss which jobs are increasingly in demand, education requirements for jobs students are specifically interested in, and the changes he or she has seen in the work world in the past 10 years.

TEACHER'S MANUAL

Chapter 2 Thinking About Work

Chapter Outline

Chapter Overview

In Chapter 2, students will be asked to begin thinking about work, jobs, and careers. They will discover why people work and how work affects their lives. They will learn that different jobs can be a career path and that careers change over time.

In this chapter, students will also learn how the world of work is changing because of a global economy, changing technology, and social changes. They will begin to see themselves as part of the world of work of the future.

LESSON 2-1

Focus

Objectives: After completing this lesson, the students will have learned:
1. why people work and
2. how work affects people's lives.

Preteaching the Vocabulary: Write on the board the Key Terms: *job, career, full-time,* and *lifestyle.* Ask students to define each of these terms or use each in a sentence.

🔔 **Bell Ringer:** Write these instructions on the board: "Spend the next three to four minutes making a list of 10 jobs or careers you want to know more about."

Introducing the Lesson: Ask several students to name one job or career on their Bell Ringer activity list and explain why it interests them. Discuss how these jobs or careers might affect the way a person lives.

Teach
Guided Practice

Critical Thinking: Introduce students to the idea that there are thousands of kinds of jobs in this country by having each student write a list of the various jobs that are part of creating a textbook. Then, as a class, compile lists so students can share their ideas.

Implementing Teamwork: Have students work in pairs to create a possible path for a career that interests them both. Have them make a poster of the path and display and discuss it with reference to the career path chosen.

Discussion Starter: Ask students to consider the following jobs: firefighter, professional baseball player, and cattle farmer. Then ask how these jobs would affect the lives of the people who do them. (Examples include: a firefighter's job can be dangerous; professional baseball players may be away from their families a great deal due to long hours and frequent travel; and cattle farmers must be available to take care of their animals every day and may not be able to travel much at all.)

Application Activity: Have students research a job or career that interests them and write a one-page paper describing a day in the life of a person with that job or career.

Teamwork Activity: Have students pair up with a classmate and choose one of the jobs in agribusiness or natural resources described in the Investigating Career Clusters on page 37. They should write a riddle that describes the work and lifestyle of a person in that job. Then, have each group read their riddle to the other groups so they can guess the job they have in mind.

Students' riddles should be based on information provided in the Investigating Career Clusters on page 37. Share examples of riddles with students to give them an idea of form and style. Emphasize that the riddle should not name the job students have in mind.

SCANS Skills—Reading: Have students read the help-wanted ads in your local newspaper. Discuss which type of jobs have the most openings.

SCANS Skills—Organizing and Maintaining Information: Students should imagine that they have been offered a job working 10 hours a week. They may work either after school or on weekends. Have them create a schedule for one week that includes time for school, work, homework, chores at home, and leisure activities. Also include time for meals and sleeping. Compare schedules with a partner.

In their schedules, students should allot a reasonable amount of time for each of the activities listed.

Independent Practice

Research Activity: Have students read Investigating Career Clusters on page 37 and complete the Research Activity.

Assess

Reteaching: Have students review the difference between a job and a career. Ask them to explain how different jobs can make up a career.

Enrichment: Invite the school principal, librarian, or counselor to talk to the class about his or her career path. Ask him or her to discuss when and where along the path choices and changes had to be made.

Assessment: Have students complete the Lesson 2-1 Review and Activities.

Close

Have students complete this statement: *"When thinking about a career, I will consider the kind of life I want to live because...."*

LESSON 2-2

Focus

Objectives: After completing this lesson, the students will have learned:

1. how the global economy affects jobs,
2. how technology is changing the way people work,
3. how the working population is changing, and
4. other recent changes in the workplace.

Preteaching the Vocabulary: Write on the board the Key Terms: *economy, goods, services, global economy, job market,* and *workplace.* Ask students to define each of these terms or use each in a sentence.

🔔**Bell Ringer:** Write these instructions on the board: "Spend the next five minutes to develop two lists—one titled 'Jobs of Yesterday' and the other 'Jobs of Today.' Think about which jobs people no longer do and why."

Introducing the Lesson: Discuss students' answers to the Bell Ringer activity. Ask two volunteers to compile the lists on the board.

Teach

Guided Practice

Discussion Starter: Ask students what skills or knowledge they might need to work for a company that has offices around the world.

Critical Thinking: Ask students this question: If a *market* is a place where buying and selling takes place, how does this help you describe a *job market*?

Implementing Teamwork: Divide the class into small groups. Give each group a list of jobs and have the groups identify the place of work and work time. As a class, discuss whether or not students would consider these factors when thinking about the type of work they would like to do.

Application Activity: Bring in, or have students bring in, several sections of classified ads for jobs. In small groups or pairs, have students identify different jobs that require knowledge of or experience with new technologies, such as the most recent computers and software, new medical technology, or state-of-the art office equipment.

Community Involvement Activity: Have students select two businesses in their community and find out the following about each: years in business, kinds of goods or services provided, kinds of jobs there, and career cluster(s) the jobs represent. Have them write a short description of each that includes this information. In groups,

they should put together a community business directory.

Students should visit or telephone the businesses to get the information they need about length of time in operation, goods or services provided, and nature of jobs. They should consult the list of career clusters on page 57 in Chapter 3 and the case studies of career clusters in Chapters 2-16 to identify the clusters represented by jobs in particular businesses. Keep the directory students compile in a convenient place in the classroom for easy reference.

SCANS Skills—Writing: Have students write a few paragraphs about their future. Be sure they describe where in the world they might be working, the kinds of technology they might be using, and their workplace setting.

SCANS Skills—Applying Technology to Task: Have the students keep track of all their tasks, or pieces of work they have to do, for a few days, including tasks at home and at school. They should record each task, writing down when they did it and why. Also, they should write whether they used some kind of technology to do it. If they did not, make notes about what kind of technology, if any, would have been helpful. Then, have students compare notes with each other, and share ideas about the kinds of new technology that would be useful for different tasks.

Urge students to list all forms of technology they use. Students should suggest creative technological methods or solutions for tasks for which they don't use technology.

Independent Practice

Research Activity: Have students research the topic *exploring careers* using the Internet, a CD-ROM database, the on-line catalog of your public library, or the *Reader's Guide to Periodical Literature*. Their research should give the title and a summary of two articles or one book.

Assess

Reteaching: In small groups, have students research the technology used for a career area in which they are interested. They should find out if the technology is changing and what kind of training is necessary to learn the technology. Have them present their findings to the class.

Enrichment: Invite a senior citizen from the community to talk about the advances in technology that he or she has experienced during his or her lifetime. (Perhaps a retired teacher would be willing or the local AARP could assist you.) Ask the senior citizen to include information about the effects technology has had on his or her lifestyle and jobs.

Assessment:

1. Have students complete the Lesson 2-2 Review and Activities.
2. Have students complete the Chapter 2 Review.
3. Assign the Chapter 2 Test for students to complete.

Close

Have students complete this statement: *"By exploring careers and thinking about the work world, I hope to learn...."*

LESSON 2-1 REVIEW ANSWERS

Vocabulary Review

Students should write four headlines, each incorporating one of the key terms. Students' headlines should be concise and catchy and accurately represent the meanings of the terms.

Check Your Understanding

1. F; a job is work done for which payment is received. A career is one or more jobs in the same area of interest.
2. T
3. F; housing, transportation, and food.

Critical Thinking

1. Students may cite a reason mentioned in the text or a reason they've thought of on their own. Students should explain their responses.
2. Students may observe that your income can determine the kind of home you have, where it is located, other things you can afford to buy, how you spend your spare time, and the kind of education your children have; they may also observe that work responsibilities can affect how much time you have to spend with friends and family and to pursue other interests.

Connecting to the Workplace

Make sure students follow the directions for the survey carefully. Suggest that they ask adult friends, family members, or neighbors to complete the survey. Students should not only report the results of the survey but also interpret them.

Community Involvement

Students' charts should feature at least 10 jobs in their community categorized under the relevant headings. Students should support their choice of a particular job by explaining why they would like to work at the job.

LESSON 2-2 REVIEW ANSWERS

Vocabulary Review

Students' speeches should incorporate the key terms for the lesson and reflect the content of the lesson. The speeches should be informative and well organized.

Check Your Understanding

1. c   2. b

Critical Thinking

1. Students should name careers of interest to them and then describe technological changes that have affected one of those careers.

Prompt students to hypothesize about what work was like in that career before more recent technology was introduced.

2. Students may observe that people of different backgrounds may introduce different ways of working and thinking as well as other aspects of their different cultures to the workplace.

3. Answers will vary; students should support their answers. Many students may cite telecommuting and explain that it has allowed more people to work at home.

Connecting to the Workplace

The ads students collect must mention some form of technology. Use the ads students' post as a springboard to discussion of kinds of technology changing the workplace.

Teamwork

Direct students to library resources such as the *Occupational Outlook Handbook* and the *Occupational Outlook Quarterly* as well as the *Reader's Guide to Periodical Literature*, to locate pertinent magazine articles. Suggest keywords that students can use to search the Internet. Students should gather information both about the career itself and about how work in the career is changing. All members of the group may participate in the actual documentary, or some may prepare the text and visuals, and others may share them in the documentary.

CHAPTER 2 REVIEW ANSWERS

Recalling Key Concepts

1. Answers will vary but may include the following: to make a contribution, to help others, to use skills and talents, to meet other people, to avoid boredom, to challenge the mind, to feel good about themselves.

2. A lifestyle is the way you use your time, energy, and other resources.

3. The global economy is the entire world's economies and how they are linked. The global economy affects the need for workers and the kinds of work available to them in different countries of the world.

4. More and more women are working, more people of different backgrounds are entering the world of work, and people are staying in the work world longer.

5. Today, people in companies often work in teams, work that was once done in one business location is now done in many locations, and more people are working at home than ever before.

Thinking Critically

1. It would help to have careers in mind when considering different jobs so that your jobs would have a purpose. You can get experience or training in an area of interest in a job and find out if you're really interested in a career in that area.

2. Many people spend much of their time and energy at work because they like what they do and want to do a good job at it. Others spend much of their time and energy at work to earn the money they need for their wants and needs.

3. The global economy connects people around the world who work and who buy and sell goods, making the world seem smaller.

4. Some people may be afraid of technology because it is new to them and they have trouble adjusting to change.

5. An older person might choose to continue to work for the same reasons people choose to work in the first place. He or she may need to

earn money or may want to make a contribution, help others, use skills and talents, meet other people, avoid boredom, challenge the mind, or feel good about him- or herself.

▶ Building Skills

1. Provide students with copies of a daily newspaper for one week. Students should read each other's summaries of news about the global economy and compare others' summaries to their own.

2. Students should record the specific tasks they did in each job and the specific skills they used. Pair or group students for more convenient sharing.

▶ Applying Academic Skills

1. Direct students to library resources and Internet sites where they might find information about state and local agencies that help people who've lost their jobs get back on their feet. Compile students' lists in a master list.

2. $\$900,000 \div 200,000 = 4.5 \times 4 = 18$ people

▶ Discovery Portfolio

Encourage students to illustrate their dream lifestyle. Provide old magazines for students to skim for pictures and words and phrases.

▶ Career Exploration

Before selecting a career in the agribusiness and natural resources career cluster, have students review the Investigating Career Clusters on page 37. Students may research the career they choose in library resources, such as encyclopedias and references published by the U.S. Department of Labor, including the *Dictionary of Occupational Titles*, the *Occupational Outlook Handbook*, the *Guide for Occupational Exploration*. They may also do research on the Internet. If students are confused about the kinds of information they need to locate, have them reread Investigating Career Clusters on page 37 for clarification.

LESSON 3-1 ● Career Choices

Lesson Objectives: After completing this lesson, the students will have learned:

1. which career clusters, or groups of related careers, interest them, and
2. career interest areas, or kinds of activities, that can direct them toward specific careers.

Lesson 3-1 Features	**Lesson 3-1 Resources**
The Global Workplace, p. 43 Career Opportunities, p. 45	• Lesson 3-1 Activities, p. 49 • Student Activity Workbook, Activities 1 and 2 • Transparencies 7 and 8 • Transparency Lesson Plan

LESSON 3-2 ● How to Get Information

Lesson Objectives: After completing this lesson, the students will have learned:

1. key questions to ask about careers that interest them and
2. where to get information about careers.

Lesson 3-2 Features	**Lesson 3-2 Resources**
The Right Attitude, p. 51 Career Q & A, p. 53 Investigating Career Clusters, p. 57	• Lesson 3-2 Activities, p. 56 • Student Activity Workbook, Activities 3, 4, 5, and 6

CHAPTER 3 RESOURCES

Assessment

• Lesson 3-1 Review, p. 49
• Lesson 3-2 Review, p. 56
• Chapter Review, p. 58
• Chapter 3 Reproducible Test and Testmaker Software

Extension

• Teacher's Manual, p. TM54
• Teacher's Resource Binder:
  – Teacher's Lesson Plans
  – Career Cluster Activities
  – Spanish Resources
  – Involving Parents and Family Resources

Multimedia

• Workforce 2000 Video Library, Segment 3
• Exploring the World of Work CD-ROM
• Teacher's Resource Binder:
  – Internet Resources, Chapter 3

TEACHER'S MANUAL

SCANS CORRELATION CHART ....

FOUNDATION SKILLS

Basic Skills	Reading	Writing	Math	Listening	Speaking

Thinking Skills	Creative Thinking	Decision Making	Problem Solving	Seeing Things in the Mind's Eye	Knowing How to Learn	Reasoning

Personal Qualities	Responsibility	Self-Esteem	Sociability	Self-Management	Integrity/Honesty

WORKPLACE COMPETENCIES

Resources	Allocating Time	Allocating Money	Allocating Material and Facility Resources	Allocating Human Resources

Information	Acquiring and Evaluating Information	Organizing and Maintaining Information	Interpreting and Communicating Information	Using Computers to Process Information

Interpersonal Skills	Participating as a Member of a Team	Teaching Others	Serving Clients/ Customers	Exercising Leadership	Negotiating to Arrive at a Decision	Working with Cultural Diversity

Systems	Understanding Systems	Monitoring and Correcting Performance	Improving and Designing Systems

Technology	Selecting Technology	Applying Technology to Task	Maintaining and Troubleshooting Technology

TEACHER'S MANUAL

ENRICHMENT AND APPLICATION ACTIVITIES

Internet Activity

Ask students to use the Internet to find government publications on job searching. They should write a brief paragraph describing one or two publications and give the URLs. Suggested Internet sites and search words:

careers   find a job

http://www.bls.gov.ocohome.htm
http://www.dol.gov

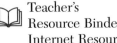 Teacher's Resource Binder: Internet Resources

Field Trip Activity

Visit a library in your area. Arrange for a librarian to acquaint students with the reference section of the library and show where publications, such as the *Dictionary of Occupational Titles*, *Occupational Outlook Handbook*, and *Reader's Guide to Periodical Literature* can be found. Also ask the librarian to give a demonstration that shows how to access the library's cataloging system (electronic or manual) and any on-line research systems, such as CD-ROM databases and the Internet.

Guest Speaker Activity

Invite a high school counselor to speak to the class about the courses available, such as marketing or accounting, for area high school students interested in business or office careers. Ask him or her to speak about any groups or associations, such as DECA, that contribute to students' learning experience.

Chapter Outline

Chapter Overview

In this chapter, students will begin to explore careers. They will read about career clusters (groups of related careers) and career interest areas (general kinds of activities people do in many careers), which will help them begin the process of looking at careers with respect to their skills and interests.

Students will also read about different ways to research careers. They will be introduced to the publications of the Department of Labor, as well as the Internet and other sources of information.

LESSON 3-1

Focus

Objectives: After completing this lesson, the students will have learned:
1. which career clusters, or groups of related careers, interest them and
2. career interest areas, or kinds of activities, that can direct them toward specific careers.

Preteaching the Vocabulary: Write on the board the Key Terms: *career clusters* and *career interest areas*. Ask students to define the terms and tell how they may relate to students' career searches.

🔔 **Bell Ringer:** Write on the board: "Take three minutes to answer this question: *If you could have any job you wanted regardless of pay or training, what job would it be?*"

Introducing the Lesson: Tell students that in this lesson they will learn about career clusters and career interest areas, groups of careers and career activities that will help give them ideas about the kinds of careers they might enjoy.

Teach
Guided Practice

Discussion Starter: Ask for volunteers to tell which one of the career clusters interests them and why.

Critical Thinking: Have students look at the jobs listed in the section "Careers for All Types!" and find jobs that could require being:
- a creator and an organizer (teacher),
- an investigator and a doer (auto mechanic trying to find the problem), and
- an influencer and a helper (minister).

Application Activity: Have students review the interests, aptitudes, skills, and values recorded in their Discovery Portfolio. Then ask them to try to match these with a career cluster and a career interest area. Have them explain why they believe there is a match.

Implementing Teamwork: Divide the class into six groups. Have each group list as many jobs for each interest area as possible in a limited time (say, 10 minutes) to see which group can think of the most jobs. Allow them to use the examples from the text. Review their lists as a class.

SCANS Skills—Speaking: Assign each student to a career cluster. Each student should prepare and present a two-minute speech that discusses the contributions workers in his or her assigned cluster make to our nation's society.

Independent Practice

Research Activity: Have students read Investigating Career Clusters on page 57 and complete the Research Activity.

Assess

Reteaching: Ask students to name the job of a neighbor, relative, or friend. Have two volunteers list as many of these jobs on the board as possible. When the list is finished, try to assign a career cluster and a career interest area to each job.

Enrichment: Have each student talk with at least five adults he or she knows regarding their jobs. Students should prepare a chart assigning each job to a career interest area and to a career cluster. Allow them to display their charts.

Assessment: Have students complete the Lesson 3-1 Review and Activities.

Close

Have students complete this statement: *"The more I learn about different careers...."*

Focus

Objectives: After completing this lesson, the students will have learned:

1. key questions to ask about careers that interest them and
2. where to get information about careers.

Preteaching the Vocabulary: Write on the board the Key Terms: *research, exploratory interview, job shadowing,* and *volunteering.* Ask students to define each of these terms or use each in a sentence.

🔔 **Bell Ringer:** Have students write 10 questions they would like to ask about a job that interests them.

Introducing the Lesson: Discuss the questions students wrote in the Bell Ringer activity. Make a list of common questions on the board. Tell students that in this lesson they will learn about what questions to ask and where to find the answers about careers that interest them.

Teach

Guided Practice

Discussion Starter: Ask students to raise their hands if they have had jobs for which they have been paid. Then ask students to describe those jobs: the hours they worked, was it an ongoing job or a one-time job, the setting, did they enjoy it, and so on. Tell students that the job experiences they have now, or will have before they begin working full-time, will be helpful when researching careers.

Critical Thinking: Have students write one or two paragraphs explaining why it is important to check information when doing research.

Implementing Teamwork: In groups of two or three, have students research very unusual jobs. Each group should choose a job and its associated career and use at least three different reference publications to research them. Allow each group to briefly report on their chosen job and add to a class bulletin board on "Most Unusual Jobs."

Application Activity: Have each student name three people with whom they could conduct an exploratory interview.

SCANS Skills—Listening: Have students conduct an exploratory interview with one of the three people listed in the Application Activity above. Tell them to use the list of 10 questions on page 51 of the text and write down the answers given.

Independent Practice

Research Activity: Using at least three sources of information and the 10 questions in the text, have students choose and research a job and its related career. They should write a two- to three-page report on what they have discovered and add it to their Discovery Portfolio.

Assess

Reteaching: With textbooks closed, review with students the different ways of researching careers.

Enrichment: Have students use the *Yellow Pages* of your local telephone directory and make a list of businesses that represent one or two career clusters of interest to the student.

Assessment:

1. Have students complete the Lesson 3-2 Review and Activities.
2. Have students complete the Chapter 3 Review.
3. Assign the Chapter 3 Test for students to complete.

Close

Have students complete this statement: *"I have an interest in the area of _____ , and to research this area I will...."*

LESSON 3-1 REVIEW ANSWERS

Vocabulary Review

The definitions provided on students' flash cards should reflect the definitions of key terms as provided in the text.

Check Your Understanding

1. c   **2.** b   **3.** b

Critical Thinking

1. They involve similar kinds of work and may take place in similar settings.
2. They show your areas of strength.

Connecting to the Workplace

Students should suggest a career cluster and a career interest area that reflects David's researching, organizational, writing, or social skills.

Teamwork

Groups' brochures should provide substantive information about five careers in the chosen cluster through text and visuals.

LESSON 3-2 REVIEW ANSWERS

Vocabulary Review

Students' drawings should clearly portray the key terms.

Check Your Understanding

1. T
2. T
3. F; check any information you gather.

Critical Thinking

1. Answers will vary; students should describe both general and specific information they would like about a career of interest to them.
2. Because the work world is constantly changing, you want to base your career choices on the latest information.
3. Gaining satisfaction from helping others, and getting the opportunity to make job contacts.

Connecting to the Workplace

Students should observe that people in the chat room may have been expressing their own opinions. Unless they supported their opinions with facts, the information may not be reliable.

Community Involvement

Suggest that students prepare questions to ask when contacting organizations. Students should identify places where young people can volunteer. Encourage interested students to inquire further about the volunteer opportunities.

CHAPTER 3 REVIEW ANSWERS

Recalling Key Concepts

1. Career clusters are groups of careers that have similar job characteristics. Career interest areas are general kinds of activities people do in many different careers.
2. Students may mention kinds of information represented in the list of key questions.
3. You can find career information at the library, on the Internet, by talking with other people, and by working.
4. You can check information by evaluating its source, comparing it with other sources, and finding out how up-to-date it is.
5. You can explore working in a particular career by talking with people involved in the career, by job shadowing, and by volunteering.

Thinking Critically

1. Students may suggest that the clusters are convenient for comparison of careers.
2. You won't really know what is involved in a particular career until you've researched it.
3. Research takes time, and some people do not have the patience for it. Others might not understand why research is important or know how to do research.
4. Students may mention the following: How did you choose your career? What kind of education or training did you have? What are some of your responsibilities? What do you like most about your work?
5. You can learn about work duties and responsibilities, the work routine, working conditions, and training or skills needed. You can find out whether the career matches your own interests, values, skills, aptitudes, and personality.

Building Skills

1. Review the format of a business letter with students. Have students submit a rough draft of their letter to you. Correct spelling and punctuation and give them advice about the proper style for a business letter. Students should carefully follow the directions for the letter that are provided in the activity. Their letters should contain all elements listed.
2. In their reports, students should compare and contrast the advantages and disadvantages of researching information in library resources and on the Internet. Students' reports should demonstrate an understanding of how to use both sources of information.

Applying Academic Skills

1. Students' buttons should accurately portray some aspect of a career cluster that interests them.
2. Urge students to list as many options for learning a second language as they can find.

Discovery Portfolio

Students may refer to the chart of career clusters on page 44 while organizing the career information they've gathered. Students should add to the file as they learn more about careers.

Career Exploration

Students should review the Investigating Career Clusters feature on page 57 before selecting a career. Students should research the career using resources described in this chapter.

Planning Guide: Chapter 4

LESSON 4-1 ● Decisions! Decisions!

Lesson Objectives: After completing this lesson, the students will have learned:

1. why decision making is an important skill,
2. steps they can follow to make decisions,
3. how to deal with things that stand in the way of decisions, and
4. how to make better decisions.

Lesson 4-1 Features	Lesson 4-1 Resources
Career Opportunities, p. 66 The Right Attitude, p. 68	• Lesson 4-1 Activities, p. 69 • Student Activity Workbook, Activities 1 and 2 • Transparency 9 • Transparency Lesson Plan

LESSON 4-2 ● Important Decisions

Lesson Objectives: After completing this lesson, the students will have learned:

1. how to make decisions about careers and
2. how to check their career decisions.

Lesson 4-2 Features	Lesson 4-2 Resources
The Global Workplace, p. 73 Career Q & A, p. 74 Investigating Career Clusters, p. 77	• Lesson 4-2 Activities, p. 76 • Student Activity Workbook, Activities 3, 4, and 5

CHAPTER 4 RESOURCES

Assessment

- Lesson 4-1 Review, p. 69
- Lesson 4-2 Review, p. 76
- Chapter Review, p. 78
- Chapter 4 Reproducible Test and Testmaker Software

Extension

- Teacher's Manual, p. TM60
- Teacher's Resource Binder:
  - Teacher's Lesson Plans
  - Career Cluster Activities
  - Spanish Resources
  - Involving Parents and Family Resource

Multimedia

- Workforce 2000 Video Library, segments 5 and 9
- Exploring the World of Work CD-ROM
- Teacher's Resource Binder:
  - Internet Resources, Chapter 4

TEACHER'S MANUAL

SCANS CORRELATION CHART ....

FOUNDATION SKILLS

Basic Skills	Reading	Writing	Math	Listening	Speaking

Thinking Skills	Creative Thinking	Decision Making	Problem Solving	Seeing Things in the Mind's Eye	Knowing How to Learn	Reasoning

Personal Qualities	Responsibility	Self-Esteem	Sociability	Self-Management	Integrity/Honesty

WORKPLACE COMPETENCIES

Resources	Allocating Time	Allocating Money	Allocating Material and Facility Resources	Allocating Human Resources

Information	Acquiring and Evaluating Information	Organizing and Maintaining Information	Interpreting and Communicating Information	Using Computers to Process Information

Interpersonal Skills	Participating as a Member of a Team	Teaching Others	Serving Clients/ Customers	Exercising Leadership	Negotiating to Arrive at a Decision	Working with Cultural Diversity

Systems	Understanding Systems	Monitoring and Correcting Performance	Improving and Designing Systems

Technology	Selecting Technology	Applying Technology to Task	Maintaining and Troubleshooting Technology

---

ENRICHMENT AND APPLICATION ACTIVITIES

Internet Activity

Ask students to use America's Job Bank on the Internet to research jobs in the field of communications and media. They should pick one job ad found in the Job Bank and write a brief description of the ad. Suggested Internet sites:

http://www.dol.gov
http://www.doleta.gov

Teacher's Resource Binder: Internet Resources

Field Trip Activity

Take students to a government meeting or session to hear how government leaders make decisions. Possibilities include city council meetings, county commissioners meetings, board of education meetings, or a state legislature session.

Guest Speaker Activity

Invite a local government official, the school principal or superintendent, or a local business president to address the class about how he or she makes the decisions required in his or her position.

TEACHER'S MANUAL

Chapter Outline

I. Decisions! Decisions!
   A. Taking Charge
   B. Reaching a Decision
      1. Breaking It Down
   C. Overcoming Problems
      1. Meeting Obstacles
      2. Finding a Way
      3. Never Give Up!
   D. Making Better Choices
II. Important Decisions
   A. Taking It Step by Step
      1. Step 1. What Do I Need or Want?
      2. Step 2. What Resources Will Help Me Decide?
      3. Step 3. What Careers Seem Interesting?
      4. Step 4. What Can I Find Out About Them?
      5. Step 5. Which Choice Seems Best for Me?
      6. Step 6. What's My Decision?
      7. Step 7. How Can I Reach My Career Goal?
   B. Checking and Changing Direction
      1. Evaluate, Evaluate!
      2. Keep Asking Questions
      3. Starting Over

Chapter Overview

Decision making is a skill that can be learned and mastered through attention and practice. In this chapter, students will learn the importance of making their own decisions and how to make decisions using the seven-step decision-making process. They will learn that sometimes there may be obstacles to making decisions but that obstacles can be overcome. Then they will follow a step-by-step plan for making decisions about a career.

LESSON 4-1

Focus

Objectives: After completing this lesson, the students will have learned:

1. why decision making is an important skill,
2. steps they can follow to make decisions,
3. how to deal with things that stand in the way of decisions, and
4. how to make better decisions.

Preteaching the Vocabulary: Write on the board the Key Terms: *decision, obstacle, outcome,* and *attitude.* Ask students to define the terms or use each in a sentence.

🔔 **Bell Ringer:** On the board write: "Take the next five minutes to answer the question: Why is decision making an important skill?"

Introducing the Lesson: Tell students that in this lesson they will learn the seven steps in the decision-making process and how to make effective decisions.

Teach
Guided Practice

Discussion Starter: Ask students to raise their hands in response to the following questions. Do you know people who sit and worry when faced with a decision? Do you know people who run away from decisions? Explain to students that this is not a productive way to handle decision making. A much better approach is to break a decision down into steps, the way you solve a math problem. When decisions, especially important decisions, are handled this way, they become more manageable, and you are more likely to make the right choice.

Critical Thinking: On the board write the names of two categories: "Easy Decisions" and "Difficult Decisions." Have students identify examples for each category. Discuss with students what makes some decisions easy and others difficult.

Implementing Teamwork: Bring in articles from your local newspaper concerning community issues on which people tend to take one or another position. (An example would be whether or not to raze a park to make room for additional housing.) Have students apply the seven-step decision-making model to the issue to select a side for a debate. After the students have made their decisions, divide the class according to their position and allow student volunteers to hold a debate.

Application Activity: Have students think of a fairly important decision they have made recently, or will be making in the near future, and have them apply the seven-step decision-making process to the situation and examine the decision. Have them write their responses.

Community Involvement Activity: Have students find out how groups make decisions. They should contact a club, your town or city council, the school board, or other community group, and attend a meeting of the group to observe how they make decisions. Afterwards, have students make a diagram that compares the group's method with the seven steps. Allow students to share the diagram with the class.

Each student's diagram should compare and contrast the selected group's decision-making process with the seven-step process taught in the lesson. If students are unable to attend a meeting to observe the decision-making process, they might interview the group's leader or a member of the group about the group's decision-making methods.

SCANS Skills—Math: Assign students the following math problem. Suppose you need a six-month training program that costs $3,000. You can get a scholarship for $750 and a long-term loan for $800. How much more will you need to earn to pay for the training program? ($1,450; $3,000 – 750 – 800)

Independent Practice

Research Activity: Have students read Investigating Career Clusters on page 77 and complete the Research Activity.

Assess

Reteaching: Review Figure 4-2, What Stands in Your Way? with the class. Have students independently choose one or two common obstacles they personally recognize and write the obstacle and how to handle it on a sheet of paper to be added to their Discovery Portfolio.

Enrichment: Have students research the topic of procrastination. They can find articles and books by using the Internet, a CD-ROM database, an on-line or card catalog, or the *Reader's Guide to Periodical Literature.*

Assessment: Have students complete the Lesson 4-1 Review and Activities.

Close

Have students think back to their answer to the Bell Ringer question: *Why is decision making an important skill?* Ask them to write a paragraph or two explaining whether their answer to that question would be different — now that they have studied the lesson.

LESSON 4-2

Focus

Objectives: After completing this lesson, the students will have learned:

1. how to make decisions about careers and
2. how to check their career decisions.

Preteaching the Vocabulary: Write on the board the Key Term: *decision-making process.* Ask students to define the term and tell how it may relate to their career searches.

🔔**Bell Ringer:** Remind students that they have been learning about making decisions. Ask them to write the answer to this question: "How is making no decision actually making a decision?"

Introducing the Lesson: Ask volunteers to read their answers to the Bell Ringer activity. Discuss their answers. Explain that making no decision means deciding to leave things the way they are. Making no career decision means leaving a very important part of one's future up to chance.

Teach

Guided Practice

Critical Thinking: Ask students what it means to say, "The only failure is not to try."

Implementing Teamwork: Divide the class into small groups. Have the groups discuss how a career choice affects the following areas of a person's life: income, friends, interests or leisure-time activities, standard of living, where they live, and life goals.

Discussion Starter: Ask students what they would do if, while applying the decision-making process to choosing a career path, they couldn't find the answers to questions along the way. Remind students of the people who are available to help them answer career questions, such as their guidance counselor.

Application Activity: Assign the Explore Activity. Have students answer questions as best they can at this point in their career exploration and add it to their Discovery Portfolio.

Teamwork Activity: Work with the class to develop a Web site about careers. Break the students up into groups of three. Each group should create a page about choosing a career. Together,

they should write copy that describes the seven steps to a career decision. The page should be kept short and to the point. Then, have students make a mock-up of the page that shows the text and a simple illustration for each step. Allow students to share the mock-up with the rest of the class.

Emphasize that students must keep the text brief and interesting. Students should suggest an illustration for each step. Explain that a mock-up is a full-size model that shows text and art in position.

SCANS Skills—Math: Assign students the following math problem. Raphael is interested in exploring a career in sales and is considering two sales jobs. One job pays $9.75 per hour for 25 hours a week. The other pays $5.50 per hour for 28 hours a week plus a 5 percent sales commission. Sales at this job average $800 per week. Which job pays more on average. (The first job pays more—$243.75 per week ($9.75 x 25). The second job pays on average $194 per week ($5.50 x 28 = $154; $800 x .05 = $40; $154 + 40).

Independent Practice

Research Activity: Assign students to research and read about the following people who made successful career changes in life: Harlan Sanders, Senator Bill Bradley, Wally (Famous) Amos, Debbie Fields (Mrs. Fields Cookies), and Mary Kay Ash (Mary Kay Cosmetics). Each student should summarize their findings in a 150-word essay that emphasizes the way each of these people made a successful career decision.

Assess

Reteaching: Below is a brief story about a young man who didn't do too well along the career decision path. Read Clint's situation to the class. Then have students discuss the mistakes Clint made. Have them suggest ways Clint could have avoided or at least improved his situation. Clint enrolled in a two-year vocational program after high school graduation. He liked the program, but a job as an assembler tempted him so much that he took it before completing the program. Clint thought the $17,000 assembler job was better than the $10,000 part-time job he was doing while enrolled in the program. After six months, Clint got laid off from the assembler job. He found another job as a farm worker. The farm job is boring for him. It requires working 14 hours many days and weekends. Other times there isn't much work.

Enrichment: In pairs or small groups, have students write a fictitious career decision history. Allow them to share their stories so students can discuss good and poor decisions.

Assessment:

1. Have students complete the Lesson 4-2 Review and Activities.

2. Have students complete the Chapter 4 Review.

3. Assign the Chapter 4 Test for students to complete.

Close

Have students write several paragraphs that describe some career choices and decisions they think they might be making before they graduate from high school.

LESSON 4-1 REVIEW ANSWERS

Vocabulary Review

Students' articles should include all four terms and reflect an understanding of their meaning and relevance to decision making.

Check Your Understanding

1. b **2.** a

Critical Thinking

1. Decisions are an important part of life. If you want a say about your life, you need to take control and make decisions about what affects you. You can't get where you want to go in life without making decisions.

2. Answers will vary. Students' responses should demonstrate a grasp of the seven steps in the decision-making process. Students should support their opinions with logical reasoning.

3. Answers will vary. Students should demonstrate an understanding of what an obstacle is and how obstacles to decisions can be handled.

4. Students should observe that your attitude might prevent you from accepting and evaluating an outcome of a decision that is different from what you wanted or hoped, and so you would not be able to learn from the decision.

Connecting to the Workplace

Students' charts should include all seven steps in the decision-making process and show in detail how they arrived at their choice between the two classes.

Teamwork

Urge students to think of as many excuses as possible and to record them exactly as they might be expressed. Students' posters should also advertise why making decisions is important.

LESSON 4-2 REVIEW ANSWERS

Vocabulary Review

Students should cover the seven steps of the decision-making process in their paragraphs, explaining how the steps can lead to a career decision and a strategy for carrying out the decision. Make sure students use the term *decision-making process* at least once in their paragraphs.

Check Your Understanding

1. T
2. T
3. F; you should evaluate your decisions and where you are, then continue to evaluate new experiences and information along your career path.
4. F; continue to evaluate your decision to make sure it still has meaning for you.

Critical Thinking

1. To make career decisions, you follow the same seven steps you would for other important decisions.
2. The decision-making process will help you identify and evaluate choices.
3. Never; you should continue to evaluate the career you've chosen to make sure it still meets your needs and wants.

Connecting to the Workplace

Students should observe that no career plan is ever wasted. Gaby pursued one of her interests in art school and gained valuable experience. She might not have discovered her interest in the restaurant business if she had not worked as a waitress to pay her expenses at art school.

Community Involvement

Students' interviews should focus on career decisions. Make sure students report responses to the questions included in the activity.

CHAPTER 4 REVIEW ANSWERS

▶ Recalling Key Concepts

1. The seven steps in the decision-making process are (1) defining your needs or wants, (2) analyzing your resources, (3) identifying your options, (4) gathering information, (5) evaluating your options, (6) making a decision, and (7) planning how to reach your goal.

2. If you run into an obstacles while making a decision, you should look for a way around them and try to make what is important to you happen.
3. You can learn how to make a better decision next time.
4. It's important to evaluate your decision after you've completed the decision-making process.
5. You can check your career decision by asking questions.

▶ Thinking Critically

1. When you don't make a decision, you decide not to decide. You also decide to leave things the way they are, or to others, or to chance.
2. When you say, "I'll go if you go" or "I'll do it if you do," you let someone else make your decision instead of taking charge yourself.
3. Accept all responses students can support with sound reasoning. Suggest that each step in the process has a purpose and leads to the next step, so that you achieve the best results when you follow all the steps.
4. If you gather information and make a plan for reaching your goal, you don't need to think about luck.
5. Some people are unhappy in their careers because they didn't give their career decision enough time and thought, or they haven't taken time to evaluate their career decision. They might be staying in a career because they are afraid of change and starting over.

▶ Building Skills

1. Students should follow the seven steps to make a decision, and make notes on its outcome to use as a reference for other decisions.
2. Students' charts should show how Carrie would proceed through the seven steps of the process to make a decision and plan of action for dealing with her customers. Ask for volunteers to explain their charts to the class.

▶ Applying Academic Skills

1. The bike repair job pays more per hour than the job as a cashier (bike repair = $5.25/hour; cashier = $5.00/hour). The cashier job pays more each week (cashier = $100.00/week; bike repair =$84.00/week [16 hours x $5.25/hour = $84.00]). Students should name other factors that might influence the decision, such as connection to a skill or interest, relevance to a career, number of hours on the job, working conditions, and so on. Students should use sound reasoning to support their choice.

2. Students may look into price, brands, and ease of use. Use computer mail-order companies, computer stores, computer magazines, and other computer users as sources of information. Students' plans should include questions they have about their software options and likely places to find answers.

▶ Discovery Portfolio

Students' lists should include important decisions many people face in life along with important decisions more specific to students' own age, circumstances, hopes, and dreams. Urge students to look at the list as a reminder to use the seven-step process to make important decisions.

▶ Career Exploration

Suggest that students review the Investigating Career Clusters feature on page 77 before selecting a career. Students should use the various resources named to research the career they choose.

LESSON 5-1 ● How Planning Helps

Lesson Objectives: After completing this lesson, the students will have learned:
1. why planning is important and
2. what a career plan should include.

Lesson 5-1 Features
The Global Workplace, p. 83
Career Opportunities , p. 88
The Right Attitude, p. 90

Lesson 5-1 Resources
- Lesson 5-1 Activities, p. 91
- Student Activity Workbook, Activity 1
- Transparencies 10 and 11
- Transparency Lesson Plan

LESSON 5-2 ● Designing a Plan

Lesson Objectives: After completing this lesson, the students will have learned:
1. how to set goals they can reach,
2. different kinds of goals that lead to a career goal, and
3. how to make their own career plan.

Lesson 5-2 Features
Career Q & A, p. 93
Investigating Career Clusters, p. 99

Lesson 5-2 Resources
- Lesson 5-2 Activities, p. 98
- Student Activity Workbook, Activities 2, 3, and 4
- Transparencies 12 and 13
- Transparency Lesson Plan

CHAPTER 5 RESOURCES

Assessment
- Lesson 5-1 Review, p. 91
- Lesson 5-2 Review, p. 98
- Chapter Review, p. 100
- Chapter 5 Reproducible Test and Testmaker Software

Extension
- Teacher's Manual, p. TM68
- Teacher's Resource Binder:
  - Teacher's Lesson Plans
  - Career Cluster Activities
  - Spanish Resources
  - Involving Parents and Family Resources

Multimedia
- Workforce 2000 Video Library, Segment 5
- Exploring the World of Work CD-ROM
- Teacher's Resource Binder:
  - Internet Resources, Chapter 5

SCANS CORRELATION CHART ....

FOUNDATION SKILLS

Basic Skills	Reading	Writing	Math	Listening	Speaking

Thinking Skills	Creative Thinking	Decision Making	Problem Solving	Seeing Things in the Mind's Eye	Knowing How to Learn	Reasoning

Personal Qualities	Responsibility	Self-Esteem	Sociability	Self-Management	Integrity/Honesty

WORKPLACE COMPETENCIES

Resources	Allocating Time	Allocating Money	Allocating Material and Facility Resources	Allocating Human Resources

Information	Acquiring and Evaluating Information	Organizing and Maintaining Information	Interpreting and Communicating Information	Using Computers to Process Information

Interpersonal Skills	Participating as a Member of a Team	Teaching Others	Serving Clients/ Customers	Exercising Leadership	Negotiating to Arrive at a Decision	Working with Cultural Diversity

Systems	Understanding Systems	Monitoring and Correcting Performance	Improving and Designing Systems

Technology	Selecting Technology	Applying Technology to Task	Maintaining and Troubleshooting Technology

ENRICHMENT AND APPLICATION ACTIVITIES

Internet Activity

Ask students to use the Internet to find out about education opportunities in your area. They should note courses offered, times offered, and cost. Suggested search words:

colleges   education

GO TO Teacher's Resource Binder: Internet Resources

Field Trip Activity

Visit a technical school or college campus in your area. Arrange for a tour and for students to receive whatever printed material is available for prospective students.

Guest Speaker Activity

Invite a representative from a local adult education or continuing education program to talk to the class about the programs available, completion requirements for various programs, financial aid, and job placement assistance.

Chapter 5 Your Career Plan

Chapter Outline

I. How Planning Helps
   A. Why Plan?
      1. Manage Your Time
      2. Remember Important Events
      3. Sort Out What's Important
      4. Reach Goals
   B. What Goes into a Plan?
      1. Education and Training
      2. Jobs Along the Way
      3. Career Research
      4. Covering All the Bases
II. Designing a Plan
   A. How to Reach Your Goals
   B. Setting Goals
      1. Stepping Stones to a Career
   C. Now You Do It
      1. Mapping It Out

Chapter Overview

In this chapter, students will take their first stab at developing their own career plan. They will learn how planning helps to reach career goals and how to design a career plan.

Encouraging students to write down their goals and career plans is important because it helps to make plans seem more concrete and attainable. However, it is also important to stress that a career plan is not etched in stone. It must be flexible enough to react to the changes that will inevitably occur as each student gains experience and as new opportunities arise.

LESSON 5-1

Focus

Objectives: After completing this lesson, the students will have learned:

1. why planning is important and
2. what a career plan should include.

Preteaching the Vocabulary: Write on the board the Key Terms: *procrastinate, prioritize, internship, part-time job,* and *temporary job.* Ask students to define each of these terms or use each in a sentence.

🔔 **Bell Ringer:** Have students write down a goal they achieved in the past year and the steps that they took to achieve that goal.

Introducing the Lesson: Tell students that in this lesson they will learn how planning helps you achieve your goals and how a career plan will help you achieve your career goals.

Teach
Guided Practice

Critical Thinking: Ask volunteers to explain the expressions *American dream* and *from rags to riches.* Then ask students if it is still possible to go from rags to riches today. Tell them to explain how values, goals, and a plan of action relate to the American dream.

Implementing Teamwork: Assign students to small groups of five or six students. Tell the groups they are going to plan an end-of-class theme party. Have each group choose a theme and make a list of everything that will need to be done to make the party a success. Make sure the groups hold on to their lists because they will be needed in the next lesson.

Discussion Starter: Photocopy a page or two from the *Yellow Pages* so students can see listings and ads for temporary job services. (See "Employment Contractors—Temporary Help.") After looking at the ads and listings, ask students how temporary jobs could fit into a career plan and help accommodate personal responsibilities.

Application Activity: Introduce students to an imaginary person named Judd who hopes to own and run a veterinary practice for farm animals. At present Judd lives in a large city, is in the tenth grade, has no money for college, and gets very good grades in school. Have students determine as many steps as possible that Judd could take to achieve his career goal. (It is not necessary to order them chronologically.) Make a list on the board.

Community Involvement Activity: Have students choose a community worker they respect, and research the education, training, and jobs that led to his or her career. They should gather information at the library or through an interview with the person. Then have students make a poster that shows the path the community worker took to his or her career. Allow students to explain their posters to their classmates.

Students may select community workers such as teachers, police officers, and town or city officials. Their posters should provide specific information about the education, training, and jobs that will help someone reach the career featured.

SCANS Skills—Writing: Write on the board: *Who, What, Where, When,* and *How.* Tell students that a good newspaper article begins by answering these questions in the first paragraph or two with details coming in later paragraphs. Then tell them to assume they are writing an article for a school newspaper, and the editor wants an article about why planning, especially career planning, is important. Have students write the article.

SCANS Skills—Math: Tell students that they have decided to attend a local community college and get a two-year degree. They plan to borrow $4,000 the first year and $5,500 the second year. The interest on a student loan is 8 percent. Have students calculate the total amount they will owe at the end of two years. ($4,000 x 0.08= $320 x 2= $640 + $4,000 = $4,640; $5,500 x 0.08 = $440 x 2 = $880 + $5,500 = $6,380; $4,640 + $6,380 = $11,020)

Independent Practice

Research Activity: Have students read Investigating Career Clusters on page 99 and complete the Research Activity.

Assess

Reteaching: Have students write definitions for the Key Terms *procrastinate, prioritize, internship, part-time job,* and *temporary job* and explain how each term relates to career planning.

Enrichment: Ask for volunteers to take roles in a play for the class. The first student plays a student who is very reluctant to begin any career planning. The second student plays a student who sees the value in career planning and wants to encourage the first student. The second should think of as many good reasons as possible to try to convince the first student. Allow others to role-play as time permits.

Assessment: Have students complete the Lesson 5-1 Review and Activities.

Close

Have students complete this statement: *"The purpose of my career plan is to...."*

LESSON 5-2

Focus

Objectives: After completing this lesson, the students will have learned:

1. how to set goals they can reach,
2. different kinds of goals that lead to a career goal, and
3. how to make their own career plan.

Preteaching the Vocabulary: Write on the board the Key Terms: *short-term goal, medium-term goal, long-term goal,* and *chronological order.* Ask students to define each of these terms or use each in a sentence.

🔔 **Bell Ringer:** Have students draw a simple map that shows their path of career exploration. It should begin with this class and lead to a career goal. It should also briefly describe the experiences, education, and/or training that the path passes.

Introducing the Lesson: Remind students that in the first lesson they learned about the importance of career planning, and in this lesson they will learn how to prepare a career plan of their own.

Teach

Guided Practice

Critical Thinking: There is an old saying about three bones that goes, "If you remember the three bones, you will always get along. The wishbone keeps you going after things. The jawbone helps you find out how to go after them when there's something you don't know. It is the backbone that keeps you at it until you get there." Have students discuss this analogy as it relates to establishing career goals and the need for making a plan and following through with it.

Implementing Teamwork: Organize the class into the same small groups that they were

in for the Teamwork activity from Lesson 5-1. Using the theme party lists, have students design a plan for their theme party putting their plans in chronological order. If possible, choose the best organized plan and allow the students to put on their party for the rest of the class.

Discussion Starter: Ask students if anyone thinks designing a career plan is just busy work. Ask them to explain why or why not. Emphasize, if necessary, that writing down a career plan will really help them become successful at whatever career they choose.

Application Activity: Have students write and present a two-minute speech describing one or two of their long-term goals and the steps necessary to achieve those goals.

Teamwork Activity: Have students form groups. Each group should select a career in the construction career cluster and research it. They should find out what education and training are needed, as well as identify the different jobs in the field of construction. Then, students should sketch a career plan on the board that shows short-, medium, and long-term goals.

Students should use the research tools described in Chapter 3 to gather information about the construction career they've chosen. Have students explain the steps in the career plan they devise to the rest of the class.

SCANS Skills—Listening: Read to the class an excerpt from Studs Terkel's *Working.* Have the class discuss the person's outlook on work, how the work experience would help in choosing a career, and how work experience would fit into a career plan.

SCANS Skills—Using Computers to Process Information: Have students use a database program to create a file of career references. For each career choice, have them collect the following information: schools/training programs;

names and addresses of companies offering jobs, and names and telephone numbers of human resource personnel; career counseling contacts, such as teachers, school counselors, friends, relatives, or businesspeople; Internet addresses for helpful sites; job search references, including books, magazines, and databases; and any other category students want to include.

Have students print out their databases and discuss how to use them to access career search information in an organized fashion.

Independent Practice

Research Activity: Have students research information about education and training available through the military services and find out if any of the programs relate to their own career goals. They can find information via the Internet, use a CD-ROM database, or look up the topic in the *Reader's Guide to Periodical Literature* or the library's on-line or card catalog. They may also contact a recruitment office.

Assess

Reteaching: Review with students the pointers for reaching your goals on pages 92 and 93. Answer any questions they may still have.

Enrichment: Have each student set a goal for the grade he or she wants to earn for this course. Have them identify at least one reason why they chose the grade and the steps they intend to take to achieve it. Students should, at the end of the course, discuss reasons why the goal was achieved, not achieved, or changed.

Assessment:

1. Have students complete the Lesson 5-2 Review and Activities.
2. Have students complete the Chapter 5 Review.
3. Assign the Chapter 5 Test for students to complete.

Close

Have students complete this statement: *"My career plan includes or will include...."*

LESSON 5-1 REVIEW ANSWERS

Vocabulary Review

Students' speeches should focus on making a career plan and should include and demonstrate an understanding of the terms listed.

Check Your Understanding

1. b   **2.** b

Critical Thinking

1. Answers will vary but may include the following: you may forget or miss out on activities, you may run out of time and miss an opportunity, you may not pay attention to what's really important to you, and you may feel as though you never get anywhere with anything you do.
2. Answers will vary. Students should cite one of the following: education and training, work experience, career research, money and personal issues. Students should support their answers with logical reasoning.
3. Temporary jobs are good ways to develop job skills you may need. Because they only last a short while you can do them during vacation breaks.

Connecting to the Workplace

No; he gave up his career plan to make more money right away in a job in which he might not have a future. If he had stayed with his plan, he would eventually have reached his goal and made more money.

Teamwork

Each team should focus on a vocational-technical center, trade school, community college, technical college, or four-year college or university. Encourage students to review the materials in the display and refer to them as needed as they proceed through the chapter.

LESSON 5-2 REVIEW ANSWERS

Vocabulary Review

Paragraphs of the students should reflect an understanding of the differences between short-, medium-, and long-term goals and the contribution of each to reaching a career goal.

Check Your Understanding

1. T   2. T   3. T
4. F; a medium-range goal is usually more challenging.

Critical Thinking

1. Short-, medium-, and long-term goals help you reach your career goal in stages or steps that you can handle one at a time.
2. When you're specific, you know exactly what you're aiming to do and will know when you've achieved it.
3. No goal is ever set in stone. You must continue to evaluate your goals as you learn and grow so they meet your needs.
4. You should write down your career plan so that you have a clear picture of your short-, medium-, and long-term goals, can check on your progress, and can make changes as needed.

Connecting to the Workplace

Students should work together to identify short-, medium-, and long-term goals for each career choice. Encourage students to look at the career plans of their classmates as an opportunity to explore careers.

Community Involvement

Students might contact service, religious, scout, or other groups in their community. Suggest that students create a visual to accompany their oral report to the class.

CHAPTER 5 REVIEW ANSWERS

▶ Recalling Key Concepts

1. Planning helps you organize your activities and manage your time so that you don't miss out on anything; it helps you remember when you need to do things; it helps you prioritize, or put tasks in order; and it gives you a feeling of accomplishment as you work toward and reach your final goal.
2. Most career plans include education and training, jobs, career research, and ways of dealing with money issues and personal responsibilities.
3. You set and meet short-, medium-, and long-term goals on the way to your ultimate career goal.
4. Without a plan, you've just got an idea or dream. With one, you're headed toward your career goal, step by step.

▶ Thinking Critically

1. On the basis of what they've learned about why planning is important, students should respond that it's important to plan time for rest and relaxation because that is the best way to make sure that they don't miss out on them.
2. Achieving an important goal would give you a positive attitude toward other goals and make you believe that you could achieve them too.
3. A part-time job would leave time for you to take classes and study.

4. Your goals are realistic if you define short-, medium-, and long-term goals in specific detail and are able to set plans to achieve them.

▶ Building Skills

1. Students should pay careful attention to their friend's description of his or her goals and should select one goal to feature in a picture. Make sure the friend provides feedback about whether the picture is an accurate representation of a goal that he or she described.

2. Students should decide on a practical project, determine the intermediate goals needed to accomplish it, and then act on their plan as a team.

▶ Applying Academic Skills

1. He earns $480 a week at the factory ($12 x 40 hours = $480). He would have earned $520 more a week as a master plumber ($25 x 40 hours = $1,000; $1,000 − $480 = $520).

2. Students should use library resources and the Internet to research the steps in becoming a physical therapist. Students should speak without notes.

▶ Discovery Portfolio

Students may use this exercise as a way to explore interesting careers and to begin thinking about the intermediate goals on the way to a career goal. The exercise will also give students practice in organizing and ordering tasks. The purpose of the essay is to build self-esteem and confidence. When students acknowledge that they've achieved other goals, they will be more likely to have a positive attitude toward goals that lie ahead of them. Urge students to update the career plan they formulated and to use it as a model for additional career plans.

▶ Career Exploration

Have students reread the Investigating Career Clusters feature on page 99 before choosing a career to research. Students should use various resources and personal interviews to gather information about the career. Students should use various visual formats to present their findings.

LESSON 6-1 ● Gathering Leads

Lesson Objectives: After completing this lesson, the students will have learned:

1. what is involved in a job search,
2. how talking with people can turn up job leads, and
3. other ways to find out about job openings.

Lesson 6-1 Features
Career Opportunities, p. 105
Career Q & A, p. 110

Lesson 6-1 Resources
- Lesson 6-1 Activities, p. 112
- Student Activity Workbook, activities 1, 2, 3, and 4
- Transparency 14
- Transparency Lesson Plan

LESSON 6-2 ● Organizing Your Job Search

Lesson Objectives
After completing this lesson, the students will have learned:

1. how to keep track of job leads and
2. how to gather information about jobs and businesses.

Lesson 6-2 Features
The Right Attitude, p. 114
The Global Workplace, p. 119
Investigating Career Clusters, p. 121

Lesson 6-2 Resources
- Lesson 6-2 Activities, p. 120
- Student Activity Workbook, Activity 5
- Transparency 15
- Transparency Lesson Plan

CHAPTER 6 RESOURCES

Assessment
- Lesson 6-1 Review, p. 112
- Lesson 6-2 Review, p. 120
- Chapter Review, p. 122
- Chapter 6 Reproducible Test and Testmaker Software

Extension
- Teacher's Manual, p. TM76
- Teacher's Resource Binder:
  - Teacher's Lesson Plans
  - Career Cluster Activities
  - Spanish Resources
  - Involving Parents and Family Resources

Multimedia
- Workforce 2000 Video Library, Segment 6
- Exploring the World of Work CD-ROM
- Teacher's Resource Binder:
  - Internet Resources, Chapter 6

SCANS CORRELATION CHART ....

FOUNDATION SKILLS

Basic Skills	Reading	Writing	Math	Listening	Speaking

Thinking Skills	Creative Thinking	Decision Making	Problem Solving	Seeing Things in the Mind's Eye	Knowing How to Learn	Reasoning

Personal Qualities	Responsibility	Self-Esteem	Sociability	Self-Management	Integrity/Honesty

WORKPLACE COMPETENCIES

Resources	Allocating Time	Allocating Money	Allocating Material and Facility Resources	Allocating Human Resources

Information	Acquiring and Evaluating Information	Organizing and Maintaining Information	Interpreting and Communicating Information	Using Computers to Process Information

Interpersonal Skills	Participating as a Member of a Team	Teaching Others	Serving Clients/ Customers	Exercising Leadership	Negotiating to Arrive at a Decision	Working with Cultural Diversity

Systems	Understanding Systems	Monitoring and Correcting Performance	Improving and Designing Systems

Technology	Selecting Technology	Applying Technology to Task	Maintaining and Troubleshooting Technology

ENRICHMENT AND APPLICATION ACTIVITIES

Internet Activity

Ask students to use the Internet to find out what kinds of job sites are available on-line. They should note how they located various jobs they are interested in and bookmark their favorite job site. Suggested Internet sites and search words:

careers   jobs

http://www.monsterboard.com
http://www.coolworks.com

Teacher's Resource Binder: Internet Resources

Field Trip Activity

Visit the career planning and placement office associated with a university, college, or technical school. Arrange for a career counselor to explain how the placement office works.

Guest Speaker Activity

Invite a high school career counselor to speak to the class about the school-to-work program(s) available through your local high school. Or, invite a career counselor from a university, college, or technical school in your area to talk about the career planning and placement office at his or her institution.

TEACHER'S MANUAL

Chapter 6 Finding a Job

Chapter Outline

I. Gathering Leads
   A. Starting Your Search
   B. Networking
      1. How It Works
      2. How to Get Started
   C. Other Ways to Get Information
      1. Get on the Phone
      2. Check the Classifieds and Job Postings
      3. Take Your Search to the Internet
      4. Get Help and Advice
II. Organizing Your Job Search
   A. Keeping Track
      1. Setting Up a System
      2. Getting the Details Down
      3. How the System Works
   B. More Detective Work
      1. What You Are After and Why
      2. Asking Questions
      3. Getting Answers
      4. Other Paths to Information
      5. Gather Your Facts

Chapter Overview

In this chapter, students will be introduced to methods of gathering leads for job openings and organizing their job searches. One of the best ways of finding job leads is through networking. Other methods include making phone calls, checking classifieds and job postings, and the Internet.

As important as knowing where to look for a job is knowing how to look. Organization skills can be the key to finding the best possible job. In this chapter, students will be introduced to some important tools they can use to better organize their job search.

LESSON 6-1

Focus

Objectives: After completing this lesson, the students will have learned:
1. what is involved in a job search,
2. how talking with people can turn up job leads, and
3. other ways to find out about job openings.

Preteaching the Vocabulary: Write on the board the Key Terms: *work permit, job lead, networking, contact list, referral, classifieds,* and *school-to-work program.* Ask students to define each of these terms or use each in a sentence.

🔔 **Bell Ringer:** Tell students to imagine that they just found out that if they don't have some kind of job this summer, they will have to watch their kid brothers or sisters. Have students write what steps they would take to get a job this summer.

Introducing the Lesson: Ask volunteers to read their responses to the Bell Ringer activity. Discuss their responses and tell students that in this lesson they will learn about the different ways to find out about different jobs.

Teach

Guided Practice

Critical Thinking: Remind students of the resources they learned about in Chapter 3 for researching careers (books, magazines, family, friends, counselors). Now ask students how looking for a job might use similar resources, and have students brainstorm ways of gathering leads for a job.

Implementing Teamwork: Bring to class enough classified advertising sections to give each of several small groups their own section of classifieds. Assign or let students choose one kind of job, such as truck driver, carpenter, or dental or medical assistant, and have each small group create a collage using different classified ads for that group's kind of job. Have each group report on the similarities and differences among the different ads for their kind of job. What kind of skills or other requirements are common among all the different jobs discussed?

Discussion Starter: Ask students to discuss what they would do if a parent or grandparent said he or she would take care of finding a paying or volunteer job for the student—talk to friends and neighbors, make the phone calls, even talk to the prospective employer. Ask: "Why might it not be a good idea to let someone else find you a job?"

Application Activity: Have students begin a collection of interesting classified ads, Internet job postings, and job ideas. These should be included with their contact list and kept in their Discovery Portfolios.

SCANS Skills—Speaking: Have each student create a cold call situation either to find out if a job is available or to find out more about a job opening. Tell students that when they place the call they get the employer's voice mail and they have two minutes to leave a message. Then have students write a script and give the message as a speech to the class. If possible, bring in a telephone for a prop and time their messages.

Independent Practice

Research Activity: Have students read Investigating Career Clusters on page 121 and complete the Research Activity.

Assess

Reteaching: Read to the class the following conversation Kaitlin has with Mr. Martinez when she asks about job openings. Have the class identify what Kaitlin did well and where she needs to improve.

Kaitlin: "Hi, Mr. Martinez. It's nice to see you again. How's Marie doing?"

Mr. Martinez: "She's fine. She just got a job promotion, and she's a department supervisor now. We're really proud of her."

Kaitlin: "That's great! I'll tell my family the good news about her.

"Mr. Martinez, I thought you might be able to help me. I'm looking for a part-time job after school and on weekends. Since you know so many people in town, I thought you might have heard of some job openings I could try for."

Mr. Martinez: "I think it's great that you want to work, Kaitlin. I don't know of any offhand, but the manager at Speedy Burger is a friend of Marie's. His name is Dave Dromboski. You could check with him, and if I hear of anything, I'll let you know."

Kaitlin: "Thanks for the referral, Mr. Martinez. I'll give him a call."

Enrichment: Have students draw a contact tree (similar to a family tree, except that it shows the paths of various contacts). The student is the base of the tree. Students should write the names of at least four people he or she knows directly (teachers, relatives, neighbors) as the first row of branches. The second row should list two people for each of the people in the first row.

Assessment: Have students complete the Lesson 6-1 Review and Activities.

Close

Have students complete this statement: *"Learning how other people find jobs will help me...."*

LESSON 6-2

Focus

Objectives: After completing this lesson, the students will have learned:

1. how to keep track of job leads and
2. how to gather information about jobs and businesses.

Preteaching the Vocabulary: Write on the board the Key Terms: *database, employer,* and *annual report.* Ask students to define each of these terms or use each in a sentence.

🔔 **Bell Ringer:** Write on the board: "Take five minutes and sketch a picture of your ideal work setting."

Introducing the Lesson: Tell students that in this lesson they will learn how to organize their job search and how to find out if a particular place of employment or job setting is right for them.

Teach
Guided Practice

Discussion Starter: Help students discuss why organizing a job search is a key to success. Ask: "Why do you think it takes hard work to find and be successful at a job? What other projects require hard work? What can you expect to learn about yourself and others when you are willing to work hard?"

Critical Thinking: Have students write one or two paragraphs explaining why volunteering could be a good first job.

Implementing Teamwork: In small groups of three or four, have students write a fictional short story that describes a successful job search, like Jason Lee's of Roanoke, Virginia. It should include a long-term career goal, a short-term job goal that could possibly lead to the long-term goal, and the order of contacts necessary to get the short-term job. Select three or four to read to the class.

Application Activity: Give students different job opening descriptions. Have them develop a list of questions they would use to gain information about the employer and the business. Discuss how the information would be helpful to students when organizing a job search.

SCANS Skills—Reading: Have students read at least two magazine articles about finding a job. By using a CD-ROM database or the *Reader's Guide to Periodical Literature*, students can locate articles using topics such as "finding a job" or "job search."

Independent Practice

Research Activity: Have students research job ads in trade publications (publications for people in specific job areas, such as book publishing: *Publisher's Weekly*, woodworking: *Woodshop News*, or visual merchandising: *Visual Merchandising and Store Display*). If possible, have each student find a trade publication in a job or career area that interests him or her and report on the publication: whether or not jobs are listed, and if so, what the jobs are. Suggest that they make inquiries at the library (libraries large enough to have a separate periodicals section should carry some trade publications) or with people who are working in a career field they would like to investigate.

Assess

Reteaching: Have students imagine the following scenario and use the information gathered to fill out a job lead card(s).

Your Aunt Alice has suggested that you call her old college roommate, Liz Naples, about a volunteer position at the animal shelter. She used to volunteer there. Her phone number is 555-1633.

When you call Ms. Naples, she tells you the volunteer coordinator there is Brian Alexander, the shelter is on Wellington Road, and she can't remember the phone number, but it's in the book.

You look up the number in the phone book and find that it is 555-7788. Mr. Alexander tells you to come in and fill out an application. Although they don't need new volunteers right now, they keep applications on file and have an orientation for new volunteers every six months.

Enrichment: Invite a representative from a temporary job service agency, like Olsten Staffing Services or Kelly Services, to talk to the class about the kinds of temporary jobs that are available to young people through the agency. Also ask the representative to discuss any requirements his or her agency may have.

Assessment:
1. Have students complete the Lesson 6-2 Review and Activities.
2. Have students complete the Chapter 6 Review.
3. Assign the Chapter 6 Test for students to complete.

Close

Have students write a 250-word report describing how to organize a job search.

LESSON 6-1 REVIEW ANSWERS

Vocabulary Review
Students' letters should accurately reflect the lesson content and incorporate all of the key terms.

Check Your Understanding
1. b   2. b

Critical Thinking
1. You need to have some idea of the kind of job you want.
2. because you can get inside information about job openings by networking, and people you meet by networking may also recommend you for a job
3. so that you don't miss out on job leads available through other sources

Connecting to the Workplace
Provide students with the classifieds section of the newspaper if necessary. Clarify abbreviations commonly used in job ads. Students' ads should incorporate the kinds of information included in the job ads they've reviewed in the paper. Ask for volunteers to read their paragraphs about the jobs that interest them.

Teamwork
To research their chosen job, students should use at least two of the methods explained in the lesson: networking, telephone, classifieds, Internet, school counselor or teacher, or placement office.

LESSON 6-2 REVIEW ANSWERS

Vocabulary Review
Definitions supplied by students should reflect those provided in the text.

Check Your Understanding

1. F; the best way to keep track of job leads is to keep a database or card file.
2. T
3. T

Critical Thinking

1. so that you keep track of all your job leads and where they are heading, so that you don't forget your conversations with people, and so that you don't lose information you've gathered
2. Answers will vary but should reflect the basic questions listed in the lesson. Students should support their response with sound reasoning.
3. A database allows you to organize your information quickly. It can be reorganized as needed. However, you may not have enough leads to warrant a database.

Connecting to the Workplace

Students should select a part-time or volunteer job that a person their age could do. Students should follow the steps for organizing a job search outlined in the lesson.

Community Involvement

Make sure students focus on a business in the family and consumer services career cluster. Suggest that in their list they include both basic questions and questions more specific to the business.

CHAPTER 6 REVIEW ANSWERS

Recalling Key Concepts

1. Networking is communicating with people you know or can get to know to share information and advice.
2. Contacts you make through networking may have information about a job or job opening.

3. You can get job leads by telephoning businesses you'd like to work for, by checking the classifieds, by looking for job postings in your community, by searching for job listings on the Internet, by talking with a counselor or teacher who helps students with career plans, and by taking part in a school-to-work program.
4. You can use index cards or sheets of paper to create a database to keep track of your job leads.
5. You can gather information about jobs and businesses by talking with workers and customers; by visiting the business; by asking for the company magazine, newsletter, or annual report; and by checking out the business' Web site.

Thinking Critically

1. Employers might like to hire people referred to them through a network because they trust the judgment of their own contacts and believe that people that come to them through a network are more likely to be well qualified for jobs that are open.
2. Answers will vary. Students should select one of the sources for job leads described in the text and explain their choice.
3. Answers will vary. Students should be prepared to support their answer. Many students will name networking and explain that it requires you to take an active part in searching for a job and can be done continuously.

Building Skills

1. Have the pairs role-play in front of the class and have the class critique each pair's conversations. Make suggestions for how students might improve their speaking skills.

2. Students should take time to explore job list-ings on-line, using a variety of keywords to start their search. Suggest that students iden-tify at least five Web sites that list job open-ings. Urge students to consult each other's files and follow the advice they find to do an on-line job search.

▶ Applying Academic Skills

1. There will be 100 people on Steve's list (20 x 2 = 40; 40 x 1 = 40; 20 + 40 + 40 = 100).
2. Assist students in deciphering the abbrevia-tions they find in the classifieds. Using the master list of abbreviations and various classified job ads as models, students should write a job ad that incorporates common abbreviations.

▶ Discovery Portfolio

Remind students to update their contact list regularly. Urge them to use it to explore career ideas. Ask students to share an interesting item from their job-hunting file with the rest of the class.

▶ Career Exploration

Have students reread the Investigating Career Clusters feature on page 121 before choosing a career. Students should use the vari-ous resources named to research the career they choose. Encourage students to include pictures in their brochures for visual interest.

LESSON 7-1 ● Presenting Yourself

Lesson Objectives: After completing this lesson, the students will have learned:

1. how to organize information about themselves in a résumé,
2. what a cover letter is and why it is important, and
3. tips for filling out job applications.

Lesson 7-1 Features
Career Q & A, p. 130

Lesson 7-1 Resources
- Lesson 7-1 Activities, p. 134
- Student Activity Workbook, Activities 1, 2, 3, 4, and 5
- Transparencies 16, 17, and 18
- Transparency Lesson Plan

LESSON 7-2 ● Putting Your Best Foot Forward

Lesson Objectives: After completing this lesson, the students will have learned:

1. how to prepare for an interview,
2. what happens in an interview, and
3. how to follow up after an interview.

Lesson 7-2 Features
The Right Attitude, p. 139
The Global Workplace, p. 143
Career Opportunities, p. 142
Investigating Career Clusters, p. 145

Lesson 7-2 Resources
- Lesson 7-2 Activities, p. 144
- Student Activity Workbook, Activities 6, 7, and 8
- Transparency 19
- Transparency Lesson Plan

CHAPTER 7 RESOURCES

Assessment
- Lesson 7-1 Review, p. 134
- Lesson 7-2 Review, p. 144
- Chapter Review, p. 146
- Chapter 7 Reproducible Test and Testmaker Software

Extension
- Teacher's Manual, p. TM84
- Teacher's Resource Binder:
  - Teacher's Lesson Plans
  - Career Cluster Activities
  - Spanish Resources
  - Involving Parents and Family Resources

Multimedia
- Workforce 2000 Video Library, Segment 6
- Exploring the World of Work CD-ROM
- Teacher's Resource Binder:
  - Internet Resources, Chapter 7

SCANS CORRELATION CHART ....

FOUNDATION SKILLS

Basic Skills	Reading	Writing	Math	Listening	Speaking

Thinking Skills	Creative Thinking	Decision Making	Problem Solving	Seeing Things in the Mind's Eye	Knowing How to Learn	Reasoning

Personal Qualities	Responsibility	Self-Esteem	Sociability	Self-Management	Integrity/Honesty

WORKPLACE COMPETENCIES

Resources	Allocating Time	Allocating Money	Allocating Material and Facility Resources	Allocating Human Resources

Information	Acquiring and Evaluating Information	Organizing and Maintaining Information	Interpreting and Communicating Information	Using Computers to Process Information

Interpersonal Skills	Participating as a Member of a Team	Teaching Others	Serving Clients/Customers	Exercising Leadership	Negotiating to Arrive at a Decision	Working with Cultural Diversity

Systems	Understanding Systems	Monitoring and Correcting Performance	Improving and Designing Systems

Technology	Selecting Technology	Applying Technology to Task	Maintaining and Troubleshooting Technology

ENRICHMENT AND APPLICATION ACTIVITIES

Internet Activity

Ask students to use the Internet to find more information about writing résumés. They should summarize the kind of information that is available on-line and make note of appropriate Web sites. Suggested Internet sites and search words:

résumés

http://www.studentcenter.com
http://www.monsterboard.com

Teacher's Resource Binder: Internet Resources

Field Trip Activity

Arrange for students to visit the human resource department of a mid-size or large business and have someone from the department explain their application and interview process.

Guest Speaker Activity

Invite the manager or supervisor of a smaller company who interviews applicants to speak to the class about how he or she processes applications and conducts interviews. Encourage students to look for the similarities and differences between interviewing with smaller and larger companies.

TEACHER'S MANUAL

Chapter Outline

I. Presenting Yourself
 A. Putting a Résumé Together
  1. Wanted: Information about You
  2. Two Different Formats
  3. Which Format Is Better?
  4. Don't Forget the Details!
  5. Electronic Résumés
 B. Covering Yourself
 C. Tackling Job Applications
II. Putting Your Best Foot Forward
 A. Getting Ready for an Interview
  1. Know Before You Go
  2. Practice Makes a Difference
  3. Dress the Part
 B. The Interview Itself
  1. A Winning Attitude
  2. A Good Conversation
  3. Watch Your Body Language
 C. After You Say Good-Bye
  1. Take Time to Say Thanks
  2. Take Stock
  3. Take It in Stride

Chapter Overview

In this chapter, students will learn about the steps to take to successfully apply and interview for a job. The first lesson discusses the application process, which includes organizing a résumé, writing a cover letter, and filling out applications.

The second lesson focuses on interviews: how to prepare for one, what an interview is like, and what to do after an interview. The point is made

that the interview should be a learning experience. Even if you don't get the job, you can use what you learn from the interview to prepare for your next application and interview.

LESSON 7-1

Focus

Objectives: After completing this lesson, the students will have learned:
1. how to organize information about themselves in a résumé,
2. what a cover letter is and why it is important, and
3. tips for filling out job applications.

Preteaching the Vocabulary: Write on the board the Key Terms: *résumé, format, cover letter, job application*, and *references*. Ask students to define each of these terms or use each in a sentence.

🔔 **Bell Ringer:** Ask students to make a list of the information about themselves they would want to give to a prospective employer.

Introducing the Lesson: Tell students that in this lesson they will be learning how to present information about themselves to prospective employers.

Teach
Guided Practice

Critical Thinking: Have students compare the two types of résumés—chronological and skills. Discuss how they are alike and how they are different.

Application Activity: Have students choose one of the résumé formats and begin filling in the résumé with the personal information they have been working on in these past few chapters. Have them explain why they chose the format they chose.

Implementing Teamwork: In pairs, have students compare their beginning résumé with their partner's. Has one included information the other has not? Allow them to exchange ideas for improving their résumés.

Discussion Starter: Write on the board: "In the world of work, first impressions count." Discuss with students what this means. How does this affect how you present yourself to prospective employers?

SCANS Skills—Writing: Have students practice writing cover letters by letting each student choose an interesting job ad and write a creative cover letter. The information may be fictitious, but the format should follow the sample cover letter in the chapter.

Independent Practice

Research Activity: Have students read Investigating Career Clusters on page 145 and complete the research activity.

Assess

Reteaching: As a class, write definitions for *résumé, cover letter*, and *application* on the board.

Enrichment: Have students interview an adult with a job, volunteer or paying, and find out what steps he or she took to get the job. Students should ask if the adult sent a résumé and cover letter or filled out an application. They should also ask what advice the adult might give to others looking for a similar job. Allow students to share their findings.

Assessment: Have students complete the Lesson 7-1 Review and Activities.

Close

Have students complete this statement: *"By learning how to present myself to an employer...."*

Focus

Objectives: After completing this lesson, the students will have learned:

1. how to prepare for an interview,
2. what happens in an interview, and
3. how to follow up after an interview.

Preteaching the Vocabulary: Write on the board the Key Terms: *interview* and *body language*. Ask students to define each of these terms or use each in a sentence.

🔔 **Bell Ringer:** Have each student sketch a picture of him- or herself during a job interview. What do they imagine an interview would be like?

Introducing the Lesson: Ask volunteers to describe their pictures. What is the job for which they are being interviewed? Where does the interview take place? How is the student dressed? What is the interviewer like? Tell students that in this lesson they will be learning about interviews.

Teach

Guided Practice

Critical Thinking: Describe the following situation to the class and ask them to respond. Marla's counselor has advised her to cut and recolor her long fuchsia fingernails before her next job interview, but Marla refuses even to trim them. What can you conclude about Marla's work values? What would you suggest to Marla?

Discussion Starter: To discuss the importance of telling the truth during an interview, ask students the following questions:

Why is it important to tell the truth during an interview? Why should you admit you don't know an answer? Why might it be difficult to admit you don't know an answer?

Implementing Teamwork: Have students work in pairs to create a role-play in which the interviewer is asking about related work experience and the prospective employee doesn't have any related work experience. Each pair should create one role-play that gives an honest answer and one that gives a dishonest answer. Challenge them to show how you can give an honest answer that is still positive. Also, have them show how a dishonest answer can create problems.

Application Activity: Divide the class into small groups and have each group create a visual presentation of the best and worst ways to present yourself for an interview. Students can make a poster, perform a skit, or write a short story.

SCANS Skills—Math: Imagine that you have a job interview at 2:30 one afternoon. You will be driving to the interview, and you estimate that the drive will take you 25 minutes. You are not sure about parking, so you want to allow 10 minutes to park your car and 5 more minutes to get from your car to the office. What time should you leave your home if you want to arrive 5 minutes early? ($25 + 10 + 5 + 5 = 45$ minutes; $2:30 - 45$ minutes = $1:45$)

Independent Practice

Research Activity: Have students research interviewing skills. They can use the subject interviewing to search the Internet, a CD-ROM database, on-line or manual card catalog, or the *Reader's Guide to Periodical Literature*.

Assess

Reteaching: Have students make an outline of this lesson (Lesson 7-2) using the headings. (It should look like the second half of the outline given in this lesson plan.) Discuss what they learned about interviewing from each section of the outline.

Enrichment: Have students talk to at least two adults who have been through the interview process about their interview experiences. Then have students write a one- to two-page report comparing the different interview experiences.

Assessment:

1. Have students complete the Lesson 7-2 Review and Activities.

2. Have students complete the Chapter 7 Review.

3. Assign the Chapter 7 Test for students to complete.

Close

Have students write an outline that briefly describes each step they would take to apply for a job.

LESSON 7-1 REVIEW ANSWERS

Vocabulary Review

Students' posters should feature all six key terms and show what each has to do with presenting oneself to an employer.

Check Your Understanding

1. b   2. c

Critical Thinking

1. Students should identify strengths of theirs that would not be described in other sections of a chronological résumé; they should explain that the skills and abilities they have identified would be relevant or useful in the workplace in general or for a particular job.

2. because in a cover letter you identify the job you're applying for and can add additional personal information as well as personal touches to your application to make an impression on an employer

3. how neat someone is, how thorough the person is, whether he or she can read well and follow directions, whether the person pays attention to detail, and, ultimately, how interested he or she is in the job

Connecting to the Workplace

Suggest that students closely follow the format of the skills résumé on page 129. Students' résumés should include the same headings as that model. If necessary, brainstorm skills categories with students to give them ideas for the subheads under *Skills and Abilities*. Be sure students include a job objective and orient their résumé toward a particular part-time or volunteer job.

Teamwork

The groups' guides should demonstrate an understanding of the material presented in the lesson. Students should apply the material to part-time and volunteer jobs.

LESSON 7-2 REVIEW ANSWERS

Vocabulary Review

Students' paragraphs should draw on the lesson text and Figure 7-4 to explain positive and negative messages which can be sent by body language to an employer during an interview.

Check Your Understanding
1. F; both parts are important to prepare for.
2. T
3. T

Critical Thinking
1. office: skirt or pants, blouse, jacket (girls); pants, shirt, jacket, and tie (boys); babysitting, volunteer at senior citizens' home, newspaper delivery: casual clothes that are neat and clean
2. Answers will vary but should include the idea that the employer will be asking about skills and past work experience that qualifies the applicant for the job.

3. Questions students ask should focus on the company or organization, the job itself, their responsibilities in the job, and opportunities for growth in the company or organization.
4. Students should respond that as with any contact, they would call the employer to follow up. Point out that a follow-up call is a good opportunity to offer additional information that might help the employer come to a decision.

Connecting to the Workplace

Prompt students to comment especially on what they learned from the person's responses to their questions. Would they have answered the questions in the same way?

Community Involvement

Students should follow the tips offered in this lesson about how to prepare for, handle, and follow up an interview. Emphasize that informational interviews are a good way to practice for job interviews.

CHAPTER 7 REVIEW ANSWERS

Recalling Key Concepts
1. The format you choose will depend on the job you're looking for and whether you want to emphasize work experience or skills.
2. The three main parts of a cover letter are the opening, the body, and the closing. In the opening, you should introduce yourself and state the job you're applying for and how you found out about it; in the body, you should sell yourself by describing your skills and experience and explaining how they match the job; in the closing, you should thank the interviewer, request an interview, and tell how you're going to follow up.
3. You need to line up references before you fill out a job application because you need to ask their permission to list them as references.

4. Your attitude tells an employer whether you can be counted on to do the job.

5. You should make notes so that you can remember how the interview went and learn from what happened. That way you'll have an even better interview next time.

Thinking Critically

1. Students may name computer skills, math skills, writing skills, and people skills.

2. Students should name other people who would know them or their work well, such as the school principal, a guidance counselor, a sports coach, or an adult who leads a club or group they belong to.

3. If you ask questions that focus on yourself, you will give an employer the impression that you are more interested in yourself and what the job can do for you than in the business, the job, and what you can contribute.

4. If you do not make eye contact, an interviewer may think you're shy, bored, or not paying attention.

Building Skills

1. Students should respond that it is important to be honest and provide accurate information in a résumé. Prompt students to suggest ways their friend might present herself in a positive light without work experience. Students may suggest that she describe skills she has that would enable her to do the job, or that she emphasize that she is a quick learner and could acquire the skills and experience she needs quickly.

2. Students may use either format. They should follow the tips provided in the text for creating a computer-friendly résumé. If a scanner is not available, have students compare their computer-friendly résumé with the appropriate résumé on pages 128-129 and comment on differences and similarities.

Applying Academic Skills

1. September 1999–present
   June–August 1999
   December 1998–January 1999
   July–September 1998
   January–June 1998
   October–December 1997
   June–August 1997

2. Suggest that students use month and year to plot events. Besides work experience or in place of it, students should include skills developed in different contexts: home, school, as part of a team or other group (community service, for example).

Discovery Portfolio

Students may use the contents of the file to create and update a résumé and may refer to it before filling out a job application or going to an interview. The file will also increase students' self-esteem and give them the confidence to apply for any job that interests them.

Suggest that students ask a variety of people to write letters of recommendation for them: teachers, neighbors, coaches, scout leaders, and other adults who know them well.

Career Exploration

Students should review the Investigating Career Clusters feature on page 145 before selecting a career. Students should research the career using resources described in Chapter 3. Suggest that in their pamphlets students also use visuals to provide information.

Employment Skills

Overview

In Unit 2, students will explore the workplace environment. They will learn about job benefits and workplace expectations. They will discover why basic skills are important to workplace success. They will learn how to make healthful choices for life and they will discover ways to make the workplace safe. Finally, they will think about ways to move ahead on the job.

Unit Introduction

Lead a discussion on employment skills by asking students the following questions:

1. Ask students what they expect from a job. What do they think the first day on the job would be like? Ask students to tell how expectations on the job are different from expectations at school.

2. Have students think about ways that they currently work with others. What makes it easier to work together? What are ways to work as a team? Explain to them that the same teamwork skills used at school will help them in the workplace.

3. Ask students to discuss ways in which basic skills such as reading, writing, math, and science might be used on the job. List the answers on the board. Elaborate on their answers by offering other potential ways that skills might be used.

4. Ask students for tips on how to stay healthy. Ask them to brainstorm ways to reduce stress. Ask them why the workplace might be stressful.

5. Ask students to come up with a list of school safety issues. Ask them to come up with ways to make their school safer. Explain how these same issues are relevant to the workplace.

6. Have students describe times they have had to change a plan they had made. Ask them why it is important to reevaluate your goals. Explain that in the workplace goals will be constantly changing.

Discuss student's answers and explain to them that they will learn more about these areas in this unit of the text.

Unit Closure

Have students write a 250-word description on their ideal workplace. Ask them to include what the environment would be like, how many employees they would work with, and the skills they would use.

Evaluation

Administer the reproducible Unit 2 Test found in the *Teacher's Resource Binder.*

Chapters within the Unit

Chapter 8
On the Job

Chapter 9
Working with Others

Chapter 10
Basic Skills Count

Chapter 11
Staying Healthy and Safe

Chapter 12
Moving toward Your Goals

LESSON 8-1 ● What You Can Expect

Lesson Objectives: After completing this lesson, the students will have learned:

1. how to handle their first day at a job,
2. ways they may be paid and benefits they may receive, and
3. how they can expect to be treated at work.

Lesson 8-1 Features	Lesson 8-1 Resources
Career Q & A, p. 151 The Global Workplace, p. 153	• Lesson 8-1 Activities, p. 159 • Student Activity Workbook, Activities 1 and 2 • Transparency 20 • Transparency Lesson Plan

LESSON 8-2 ● What an Employer Expects of You

Lesson Objectives: After completing this lesson, the students will have learned:

1. qualities employers look for in employees,
2. how to behave in the workplace, and
3. how their work is evaluated.

Lesson 8-2 Features	Lesson 8-2 Resources
The Right Attitude ,p. 161 Career Opportunities, p. 166 Investigating Career Clusters, p. 169	• Lesson 8-2 Activities, p. 168 • Student Activity Workbook, Activities 3, 4, and 5 • Transparency 21 • Transparency Lesson Plan

CHAPTER 8 RESOURCES

Assessment

- Lesson 8-1 Review, p. 159
- Lesson 8-2 Review, p. 168
- Chapter Review, p. 170
- Chapter 8 Reproducible Test and Testmaker Software

Extension

- Teacher's Manual, p. TM92
- Teacher's Resource Binder:
  - Teacher's Lesson Plans
  - Career Cluster Activities
  - Spanish Resources
  - Involving Parents and Family Resources

Multimedia

- Workforce 2000 Video Library, segments 7, 8, and 9
- Exploring the World of Work CD-ROM
- Teacher's Resource Binder:
  - Internet Resources, Chapter 8

SCANS CORRELATION CHART ....

FOUNDATION SKILLS

Basic Skills	Reading	Writing	Math	Listening	Speaking

Thinking Skills	Creative Thinking	Decision Making	Problem Solving	Seeing Things in the Mind's Eye	Knowing How to Learn	Reasoning

Personal Qualities	Responsibility	Self-Esteem	Sociability	Self-Management	Integrity/Honesty

WORKPLACE COMPETENCIES

Resources	Allocating Time	Allocating Money	Allocating Material and Facility Resources	Allocating Human Resources

Information	Acquiring and Evaluating Information	Organizing and Maintaining Information	Interpreting and Communicating Information	Using Computers to Process Information

Interpersonal Skills	Participating as a Member of a Team	Teaching Others	Serving Clients/ Customers	Exercising Leadership	Negotiating to Arrive at a Decision	Working with Cultural Diversity

Systems	Understanding Systems	Monitoring and Correcting Performance	Improving and Designing Systems

Technology	Selecting Technology	Applying Technology to Task	Maintaining and Troubleshooting Technology

TEACHER'S MANUAL

ENRICHMENT AND APPLICATION ACTIVITIES

Internet Activity

Ask students to use the Internet to find articles in publications on ethics in business. They should note the name of the publication and article, when it was published, and a summary of its contents. Suggested Internet sites or search words:

ethics

http://www.businessweek.com
http://www.cnnfn.com

Teacher's Resource Binder: Internet Resources

Field Trip Activity

Arrange for your class to tour a local manufacturing company. Many businesses offer tours of certain areas of their company. Encourage students to take note of the employees' working conditions and attitudes toward their work.

Guest Speaker Activity

Invite a representative from the human resources department of a mid- to large-sized company to talk to the class about his or her company's expectations of new employees, evaluation policies, orientation programs, and so on.

Chapter 8 On the Job

Chapter Outline

I. What You Can Expect
  A. Your First Day on the Job
    1. Getting Ready
    2. What's Waiting for You
    3. Getting It Right
  B. How Will You Be Paid?
    1. Forms of Payment
    2. Kinds of Benefits
  C. Honest and Fair Treatment
II. What an Employer Expects of You
  A. What Employers Want
    1. Working Well with Others
    2. Following Directions
    3. Doing What Needs to Be Done
    4. Taking on More Responsibility
    5. Continuing to Learn
  B. Working by the Rules
    1. Right Ways to Behave
    2. Why Is Ethics Important?
    3. Ethics and You
  C. How Are You Doing?

Chapter Overview

In this chapter, students will learn more about life in the workplace. They will learn what to expect on the first day of work, including how to prepare for it. They will learn about different ways of being paid and the different types of benefits many employers offer. They will also learn about the expectations employers have of their employees. Students will discover what personal qualities they can work on to become better employees. Finally, they will learn more about the evaluation process on the job and how it helps them be better employees.

LESSON 8-1

Focus

Objectives: After completing this lesson, the students will have learned:
1. how to handle their first day at a job,
2. ways they may be paid and benefits they may receive, and
3. how they can expect to be treated at work.

Preteaching the Vocabulary: Write on the board the Key Terms: *employee, orientation, coworkers, supervisor, wages, entry-level, overtime, salary, commission, benefits, minimum wage, discriminate*, and *disability*. Ask students to define each of these terms or use each in a sentence.

🔔**Bell Ringer:** Write on the board: "Take five minutes and write how you felt on the first day of attending middle school."

Introducing the Lesson: Ask volunteers to read their responses to the Bell Ringer activity. Then tell students that in this lesson they will be learning what to expect on their first day of a new job.

Teach
Guided Practice

Discussion Starter: Ask students to recall specific skills or activities that are now easy for them. Ask: "What mistakes did you make when you first tried them? What did you learn from your mistakes? How long did it take to overcome your mistakes?" Discuss how they can apply this knowledge about themselves to the first days on a job.

Critical Thinking: Tell students that most first jobs are entry-level jobs and ask: "How can keeping your career goals in mind help you accept and appreciate a job at the beginning level?"

Implementing Teamwork: Divide the class into small groups and have each group make up a math problem for each of the following forms of payment: wages with overtime, salary, and salary plus commission. Give each group a copy of the other groups' problems and time them to see which group can solve the other groups' problems fastest.

Application Activity: Bring some play money to class to help demonstrate different methods of payment. Ask three students to volunteer. One student will be paid a salary; one will be paid commission plus salary; and one will be paid wages. Ask the class to calculate how much each student will be paid for one week: salary $14,500 per year; commission plus salary, $10,000 per year plus 10 percent of $500 sales; and wages, $15 per hour for 40 hours. ($279, $242, and $600) Discuss with students that some levels of pay sound higher than they actually are.

SCANS Skills—Math: Have students calculate the cash value that benefits contribute to an income in the following situation.

Independent Practice

Amber makes $13 an hour as a lab technician and works 8 hours a day, 40 hours per week. She shares the cost of her health insurance with her employer; she pays $50 per month. The same coverage for herself and her two-year-old daughter, if purchased independently, would cost $133 per month. During the first week of July she was paid for a July 4th holiday. She contributes $30 per month to a retirement plan in which her employer offers matching funds. She brings her daughter to the on-site daycare center and pays $35 per week. The daycare center in her neighborhood costs $85 per week. Her company also offers educational assistance, but she is waiting for the fall semester to take a class.

What is the additional cash value of these benefits to Amber for the month of July? ($417: 133 − 50 = 83; 13 x 8 = 104; (85 − 35) x 4 = 200; 83 + 104 + 30 + 200 = 417)

Research Activity: Have students read Investigating Career Clusters on page 169 and complete the research activity.

Assess

Reteaching: Divide the class into small groups of five or six students. Allow each group to choose the type of small business it will become and the company's name. Give each group the guidelines that they are a small business with 20 or fewer employees; they represent the management of the company; and the company is moderately profitable. Have the students, as the management of their business, decide the following issues:

- the form of payment for each kind of employee
- the kinds of benefits to be offered
- the type of orientation to be given

Allow each group to present their decisions and discuss how they came to their decisions.

Enrichment: Ask students to interview employed people about how most of the employees at their company are paid. (Emphasize that they are not to ask the *amount* people are paid but the *method* of payment, such as wages, salary, and commission). Have them share their findings with the class. The following questions may be helpful:

- Are most of the employees paid a salary or a wage?
- Are any people paid by commission? How do the commission sales work? Do people working on commission have a base pay?

- Is it possible to earn overtime pay? How does overtime work?
- What are the advantages and disadvantages of the method of payment your company uses?

Assessment: Have students complete the Lesson 8-1 Review and Activities.

Close

Have student complete the following statement: *"On my first day of work, I can probably expect...."*

LESSON 8-2

Focus

Objectives: After completing this lesson, the students will have learned:

1. qualities employers look for in employees,
2. how to behave in the workplace, and
3. how their work is evaluated.

Preteaching the Vocabulary: Write on the board the Key Terms: *cooperate, initiative, ethics,* and *performance reviews.* Ask students to define each of these terms or use each in a sentence.

🔔 **Bell Ringer:** Write on the board: "List at least four things your teachers expect of you and four things you expect of your teachers."

Introducing the Lesson: Discuss students' responses to the Bell Ringer activity and how the expectations of their teachers may be similar to the expectations of future employers. Then tell students that in this lesson they will learn the qualities employers look for in employees and how to behave in the workplace.

Teach

Guided Practice

Implementing Teamwork: Divide the class into five groups giving each one of the following team names: Won't Cooperate, Can't Follow Directions, Lacks Initiative, Shuns Responsibility, and Doesn't Learn. Have each group write a comedy skit that describes a work situation with their team name. After each group has performed their skit, discuss how difficult a work environment could be if the employees displayed these negative qualities.

Discussion Starter: Present the following ethical situation to students and ask for their reactions. Make sure that they understand who is affected by their decision and how that party is affected.

Imagine that you work for a large department store like Macy's or Sears. After you have worked there for a couple of weeks, you notice that some of your coworkers take home store supplies, like hangers, bags, notepads, and pens. Decide whether you would:

1. Do the same. Nobody seems to mind.
2. Tell your supervisor about what you've seen.
3. Keep your mouth shut and your hands off the supplies, even though you think your coworkers' activities are wrong.

Application Activity: Have students create student performance evaluation forms for this class in pairs or small groups. Suggest they start by listing qualities that a student should have to be successful in this class (ability to cooperate, follows directions, etc.) and make a space for how well the student demonstrates those qualities (satisfactory, unsatisfactory, etc.). Post the different forms and allow students to discuss them.

Critical Thinking: Ask students why a worker might be fearful of performance evaluations? What could they suggest to help an employee overcome this fear?

SCANS Skills—Speaking: Have each student give a two-minute speech about ethics in the workplace.

Independent Practice

Research Activity: Have students research the problems and concerns of business owners. They can use the Internet, a CD-ROM database, on-line or manual card catalogs at the library, or the *Reader's Guide to Periodical Literature* to perform searches using topics such as "Business," "Entrepreneurs," "Free Enterprise," and "Capitalism."

Assess

Reteaching: Write the five personal qualities that employers value most on the board: "Works Well with Others," "Follows Directions," "Does What Needs to Be Done," "Takes on More Responsibility," and "Continues to Learn." Ask students to write an example from their daily lives that demonstrates each quality.

Enrichment: Ask students to interview at least one employer in the community on how employee evaluations are handled. The following, or similar questions, may be used:

* How are employee evaluations handled in your business? Are they written or informal?
* What should an employee do to prepare for an evaluation?
* What are the most important points you stress in evaluations?
* If an employee does not receive a good evaluation, what is done?
* How often are employees evaluated?
* If a written evaluation is used, may I have a sample copy to share with the class?

Assessment:

1. Have students complete the Lesson 8-2 Review and Activities.
2. Have students complete the Chapter 8 Review.
3. Assign the Chapter 8 Test for students to complete.

Close

Have student complete the following statement: *"An employer can expect that I will...."*

LESSON 8-1 REVIEW ANSWERS

Vocabulary Review

Students' work should demonstrate a grasp of the lesson content and reflect an understanding of the key terms.

Check Your Understanding

1. b 2. a

Critical Thinking

1. Students should draw on their own experience to answer the question. They should demonstrate an understanding of the purpose of orientation and should support their response with sound reasoning and examples from their own experience, if possible.
2. Answer will vary but should include the ideas that asking questions can clear up uncertainties and give you a clear idea of what is expected of you.
3. someone who is outgoing and gets along well with others, someone with high self-esteem
4. In addition to wages or commission, a full-time sales job would probably include health insurance, paid time off, and a retirement plan. It might also include child care and education assistance, as well as a company discount.
5. Students may respond that laws have been passed to make sure everyone has the opportunity to work regardless of their race, religion, nationality, gender, age, or physical appearance or disability.

Connecting to the Workplace

Students should respond that they would have gone ahead and asked questions if they had been in Tyrone's situation. Students should observe that Tyrone may not do his job well if he is confused about his job responsibilities.

Teamwork

Students should use what they have learned about company orientations to prepare an orientation program. Encourage them to be creative and to use various media to welcome new employees.

LESSON 8-2 REVIEW ANSWERS

Vocabulary Review

Students' letters should recap material presented in the lesson and should include the key terms.

Check Your Understanding

1. T
2. F; employers do expect their employees to behave ethically.

Critical Thinking

1. Answers will vary but should include the following: ability to cooperate, ability to follow directions, initiative, willingness to take on more responsibility, willingness to learn. Urge students to take time to evaluate their personal qualities before responding.
2. Answers will vary but may include the following: at home you might do the dishes or other chores without being asked; at school you might work on something for extra credit or bring in information on items that pertain to something you're studying in class.
3. Students should identify one area of ethical behavior as a challenge and support their choice with sound reasoning.

4. Students should observe that performance reviews offer valuable feedback that can help workers improve their performance and set career goals.
5. Answer will vary but should include the idea that self-evaluation allows you to identify strengths and weaknesses, therefore giving you useful information about how to make improvements.
6. Students may respond that they would find it hard to hear criticism of their work.

Connecting to the Workplace

Students should respond that they should behave ethically in the situation by being honest about both time and money. They should report to their employer that they have been overpaid, and ask what can be done to correct the error.

Community Involvement

Students should identify an appropriate community service project and should work as a group to carry it out. Allow time for students to report on their projects.

CHAPTER 8 REVIEW ANSWERS

Recalling Key Concepts

1. Companies provide orientation for new employees to explain company policies and procedures. Orientation is also an opportunity to tour the work environment and meet coworkers.
2. Wages are a fixed amount of money paid for each hour worked. A salary is a fixed amount of money for a certain period of time, such as a year.
3. Initiative is when you take the first step in doing or beginning something. You do what needs to be done without being told to do it.

4. Answers will vary but should include three of the following: honesty about time, honesty about money, respecting employer's property, confidentiality, and fairness.

5. The purpose of a performance review is to evaluate how well you're doing your job.

▶ Thinking Critically

1. Allow students to share worries or concerns they anticipate having on the first day at a new job. Discuss strategies for dealing with nervous or anxious feelings.

2. For many people, benefits are an important reason for working because they fill important needs and employers cover their cost or share it with employees.

3. People who are treated with honesty and fairness are more likely to care about their work and to work well with others.

▶ Building Skills

1. Students posing as new employees should prepare general questions about their first day and a few specific questions about the job. Students posing as employers should welcome the new employee and provide some general information about the first day.

2. Have students use their lists to participate in a class discussion about getting to know new people at work and fitting in at the workplace.

3. The purpose of the activity is to increase students' awareness of the diversity of people in various settings, including the workplace. Discuss what diversity contributes to the classroom and workplace.

▶ Applying Academic Skills

1. Students' collages should feature at least five careers in the fine arts and humanities. Students should use both pictures and words to illustrate the careers. Have students explain their collages to the class.

2. Commission: $1,200; total earnings for the month: $3,600.

▶ Discovery Portfolio

Goals students set should be based on conferences, report cards, or both. Remind students to check their progress in reaching their goals.

▶ Career Exploration

Suggest that students review the Investigating Career Clusters on page 169 before selecting a career. Students should use the various resources named to research the career they choose.

LESSON 9-1 ● Building Relationships

Lesson Objectives: After completing this lesson, the students will have learned:

1. the basics of working well with others,
2. how to build work relationships, and
3. how to deal with conflicts when they arise.

Lesson 9-1 Features
Career Opportunities, p. 179

Lesson 9-1 Resources
- Lesson 9-1 Activities, p. 182
- Student Activity Workbook, Activities 1, 2, and 3
- Transparency 22
- Transparency Lesson Plan

LESSON 9-2 ● Teamwork

Lesson Objectives: After completing this lesson, the students will have learned:

1. why teamwork is important,
2. the steps involved in teamwork, and
3. problems teams face and how to handle them.

Lesson 9-2 Features
The Global Workplace, p. 187
Career Q & A, p. 189
The Right Attitude, p. 190
Investigating Career Clusters, p. 193

Lesson 9-2 Resources
- Lesson 9-2 Activities, p. 192
- Student Activity Workbook, Activities 4 and 5

CHAPTER 9 RESOURCES

Assessment
- Lesson 9-1 Review, p. 182
- Lesson 9-2 Review, p. 192
- Chapter Review, p. 194
- Chapter 9 Reproducible Test and Testmaker Software

Extension
- Teacher's Manual, p. TM100
- Teacher's Resource Binder:
  - Teacher's Lesson Plans
  - Career Cluster Activities
  - Spanish Resources
  - Involving Parents and Family Resources

Multimedia
- Workforce 2000 Video Library, segments 9 and 13
- Exploring the World of Work CD-ROM
- Teacher's Resource Binder:
  - Internet Resources, Chapter 9

SCANS CORRELATION CHART ....

FOUNDATION SKILLS

Basic Skills	Reading	Writing	Math	Listening	Speaking

Thinking Skills	Creative Thinking	Decision Making	Problem Solving	Seeing Things in the Mind's Eye	Knowing How to Learn	Reasoning

Personal Qualities	Responsibility	Self-Esteem	Sociability	Self-Management	Integrity/Honesty

WORKPLACE COMPETENCIES

Resources	Allocating Time	Allocating Money	Allocating Material and Facility Resources	Allocating Human Resources

Information	Acquiring and Evaluating Information	Organizing and Maintaining Information	Interpreting and Communicating Information	Using Computers to Process Information

Interpersonal Skills	Participating as a Member of a Team	Teaching Others	Serving Clients/ Customers	Exercising Leadership	Negotiating to Arrive at a Decision	Working with Cultural Diversity

Systems	Understanding Systems	Monitoring and Correcting Performance	Improving and Designing Systems

Technology	Selecting Technology	Applying Technology to Task	Maintaining and Troubleshooting Technology

ENRICHMENT AND APPLICATION ACTIVITIES

Internet Activity

Ask students to use the Internet to find information on teamwork in the workplace. They should see what kinds of information are available on-line and make note of appropriate Web sites. Suggested Internet search words:

    teamwork
    team leader
    group leader
    team planning

GO TO Teacher's Resource Binder: Internet Resources

Field Trip Activity

Depending on what's available in your area, have students meet with a member or members of a team at your local hospital, fire station, or business. Have students ask questions and share their impressions when they return to the classroom.

Guest Speaker Activity

Invite an arbitrator or mediator at a local business or industry to speak to the class. Ask this person to discuss some specific skills required for the job and his or her background and training.

Working with Others

Chapter Outline

I. Building Relationships
   A. Respect Is the Key
   B. Getting Along with Others
      1. Ways to Build Relationships
   C. Getting Along with Yourself
   D. Dealing with Conflict
      1. Causes of Conflicts
      2. Resolving Conflicts
      3. Preventing Conflicts
II. Teamwork
   A. Why Work as a Team?
      1. Teams in the Work World
   B. Team Planning
      1. Setting Goals
      2. Assigning Roles and Tasks
      3. Assessing
   C. Dealing with Problems

Chapter Overview

In this chapter, students will learn the importance of working well with others. First they will look at their own relationships with friends, family, and people in their community. They will learn that showing respect for others is a basic skill that employers look for in employees. Then they will learn how to build good relationships and what can be done should conflict occur. To deal with conflict, problem-solving skills can be used, but the best approach is to prevent conflict in the first place.

Students will also learn the importance of teamwork in the workplace. They will identify ways in which they already work on teams and observe the skills that are required for successful cooperation. Different roles, special skills, good communication, and responsibility are all required in setting and achieving goals within a group.

After this chapter, students will begin to see the benefits of working well with others. Conflict and problems may be a part of teamwork in the workplace, but meeting the challenge can even be fun.

LESSON 9-1

Focus

Objectives: After completing this lesson, the students will have learned:
1. the basics of working well with others,
2. how to build work relationships, and
3. how to deal with conflicts when they arise.

Preteaching the Vocabulary: Write on the board the Key Terms: *relationships, respect, empathize, self-esteem, conflict, prejudice mediator, compromise,* and *conflict resolution.* Ask students to define each of these terms.

🔔 **Bell Ringer:** Write on the board: "Take five minutes to list some examples of your experience working with others, such as on an athletic team, a committee, etc."

Introducing the Lesson: Ask volunteers to name some group experiences named in the Bell Ringer activity. Tell students that these experiences will be valuable as preparation for the workplace.

Teach

Guided Practice

Critical Thinking: Write the following words on the board as column headings: *respect, empathize, compromise.* Ask students to give word associations for each heading and list them under each heading. You may need to discuss with students. How, for example, does *sympathize* differ from *empathize*? Point out that without respect for others and the ability to put oneself in another's shoes, a compromise cannot be reached.

Implementing Teamwork: Divide the class into small groups. Give each group one of the following problems to solve. Have each group read their assigned problem and its solution to the rest of the class.

Problem A. Dan is beginning his second week of work, and he is feeling lonely. Others have not given him any sign that they want to get to know him. Everyone at work is older than Dan, but he doesn't feel this should keep them from being friendly.

Problem B. George is on his second day of work. He is having a problem talking to his coworkers. What suggestions would you offer George?

Problem C. Catherine reported to work on her first day in a pair of slacks and a jacket. After she got to work, she realized that other female employees did not wear slacks. What should Catherine do?

Problem D. It was time for Hugh to go to lunch. Since it was his first day on the job, he wasn't sure of how much time he had or where to eat. How should he handle this problem?

Discussion Starter: Ask the students to compare the challenges they find in getting along with others at school to the challenges they expect on the job. Is either set of relationships more important than the other? Why?

Application Activity: On the board list some of the general strategies suggested for getting along with others:

- Treat people as you would like to be treated.
- Try to understand the other person's side.
- Speak carefully.
- Be friendly.
- Have a sense of humor.

Ask students to cite examples of how they have used these strategies successfully in the past. How can the use of these and similar strategies benefit them when they work?

Community Involvement Activity: Have students make arrangements to job shadow someone in their community for half a day. They should observe and take notes on the person's interactions, or dealings, with other people. Then, have them write a report that focuses on the importance of getting along with others in the job they observed. Allow students to read their reports to the class.

Emphasize that students should focus on the person's interactions with others. In their reports students should comment on the importance of getting along with others in the job they observed.

SCANS Skills—Math: Tell students that they are employed by the Collins Moving Company, which uses teams to handle different parts of the move—for example, packing, loading, driving, and unloading. Collins has given an estimate to one client that it will take a team of four people nine hours to move her belongings. What is the total of hours required? If each packer is paid $12.50 per hour, how much will each person earn for this job? (36 hours; earnings, 9 x $12.50 = $112.50 each)

Independent Practice

Research Activity: Have students read Investigating Career Clusters on page 193 and complete the Research Activity.

Assess

Reteaching: With textbooks closed, review causes that may lead to conflict in the workplace, such as poor communication, differences in beliefs, jealousy, and prejudice. Take one cause and list on the board some possible problem-solving skills.

Enrichment: Divide the class into small groups of three or four students. Have each group design a bulletin board display or a mural depicting people in both positive and negative work situations. Suggest students use pictures and headlines from magazines and newspapers as well as their own illustrations and captions to show examples of pleasant and unpleasant work situations.

Assessment: Have students complete the Lesson 9-1 Review and Activities.

Close

Have students complete this statement: *"Because many problems on the job stem from relationships with other people, it is important to treat others...."*

LESSON 9-2

Focus

Objectives: After completing this lesson, the students will have learned:
1. why teamwork is important,
2. the steps involved in teamwork, and
3. problems teams face and how to handle them.

Preteaching the Vocabulary: Write on the board the Key Terms: *team planning* and *assess*. Ask students to define these terms and tell about their importance in the success of teamwork.

Bell Ringer: Remind students that human relationships are vital in the work world. Ask them to list at least three tips for getting along as a member of a team.

Introducing the Lesson: Ask volunteers to read their tips from the Bell Ringer activity. Emphasize that successful use of team skills can make the difference between success and failure in the working world.

Teach
Guided Practice

Critical Thinking: Have students write a short paper (75–100 words) describing the interpersonal skills needed by team members. Answers might include cooperativeness, responsibility, initiative, listening to the ideas of others, and accepting constructive criticism.

Implementing Teamwork: Ask a student to volunteer a problem he or she has had at work or school. Allow time for students to ask questions to clarify the problem described. Divide the class into small groups. List the steps in the problem-solving process on the board and have each group decide on one way they would try to solve the problem. Stress the value of the process itself, and have students notice that there may be more than one workable solution to a problem.

Discussion Starter: Ask students who play on sports teams to share their thoughts about how teamwork helps them to perform better. Then have students with part-time jobs share their teamwork experiences. Ask students to compare the two situations.

Application Activity: Have students decide which of the roles mentioned in the Explore Activity on page 188 they would prefer. Reasons can be recorded in their Discovery Portfolios.

Teamwork Activity: In teams of five students, have each group plan a fund-raiser such as a bake sale, car wash, or bazaar. Their goal will be to raise money for a field trip.

They should decide what tasks need to be done and assign roles within the team. Students should make a schedule for assessing their progress. Then, have them present their plan to the class. Students should compare their plan to those of the other teams. Which plan does the class think is most workable? Why?

Each team should compile a detailed fund-raising plan. Have the class vote on the most workable plan. Discuss why one plan is more workable than another.

SCANS Skills—Interpreting and Communicating Information: Assign students to teams of four or five to plan a class newsletter on career advice. Tell students they have two months to complete this project and they are to set short-, medium-, and long-term goals. Have students compare their completed goals in class.

Independent Practice

Research Activity: Have each student find and read an article about how to improve team performance. Have students take notes about suggestions they find and discuss their findings in class.

Assess

Reteaching: Working in teams of four or five, have students imagine that they have been assigned to teams that will work together for several months. Have them list rules for how the team members should work together. For example, one rule might be that all team members must participate. Have teams share their rules, and then discuss how cooperation helps teams accomplish goals.

Enrichment: Have students write about a dramatic situation involving teamwork, such as a car crash, a fire, or an earthquake.

Assessment:

1. Have students complete the Lesson 9-2 Review and Activities.
2. Have students complete the Chapter 9 Review.
3. Assign the Chapter 9 Test for students to complete.

Close

Have students complete this sentence: *"When I work as a team member in a future job, I will remember to...."*

LESSON 9-1 REVIEW ANSWERS

Vocabulary Review

Students should write a sentence for each key term. Students' sentences should demonstrate an understanding of the meaning of the key terms and relate the terms to their own experience.

Check Your Understanding

1. c   **2.** b

Critical Thinking

1. Students may observe that they feel hurt or insulted.
2. Students should support their choice with sound reasoning.
3. When you learn to do something new, you realize what you are capable of doing, and the experience gives you confidence in yourself.
4. Students may name strategies mentioned in the text or offer strategies of their own for avoiding a conflict.

Connecting to the Workplace

Supply students with newspapers or have them check a newspaper at home. Students should base their summaries on information provided in the ad. Although the ad may not include specific information about people skills, students should be able to surmise what people skills would be useful for the job.

Teamwork

As necessary, elaborate on the concept of peer mediation. Direct students to teachers or counselors at school who may be able to help them learn more about peer mediation and set up a program for use in the school.

LESSON 9-2 REVIEW ANSWERS

Vocabulary Review

Students' posters should incorporate the two key terms and illustrate the three main steps in team planning: setting goals, assigning roles and tasks, and assessing. Set aside time for students to explain their posters to the class.

Check Your Understanding

1. F; team planning involves setting goals, assigning tasks, and communicating regularly about how things are going.
2. F; it helps everyone move in the same direction.
3. T

Critical Thinking

1. Students should respond that teamwork is important in school because they work in many kinds of groups and must cooperate to complete projects in class. Students should observe that knowing how to work on a team may be important to them in a job in the future.

2. Answers should include specific interests and skills that would make the student a key player on the leadership team.
3. Assessing the outcome of a project helps you evaluate your work and determine what you could do better next time.
4. Answers will vary, but students may name problems identified in Figure 9-2. Allow students time to explain how they handled problems they faced in a group.

Connecting to the Workplace

Students should report on teamwork in a health career or career of interest to them. Students should use as many resources as possible to gather information.

Community Involvement

Urge each student to find at least one article about teamwork in the community. Have students gather in small groups to share interesting examples of teamwork.

CHAPTER 9 REVIEW ANSWERS

▶ Recalling Key Concepts

1. Respect is consideration for others.
2. Students should name five of the following as causes of conflict: misunderstandings, different beliefs or opinions, gossip, teasing, jealousy, and prejudice.
3. You might ask a third party to make the decision that will end a conflict if both sides want a solution but cannot agree on what it should be.
4. Team planning involves setting goals, assigning tasks, and communicating regularly about how things are going.
5. Unclear goals, misunderstandings about decision making and leadership, competitiveness among team members, team members not

doing their share of work, and bad feelings because individual effort is not recognized are among the problems teams often face.

▶ Thinking Critically

1. A sense of humor helps you look at the light side of a situation. When you have a sense of humor, you are able to take things less seriously and so get along more easily with others.

2. Answers will vary; students should explain their answers and discuss strategies for developing a positive attitude toward themselves.

3. Students should observe that although close friends have much in common, they are still unique individuals with their own points of view and ideas.

4. Students should name specific projects they have completed with others that would not have been possible for themselves or any individual to do alone.

5. Students may suggest calling a meeting of the team to assess the group's progress and individual roles in the group.

▶ Building Skills

1. Students should suggest two solutions that are fair to both boys, such as having Josh do his homework in another room or having Matt use earphones to listen to music while Josh is working, and having Matt go to another room when Josh wants to sleep or having Josh wear an eye mask when he is trying to sleep.

2. Suggest that students follow the steps in team planning to prepare their newscast. Assess the newscast for students or have the class assess each team's presentation.

▶ Applying Academic Skills

1. Students should gather a variety of examples of conflicts from the newspaper. The letters they write should offer a constructive solution to the conflict they select.

2. Students' comic strips should focus on ways to build relationships. Encourage students to critique each other's work as instructed.

▶ Discovery Portfolio

Ask for volunteers to share their short stories, poems, or songs with the class. Students' compositions should focus on relationships.

▶ Career Exploration

Suggest that students review the Investigating Career Clusters feature on page 193 before selecting a career. Students should use the various resources named to research the career they choose. They should present their findings in a mock ad and use the interview setting to share additional information about the career.

LESSON 10-1 ● Getting Your Message Across

Lesson Objectives: After completing this lesson, the students will have learned:

1. how to apply the basics of speaking,
2. how to listen effectively,
3. how to improve reading and writing skills, and
4. how to use images, or pictures, to present ideas.

Lesson 10-1 Features

The Right Attitude, p. 199

The Global Workplace, p. 209

Lesson 10-1 Resources

- Lesson 10-1 Activities, p. 210
- Student Activity Workbook, Activities 1, 2, 3, and 4
- Transparencies 23 and 24
- Transparency Lesson Plan

LESSON 10-2 ● Applying Other Skills

Lesson Objectives: After completing this lesson, the students will have learned:

1. how to strengthen their math and science skills, and
2. how to build their computer skills.

Lesson 10-2 Features

Career Q & A, p. 212

Career Opportunities, p. 216

Investigating Career Clusters, p. 219

Lesson 10-2 Resources

- Lesson 10-2 Activities, p. 218
- Student Activity Workbook, Activity 5

CHAPTER 10 RESOURCES

Assessment

- Lesson 10-1 Review, p. 210
- Lesson 10-2 Review, p. 218
- Chapter Review, p. 220
- Chapter 10 Reproducible Test and Testmaker Software

Extension

- Teacher's Manual, p. TM108
- Teacher's Resource Binder:
  - Teacher's Lesson Plans
  - Career Cluster Activities
  - Spanish Resources
  - Involving Parents and Family Resources

Multimedia

- Workforce 2000 Video Library, segments 14, 15, and 16
- Exploring the World of Work CD-ROM
- Teacher's Resource Binder:
  - Internet Resources, Chapter 10

TEACHER'S MANUAL

SCANS CORRELATION CHART ....

FOUNDATION SKILLS

Basic Skills	Reading	Writing	Math	Listening	Speaking

Thinking Skills	Creative Thinking	Decision Making	Problem Solving	Seeing Things in the Mind's Eye	Knowing How to Learn	Reasoning

Personal Qualities	Responsibility	Self-Esteem	Sociability	Self-Management	Integrity/Honesty

WORKPLACE COMPETENCIES

Resources	Allocating Time	Allocating Money	Allocating Material and Facility Resources	Allocating Human Resources

Information	Acquiring and Evaluating Information	Organizing and Maintaining Information	Interpreting and Communicating Information	Using Computers to Process Information

Interpersonal Skills	Participating as a Member of a Team	Teaching Others	Serving Clients/ Customers	Exercising Leadership	Negotiating to Arrive at a Decision	Working with Cultural Diversity

Systems	Understanding Systems	Monitoring and Correcting Performance	Improving and Designing Systems

Technology	Selecting Technology	Applying Technology to Task	Maintaining and Troubleshooting Technology

ENRICHMENT AND APPLICATION ACTIVITIES

Internet Activity

Ask students to use the Internet to gather information about reading programs. Have them look for different levels of reading courses in community classes, volunteer programs, and private reading workshops. Suggested Internet search words:

reading
speed reading

GO TO Teacher's Resource Binder: Internet Resources

Field Trip Activity

Arrange to visit a company that does business abroad. Ask a company representative to explain how the Internet, faxes, and high-tech communication affect the business.

Guest Speaker Activity

Find a person who works at home, such as a freelance writer, who can explain some of the advantages of not having to "go to work." How has technology changed his or her life? Have students write down some of the pros and cons of working with a computer at home.

Chapter 10 Basic Skills Count

Chapter Outline

Chapter Overview

In this chapter, students will discover why the basic skills of speaking, listening, reading, and writing are important in the workplace. They will gather tips for improving these skills in order to prepare for the types of situations they will meet at work. Reading and writing skills are needed both to apply for a job and on the job.

Students will also discover that math and science skills are among the most important tools used in careers today. Math and science skills help develop logical thinking skills and habits of observation, as well as teach how to solve problems. Students will realize that computer skills are important in today's work world.

LESSON 10-1

Focus

Objectives: After completing this lesson, the students will have learned:
1. how to apply the basics of speaking,
2. how to listen effectively,
3. how to improve reading and writing skills, and
4. how to use images, or pictures, to present ideas.

Preteaching the Vocabulary: Write on the board the Key Terms: *communication, purpose, audience, subject, active listening, previewing, skimming, context clues,* and *images.* Ask students to define each term and explain how the first three are closely connected.

Bell Ringer: Ask students which skills (speaking, listening, reading, writing) they spent the most time on today. Which one do they think they will spend the most time on in the workplace?

Introducing the Lesson: Tell students that the basic skills are essential tools in pursuing a career. In this lesson they will learn about the basics of speaking and listening, how to improve reading and writing skills, and how to use images to present ideas.

Teach
Guided Practice

Discussion Starter: Ask students: "If all they ever need to write is a short note to their supervisor or a coworker, would good writing skills be necessary? What might happen if the reader has trouble understanding a request for some time off? What other written messages might be too important to risk a misunderstanding?"

Critical Thinking: Ask students how an image expresses what cannot be said in words. Is the message of an image clearer or less clear than a written message?

Application Activity: Have students take a piece of their own writing (a letter, essay, or report) and explain to whom the writing is directed (audience). What "voice" or tone is used in the piece? (Businesslike, objective, emotional, persuasive, etc.)

Implementing Teamwork: Ask students to form teams of three people. Have the teams compare two brands of word-processing or spreadsheet software. Students should research the software by reading magazines, talking with store owners, or talking with users. Then ask the teams to make a chart comparing the two products. The chart can be divided into strong points and weak points.

Community Involvement Activity: Have students volunteer to help out in an elementary school class or after-school program one day a week. They should work on their speaking and listening skills with the children. Have students keep a journal to record their experiences. They should compare and contrast speaking and listening to children with speaking and listening to people their own age or older. Which skill comes most easily to them? Which takes the most practice? Then, have them discuss their ideas with you.

Review students' journal entries. Discuss their evaluation of their experience. Students should observe that good speaking habits and active listening are useful when speaking or listening to anyone. Students may describe ways they speak differently to people of different ages.

SCANS Skills—Speaking: Ask each student to give a three-minute oral presentation that outlines the features of his or her favorite computer software (including games). If you have computers in the classroom, students might give a brief demonstration.

SCANS Skills—Listening: Invite a math teacher to make a short presentation about improving math skills. Tell students to practice active listening during the presentation. They may take notes if they wish, and ask questions after the presentation. Then, have them write a paragraph summarizing the teacher's suggestions.

Students should review the guidelines for active listening, taking notes, and writing well. Students' paragraphs should cover the main points of the teacher's presentation.

Independent Practice

Research Activity: Have students read Investigating Career Clusters on page 219 and complete the Research Activity.

Assess

Reteaching Activity: Help students to imagine a work situation requiring the four basic skills. Emphasize that listening may be one of the hardest skills to learn. Review ways in which listening can be an "active" skill.

Enrichment: Tell students to listen to a well-known speech and analyze its purpose, audience, subject, and tone.

Assessment: Have students complete the Lesson 10-1 Review and Activities.

Close

Have students complete this statement: *"A truly important skill for my future career is...."*

LESSON 10-2

Focus

Objectives: After completing this lesson, the students will have learned:

1. how to strengthen their math and science skills, and

2. how to build their computer skills.

Preteaching the Vocabulary: Write on the board the Key Terms: *mathematics, science, spreadsheet, netiquette,* and *emoticons*. Ask students how the first two are related. Have students who are especially computer literate explain the last three terms to the rest of the class.

Bell Ringer: Ask students who have received paychecks for jobs they have done if they used their math skills to understand their paychecks.

Introducing the Lesson: Remind students that math, science, and the computer are already an active part of everyday life for them. Tell students that basic skills in these areas are among the most important tools people use in careers today.

Teach
Guided Practice

Critical Thinking: Ask students what a credit card is. Ask them how technology makes credit cards possible. Why is it a good thing to have strong math skills when dealing with personal finances, such as the use of credit cards?

Implementing Teamwork: Divide the class into small groups and assign each group an everyday activity, for example, shopping, gardening, using machines, cooking, sewing, or building. Have each group come up with a list of ways in which math skills are needed in these areas. Have groups compare the length of their lists.

Discussion Starter: Before the students begin reading, ask them about their math skills. How would students rate their attitude to math and science — involved, not as involved as they would like to be, or can't relate to math and science problems. Do students think that a career will motivate them to improve their math skills or become more involved in science?

Application Activity: To introduce the necessity of having or improving math skills, ask students to give examples of when math might be used at the office. Discuss their ideas and include examples, such as analyzing bills and making out paychecks, in the discussion.

Teamwork Activity: Have students work in small groups to make booklets about how to build computer skills for the future. They should use information from their textbooks and other sources to write the text for their booklet. Tell students to ask you for help locating and using desktop publishing software to design and print their booklets.

Students who have worked with desktop publishing software before may lead their groups. Urge students also to include images in their booklets. In creating the text for the booklet, students should follow the writing guidelines provided in Lesson 1. Publish enough copies to distribute to students at the grade level you teach in school.

SCANS Skills—Math: Have students imagine they have started a job. They will be earning $15.00 per hour for an 8-hour day. Have them set up a budget for lunches and snacks per day.

SCANS Skills—Interprets and Communicates Information: Have students pair up and make a poster showing five terms that Internet users should know. Possible terms include *browser, download, freeware, home page, HTML, hyperlink, log in* or *on, shareware, spam, thread, URL.* They should find the definitions of the Internet terms, then use words and images to explain the terms.

Suggest students look for definitions of the terms in an up-to-date, comprehensive dictionary, or in books on using the Internet, such as *The Internet for Busy People* by Christian Crumlish. Students should present the terms in a clear and understandable form on a poster.

Independent Practice

Research Activity: Have several students do research about math games. Take some time to play these games in class.

Assess

Reteaching: Remind students that by improving math, science, and computer skills, they will enjoy greater success in their careers. Then have students list ways they can improve their science skills.

Enrichment: Invite someone with a job in the hospitality and recreation field to speak to the class on the topic of how computer skills are used in this career.

Assessment

1. Have students complete the Lesson 10-2 Review and Activities.

2. Have students complete the Chapter 10 Review.

3. Assign the Chapter 10 Test for students to complete.

Close

Have students complete this sentence: *"I am interested in improving my computer skills because...."*

LESSON 10-1 REVIEW ANSWERS

Vocabulary Review

Students should think about their purpose, audience, and subject as they prepare their talk; their talk should incorporate the terms listed and demonstrate an understanding of the meaning of each term.

Check Your Understanding

1. b   2. a

Critical Thinking

1. You might ramble and lose the interest of your listeners.

2. Answers will vary; students should explain why a particular kind of image especially appeals to them.

Connecting to the Workplace

Students should use good writing skills to summarize clearly the essential information contained in the message.

Teamwork

Students may refer to the Investigating Career Clusters on page 219 to identify a career in hospitality or recreation. They should use words and images on their posters to tell about the importance of communication skills in the career they have selected.

LESSON 10-2 REVIEW ANSWERS

Vocabulary Review

Students' questions should include the key terms and focus on main ideas in the lesson. Partners may use each other's questions to review the lesson.

Check Your Understanding

1. T
2. T
3. F; do not type in all capital letters.
4. T

Critical Thinking

1. Students should describe the application of thinking skills such as sequencing, observing, and problem solving in a career of interest to them.
2. Students may respond that computers are part of everyday life and computer skills are as basic to work as speaking, listening, reading, writing, math, and science.

Connecting to the Workplace

Students should identify a work activity involving a computer, such as writing, editing, drawing or designing, solving mathematical problems, or organizing information, and then research a job in which they might engage in this activity. Besides career reference books, students might skim the Investigating Career Clusters in each chapter for ideas for jobs. Ask for volunteers to share their paragraphs with the class.

Community Involvement

Discuss the concept of a virtual community. Have students pool what they learn about other principles of netiquette to supplement the rules outlined in their textbook.

CHAPTER 10 REVIEW ANSWERS

▶ Recalling Key Concepts

1. When you know your purpose, or overall goal, in speaking, you are more likely to achieve it. When you know who your listeners are, you can choose the best way to reach them with your words and ideas. You need to know your subject to speak on it well and capture the attention of your audience.
2. Previewing and skimming can be helpful when you need to read a lot of material.
3. Math and science teach you how to put things or events in order, how to do things one step at a time, how to organize information, how to observe things and events, and how to solve problems.
4. Netiquette is important because following rules is a key part of being a good citizen whether you're in cyberspace or elsewhere.

▶ Thinking Critically

1. Speaking, listening, reading, and writing are called basic skills because they create the foundation on which all daily activities are based, including activities in your personal life as well as those in the workplace.
2. You can practice active listening on the telephone by making comments and asking questions to show your interest.
3. When you solve math problems without a calculator, you learn how you arrive at solutions.
4. Students may cite one of the following or some other business use of the Internet: to find information, to communicate by E-mail, to send long documents and images quickly and inexpensively, to advertise and sell products, to provide information and help to customers, and to post job openings and locate job applicants. Be sure students explain their answers.

▶ Building Skills

1. Allow time for students to assess the game and to discuss how they might improve their speaking and listening skills.

2. Students should consult the sources listed to gather information about the software. Allow time for the groups to present their charts to the class.

▶ Applying Academic Skills

1. This exercise will test students' reading and writing skills and ability to translate written directions to a visual format.

2. Students should use this activity to build various basic skills. Encourage them to work closely with you or another teacher as they create their Web page, asking questions and seeking help as needed.

▶ Discovery Portfolio

Emphasize that a good way to build reading skills is to read extensively. Encourage students to add to both lists frequently.

▶ Career Exploration

Have students reread the Investigating Career Clusters feature on page 219 before choosing a career. Students should use the various resources named to research the career they choose. In their letters students should cover all the items listed.

LESSON 11-1 ● It's Your Health

Lesson Objectives: After completing this lesson, students will have learned:
1. what it takes to be healthy and
2. what stress is and how they can deal with it.

Lesson 11-1 Features
Career Opportunities, p. 232

Lesson 11-1 Resources
- Lesson 11-1 Activities, p. 233
- Student Activity Workbook, Activities 1 and 2
- Transparency 25
- Transparency Lesson Plan

LESSON 11-2 ● Make Safety Your Business

Lesson Objectives: After completing this lesson, the students will have learned:
1. what they can do to stay safe and prevent accidents,
2. how the government, employers, and employees make the workplace safe, and
3. how to respond to an emergency.

Lesson 11-2 Features
The Right Attitude, p. 235
The Global Workplace, p. 237
Career Q & A, p. 238
Investigating Career Clusters feature, p. 243

Lesson 11-2 Resources
- Lesson 11-2 Activities, p. 242
- Student Activity Workbook, Activities 3 and 4
- Transparency 26
- Transparency Lesson Plan

CHAPTER 11 RESOURCES

Assessment
- Lesson 11-1 Review, p. 233
- Lesson 11-2 Review, p. 242
- Chapter Review, p. 244
- Chapter 11 Reproducible Test and Testmaker Software

Extension
- Teacher's Manual, p. TM116
- Teacher's Resource Binder:
  - Teacher's Lesson Plans
  - Career Cluster Activities
  - Spanish Resources
  - Involving Parents and Family Resources

Multimedia
- Workforce 2000 Video Library, Segments 10 and 11
- Exploring the World of Work CD-ROM
- Teacher's Resource Binder:
  - Internet Resources, Chapter 11

TEACHER'S MANUAL

SCANS CORRELATION CHART ....

FOUNDATION SKILLS

Basic Skills	Reading	Writing	Math	Listening	Speaking

Thinking Skills	Creative Thinking	Decision Making	Problem Solving	Seeing Things in the Mind's Eye	Knowing How to Learn	Reasoning

Personal Qualities	Responsibility	Self-Esteem	Sociability	Self-Management	Integrity/Honesty

WORKPLACE COMPETENCIES

Resources	Allocating Time	Allocating Money	Allocating Material and Facility Resources	Allocating Human Resources

Information	Acquiring and Evaluating Information	Organizing and Maintaining Information	Interpreting and Communicating Information	Using Computers to Process Information

Interpersonal Skills	Participating as a Member of a Team	Teaching Others	Serving Clients/ Customers	Exercising Leadership	Negotiating to Arrive at a Decision	Working with Cultural Diversity

Systems	Understanding Systems	Monitoring and Correcting Performance	Improving and Designing Systems

Technology	Selecting Technology	Applying Technology to Task	Maintaining and Troubleshooting Technology

---

ENRICHMENT AND APPLICATION ACTIVITIES

Internet Activity

Ask students to make an outline of some basic information about the Occupational Safety and Health Administration of the U.S. Department of Labor (OSHA). Suggested Internet sites and search words:

OSHA
safety
workers' compensation

GO TO Teacher's Resource Binder: Internet Resources

Field Trip Activity

Arrange for a class visit to a workplace cafeteria. Have students observe the foods and write down the healthiest selection they can make for a well-balanced meal.

Guest Speaker Activity

Have a doctor, nurse, or other health-care professional address the class on the value of preventive health care. The speaker may wish to include the need for emotional well-being in an overall view of health.

Staying Healthy and Safe

Chapter Outline

Chapter Overview

In this chapter, students will learn how to make healthful choices about diet, exercise, and hygiene. They will learn the value of caring for themselves by getting sufficient sleep and regular checkups, and by avoiding extreme eating habits as well as guarding against addiction to tobacco, alcohol, or drugs. Students will also learn that stress is not always a bad thing, but if it doesn't go away that there are ways of handling it.

Additionally, students will discover what they can do to stay safe and prevent accidents in the workplace. They will find out how the government, employers, and employees all contribute to making the workplace a safe place to be. Should an emergency occur, students will learn how they can respond.

LESSON 11-1

Focus

Objectives: After completing this lesson, students will have learned:
1. what it takes to be healthy, and
2. what stress is and how they can deal with it.

Preteaching the Vocabulary: Write on the board the Key Terms: *health, nutrients, Food Guide Pyramid, sedentary, hygiene, eating disorder, addiction,* and *stress.* Ask students to define each term and to use *sedentary, addiction,* and *stress* in sentences.

Bell Ringer: Draw a large pie divided into four pieces on the board: nutrition, exercise, sleep, prevention. Title the chart "A Healthy Lifestyle." Have students copy it and, for each piece, write three things they do to lead healthy lives.

Introducing the Lesson: Tell students that in this lesson they will learn what preventive measures they can take to protect their health and what remedies exist for handling stress.

Teach

Guided Practice

Critical Thinking: Ask students to explain the statement, "Some people in the United States abuse their health." Have students list some abuses, such as lack of exercise, substance abuse, and so on.

Implementing Teamwork: Divide the class into groups of four or five students and have each group prepare a report on the effects of tobacco, alcohol, and various drugs. Encourage the groups to use a variety of media to present their report, such as posters, overhead transparencies, and models.

Discussion Starter: Ask students how being healthy and fit helps people succeed in their careers. What are two important ways to be sure you protect your health?

Application Activity: Have pairs of students role-play conversations about changing unhealthful eating habits. Each pair will choose a habit or behavior and discuss reasons why one might follow this behavior and the other argue against it. Afterward, ask students which reasons for stopping unhealthful behavior seemed most valid and whether students' attitudes have been changed as a result.

Community Involvement Activity: Many people don't have time to do the shopping and cooking it takes to eat wisely. Have students design a Food Guide Pyramid poster that could be displayed at the local grocery store. They should include foods that can be found quickly at the store, and are easy to prepare. Have them inquire whether or not they can display their posters somewhere in the local store.

Students' posters should accurately represent the Food Guide Pyramid and be visually appealing.

SCANS Skill—Math: Tell students that they've invited three friends from work to dinner. They plan to serve chicken. If a roasted chicken has a cooked weight of one pound, five ounces, and a serving is three ounces, how many servings are in the chicken? (chicken — 7 servings total: 16 ounces + 5 = 21 ÷ 3)

Independent Practice

Research Activity: Have students read the Investigating Career Clusters feature on page 243 and complete the Research Activity.

Assess

Reteaching: Have students write down the terms *eating disorder, addiction,* and *stress*. Can students tell you ways of handling these problems?

Enrichment: Invite a representative from an organization such as the American Cancer Society to discuss health and safety issues involved with tobacco use. Ask the representative about the latest research on diet and prevention of cancer.

Assessment: Have students complete the Lesson Review and Activities.

Close

Have students complete this statement: *"I can help protect my own health and safety by...."*

LESSON 11-2

Focus

Objectives: After completing this lesson, the students will have learned:

1. what they can do to stay safe and prevent accidents,
2. how the government, employers, and employees make the workplace safe, and
3. how to respond to an emergency.

Preteaching the Vocabulary: Write on the board the Key Terms: *Occupational Safety and*

Health Administration (OSHA), workers' compensation, emergency, and *first aid.* Ask students what they know about these terms. Ask them to use *emergency* in a sentence.

🔔 **Bell Ringer:** Have students list all of the safety precautions they can think of. Give as an example, orange traffic cones that alert motorists to roadwork and help protect highway workers.

Introducing the Lesson: Ask students to share their lists from the Bell Ringer activity. Point out that safety is not just a matter of cost to a business. Hundreds of people are killed or injured on the job each year.

Teach

Guided Practice

Critical Thinking: Ask students what they would do if they were asked to operate a potentially dangerous piece of equipment without being fully trained. The factory they are working in is on a tight production schedule.

Implementing Teamwork: Divide the class into small groups that represent the management of a large company. Have each group design the company's policies and procedures regarding employee tobacco and alcohol use and drug abuse. Remind students of the effects of these substances and how they affect the health and safety of other workers. Also have students consider the types of education and counseling programs management could offer employees.

Discussion Starter: Ask students what they would like to know about the safety of working conditions before accepting a job. How could they get that information?

Connecting to the Workplace: Have each student interview a safety administrator in a local manufacturing company. Tell students to ask about the specific workplace hazards and the safety precautions the company takes to make the environment safe (for example, use of eye guards or other safety equipment). Have students write reports on their findings, then share their information in class.

Application Activity: Have students prepare a short report on how toxic waste is disposed of in their town or area. What safety precautions are used?

Teamwork Activity: Have students form a small group with others who enjoy a particular outdoor activity. For the activity, they should make a poster of safety precautions. For example, they can describe clothing or equipment needed for protection, and list safety rules. They can also include illustrations that show people enjoying the activity safely. Display the poster in the classroom. Then allow students to invite others interested in trying the activity to discuss it with them. During their discussions, students should answer the questions of their peers and share additional safety tips.

Students' posters should illustrate how people can enjoy the activities safely. Students may use their posters to share information about their favorite activities with others.

SCANS Skill—Reading: Have students read an article about working conditions in another country (perhaps a developing country). Ask them to compare the conditions in that country with those in the United States.

SCANS Skill—Acquiring and Evaluating Information: Have each student develop a questionnaire to use in interviewing three to five people about how they relieve job-related stress. Students may want to ask about the type of work the person does and how it creates stress, as well as exercises or relaxation techniques the person follows.

After students have conducted the interviews, ask them to share their results in class. Take a poll to see which methods of relieving stress are used most and the proportion of interviewees who do nothing. What advice might students offer to those people?

SCANS Skill—Working with Cultural Diversity: Different cultures have unique ways of relieving stress. (For example, Hindu society practices yoga as a form of healthful relaxation.) Have students research yoga or similar practices from other cultures and write 150-word articles for the school newspaper. Students' articles should describe the specific practice, its origins, and local classes one can take to learn the practice. (Other cultures/practices to research might include the Chinese tai chi or the Korean tae kwon do.)

Independent Practice

Research Activity: Ask students to research protection of the environment. Have students name two current laws protecting the environment. Ask students to write a short essay comparing safety in the workplace and safety in the environment.

Assess

Reteaching: Review with students the ways in which they can stay healthy and safe on the job. Answer any questions they may still have about the government's role in protecting the work environment. Have students enter in the Discovery Portfolio three ways they can establish healthy habits for a future career.

Enrichment: Invite a member of the American Red Cross to talk to the class about emergencies.

Assessment:
1. Have students complete the Lesson 11-2 Review and Activities.
2. Have students complete the Chapter 11 Review.
3. Assign the Chapter 11 Test for students to complete.

Close

Have students complete the following statement: *"The best thing I can do in an emergency is to...."*

LESSON 11-1 REVIEW ANSWERS

Vocabulary Review

Students' articles should incorporate the terms listed and demonstrate an understanding of the material presented in the lesson.

Check Your Understanding
1. b   2. c   3. b

Critical Thinking
1. Students should identify one or more of the areas of health described in the lesson (diet, exercise, rest, and guarding health) and use what they have learned to explain how they can improve in the areas they have identified.
2. Students should describe methods they use to deal with stress at school.

Connecting to the Workplace

Students should identify three forms of exercise employees might do at the workplace as part of a wellness program, such as yoga, stretching, aerobics, running, walking, and tai chi.

Teamwork

Each team should make three signs that offer clear and concise health tips.

LESSON 11-2 REVIEW ANSWERS

Vocabulary Review

Students' articles should reflect the lesson content on the cooperation of government, employers, and employees, and include the key terms in the lesson.

Check Your Understanding

1. T
2. F; government, employers, and employees share responsibility for creating a safe workplace.
3. T

Critical Thinking

1. Encourage students to share home safety precautions with each other, such as not answering the door when an adult is not home, not telling unfamiliar callers that an adult is not home, keeping doors locked, and turning off the stove and other appliances after use.
2. Students may suggest that the government sets safety standards so that all workers are protected on the job, no matter what their job or where they work.
3. You need to survey the scene of an accident to figure out what happened, what may happen, what you should do, and how to protect your own safety.

Connecting to the Workplace

Students should identify five part-time jobs open to people their age, hypothesize about emergencies that might arise in the jobs, suggest safety precautions for the jobs, and describe how they would respond to the emergencies they have identified. Use class discussion to check students' reasoning.

Community Involvement

Make sure that students write a thank-you note after the Red Cross representative's visit. Students should incorporate in their bulletin-board display what they have learned about the Red Cross from the visit.

CHAPTER 11 REVIEW ANSWERS

▶ Recalling Key Concepts

1. The six groups of food in the Food Guide Pyramid are fats, oils, and sweets; milk, yogurt, and cheese; meat, poultry, fish, dried beans, eggs, and nuts; vegetables; fruit; bread, cereal, rice, and pasta.
2. You can protect your health by practicing good hygiene, getting regular checkups, seeking help for eating disorders, and guarding against tobacco, alcohol, and drug addiction.
3. Stress is the mental or physical tension that is the body's natural response to conflict.
4. OSHA is the Occupational Safety and Health Administration, a special branch of the U.S. Department of Labor that sets safety standards and inspects places of work to see that the standards are being followed.
5. *AID* helps you remember to ask for help, intervene, and do no further harm.

▶ Thinking Critically

1. Students should suggest a variety of foods from different food groups, such as eggs, toast, and juice; cereal, milk, and juice; fruit, yogurt, and a muffin.
2. Answers will vary but may include the following: doing homework earlier, limiting the amount of television watched.
3. Answers will vary but should demonstrate a grasp of basic techniques for managing stress; students should support their response with logical reasoning.

4. Students may suggest that many young people take risks because they don't care about themselves or think no one cares about them.

5. When you think clearly, you are able to assess situations, set priorities, and do what needs to be done.

▶ Building Skills

1. Students should record what they eat and compare it to the recommendations included in the Food Guide Pyramid. Call on students to describe what they discovered about their eating habits and how they plan to change them.

2. Students should take time to assess themselves carefully. Their lists should reflect a basic understanding of safety and safety precautions. Point out that the exercise serves no purpose if students do not put the items on their lists into practice.

▶ Applying Academic Skills

1. In their reports, students should define ergonomics and explain its purpose. They should also describe the contribution of OSHA to ergonomics.

2. Students should use what they have learned about good health to design a schoolwide wellness program. Enlist the help of other teachers and school staff as well as interested parents and adults outside the school.

▶ Discovery Portfolio

Remind students of the importance of matching careers to their interests, values, and life goals. Emphasize that they should frequently review and update their views on basic topics such as health and fitness. They should determine whether their views are compatible with career choices they have made.

▶ Career Exploration

Have students reread the Investigating Cluster Clusters feature on page 243 before choosing a career. Students should use the various resources named to research the career they choose. Students' collages should illustrate all the items listed.

LESSON 12-1 ● Learning and Growing

Lesson Objectives: After completing this lesson, the students will have learned:

1. how to grow in all their experiences, including a job, and
2. how to get and handle more responsibility on the job.

Lesson 12-1 Features
The Right Attitude, p. 250
Career Opportunities, p. 254

Lesson 12-1 Resources
- Lesson 12-1 Activities, p. 256
- Student Activity Workbook, Activities 1, 2, and 3

LESSON 12-2 ● Reevaluating Your Goals

Lesson Objectives: After completing this lesson, the students will have learned:

1. why it is important for them to reevaluate their goals, and
2. why they might make changes in a career plan.

Lesson 12-2 Features
The Global Workplace, p. 261
Career Q & A, p. 265
Investigating Career Clusters, p. 267

Lesson 12-2 Resources
- Lesson 12-2 Activities, p. 266
- Student Activity Workbook, Activities 4 and 5
- Transparencies 27 and 28
- Transparency Lesson Plan

CHAPTER 12 RESOURCES

Assessment
- Lesson 12-1 Review, p. 256
- Lesson 12-2 Review, p. 266
- Chapter Review, p. 268
- Chapter 12 Reproducible Test and Testmaker Software

Extension
- Teacher's Manual, p. TM124
- Teacher's Resource Binder:
  - Teacher's Lesson Plans
  - Career Cluster Activities
  - Spanish Resources
  - Involving Parents and Family Resources

Multimedia
- Workforce 2000 Video Library, segments 9 and 17
- Exploring the World of Work CD-ROM
- Teacher's Resource Binder:
  - Internet Resources, Chapter 12

SCANS CORRELATION CHART ....

FOUNDATION SKILLS

Basic Skills	Reading	Writing	Math	Listening	Speaking

Thinking Skills	Creative Thinking	Decision Making	Problem Solving	Seeing Things in the Mind's Eye	Knowing How to Learn	Reasoning

Personal Qualities	Responsibility	Self-Esteem	Sociability	Self-Management	Integrity/Honesty

WORKPLACE COMPETENCIES

Resources	Allocating Time	Allocating Money	Allocating Material and Facility Resources	Allocating Human Resources

Information	Acquiring and Evaluating Information	Organizing and Maintaining Information	Interpreting and Communicating Information	Using Computers to Process Information

Interpersonal Skills	Participating as a Member of a Team	Teaching Others	Serving Clients/ Customers	Exercising Leadership	Negotiating to Arrive at a Decision	Working with Cultural Diversity

Systems	Understanding Systems	Monitoring and Correcting Performance	Improving and Designing Systems

Technology	Selecting Technology	Applying Technology to Task	Maintaining and Troubleshooting Technology

---

ENRICHMENT AND APPLICATION ACTIVITIES

Internet Activity

Ask students to find out how the Internet could help them if they lost their jobs. They should note what kinds of services are available on-line and make note of appropriate Web sites. Suggested Internet search words:

   job-search
   unemployment benefits

GO TO → Teacher's Resource Binder: Internet Resources

Field Trip Activity

Have students find out where the local unemployment office is. What information can they obtain from a representative about how to apply for benefits? How long are benefits paid? How is a person eligible in the first place?

Guest Speaker Activity

Ask someone from the work world to speak to the class about networking. Have students ask how important networking has been in that person's career.

Chapter 12 Moving Toward Your Goals

Chapter Outline

I. Learning and Growing
  A. Getting the Most out of All You Do
    1. The Right Attitude
    2. Always Give Your Best
    3. Growing on the Job
  B. More Responsibility
    1. Who Gets Promoted?
    2. Do You Want More Responsibility?
    3. Can You Handle More Responsibility?
    4. Yes or No?
II. Reevaluating Your Goals
  A. Reviewing Your Career Plan
  B. Making Changes
    1. Changing Direction
    2. Changing Jobs
    3. Bowing Out
    4. Changing Careers

Chapter Overview

In Chapter 12, students will learn that getting the most out of what they do means having the right attitude and always giving their best. Learning goes on not just at school but over a lifetime. Looking for opportunities is part of growing on the job. They will learn what qualities employers look for before promoting employees and that more responsibility comes with promotion. Students will consider what it takes to handle more responsibility. They will come to realize that a promotion does not have to be accepted if it is not right for that employee. Just because a person is not ready now doesn't mean he or she won't be ready later.

Students will also learn in this chapter that it is important to check progress towards their goals. They can change jobs and direction in the careers if necessary. They will learn what is required to give notice if they decide on change. They will begin to see that discovering what they want to do is a lifelong process.

LESSON 12-1

Focus

Objectives: After completing this lesson, the students will have learned:
1. how to grow in all their experiences, including a job, and
2. how to get and handle more responsibility on the job.

Preteaching the Vocabulary: Write on the board the Key Terms: *promotion* and *raise*. Ask students to define each of these terms or use each in a sentence.

🔔**Bell Ringer:** Ask students to think about the times they *feel* most bored. How do they get over this feeling? What are some positive antidotes? (If necessary, explain antidote.)

Introducing the Lesson: Take one of the antidotes to boredom from the Bell Ringer activity, such as giving oneself a challenge, and suggest how this habit can improve chances of promotion in the work world. Finding opportunities to grow will always be there on the job.

Teach

Guided Practice

Critical Thinking: Write the following words on the board as column headings: *loyalty* and *networking*. Ask students if a person can be loyal to his or her company and still share information with others. Remind students that networking takes place both inside and outside your work or company.

Implementing Teamwork: Divide the class into small groups. On slips of paper, list factors to consider when accepting a promotion. Have each group debate the advantages and disadvantages of each factor. (Examples are: new and more work to do; supervision of people; more money; chances to relocate.) Emphasize during the discussion that the person who is given a promotion must decide if a factor is an advantage or disadvantage.

Discussion Starter: Ask students whether they think a person should play it safe by staying in a career that offers good pay and opportunities, even if he or she is not particularly interested in that career.

Application Activity: Read the following situation to the class. Have the students suggest several ways for Margaret to leave her position, deciding whether each suggestion is appropriate or inappropriate. In the follow-up discussion, have students explain why the alternatives were or were not appropriate.

Margaret had worked in her present position for almost two years. As time passed, it became obvious to her that there wasn't much opportunity for her to receive a promotion to a more responsible position. She wanted to become an office manager eventually, but the business where she was working was too small and did not provide that opportunity. Margaret began looking for other jobs. In doing so, she was careful about scheduling interviews. She was able to take one day of personal leave and to have the other interviews during her lunch hour and after work. Finally, she found a position she wanted that provided the opportunity for moving up to a more responsible position. The only problem was the new employer wanted someone to begin work in one week. What should Margaret do? What is the best way for her to handle this situation?

SCANS Skill—Math: Have each student ask at least two adults these questions: "How many years have you been employed? How many different jobs have you held during those years?" Have each student calculate the average length of time each adult spent at a single job (number of years ÷ number of jobs).

Independent Practice

Research Activity: Have students read Investigating Career Clusters on page 267 and complete the Research Activity.

Assess

Reteaching: Write on the board the ways a person could grow on the job. (Do your job as well as you can; volunteer to do more; look for opportunities to learn on the job, get more education or training; be willing to try new things.) After each way ask students to give some examples. One example might be a word-processing operator who wanted to work in advertising. He or she could take a class on desktop publishing.

Enrichment: Ask someone from a local company who was promoted during a downsizing, what difference the downsizing has made to the remaining employees' workloads. How did that person feel when others were laid off.

Assessment: Have students complete the Lesson 12-1 Review and Activities.

Close

Have students complete this statement: *"To get more responsibility on a job, I must...."*

LESSON 12-2

Focus

Objectives: After completing this lesson, the students will have learned:

1. why it is important for them to reevaluate their goals, and

2. why they might make changes in a career plan.

Preteaching the Vocabulary: Write on the board the Key Terms: *notice* and *letter of resignation*. Have students write sentences for each word making the meaning clear and showing the difference between the two terms.

Bell Ringer: Ask students to think of some famous people they have heard or read about who have had long careers (perhaps in the entertainment world or in the arts). Did age make much difference to the performance of these peoples' skills? How long do students wish to go on working?

Introducing the Lesson: Tell the students that in this lesson they will find out that making changes is part of having a career. Sometimes the changes are relatively minor, such as changing jobs, and sometimes they are major, such as changing careers. Stopping to check on your progress is essential for lifelong learning.

Teach

Guided Practice

Critical Thinking: Ask students to tell why it matters what they do now if their future career may be along completely different lines? Are skills and good attitudes ever really "wasted"?

Implementing Teamwork: Divide the class into groups of five or six. Ask each group to set up a job counseling service. Each group should brainstorm the types of assistance it could provide (for example, training, assessment, interview skills) and the career target areas. Ask each group to give a presentation about its counseling service.

Discussion Starter: If you decide to change your job, why is it important to maintain a good relationship with an employer you are leaving?

Application Activity: Have students imagine they are quitting a job to take a better position. Have them write three paragraphs on when they are handing in their notice, what they will try to stress in their letters of resignation, and what other "bowing out" steps they will think about.

SCANS Skill—Listening: Read to the students Robert Frost's poem, "The Road Not Taken." Discuss what the poet might have meant by "the one less traveled by." Ask students to write their reaction to the poem in their Discovery Portfolio.

Independent Practice

Research Activity: Have students look up in newspaper ads and school catalogues educational and training programs that can help them make progress toward their career goals. Have them list the career goal, the possible program, and where and how it is available.

Assess

Reteaching: Review with students how to change a job and how to explore career goals.

Enrichment: Divide students into pairs and have each pair role-play a conversation between a supervisor and an employee who is giving notice.

Assessment:

1. Have students complete the Lesson 12-2 Review and Activities.

2. Have students complete the Chapter 12 Review.

3. Assign the Chapter 12 Test for students to complete.

Close

Have students complete this statement: *"Some steps I can take to reevaluate my goals are..."*

Vocabulary Review

Students' written remarks should demonstrate an understanding of the lesson content and incorporate an explanation of the key terms.

Check Your Understanding

1. c   2. b

Critical Thinking

1. Students should describe an experience they had that would have been improved by a positive attitude.

2. You may find that by trying something new you get new ideas and you learn a better way of doing things. If you want to grow, you need to be open to new things. For example, if you are an athlete, you might want to try a new position on a team. You might find that you learn more about the sport.

3. Answers will vary but may include the following: perform your new tasks with a good attitude and to the best of your ability, show some initiative, be cooperative and adaptable, ask about special training you may need.

Connecting to the Workplace

Urge students to role-play the situation as they believe Linette should handle it. In the discussion that follows, consider other ways of handling the situation.

Teamwork

Each team should adopt one or the other point of view and prepare arguments to support it in a debate. Moderate debates between teams of opposing points of view.

Vocabulary Review

Students' paragraphs should demonstrate a grasp of the concept of notice and should clearly explain the key terms.

Check Your Understanding

1. T

2. F; a career plan can change. People change direction and jobs in the course of a career.

3. F; it is proper to give two weeks notice.

4. T

Critical Thinking

1. You should review your career plan periodically to make sure it still reflects where you are going or want to go.

2. Students should name one or more careers they think they might pursue in their lifetime.

3. Checking your career progress is important because it allows you to continue exploring your interests and expanding your skills.

Connecting to the Workplace

Students' letters should explain why they are unable to take their old job and should be gracious and polite in tone.

Community Involvement

Hold a "Career Change Day/Week" in which students' guests can discuss their career changes and field questions from the class.

▶ Recalling Key Concepts

1. When you give your best, you have the satisfaction of knowing you gave your all to something.
2. The education and training you get can increase your career options.
3. You might have to move to a new place, travel more, or live far from family and friends.
4. People change careers because they have come to the end of a career plan, their career plan is no longer right for them, they want to pursue personal interests, or they want to run their own business.

▶ Thinking Critically

1. Students may make correlations between positive or negative attitudes toward school and their performance at school.
2. Answers will vary but may include the following: you are ready for more responsibility, you want new challenges, you want more say in projects or company business, you have ideas for new projects.
3. You might decline a promotion if you don't want to make the personal sacrifices involved, if the new position doesn't help you move toward your goals, or if the position doesn't fit your interests or skills.
4. Answers will vary but may include the following: when your goals change, when you develop new interests, when you are thinking about changing your job or are offered a promotion.
5. Answers will vary; students may cite the following as advantages: you can pursue different interests, you can use new skills. Students may cite the following as drawbacks: you may have to make completely new contacts in your new career field; it may take time to reach higher positions in the field or earn the salary you want.

▶ Building Skills

1. Students should list at least three ways they can do each of the following at home: help others, show initiative.
2. Students may respond that they would explain to Paul that they are only doing their job, that in their new position they have more responsibility and authority, and that it is their job to oversee Paul's work.

▶ Applying Academic Skills

1. $1,875 a summer ÷ 2.5 months = $750 a month x .04 raise = $30 more a month; $780 a month x 2.5 months = $1,950 for the summer.
2. Students' speeches should focus on the theme and should address the importance of giving your best throughout your life.

▶ Discovery Portfolio

Students should review the career plans they made in Chapter 5 and make changes in them on the basis of what they've learned in this chapter. Urge students to create career plans for other careers that interest them.

▶ Career Exploration

Before selecting a career in the marine science career cluster, have students review the Investigating Career Clusters feature on page 267. Students may research the career they choose in library resources, such as encyclopedias and references published by the U.S. Department of Labor, including the *Dictionary of Occupational Titles*, the *Occupational Outlook Handbook*, and the *Guide for Occupational Exploration*. They may also do research on the Internet. If possible, they should interview someone with a job in the field. Students' profiles should include information on each topic listed.

Unit 3

Lifelong Learning

Overview

In Unit 3, students will investigate our economic system. They will learn why it is important to balance the different parts of one's life, and how to make time for school, work, family, and friends.

They will look ahead to see what life changes they may expect. They will learn how they can handle personal and job- or career-related changes, as well as find out ways they can look at and prepare for change.

Unit Introduction

Lead a discussion on career exploration by asking students the following questions:

1. Ask students to think of ways in which they are a part of our economic system. Ask them whether they have ever earned their own money. Ask them if they spend the money they earn. Tell students in both ways they are a part of the economic system.

2. Ask students how making a budget and making a career plan are linked. (Both help a person plan for the future.) Ask students for specific examples. (How much you want to make may be based on a specific purchase or goal such as college. Which jobs you consider taking may require a certain amount of pay.)

3. Ask students to identify one way in which they balance school work and home life.

4. Ask students to think of one change that has already happened in their lives. Ask them to think of types of changes that might take place in the next year or two. Ask students to think of ways that they can prepare for these changes.

Discuss student's answers and explain to them that they will learn more about these areas in this unit of the text.

Unit Closure

Have students create a collage with art and text depicting how they are involved in our economic system, how they manage their money, ways that they balance their lives, and where they see themselves in the future.

Evaluation

Administer the reproducible Unit 3 Test found in the *Teacher's Resource Binder.*

> **Chapters within the Unit**
>
> **Chapter 13**
> Our Economic System
>
> **Chapter 14**
> Managing Your Money
>
> **Chapter 15**
> Living a Balanced Life
>
> **Chapter 16**
> Looking Beyond Today

TEACHER'S MANUAL

TEACHER'S MANUAL

LESSON 13-1 The Free Enterprise System

Lesson Objectives: After completing this lesson, the students will have learned:

1. the meaning of free enterprise,
2. how the free enterprise system works, and
3. how they fit into our economic system.

Lesson 13-1 Features	**Lesson 13-1 Resources**
The Right Attitude, p. 273	• Lesson 13-1 Activities, p. 280
Career Q & A, p. 276	• Student Activity Workbook,
The Global Workplace, p. 278	Activities 1, 2, and 3

LESSON 13-2 Being Your Own Boss

Lesson Objectives: After completing this lesson, the students will have learned:

1. the rewards and challenges of working for yourself, and
2. how to start their own businesses.

Lesson 13-2 Features	**Lesson 13-2 Resources**
Career Opportunities, p. 282	• Lesson 13-2 Activities, p. 288
Investigating Career Clusters, p. 289	• Student Activity Workbook, Activities 4, 5, and 6
	• Transparency 29
	• Transparency Lesson Plan

CHAPTER 13 RESOURCES

Assessment

• Lesson 13-1 Review, p. 280
• Lesson 13-2 Review, p. 288
• Chapter Review, p. 290
• Chapter 13 Reproducible Test and Testmaker Software

Extension

• Teacher's Manual, p. TM132
• Teacher's Resource Binder:
  – Teacher's Lesson Plans
  – Career Cluster Activities
  – Spanish Resources
  – Involving Parents and Family Resources

Multimedia

• Workforce 2000 Video Library, Segments 4, 12, and 18
• Exploring the World of Work CD-ROM
• Teacher's Resource Binder:
  – Internet Resources, Chapter 13

SCANS CORRELATION CHART ....

FOUNDATION SKILLS

Basic Skills	Reading	Writing	Math	Listening	Speaking

Thinking Skills	Creative Thinking	Decision Making	Problem Solving	Seeing Things in the Mind's Eye	Knowing How to Learn	Reasoning

Personal Qualities	Responsibility	Self-Esteem	Sociability	Self-Management	Integrity/Honesty

WORKPLACE COMPETENCIES

Resources	Allocating Time	Allocating Money	Allocating Material and Facility Resources	Allocating Human Resources

Information	Acquiring and Evaluating Information	Organizing and Maintaining Information	Interpreting and Communicating Information	Using Computers to Process Information

Interpersonal Skills	Participating as a Member of a Team	Teaching Others	Serving Clients/ Customers	Exercising Leadership	Negotiating to Arrive at a Decision	Working with Cultural Diversity

Systems	Understanding Systems	Monitoring and Correcting Performance	Improving and Designing Systems

Technology	Selecting Technology	Applying Technology to Task	Maintaining and Troubleshooting Technology

ENRICHMENT AND APPLICATION ACTIVITIES

Internet Activity

Ask students to use Internet resources to find information on women starting new businesses in the last two years. They should note what kinds of information are available on the numbers of women involved. Suggested Internet search words:

women in small businesses

women's businesses

 Teacher's Resource Binder: Internet Resources

Field Trip Activity

Have students visit a local mall to do a survey of businesses. Students should count the number of stores owned by corporations (such as department store chains) and the number owned and operated by entrepreneurs. Have them write a brief report about their findings.

Guest Speaker Activity

Ask a representative from the local Kinko's (or another local business operated by entrepreneurs) to speak to the class on how that business got started.

Chapter 13 Our Economic System

Chapter Outline

I. The Free Enterprise System
   A. What Is Free Enterprise All About?
   B. How Our Economy Works
      1. Producers and Consumers
      2. Making a Profit
      3. One Producer's Experience
      4. Changing Prices
   C. Looking at the Big Picture
II. Being Your Own Boss
   A. Rewards and Challenges
   B. Launching Your Own Business
      1. What's Involved
      2. Putting an Idea on Paper

Chapter Overview

In this chapter, students will find out how they already take part in the economic system and what free enterprise means. They will find out how our economy works, how producers and consumers operate (producers make a profit and consumers get the most for their money), and how supply and demand affect competition.

Students will also read about the rewards and challenges of working for oneself, what qualities an entrepreneur needs, and what is involved in going into business for oneself. They will understand that a business plan is hard work but essential if a person wants to be his or her own boss. Running one's own business can be an adventure.

LESSON 13-1

Focus

Objectives: After completing this lesson, the students will have learned:
1. the meaning of free enterprise,
2. how the free enterprise system works, and
3. how they fit into our economic system.

Preteaching the Vocabulary: Write on the board the Key Terms: *economics, economic system, capitalism, free enterprise, regulate, consumers, producers, profit, supply,* and *demand.* Group terms in pairs. Ask students the connection between the paired terms.

🔔 **Bell Ringer:** Write the word *choice* on the board. Have the students write a definition of the word. Next, write the words *free enterprise.* Ask students to define each word and then the whole term.

Introducing the Lesson: Have students brainstorm a list of the economic choices we make in the United States under a free enterprise system (for example, we can choose what to buy and where to buy it).

Teach

Guided Practice

Critical Thinking: Ask students if the words *economics* and *economical* are related. Can being *economical* result from a knowledge of *economics*?

Critical Thinking: Tell students that they are writing to a teen living in a country that has a traditional or command economic system in which the government decides what products will be available to the public. Have students describe the U.S. free enterprise system to the teen.

Implementing Teamwork: Organize students in pairs and have each pair design an advertisement to attract teens to their new business. They may use any medium to design the ads. Once completed, display the ads and ask students to choose the most appealing ones.

Discussion Starter: Have students name some way the condition of the economy affects them individually. They may choose among goods and services.

Application Activity: Have students write their answers to the Discussion Starter independently. If time permits, read some answers.

Community Involvement Activity: Have students make a directory of at least five producers in your community. They should organize the businesses in two categories: goods and services. Then, have them write the name and a one-sentence description of each business at the top of a separate sheet of paper, leaving space below. Help them bind the sheets together, and circulate the directories in class. Ask students to make a check mark on the page of each business they have visited or used. Also have them make comments about what they liked or disliked about the businesses. Students should tally and report on which local producers the class visits or uses most and why.

The directories students assemble should list at least five local producers and describe the goods or services they offer. As a class, discuss the results of students' surveys.

SCANS Skills—Math: Ask students to take the business idea they chose from Figure 13-3 and to create a schedule of their activities for the day. How many hours would they be working per week with this daily schedule?

SCANS Skills—Problem Solving: Assign students to work in small groups to discuss whether price should be *the* major consideration when making a purchase. Tell students to

consider how quality and function enter into the final decision to buy. Ask them if they have ever been disappointed with a product for which they paid a top price. How do they decide if something is a bargain? Have students share their comments in class.

Independent Practice

Research Activity: Have students read Investigating Career Clusters on page 289 and complete the Research Activity.

Assess

Reteaching: Outline this section of the chapter (Lesson 13-1) by writing the major headings and subheadings on the board. Have students explain the meaning of each one.

Enrichment: Have an economics teacher from a school in the area explain to your class some basic aspect of our economic system, such as supply and demand.

Assessment: Have students complete the Lesson 13-1 Review and Activities.

Close

Have students complete this statement: *"I take part in our economic system by...."*

LESSON 13-2

Focus

Objectives: After completing this lesson, the students will have learned:

1. the rewards and challenges of working for yourself, and

2. how to start their own businesses.

Preteaching the Vocabulary: Write on the board the Key Terms: *entrepreneur, business plan,* and *marketing.* Ask students to define each term or use each in a sentence.

🔔 **Bell Ringer:** Tell students to imagine that they have decided to invest money in a business. Have them write a sentence or two telling whether they prefer to start a business on their own or with a partner.

Introducing the Lesson: Have students explain what they wrote about in the Bell Ringer activity. Do they think they want to run their own businesses, and do they see this as part of their future?

Teach

Guided Practice

Critical Thinking: Ask students if working in a family business would be good training for becoming an entrepreneur or not. What would be some advantages and disadvantages?

Discussion Starter: Ask students if they have ever had a creative idea for a new product or service that they thought they could market. Have volunteers give their ideas.

Implementing Teamwork: Divide the class into small groups. Have each group think of an innovative product or service. Some of the ideas volunteered in the Discussion Starter may be used, but students will need to come up with others. Then have groups make a presentation to the class. Allow students to be creative, and have the class vote on the top five ideas based on the information in the text.

Application Activity: Ask students to write a short essay on why they would like to be entrepreneurs or why they would rather not.

Teamwork Activity: In teams of four, students should create a plan for a business designing T-shirts. Have them decide what products to sell and what prices to charge. Also, have them figure out where they could make and sell the T-shirts. Students should consider what other decisions they would need to make and list them.

Then, allow them to present their plan, including visuals, to the rest of the class.

For this activity, students should gather the kinds of information that would be included in a business plan. Encourage teams to research prices and other information they need.

SCANS Skills—Writing: Have students express in their own words the skills an entrepreneur must have. They may use the headings "Motivation," "Sight and Foresight," "Decision Making" and "Human Relations" but not the words of the textbook. They may use examples if they wish.

SCANS Skills—Teaching Others: Divide students into five groups and assign each group one of these information sources: the local Chamber of Commerce, the Small Business Administration, the library, an accountant, and a bank loan officer. Have the groups gather information about the needs of a new business and then have them teach others what they learned.

Independent Practice

Research Activity: Have students research the zoning laws in their community. Ask them to find out where a person can operate certain kinds of businesses and which parts of town are zoned for commercial use.

Research Activity: Have students interview a local representative of the Small Business Administration to obtain information about the services provided to local businesses and the percentage of services provided for each type of business ownership.

Assess

Reteaching: Have students recall what qualities an entrepreneur must have. What are some risks entrepreneurs face? How important is making a business plan if you want to run a successful business? What are some factors to consider when developing a business plan?

Enrichment: Invite a representative from a local bank to talk to the class about how a person applies for and receives a loan to start a small business. Have the representative talk about his or her bank's requirements for lending money.

Assessment:

1. Have students complete the Lesson 13-2 Review and Activities.
2. Have students complete the Chapter 13 Review.
3. Assign the Chapter 13 Test for students to complete.

Close

Have students complete this sentence: *"If I were going into business for myself, I would like to...."*

LESSON 13-1 REVIEW ANSWERS

Vocabulary Review

Questions and answers students formulate should demonstrate an understanding of the key terms.

Check Your Understanding

1. a
2. c

Critical Thinking

1. Students may respond that the government regulates some prices and wages to protect both consumers and producers.
2. Yes; any person who buys and uses goods and services is a consumer. That same person might also provide goods or services as a producer in his or her job.
3. You might find people who can teach you about our economic system at school, at work, on television, and on the radio. Producers

lower prices when supply is greater than demand. They raise prices when demand is greater than supply.

4. Prices go down when supply is greater than demand because producers have an excess amount of goods or services available; prices go up when demand is greater than supply because consumers want more goods or services than are available for sale.

Connecting to the Workplace

Students may suggest that Miguel should make some kinds of jewelry the others do not make and that he should price his pieces competitively, ideally with some priced under $12.

Teamwork

Students should create an oral presentation with visuals that reteaches the lesson content to a younger audience. Help students make arrangements to give their presentations to elementary school students.

LESSON 13-2 REVIEW ANSWERS

Vocabulary Review

Students should present an original idea for a business and use the key terms in their description of it.

Check Your Understanding

1. T
2. F; almost two of every three new businesses fail within their first four years.
3. T

Critical Thinking

1. Answers will vary; students may wish to review the section of the lesson on the rewards and challenges of being an entrepreneur.
2. Students should demonstrate a grasp of both the rewards and the challenges of being an entrepreneur and should be able to express and support their points of view.

3. Students should refer to the qualities listed in Figure 13-2 and should be able to support their points of view.

4. Students may suggest the following: whether you need to be near customers or services, where your competition is located, the cost of property, the condition of streets and buildings, and the types of businesses in the area.

5. Students should identify a business they'd like to own and run later in their lives and explain the choice.

Connecting to the Workplace

Students should make a creative flyer or business card to advertise to neighbors Lori's business as an obedience trainer.

Community Involvement

Students' essays should include all the reasons the entrepreneur gave for the business' success.

CHAPTER 13 REVIEW ANSWERS

▶ Recalling Key Concepts

1. The economic system of the United States is known as capitalism or the free enterprise system.

2. Students should respond that they will be consumers, producers, and voters.

3. An entrepreneur is someone who organizes and runs a business.

4. A business plan should give the following specific information: the goods or services your business will offer, where your business will be located, what your goals for the business are, a timetable for meeting them, who you expect your customers will be, what kind of marketing you will do, how much it will cost to start and run your business, how many employees you need, if any, what you will pay them, and what your profits will be.

▶ Thinking Critically

1. Other economic systems may differ from the free enterprise system in the amount of control the government has over the economy and in the choices consumers and producers have.

2. When there is more competition among producers, consumers have a greater choice of goods and services. To get their business, producers must keep prices low.

3. Students should identify qualities that employees share with entrepreneurs and explain why the qualities are important when working for someone else.

▶ Building Skills

1. Students should identify a realistic need, and in their summaries describe the need, and how they would fill it by starting a business. After the vote, ask students who voted for the winning business idea to explain why they thought it was creative.

2. Students should identify a variety of economic systems.

▶ Applying Academic Skills

1. Her profit was $86 ($50 [100 x $.50 = $50] + $67.50 [90 x $.75 = $67.50] = $117.50; $100 [100 x $1 = $100] + $135 [90 x $1.50 = $135] = $235; $235 − $117.50 = $117.50; $117.50 − $31.50 = $86).

2. Answers will depend on the countries students select.

▶ Discovery Portfolio

Students' journal entries should exhibit a grasp of the material in the chapter and should make connections between what they have learned and the world of work; students should also answer the questions and explore others. Students should keep an ongoing list of business ideas in their portfolios; urge them to add to the list frequently. Ask students to share with their classmates other interesting information they have found about entrepreneurship.

▶ Career Exploration

Before they select a career in the marketing and distribution career cluster, have students review the Investigating Career Clusters feature on page 289. Students may research the career they choose in library resources, such as encyclopedias and references published by the U.S. Department of Labor, including the *Dictionary of Occupational Titles*, the *Occupational Outlook Handbook*, and the *Guide for Occupational Exploration*. They may also do research on the Internet. If possible, they should interview someone with a job in this field. Students should make and share observations about how the marketing and distribution career might affect or influence consumers.

LESSON 14-1 ● The Money You Earn

Lesson Objectives: After completing this lesson, students will have learned:

1. what their sources of income are and
2. how to make a plan for spending and saving money.

Lesson 14-1 Features

Career Opportunities, p. 297

The Global Workplace, p. 298

Career Q & A, p. 300

Lesson 14-1 Resources

- Lesson 14-1 Activities, p. 303
- Student Activity Workbook, Activity 1

LESSON 14-2 ● You, the Consumer

Lesson Objectives: After completing this lesson, students will have learned:

1. how they can get the most for their money and
2. ways that people pay for purchases.

Lesson 14-2 Features

The Right Attitude, p. 309

Investigating Career Clusters, p. 313

Lesson 14-2 Resources

- Lesson 14-2 Activities, p. 312
- Student Activity Workbook, Activities 2, 3, 4, and 5
- Transparency 30
- Transparency Lesson Plan

CHAPTER 14 RESOURCES

Assessment

- Lesson 14-1 Review, p. 303
- Lesson 14-2 Review, p. 312
- Chapter Review, p. 314
- Chapter 14 Reproducible Test and Testmaker Software

Extension

- Teacher's Manual, p. TM142
- Teacher's Resource Binder:
  - Teacher's Lesson Plans
  - Career Cluster Activities
  - Spanish Resources
  - Involving Parents and Family Resources

Multimedia

- Workforce 2000 Video Library, Segments 19 and 20
- Exploring the World of Work CD-ROM
- Teacher's Resource Binder:
  - Internet Resources, Chapter 14

TEACHER'S MANUAL

SCANS CORRELATION CHART ....

FOUNDATION SKILLS

Basic Skills	Reading	Writing	Math	Listening	Speaking

Thinking Skills	Creative Thinking	Decision Making	Problem Solving	Seeing Things in the Mind's Eye	Knowing How to Learn	Reasoning

Personal Qualities	Responsibility	Self-Esteem	Sociability	Self-Management	Integrity/Honesty

WORKPLACE COMPETENCIES

Resources	Allocating Time	Allocating Money	Allocating Material and Facility Resources	Allocating Human Resources

Information	Acquiring and Evaluating Information	Organizing and Maintaining Information	Interpreting and Communicating Information	Using Computers to Process Information

Interpersonal Skills	Participating as a Member of a Team	Teaching Others	Serving Clients/ Customers	Exercising Leadership	Negotiating to Arrive at a Decision	Working with Cultural Diversity

Systems	Understanding Systems	Monitoring and Correcting Performance	Improving and Designing Systems

Technology	Selecting Technology	Applying Technology to Task	Maintaining and Troubleshooting Technology

---

ENRICHMENT AND APPLICATION ACTIVITIES

Internet Activity

Credit unions are a popular alternative to banks. Ask students to find out more about them through the Internet. They should note what kinds of services they offer, how they are different from banks, and how to become eligible to participate. Suggested Internet search words:

    credit unions
    bank alternatives

GO TO Teacher's Resource Binder: Internet Resources

Field Trip Activity

As a class, visit a local business and speak with an accountant or financial officer. Have students ask what the company's budgeting procedures are. Perhaps the officer will explain how the company's use of credit affects the business net earnings.

Guest Speaker Activity

Ask someone who works in the administration of a local department store to speak to the class. Have them explain what the store's policy is on refunds and exchanges; what percentage of a bill must be paid monthly; and what interest rate is charged. Allow students to discuss the information and tell if it fits with their expectations.

Chapter 14 · Managing Your Money

Chapter Outline

I. The Money You Earn
   A. Your Income
      1. What Are Your Sources of Income?
      2. Making Sense of a Paycheck
   B. Making a Budget
      1. Decide on Your Goals
      2. Make Choices
      3. Figure Out Your Income and Expenses
      4. Set Up Your Budget
      5. Staying Within Your Budget
II. You, the Consumer
   A. Becoming a Smart Shopper
      1. Gather Information
      2. Compare Quality and Price
      3. Read the Fine Print
   B. Making a Purchase
      1. Ways to Pay
      2. Refunds and Exchanges

Chapter Overview

In this chapter, students will learn the sources of income and what will be withheld from their paychecks. They will learn that making a budget is a smart method of money management and that setting up goals is an important way to decide how to spend and save money. They will also find out the best ways of staying within a budget.

Students will discover that getting the most for their money can be achieved through research and comparison shopping. The way in which one pays for items also factors into making the most of one's money.

Focus

Objectives: After completing this lesson, students will have learned:

1. what their sources of income are and
2. how to make a plan for spending and saving money.

Preteaching the Vocabulary: Write on the board the Key Terms: *income, withhold, budget, fixed expenses, flexible expenses,* and *interest.* Ask students to define each of these terms or use each in a sentence.

🔔 **Bell Ringer:** Tell students to imagine that they have $40 to spend for the next two weeks. How would they budget this money? Have them list what they will buy and how much they will spend on each item.

Introducing the Lesson: Ask students to think about their responses to the Bell Ringer activity. Would any of them have money left over? If they ran over budget, what item would they plan to do without?

Teach

Guided Practice

Discussion Starter: Ask students if they ever played "store" when they were young. Did they consider themselves to be smart shoppers? Did they feel they got the most out of their money? If so, why and how? How do they feel they spend their money now—extravagantly or carefully?

Critical Thinking: Have students ever wondered how a country or government runs its budget? Are the basic facts of money managing the

TEACHER'S MANUAL

same for an individual and for a country? What essential elements are the same? Have students write a short paragraph to explain.

Implementing Teamwork: Divide the class into small groups. Make copies of a sample blank check and distribute to all students. Have students make out the check to pay for a department store bill. Have them make up the name of the store and the amount. Have them decide as a group to include an error on the check. After endorsing the checks, have the groups exchange checks and spot the errors. Discuss the importance of accurately making out checks.

Application Activity: Obtain blank application forms for store credit cards from local stores. Discuss the information printed on the forms. Have students complete the forms as if they were applying for a credit card.

Community Involvement Activity: Have students find out where in their neighborhood or community they could open a savings account. They should identify at least two banks or credit unions nearby that offer savings accounts. Then, they should visit one of the places they've identified and ask for information about savings accounts. Students should prepare a short oral report on the kinds of savings accounts that the bank or credit union offers. Then, have students create a poster or use the board to explain the different choices.

Students should identify at least two banks or credit unions in their neighborhood or community that offer savings accounts. They should gather information about savings accounts at one of the institutions they have identified and present it in a brief oral report that clearly explains the savings choices customers of the bank or credit union have.

SCANS Skills—Thinking: Tell students that they are toy sales representatives. Their total monthly income is in the form of commission. What are some seasons of the year they might expect high or low sales? How would they adjust their budgets to account for income variations?

SCANS Skills—Decision Making: Have students list five or six things they would like to buy. Then have them divide their list into *wants* and *needs*. Tell students their needs include anything they must have or do, for instance, repairing a flat tire. Have students write a paragraph describing how they spend their money in order to both meet their needs and satisfy their wants.

Independent Practice

Research Activity: Have students read the Investigating Career Clusters feature on page 313 in this chapter and complete the Research Activity.

Assess

Reteaching: Read the following account of Bill's shopping trip. Have the class make suggestions about how Bill could improve his shopping habits.

Bill needed some clothes for his new part-time job. He didn't have much time, so he didn't bother to double-check to see what clothes he already had that he could use for work. When he arrived at the shopping mall, he saw a sale on shirts and pants. The store was crowded and he decided not to look through the racks and piles of clothes.

He did see a display of sport shoes. The leather high tops were popular now—just what everyone was wearing. They seemed a little expensive, but they were "the best." Bill thought to himself, "What the heck, I don't buy shoes every day of the week! I'll get them."

Bill had just enough money left for either a pair of jeans or two shirts. He decided on the shirts. He saw a dark blue shirt and a brown plaid one in his size. He took the two shirts to the cashier, paid for them, and left the mall just in time for work.

Enrichment: Invite the branch manager of a bank or savings and loan to talk to the class about procedures for opening a checking or savings account with his or her bank or savings and loan. Also, ask the manager to talk about personal loans and how a person qualifies for such a loan.

Assessment: Have students complete the Lesson 14-1 Review and Activities.

Close

Have students complete these two sentences: *"My number one long-term goal in managing my money is.... My number one short-term goal in managing my money is...."*

LESSON 14-2

Focus

Objectives: After completing this lesson, students will have learned:

1. how they can get the most for their money and
2. ways that people pay for purchases.

Preteaching the Vocabulary: Write on the board the Key Terms: *impulse buying, warranty, exchange,* and *refund.* Ask students to define each of these terms or to use each in a sentence.

🔔 **Bell Ringer:** Ask students what the term *impulse buying* means. Is it sometimes good to do things on impulse? How many students would consider themselves impulsive in some area of their lives? What are some problems that come with connecting impulsiveness and money in the students' view?

Introducing the Lesson: What do students think the opposite of *impulsive* is? Tell students that in this lesson they will learn some ways to

curb their impulses when dealing with money and that this will help them to stay on a budget.

Teach
Guided Practice

Critical Thinking: Tell students they are buying a shirt for everyday use in the fall. They are trying to choose between one that is sturdy, all cotton, light-colored, and machine washable, but does not have much style, and one that is stylish, dark-colored, silk and wool combined, and needs hand washing or dry cleaning. What are some considerations they would need to take into account to be smart shoppers?

Implementing Teamwork: Organize students into groups. Have each group choose a different college financing program (for example, grants and scholarships). Ask each group to write a paragraph on that source of assistance and to present their findings to the class.

Discussion Starter: Ask students if they have ever used a warranty. Were they able to return or replace the item? When is it a good idea to check out the warranty? What are some typical time periods of expiration?

Application Activity: Have each student make a budget using the following information: each student makes $1,150 per month net pay; they must either rent an apartment or pay some amount to live at home; they must buy a car, pay for utilities, clothes, and food; and they must try to save some money, even if it is a very small amount. Have students research any unknown costs by checking newspapers or asking others who already pay for such items. Check their budgets to see that their figures are realistic.

Teamwork Activity: In groups, have students create a public service announcement that offers tips for young consumers. They should write a script for the announcement, using what they have learned in this lesson about smart

shopping. Tell students to keep the announcement short and high-interest. Then, have them
deliver it as a group or select a member of the
group to give it.

Students in each group should translate the
information provided in the lesson into tips of
high interest for young consumers. Set a time
limit of two minutes for each announcement.

SCANS Skills—Math: You have a balance of
$372.54 in your checking account. During the
next two weeks, you write a check for $62.50,
make an ATM withdrawal of $20, write a check
for $19.97, deposit $136.88, write a check for
$3.15, write a check for $95.09, and make an
ATM withdrawal of $40. What is your balance
after each transaction?
(372.54 – 62.50 = 310.04; 310.04 – 20 = 290.04;
290.04 – 19.97 = 270.07; 270.07 + 136.88 =
406.95; 406.95 – 3.15 = 403.80; 403.80 – 95.09 =
308.71; 308.71 – 40 = 268.71.)

Independent Practice

Research Activity: Have students research
an item that they might be interested in buying
in *Consumer Reports*. (Examples might be a CD
player, a food processor, a vacuum, or a television.)
They should find the best buy for their item.

Assess

Reteaching: Write the four ways of paying
for purchases on the board. Have students review
some pros and cons.

Enrichment: Invite someone who works in
the "How to . . ." section of a local bookstore to
come to your class. Ask the person to guide
students to some good books on money
management.

Assessment:
1. Have students complete the Lesson 14-2
   Review and Activities.
2. Have students complete the Chapter 14
   Review.

3. Assign the Chapter 14 Test for students
   to complete.

Close

Have students complete this statement:
"To be a smart shopper, I need to...."

LESSON 14-1 REVIEW ANSWERS

Vocabulary Review

Students should use what they have learned
in this lesson to write a paragraph about managing their money. Students' paragraphs should
incorporate and demonstrate an understanding
of the key terms.

Check Your Understanding

1. c
2. b

Critical Thinking

1. Students may designate allowance, gifts, or
   earnings from part-time jobs as the main
   source of income for people their age; they
   should support their response with information, evidence, or examples.
2. Students should observe that it is important
   to be flexible about your budget because your
   wants and needs may change or something
   unexpected may happen. They should suggest
   that if you are too flexible about your budget,
   however, you may lose sight of your priorities
   and not have enough money for them.
3. Answers will vary; students may suggest that
   they would ask for a raise in their allowance
   in exchange for doing chores, get a part-time
   job, or get a second part-time job.

Connecting to the Workplace

$16 per month (10% of $40 = $4 x 4 weeks =
$16); $192 ($16 x 12 months = $192); $384 ($192
x 2 years = $384); answers will vary

Teamwork 👤👤👤

Each group should create a teen and outline his or her situation and finances. Using information in the scenario they have been given, the members of each group should follow the steps in this lesson to make a budget for the teen.

LESSON 14-2 REVIEW ANSWERS

Vocabulary Review

Students' dialogues should focus on being a smart shopper and should incorporate the key terms.

Check Your Understanding

1. T
2. F; a higher-priced item is not always a better product than a lower-priced item.
3. F; the ways to pay for a purchase include cash, check, debit card, layaway, and credit.

Critical Thinking

1. Students may respond that it is important to read about the use and care of the product before purchasing it to make sure its use and care are practical, reasonable, or appropriate for you or whoever will be using or caring for the product.
2. Price and quality are sometimes but not always linked. When comparing price and quality, you should consider whether you're getting a good buy that meets your wants or needs.
3. People like buying on credit because they do not have to wait until they have the money needed to purchase something; they can have what they want or need right away. Students may name the following risks: credit makes it easy to buy on impulse; what you purchase on credit may not fit your budget; you may not be able to keep up with payments; you may overspend.

Connecting to the Workplace 🏢

Students' checklists for shopping for a computer should include the steps in smart shopping outlined in the lesson.

Community Involvement 🏘️

Each entry in students' directories should contain the name and address of the store, a short description of the kinds of goods or services it offers, and personal comments about bargains and special offers at the store.

CHAPTER 14 REVIEW ANSWERS

▶ Recalling Key Concepts

1. Income is the amount of money you receive or earn regularly.
2. Before setting up a budget, you must decide on your goals, prioritize them, and figure out your income and expenses.
3. Every good budget includes a plan for saving.
4. You need an account at a bank or credit union.

▶ Thinking Critically

1. You need realistic figures for income and expenses when you are making a budget; if you aren't honest with yourself about your income and expenses, your budget won't be realistic and won't work.
2. Students may observe that the purpose of many ads is to influence you to buy a product; for that reason, you need to carefully evaluate information ads provide.
3. Answers will vary but may include the following: don't use your credit card for impulse buying; make sure the purchases you make on credit fit your budget.

▶ Building Skills

1. Students should set up a simple home filing system for storing sales receipts, warranties, and product instructions. Have students describe the system they design to a friend.

2. Students should not only make a budget but should monitor their use of it and make adjustments in it as necessary. Using their first budget as a guide, students should make a second, more realistic budget that spans several months.

▶ Applying Academic Skills

1. Elaborate as necessary on the concept of bartering. Encourage students to share their bartering experiences with the class.

2. $275.60 ($5 x 52 weeks = $260; 6% of $260 = $15.60; $260 + 15.60 = $275.60)

▶ Discovery Portfolio

As directed, students should make a savings plan for a major purchase. As inspiration, students should add to their portfolio a photo or drawing of the item they wish to purchase.

▶ Career Exploration

Before selecting a career in the personal services career cluster, have students review the Investigating Career Clusters feature on page 313. Students may research the career they choose in library resources, such as encyclopedias and references published by the U.S. Department of Labor, including the *Dictionary of Occupational Titles*, the *Occupational Outlook Handbook*, and the *Guide for Occupational Exploration*. They may also do research on the Internet. If possible, they should interview someone in the career. Students should use their findings to write a classified ad for a job in the career field they have chosen. Have students post their ads on a bulletin board and read each other's ads.

LESSON 15-1 ● Work Isn't Everything!

Lesson Objectives: After completing this lesson, students will have learned:

1. why it is important to balance the different parts of one's life and
2. how to make time for school, work, family, and friends.

Lesson 15-1 Features
Career Q & A, p. 320
The Right Attitude, p. 324
The Global Workplace, p. 321

Lesson 15-1 Resources
- Lesson 15-1 Activities, p. 325
- Student Activity Workbook, Activities 1 and 2
- Transparency 31
- Transparency Lesson Plan

LESSON 15-2 ● Giving Something Back

Lesson Objectives: After completing this lesson, students will have learned:

1. their responsibilities to their community and
2. how they can contribute to the life of their community.

Lesson 15-2 Features
Career Opportunities, p. 329
Investigating Career Clusters, p. 333

Lesson 15-2 Resources
- Lesson 15-2 Activities, p. 332
- Student Activity Workbook, Activities 3, 4, and 5

CHAPTER 15 RESOURCES

Assessment
- Lesson 15-1 Review, p. 325
- Lesson 15-2 Review, p. 332
- Chapter Review, p. 334
- Chapter 15 Reproducible Test and Testmaker Software

Extension
- Teacher's Manual, p. TM150
- Teacher's Resource Binder:
  - Teacher's Lesson Plans
  - Career Cluster Activities
  - Spanish Resources
  - Involving Parents and Family Resources

Multimedia
- Workforce 2000 Video Library, Segments 17 and 21
- Exploring the World of Work CD-ROM
- Teacher's Resource Binder:
  - Internet Resources, Chapter 15

SCANS CORRELATION CHART ....

FOUNDATION SKILLS

Basic Skills	Reading	Writing	Math	Listening	Speaking

Thinking Skills	Creative Thinking	Decision Making	Problem Solving	Seeing Things in the Mind's Eye	Knowing How to Learn	Reasoning

Personal Qualities	Responsibility	Self-Esteem	Sociability	Self-Management	Integrity/Honesty

WORKPLACE COMPETENCIES

Resources	Allocating Time	Allocating Money	Allocating Material and Facility Resources	Allocating Human Resources

Information	Acquiring and Evaluating Information	Organizing and Maintaining Information	Interpreting and Communicating Information	Using Computers to Process Information

Interpersonal Skills	Participating as a Member of a Team	Teaching Others	Serving Clients/ Customers	Exercising Leadership	Negotiating to Arrive at a Decision	Working with Cultural Diversity

Systems	Understanding Systems	Monitoring and Correcting Performance	Improving and Designing Systems

Technology	Selecting Technology	Applying Technology to Task	Maintaining and Troubleshooting Technology

TEACHER'S MANUAL

ENRICHMENT AND APPLICATION ACTIVITIES

Internet Activity

Ask students to use the Internet to find some nonprofit organizations (local or national) that use volunteers. Have each student choose an organization of interest to him or her and research it. Students should make note of appropriate Web sites. Suggested Internet search words:
nonprofit organizations
volunteering

GO TO Teacher's Resource Binder: Internet Resources

Field Trip Activity

Arrange for students to visit a local museum or library and to find out about volunteering or internships at that institution. Have them write down all the facts—in case they would be interested later.

Guest Speaker Activity

Ask a parent who has a particularly busy schedule and many responsibilities to share with the class how he or she copes. Students might ask how this person managed to make time to give the talk to the class.

Chapter 15 Living a Balanced Life

Chapter Outline

I. Work Isn't Everything!
   A. The Need for Balance
      1. Balancing Work and Personal Life
      2. What's Your Life About?
   B. Making Your Time Count
      1. Finding Time
      2. Being Present
II. Giving Something Back
   A. What Being a Citizen Means
      1. Respecting Others
      2. Caring for What You Share
      3. Staying Informed
      4. Making Your Voice Heard
   B. Doing Your Part
      1. Ways to Lend a Hand
      2. The Rewards of Good Citizenship

Chapter Overview

In this chapter, students will learn that as adults they will need to balance the responsibilities of home, work, and the community. They will learn that time management plays an important part in a busy life and that they will need to decide what is important to them in order to keep balance in their lives.

Students will also learn what being a citizen means and how they might contribute to making their communities better places to live.

LESSON 15-1

Focus

Objectives: After completing this lesson, students will have learned:
1. why it is important to balance the different parts of one's life and
2. how to make time for school, work, family, and friends.

Preteaching the Vocabulary: Write on the board the Key Terms: *balance, leisure,* and *time management.* Ask students to define each of these terms or use each in a sentence.

Bell Ringer: Have students think about their lives and suggest how much time they give to family and friends. Do they think it is too much or too little?

Introducing the Lesson: Have students think of other parts of their lives (not counting family and friends). Explain that all these parts have to maintain a balance in their lives. If students have part-time work, have them share with the class exactly how much time they devote to work.

Teach

Guided Practice

Critical Thinking: Have students think about what values they cherish. If these values are reflected in their choice of career, how do students think they will avoid spending too much time on the job? Discuss answers.

Implementing Teamwork: Have students role-play situations on the topic of time management. Explain that one person is overly organized and one person is irresponsible about time. Have students choose the skit that shows their own tendencies.

Discussion Starter: Write the word *compromise* on the chalkboard and ask students to suggest definitions. Remind students that compromise is a human-relations skill—a way of getting along with others. Compromising is also a way of balancing job and family responsibilities.

Community Involvement Activity: Tell students to ask a librarian for help in finding information about time management and balancing work and personal life. They should look for books and for articles in newspapers and magazines, as well as conduct a search for information on the Internet. Have students put together a bibliography, or reading list, of books, articles, and Web sites they find.

Students may work with a librarian in their school or local library to locate books and articles on time management and finding balance in life. Encourage students to ask the librarian for help in using correct bibliographical style for their reading lists. Help students identify community organizations whose members or users might find such a resource useful.

SCANS Skills—Thinking: Have students imagine they are working from home. What special problems would make the balance between home and work difficult to achieve? How would students suggest resolving these difficulties?

SCANS Skills—Responsibility: Have students list their current responsibilities. Then have each student create a bar graph or pie chart showing how he or she allocates time for each. Have them evaluate the percentage of their time that is spent on useful versus frivolous activities. Then have them discuss how allocating their time differently will allow them to spend their time more efficiently.

Independent Practice

Research Activity: Check the local library or *Reader's Guide to Periodical Literature* to look for books or articles on the topic of working from home. Have students compare and contrast their own suggestions with those they find during their research.

Assess

Reteaching: Have students review the tools and techniques for time management. Have volunteers demonstrate a day planner.

Enrichment: Have the vice principal of your school come to the class to explain scheduling school activities with a time line. Does he or she have any good suggestions for personal time management?

Assessment: Have students complete the Lesson 15-1 Review and Activities.

Close

Have students complete this statement: *"To keep a balance in my life, I must...."*

Focus

Objectives: After completing this lesson, students will have learned:
1. their responsibilities to their community and
2. how they can contribute to the life of their community.

Preteaching the Vocabulary: Write on the board the Key Term: *register*. Have students explain this term with respect to voting.

Bell Ringer: Why would students consider it necessary to give back to their families and to their communities? What does "giving back" imply?

Introducing the Lesson: Ask volunteers to suggest some ways of "giving back." Point out to students that their own lives will be enriched by becoming actively involved in their communities.

Teach

Guided Practice

Critical Thinking: Ask students if it makes sense to show respect to people they don't really like. Why should a person be accepting of those who hold different values or beliefs?

Discussion Starter: Have students suggest ways in which their own community could use help. How would providing this help exercise good citizenship?

Ask students how many of them followed the most recent local election. Had they been old enough, would they have voted in that election? Why or why not?

Application Activity: Ask students to write out the answers they came up with in the Discussion Starter. If time permits, read aloud some of the answers.

Implementing Teamwork: Have students break into small groups. Ask each group to make a list of needs the local environment may have. Have each group take one concrete need and explain in a paragraph how this need could be met.

Teamwork Activity: Have students work in groups to put together a regular newsletter about community developments. They should focus on issues and events of interest to young people. In the groups, they should divide up the tasks of gathering information, writing, editing, and producing the newsletter. Help students use word-processing and desktop-publishing software to create their newsletter. Circulate the newsletter at the school.

Students should produce a newsletter that focuses on community issues, and events of interest to young people.

Application Activity: Have students write a one-page summary of ways suggested in the chapter of "giving back."

SCANS Skills—Writing: Tell students that voting patterns show that older people are far more likely to vote than people in their twenties. Ask students why they think younger people fail to vote. How could they be encouraged to do so? Have students write a 100-word message to their peers persuading them to follow political issues and vote.

SCANS Skills—Responsibility: Ask students whether they keep informed about what's going on at school and in their community. How do they stay informed? How could they become more active citizens regarding school or community? Ask students how staying informed about activities affecting an employer might help them on the job. Tell students to summarize their thoughts in a paragraph or two.

SCANS Skills—Speaking: Have students use an example they find in the Research Activity as an example for a persuasive speech. Tell students to take off from the example and give a short (3-paragraph) speech to their audience on the topic of giving back to the community.

Independent Practice

Research Activity: Have students research the topic of volunteering. What types of volunteering opportunities are out there for students like themselves? What kinds of programs are available for those who would like to provide their services?

Assess

Reteaching: Have students review the place of good citizenship in a balanced life. How will their work benefit if they contribute to their communities?

Enrichment: Have a person who works at the voting booth during elections come to your class. Ask him or her to explain in detail the actual physical process of voting (using the machine to punch holes). Point out to students that, if they don't vote, they are letting someone else determine their lives.

Assessment:

1. Have students complete the Lesson 15-2 Review and Activities.
2. Have students complete the Chapter 15 Review.
3. Assign the Chapter 15 Test for students to complete.

Close

Have students complete this statement: *"Contributing to the life of my community will help me...."*

LESSON 15-1 REVIEW ANSWERS

Vocabulary Review

Students' diagrams should demonstrate a clear understanding of the meaning of the terms and should illustrate the connections among the concepts.

Check Your Understanding

1. c
2. a

Critical Thinking

1. Students should observe that when a job takes up a good deal of your time, setting aside time with family and friends helps keep your life balanced by giving you a break from work responsibilities.

2. Students are likely to suggest that a daily "to-do list" would help them remember to do their homework and that a schedule and/or a time line and the technique of breaking a large project into smaller pieces would help them manage a long-term project.

3. Students' answers should reflect their understanding of the suggestions from the book.

Connecting to the Workplace

Students might recommend creating a "to-do list" of tasks for the day and a schedule that will help their coworker arrive on time and complete all her tasks without rushing.

Teamwork

Students may create a time line either for an ongoing group project in which they are involved or for a group project they would like to do. Allow time for students to share their time lines with the class.

LESSON 15-2 REVIEW ANSWERS

Vocabulary Review

Students' posters should stress the importance of voting and should promote voter registration.

Check Your Understanding

1. T
2. F; citizens have rights and responsibilities.
3. F; the key to getting along with others is showing respect.
4. T

Critical Thinking

1. Answers should reflect students' understanding of showing respect to others.

2. Responsible voters use the information they've gathered about the issues to make choices when they vote.

3. Answers may include being a good role model to children, being a taxpayer, and being a responsible member of the workforce.

4. Answers will vary; students may mention library reading hours, health-care support services, soup kitchens, as well as other activities and services in their community.

5. Students should identify volunteers in their community and describe how they are working to make life better for other citizens.

Connecting to the Workplace

Students' essays should explain how each of the citizenship skills described on pages 327–330 could be applied in the workplace.

Community Involvement

Answers will vary but may include the following: you could volunteer your services by planting and maintaining some public space in your community or by mowing and caring for the yards of older people or people who cannot afford lawn and garden care; you could volunteer your services as a baby-sitter at community events, such as school open houses and plays and concerts, or to parents whose children are home alone after school.

CHAPTER 15 REVIEW ANSWERS

▶ Recalling Key Concepts

1. When you balance the different parts of your life—your work and your commitments to yourself and others—you will be happier and healthier, and you are likely to be more satisfied with everything you do.

2. Time management involves choosing how to spend your time and creating a schedule for your choices.

3. Making a "to-do list," prioritizing, breaking big projects into small steps, setting up a schedule, and making a time line are five tools or techniques of time management.

4. To vote, you must be at least 18 years old and you must register.

5. When you help someone else, you see how valuable your time and energy can be to others; that gives you a sense of self-worth.

▶ Thinking Critically

1. Students' responses should demonstrate an understanding of the concept of balance; students should cite specific examples of the balance or lack of balance in their lives.

2. Students may describe their own methods of being present with others as well as methods described in the text.

3. Students should identify various citizenship skills described in the text.

4. Answers will vary but may include the following: writing letters to elected officials and other leaders, circulating petitions, and organizing demonstrations.

▶ Building Skills

1. Accept all responses students can support with sound reasoning. Many students will observe that if they were Zach and wanted to run a business buying and selling comic books, they would buy a used table that they could use now and could bring to subsequent fairs.

2. Students should research either flextime or on-site day care and report on how it helps employees manage their job and family responsibilities.

▶ Applying Academic Skills

1. Each group should identify a problem in the community, find out what is being done about it, and join the effort or plan and carry out a strategy for dealing with it. Help students prepare and submit an account of their efforts to a local newspaper.

2. Students should compile an honest evaluation of their ability to manage time and consider ways they might change to manage their time better.

▶ Discovery Portfolio

Students may analyze a project or job. They should keep their lists in their portfolio for easy reference. Students should refer to the lists of interests and skills that they made in Chapter 1. They should match volunteer jobs with their interests and skills and pursue at least one of their job ideas. Encourage students to keep a detailed record of their experiences as volunteers in their portfolios.

▶ Career Exploration

Before selecting a career in the public services career cluster, have students review the Investigating Career Clusters feature on page 333. Students may research the career they choose in library resources, such as encyclopedias and references published by the U.S. Department of Labor, including the *Dictionary of Occupational Titles,* the *Occupational Outlook Handbook,* and the *Guide for Occupational Exploration.* They may also do research on the Internet. If possible, they should interview someone with a job in the field. Students' posters should provide information about the career in a way that will attract people's interest.

LESSON 16-1 ● Dealing with Change

Lesson Objectives: After completing this lesson, the students will have learned:

1. how to deal with personal changes beyond their control,
2. kinds of personal changes they might choose in the future,
3. how to handle job and career changes, and
4. ways of looking at and preparing for change.

Lesson 16-1 Features	**Lesson 16-2 Resources**
The Global Workplace, p. 344	• Lesson 16-1 Activities, p. 350
Career Q & A, p. 348	• Student Activity Workbook, Activities 1 and 2
	• Transparency 32
	• Transparency Lesson Plan

LESSON 16-2 ● The Future Is Coming

Lesson Objectives: After completing this lesson, the students will have learned:

1. why they should plan for the future,
2. the power of positive thinking, and
3. how they can start to move toward the future.

Lesson 16-2 Features	**Lesson 16-2 Resources**
The Right Attitude, p. 353	• Lesson 16-2 Activities, p. 356
Career Opportunities, p. 354	• Student Activity Workbook, Activities 3, 4, and 5
Investigating Career Clusters, p. 357	

CHAPTER 16 RESOURCES

Assessment

- Lesson 16-1 Review, p. 350
- Lesson 16-2 Review, p. 356
- Chapter Review, p. 358
- Chapter 16 Reproducible Test and Testmaker Software

Extension

- Teacher's Manual, p. TM156
- Teacher's Resource Binder:
  - Teacher's Lesson Plans
  - Career Cluster Activities
  - Spanish Resources
  - Involving Parents and Family Resources

Multimedia

- Workforce 2000 Video Library, Segment 21
- Exploring the World of Work CD-ROM
- Teacher's Resource Binder:
  - Internet Resources, Chapter 16

TEACHER'S MANUAL

SCANS CORRELATION CHART ....

FOUNDATION SKILLS

Basic Skills	Reading	Writing	Math	Listening	Speaking

Thinking Skills	Creative Thinking	Decision Making	Problem Solving	Seeing Things in the Mind's Eye	Knowing How to Learn	Reasoning

Personal Qualities	Responsibility	Self-Esteem	Sociability	Self-Management	Integrity/Honesty

WORKPLACE COMPETENCIES

Resources	Allocating Time	Allocating Money	Allocating Material and Facility Resources	Allocating Human Resources

Information	Acquiring and Evaluating Information	Organizing and Maintaining Information	Interpreting and Communicating Information	Using Computers to Process Information

Interpersonal Skills	Participating as a Member of a Team	Teaching Others	Serving Clients/ Customers	Exercising Leadership	Negotiating to Arrive at a Decision	Working with Cultural Diversity

Systems	Understanding Systems	Monitoring and Correcting Performance	Improving and Designing Systems

Technology	Selecting Technology	Applying Technology to Task	Maintaining and Troubleshooting Technology

---

ENRICHMENT AND APPLICATION ACTIVITIES

Internet Activity

Ask students to use the Internet to find predictions about the workplace of the future. They should make note of appropriate Web sites. Suggested Internet search words: workforce 2000 trends

Teacher's Resource Binder: Internet Resources

Field Trip Activity

Visit an industry in your area that is particularly forward-looking. Ask an officer or representative to explain what changes are anticipated in the next 10 years and how the industry is preparing adjustments for those changes.

Guest Speaker Activity

Have students meet with a leader from the community. Ask this person to speak on the changes coming for workers and members of the community. Ask students to prepare and ask questions.

Chapter Outline

I. Dealing with Change
   A. Personal Changes Beyond Your Control
      1. Family Changes
      2. Changing Places
      3. Illness and Death
      4. Dealing with What You Can't Control
   B. Choosing Change
   C. Changing Jobs or Careers
      1. Losing a Job
      2. Rethinking the Future
      3. Looking for a New Job or Career
   D. Ready for Change?
   E. Be a Lifelong Learner
      1. Get Support
II. The Future Is Coming
   A. Make Plans Now
   B. Be Positive!
      1. Trade in Your Negative Thoughts
      2. Making Things Happen
   C. Move Toward Your Vision
      1. There's No Time Like the Present
      2. Exploring Possibilities

Chapter Overview

In this chapter, students will look ahead to see what life changes they may expect. They will learn how they can handle personal and job- or career-related changes, as well as finding out ways they can look at and prepare for change.

Additionally, they will discover why making plans now for the future puts them in charge of their lives and why thinking positively increases chances of reaching a goal. Planning right now will set students on the way to achieving a bright future.

LESSON 16-1

Focus

Objectives: After completing this lesson, students will have learned:

1. how to deal with personal changes beyond their control,
2. kinds of personal changes they might choose in the future,
3. how to handle job and career changes, and
4. ways of looking at and preparing for change.

Preteaching the Vocabulary: Write on the board the Key Terms: *stepparent* and *blended family*. Ask students to define each of these terms or use each in a sentence.

🔔 **Bell Ringer:** Ask students what adjectives they can think of to describe a time of change that is unsettling or unwelcome. (Examples might be stormy, uprooting, dizzying.)

Introducing the Lesson: Tell students that while some changes are beyond their control, there are ways to handle these changes with patience and help from others. With careful consideration, any change that a person chooses to make can be positive.

Teach
Guided Practice

Critical Thinking: Tell students that in the past, catastrophic illnesses such as polio would completely change a person's career plan. Do the students consider this is less likely today? Is it possible to continue an education even when being held back by a serious illness? What qualities would such a person need to have?

Implementing Teamwork: Divide the class into small groups. Have each group compile a list of different situations that may be the source of stress. How would they deal with each of the situations? Have the groups choose and act out one situation.

Discussion Starter: *Downsizing* is a word often used in connection with the workplace today. Ask students to explain the term and to list some changes it brings about for a company. How would they personally feel about losing a job through downsizing?

Application Activity: Ask students to imagine that they have chosen a career path. Suddenly, this career is threatened by unforeseen circumstances. Have students write down their imagined career and underneath it list possible related careers that they could turn to if necessary.

Community Involvement Activity: Have students list the changes discussed in this chapter. They should identify community resources available to help people experiencing these changes. The resources may include support groups, individuals, and agencies. Tell students they can look for information in their local newspaper and telephone book. They can also talk to other people about appropriate community resources. Then, have students display their findings on a poster. Students may share and compare the information on their posters.

SCANS Skills—Writing: Have students write as if they were writing science fiction. They should write about a day in the future. How do they get to work? How are the workers communicating with their managers? Are many people or only a few working for their companies? Do students imagine this day in the future to be more or less stressful than current working days? Have students write their ideas in two or three paragraphs.

Independent Practice

Research Activity: Have students read Investigating Career Clusters on page 357 and complete the Research Activity.

Assess

Reteaching: Have students review how they would deal with difficult personal changes. Suggest that flexibility and lifelong learning would be helpful means. Have students define these terms.

Enrichment: Have students write a 1–2 page story about a person who reacts positively to a difficult personal change. The story should be fictional and imaginative but may be based on real experiences.

Assessment: Have students complete the Lesson 16-1 Review and Activities.

Close

Have students complete this statement: *"The best ways of preparing for change in personal life, jobs, and careers are...."*

LESSON 16-2

Focus

Objectives: After completing this lesson, students will have learned:
1. why they should plan for the future,
2. the power of positive thinking, and
3. how they can start to move toward the future.

Preteaching the Vocabulary: Write on the board the Key Terms: *accomplishments* and *fulfilling*. Ask students to define the terms and discuss the link between the two ideas.

🔔 **Bell Ringer:** Have students identify specific accomplishments they would like to achieve that they will keep in mind when forming a plan for the future. Remind students that stressing the positive helps a person to move forward.

Introducing the Lesson: Tell students that in the first lesson of the chapter they learned about adapting to change. In this lesson, they will be thinking about what can be done in the present for a successful future. Taking small steps toward a personal goal or a career goal will give them a feeling of success.

Teach

Guided Practice

Critical Thinking: Have students imagine they are attending a class reunion. What would they like to be able to say about themselves in 15 years' time? Ask them to write a 50-word paragraph.

Implementing Teamwork: In small groups, have students think about a career that has not been imagined before. When they have decided on their never-thought-of-before careers, have the groups act out some aspect of these careers for the rest of the class.

Discussion Starter: Ask students how they think having a plan can include changing plans. Does changing a plan mean canceling out the previous plan? Ask them to explain why or why not.

Application Activity: Have students write a two-minute speech describing one long-term goal for their careers and one small step they are taking now toward that goal.

Teamwork Activity: Have students work in small groups to make collages of what they have learned in this book. They should use words and pictures in their collages. Allow time for each group to explain their collage to the class, and answer any questions the class may have. Display their collages in the classroom or somewhere else where other students will see it.

Remind students that a collage is a collection of images from many different sources. The images are pasted onto a large piece of paper or cardboard. Students may also use words cut from magazines or newspapers, small objects, and other art materials to create their collages. Students' collages should highlight various themes of this book.

SCANS Skills—Creative Thinking: Have students imagine that, like Rip Van Winkle, they have gone to sleep for 20 years. When they awaken, the world of work will have changed. Ask students if they think the strategies for dealing with change they have learned in this lesson will still apply for them. Have them discuss why or why not.

Independent Practice

Research Activity: Tell students that experts predict traditional full-time jobs will be replaced by temporary, part-time positions in the future. Have students research this topic in the *Reader's Guide to Periodical Literature*, or find information on the Internet. Ask students to report on how a part-time position would fit into their plan for the future. How could they make plans now for this trend in the workplace?

Assess

Reteaching: Review with students the best ways of planning now for a fulfilling career in the future. (They should think about using their present accomplishments, exploring possibilities, and developing a positive attitude.)

Enrichment: Have students look for a poem, a painting, a sculpture, a movie, or some other artistic creation that seems to them to typify their dream of what the future holds.

Assessment:

1. Have students complete the Lesson 16-2 Review and Activities.
2. Have students complete the Chapter 16 Review.
3. Assign the Chapter 16 Test for students to complete.

Close

Have students complete this statement: *"My plans for a fulfilling career in the future include...."*

Vocabulary Review

Students' notes for their talk should include the key terms.

Check Your Understanding

1. a
2. b

Critical Thinking

1. Students may identify marriage and children among other personal changes they might choose one day; they may suggest preparing for their choices by asking others' advice, reading books, comparing pros and cons, and thinking about how the choices fit their plans.
2. Answers will vary but should include details about how the change was positive.
3. If you are a lifelong learner, you're always looking for ways to learn, and as a result, you know where to find the latest information and resources. Information and resources help you deal with changes.

Connecting to the Workplace

Most students will respond that John should at least tell his boss what is going on so that his boss can help him manage his work and get help if needed; students may suggest that John ask coworkers he trusts for support.

Teamwork

Students should divide up the tasks involved and invite teachers or other adults to help them produce their guide.

Vocabulary Review

Students' essays should demonstrate an understanding of the terms and focus on accomplishments in the present and future.

Check Your Understanding

1. a
2. b
3. b
4. c

Critical Thinking

1. Answers will vary but may include making plans for further schooling or for a career.
2. A positive attitude keeps you from being discouraged and helps you keep moving forward.
3. The steps you take in the present lead to the future.

Connecting to the Workplace

The contrast between the attitudes of the two characters students role-play should be clear.

Community Involvement

Students' posters, buttons, or flyers should feature catchy slogans that promote positive thinking. Help students post or distribute their work in the community.

Recalling Key Concepts

1. You might choose to move into your own place, marry, and have children.
2. You might lose a job because you were fired, your company went through downsizing, you refused a transfer, or your company was sold.
3. Teachers, school counselors, coaches, and religious leaders can help you adjust to change.

4. To be in charge of your life, you need a plan for the future.

5. You make things happen in the present, because that's where you begin to work on accomplishing your goals, step by step.

▶ Thinking Critically

1. Answers will vary but students may observe that change can be unpredictable, take you by surprise, make you feel you don't have control over your life, and turn your life upside down.

2. Answers will vary. Most students will select one of the personal changes mentioned in the chapter.

3. You can create a fulfilling life for yourself by developing a plan for your life, rather than letting life happen to you.

4. Answers will vary; students should support their answers.

5. Entertain all thoughtful responses.

▶ Building Skills

1. Answers will vary; students' plans should be broken down into small, manageable steps. The plans should also show a logical progression toward the ultimate goal.

2. Students' book reviews should focus on someone who made a difference in the world and should answer the questions in the activity.

3. Help students connect with students at the elementary level to share their books.

▶ Applying Academic Skills

1. Students may enjoy sharing their raps and poems with the rest of the class. Make sure the raps and poems offer a positive vision.

2. Students may choose to make a painting, sculpture, collage, poster, sketch, diorama, or other piece of art to celebrate their accomplishments.

▶ Discovery Portfolio

Students should develop lists of possible changes and discuss how they will handle these changes.

▶ Career Exploration

Have students begin by reviewing the Investigating Career Clusters feature on page 357. Students may research the career they chose in library resources, such as encyclopedias and references published by the U.S. Department of Labor, including the *Dictionary of Occupational Titles*, the *Occupational Outlook Handbook*, and the *Guide for Occupational Exploration*. They may also do research on the Internet. If possible, students should interview someone with a job in the career. In their oral reports, students should give information on each topic listed.

EXPLORING
CAREERS

THIRD EDITION

Joan Kelly-Plate
Career Educator
Lake Suzy, Florida

Ruth Volz-Patton
Career Consultant
Springfield, Illinois

Glencoe McGraw-Hill

New York, New York   Columbus, Ohio   Woodland Hills, California   Peoria, Illinois

Glencoe/McGraw-Hill

A Division of The **McGraw·Hill** *Companies*

Printed in the United States of America.

Send all inquiries to:
Glencoe/McGraw-Hill
21600 Oxnard Street
Woodland Hills, California 91367

ISBN 0-02-643183-1 (Student Text)
ISBN 0-02-642593-9 (Teacher's Annotated Edition)

1 2 3 4 5 6 7 8 9   027   04 03 02 01 00 99 98

Advisory Board

To best research and address the needs of today's workplace, Glencoe/McGraw-Hill assembled an advisory board of industry leaders and educators. The board lent its expertise and experience to establish the foundation for this innovative, real-world, career education program. Glencoe/McGraw-Hill would like to acknowledge the following companies and individuals for their support and commitment to this project:

Mark Ballard
Director of Human Resources
Recruitment and Development
The Limited, Inc.
Columbus, OH

Michele Bina
Michele Bina and Associates
former Manager of Organizational
    Effectiveness
The Prudential Healthcare Group
Woodland Hills, CA

Joe Bryan
Industrial Cooperative Training Coordinator
Warsaw Community Schools
Warsaw, IN

Mary Sue Burkhardt
Career Specialist
Family and Consumer Sciences
Twin Lakes High School
Monticello, IN

Mable Burton
Career Development Specialist
Office of Education for Employment
Philadelphia, PA

Lolita B. Hall, Specialist
Program Improvement
Virginia Department of Education
Richmond, VA

Liz Lamatrice
Career Education Coordinator
Jefferson County, OH

Keith Mitchell
Manager, Testing and Assessment
Abbott Laboratories
Abbott Park, IL

James Murphy
Education Relations Manager
The Boeing Company
Seattle, WA

William M. Pepito
Manager, Lake County Skills
    Development Program
Abbott Laboratories
Abbott Park, IL

William J. Ratzburg
Director, Education for Work and Careers
Racine School District
Racine, WI

Gary Schepf
Business Education Department Chair
Nimitz High School
Irving, TX

Reviewers

Toni Barrows
Teacher/Coordinator
Clay High School
Orange Park, FL

Nathan Brubaker
Putnam City High School
Oklahoma City, OK

Kimala J. Forrest
Sylvan Hills Jr. High
Sherwood, AZ

Joan F. Haas
Conway Middle School
Orlando, FL

Mary Hopple
School-to-Career Coordinator
Oxnard Union High School District
Oxnard, CA

Beverly Newton
Business Education Consultant
Nebraska Department of Education
Lincoln, NE

Table of Contents

Unit 3 Lifelong Learning

Features

CAREER OPPORTUNITIES

CAREER  Q&A

The RIGHT Attitude!

The Global Workplace

Welcome to *Exploring Careers!*

What do you enjoy? What are you good at? What do you want to do with your life? What do you dream of becoming? This book will help you begin to explore the answers to these questions.

Getting to Know You

If you really think about it, there is at least one thing, if not several things, you really enjoy. Think of the things that make time fly for you, things that make you feel good about yourself. Maybe you love playing sports or acting in plays. Perhaps you like working with computers or writing stories. The things you enjoy now and in the future will lead to various careers. Throughout this course, you will be exploring careers that match who you are. This book will help you get started.

First, you'll take a look at yourself. You'll identify your interests and values. You'll think about your skills and aptitudes. You'll imagine your ideal lifestyle. Then you'll consider how each might affect your career choices one day.

Looking at Careers

You'll learn about the many career areas and begin to think about careers that best suit you. Let's say for example that you love animals and value education. A career working as an exhibit interpreter at a zoo or aquarium might interest you. A career as an dog obedience trainer might also appeal to you. There are all kinds of career possibilities to match who you are and what you believe is important. This book will introduce you to different ways to explore these possibilities now and in the future.

Planning for the Future

In this book, you'll also learn how to make decisions, set goals, and plan for your future. You will look at the kind of education and training you will need for careers that interest you. You'll learn how to find, apply, and interview for a job.

You'll get a glimpse of what it's like to be part of the work world. You'll learn what to expect and what will be expected of you. You'll find out why it is important to develop strong people skills and basic skills. You'll discover the part health and safety play in your life now and on the job.

You'll take a look at how business is organized and operates in our country. You'll find out how to manage your money and make wise purchases. You'll get valuable tips for balancing work and personal life. You'll learn how you can give something back to your community.

Last but not least, you'll discover how to deal with the different kinds of changes that life brings. You'll learn the importance of lifelong learning, a positive attitude, and planning. What you learn will help you move toward your future with excitement and confidence.

Get ready for an exciting adventure with *Exploring Careers*. The adventure you are invited to join is just the beginning of a lifetime of exploration!

Understanding the Text Structure

You'll find the text of Exploring Careers easy to read and understand. The text is divided into three units: **Career Exploration**, **Employment Skills**, and **Lifelong Learning**. Within each unit there are chapters.

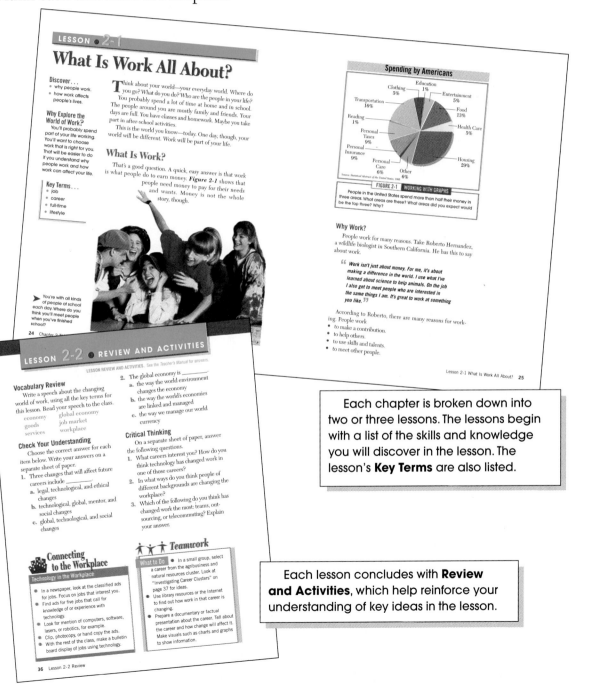

Each chapter is broken down into two or three lessons. The lessons begin with a list of the skills and knowledge you will discover in the lesson. The lesson's **Key Terms** are also listed.

Each lesson concludes with **Review and Activities**, which help reinforce your understanding of key ideas in the lesson.

To the Student

Focus on the Features

Text features in each chapter provide special insights into career topics and challenge your creativity and imagination.

The Right Attitude provides tips for building a positive attitude. These tips will come in handy on the job one day.

Career Q & A answers questions about exploring careers that might come to mind as you read the text.

The Global Workplace identifies work-related cultural differences to prepare you for the global workplace you will enter one day.

The RIGHT Attitude!

Attitude Counts

Success depends on more than hard work. In the recipe for success, in both career and life, attitude is an essential ingredient. You can start cultivating a positive attitude today. What are some positive attitude skills? Enthusiasm, asserting yourself, managing stressful situations, flexibility, self-esteem, and treating people with respect all play a part.

Apply Your Skills!

Brainstorm with a partner, a list of qualities that show a positive attitude. Come up with five or six qualities and share your list with the class. Make a list on the board of all the qualities chosen and pick 10. Write them out on a large sheet of construction paper, and post them in your classroom.

CAREER Q&A

Finding Out More About a Job

Q: What if I have the skills and aptitudes for a job, but I'm still not sure that I'll like it?

A: Talk to people who work in the job that interests you. Find out what they like about their job. What are the working conditions like? The people who actually work in the jobs that interest you can give you the best idea as to whether you might like the job yourself.

Investigating Career Clusters

Agribusiness and Natural Resources

What Is the Agribusiness and Natural Resources Cluster?
Occupations in this cluster area involve supplying consumers with raw materials for food, shelter, and clothing. Jobs center around agriculture, land and water management, mining, petroleum production, and agriculture support services.

Skills Needed
Technical communication, mathematics, safety, basic lab, and information

THE FACTS Types of Careers in This Cluster	Work Description	Career Outlook	Education
Quality control technician	Supervise the production of agriculture products	Good	H.S. diploma, On-the-job training
Farm operator	Manage the planting, harvesting, and storing of crops; tend livestock and poultry	Slower than average	H.S. diploma, On-the-job training, Bachelor's
Forester	Manage forested lands for a variety of purposes	Average	Bachelor's, Ph.D.
Petroleum engineer	Explore for and monitor recovery of oil or natural gas	Slower than average	Bachelor's
Agricultural scientist	Study farm crops and animals and develop ways of improving their quantity and quality	Good	Bachelor's, Ph.D.

Research Activity Make a list of five agribusiness and natural resources jobs that interest you. Then research the particular skills and tasks required of each job. Also investigate the job outlook and salary range for this particular job. Create a chart that summarizes your findings.

Investigating Career Clusters 37

Investigating Career Clusters offers information on one of the fifteen career clusters, or areas. The research activity at the end of the feature will help you think about how the career cluster relates to you.

Career Opportunities gives a short newspaper-ad description of a job in a particular career cluster, or area. It concludes with a critical thinking question to challenge your mind.

The Global Workplace

Business Cards Are An Essential Tool

Common business practice requires the exchange of business cards. With a card, an associate can remember your company's name and your job title and can contact you. In most of Southeast Asia, Africa, and the Middle East, it is considered rude to present a card with your left hand. In Japan, present cards with both hands. Make sure the words face the recipient and are right side up.

Exploration Activity!

Research business cards. What kind of information is listed on business cards? What do they look like? Make up a business card for a job you would like to have.

CAREER OPPORTUNITIES

Communications and Media
If you love working with computers and surfing the 'net, check out this job in communications.

Critical Thinking
Why would communication skills be important for this job?

CLASSIFIED
THURSDAY

Webmaster
Clothing store needs a webmaster to build a Web site and create an online catalog of its merchandise. Requirements: fluency in HTML, a working knowledge of Photoshop and Java, and excellent communication skills. Ability to play a leadership role essential.

Reviewing What You've Learned

At the end of each chapter is the Chapter Review.

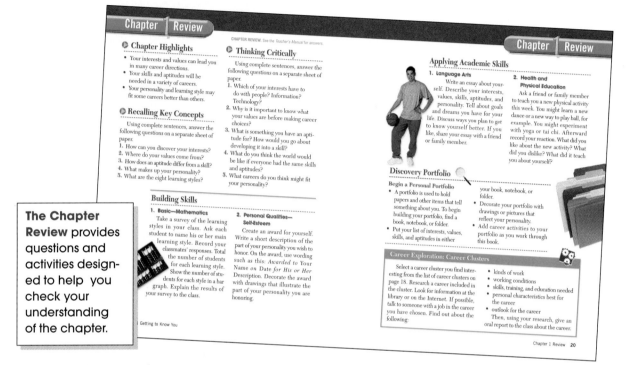

Chapter | **Review**

CHAPTER REVIEW. See the *Teacher's Manual* for answers.

Chapter Highlights

• Your interests and values can lead you in many career directions.
• Your skills and aptitudes will be needed in a variety of careers.
• Your personality and learning style may fit some careers better than others.

Recalling Key Concepts

Using complete sentences, answer the following questions on a separate sheet of paper.
1. How can you discover your interests?
2. Where do your values come from?
3. How does an aptitude differ from a skill?
4. What makes up your personality?
5. What are the eight learning styles?

Thinking Critically

Using complete sentences, answer the following questions on a separate sheet of paper.
1. Which of your interests have to do with people? Information? Technology?
2. Why is it important to know what your values are before making career choices?
3. What is something you have an aptitude for? How would you go about developing it into a skill?
4. What do you think the world would be like if everyone had the same skills and aptitudes?
5. What careers do you think might fit your personality?

Building Skills

1. **Basic—Mathematics**
Take a survey of the learning styles in your class. Ask each student to name his or her main learning style. Record your classmates' responses. Total the number of students for each learning style. Show the number of students for each style in a bar graph. Explain the results of your survey to the class.

2. **Personal Qualities—Self-Esteem**
Create an award for yourself. Write a short description of the part of your personality you wish to honor. On the award, use wording such as this: *Awarded to Your Name on Date for His or Her Description.* Decorate the award with drawings that illustrate the part of your personality you are honoring.

Getting to Know You

Chapter | **Review**

Applying Academic Skills

1. **Language Arts**
Write an essay about yourself. Describe your interests, values, skills, aptitudes, and personality. Tell about goals and dreams you have for your life. Discuss ways you plan to get to know yourself better. If you like, share your essay with a friend or family member.

2. **Health and Physical Education**
Ask a friend or family member to teach you a new physical activity this week. You might learn a new dance or a new way to play ball, for example. You might experiment with yoga or tai chi. Afterward record your reaction. What did you like about the new activity? What did you dislike? What did it teach you about yourself?

Discovery Portfolio

Begin a Personal Portfolio
• A portfolio is used to hold papers and other items that tell something about you. To begin building your portfolio, find a book, notebook, or folder.
• Put your list of interests, values, skills, and aptitudes in either

your book, notebook, or folder.
• Decorate your portfolio with drawings or pictures that reflect your personality.
• Add career activities to your portfolio as you work through this book.

Career Exploration: Career Clusters

Select a career cluster you find interesting from the list of career clusters on page 18. Research a career included in the cluster. Look for information at the library or on the Internet. If possible, talk to someone with a job in the career you have chosen. Find out about the following:

• kinds of work
• working conditions
• skills, training, and education needed
• personal characteristics best for the career
• outlook for the career
Then, using your research, give an oral report to the class about the career.

Chapter 1 Review **20**

> **The Chapter Review** provides questions and activities designed to help you check your understanding of the chapter.

Resources to Help You Learn

The **Glossary** and **Index** allow you to find definitions for terms and locate career and other topics quickly.

The Glossary provides definitions for all the Key Terms highlighted throughout the text. Following each definition in parentheses is the chapter page number on which the term is explained.

The Index lists key terms and ideas along with important graphs, charts, and other chapter illustrations.

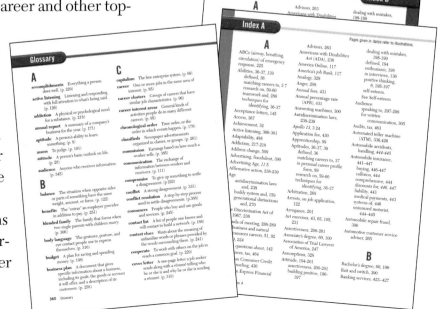

Index B

A

Advisors, 263
Americans with Disabilities

dealing with mistakes, 198-199

Index A

A

ABCs (airway, breathing, circulation) of emergency response, 225
Abilities, 36-37, 139
defined, 36
matching careers to, 3 7
research on, 59-60
teamwork and, 280
techniques for identifying, 36-37
Acceptance letters, 145
Access, 367
Achievement, 32
Active listening, 300-301
Adaptability, 488
Addiction, 217-218
Address change, 509
Advertising, fraudulent, 390
Advertising Age, 11 5
Affirmative action, 238-239
Age
antidiscrimination laws and, 238
buddy system and, 159
generational distinctions and, 270
Discrimination Act of 1967, 238
...da of meeting, 288-289
...business and natural resources careers, 51, 92
...224
...questions about, 142
...ces, tax, 464
...an Consumer Credit ...unseling, 430
...n Express Financial

Advisors, 263
Americans with Disabilities Act (ADA), 238
America Online, 117
America's job Bank, 117
Analogy, 328
Anger, 208
Annual fees, 431
Annual percentage rate (APR), 431
Answering machines, 300
Antidiscrimination laws, 238-239
Apollo 13, 3 24
Application fee, 430
Apprenticeship, 99
Aptitudes, 36-37, 39
defined, 36
matching careers to, 37
in personal career profile form, 89
research on, 59-60
techniques for identifying, 36-37
Arbitration, 268
Arrests, on job application, 122
Arrogance, 201
Art exercises, 43, 65, 105, 231
Assertiveness, 200-201
Associate's degree, 60, 100
Association of Trial Lawyers of America, 247
Assumptions, 328
Attitude, 194-201
assertiveness, 200-201
building positive, 196-197

Pages given in *italics* refer to illustrations.

dealing with mistakes, 198-199
defined, 194
enthusiasm, 198
in interviews, 136
positive thinking, 6, 195-197
self-esteem. See Self-esteem
Audience
speaking to, 297-298
for written communication, 298
Audits, tax, 463
Automated teller machine (ATM), 336,426
Automobile accidents, handling, 444-445
Automobile insurance, 441-447
buying, 446-447
collision, 444
comprehensive, 444
discounts for, 446, 447
liability, 443
medical payments, 443
systems of, 446
uninsured motorist, 444-445
Automobile repair fraud, 390
Automotive customer service adviser, 265

B

Bachelor's degree, 60, 100
Bait and switch, 390
Banking services, 423-427

A

accomplishments Everything a person does well. (p. 229)
active listening Listening and responding with full attention to what's being said. (p. 126)
addiction A physical or psychological need for a substance. (p. 218)
annual report A summary of a company's business for the year. (p. 171)
aptitude A person's ability to learn something. (p. 8)
assess To judge. (p. 101)
attitude A person's basic outlook on life. (p. 28)
audience Anyone who receives information.
(p. 345)

B

balance The situation when opposite sides or parts of something have the same weight, amount, or force. (p. 122)
benefits The "extras" an employer provides in addition to pay. (p. 251)
blended family The family that forms when two single parents with children marry. (p. 306)
body language The gestures, posture, and eye contact people use to express themselves. (p. 316)
budget A plan for saving and spending money. (p. 198)
business plan A document that gives specific information about a business, including its goals, the goods or services it will offer, and a description of its customers. (p. 258)

C

capitalism The free enterprise system. (p. 89)
career One or more jobs in the same area of interest. (p. 85)
career clusters Groups of careers that have similar job characteristics. (p. 96)
career interest areas General kinds of activities people do in many different careers. (p. 95)
chronological order Time order, or the order in which events happen. (p. 178)
classifieds Newspaper advertisements organized in classes, or groups. (p. 261)
commission Earnings based on how much a worker sells. (p. 385)
communication The exchange of information between senders and receivers. (p. 111)
compromise To give up something to settle a disagreement. (p. 222)
conflict A strong disagreement. (p. 333)
conflict resolution A step-by-step process used to settle disagreements. (p.388)
consumers People who buy and use goods and services. (p. 245)
contact list A list of people one knows and will contact to build a network. (p. 188)
context clues Hints about the meaning of unfamiliar words or phrases provided by the words surrounding them. (p. 241)
cooperate To work with others on the job to reach a common goal. (p. 220)
cover letter A one-page letter a job seeker sends along with a résumé telling who he or she is and why he or she is sending a résumé. (p. 319)

360 Glossary

Chapter 1

Getting to Know You

What You'll Learn...

- You will explore who you are.
- You will discover your interests, values, skills, and aptitudes.
- You will take a close look at your personality and ways you learn best.
- You will begin to see a link between who you are and possible careers.
- **CAREER CLUSTER** You will explore the *15 career clusters.*

LESSON 1-1
Your Interests and Values

LESSON 1-2
Your Skills and Aptitudes

LESSON 1-3
Your Personality and Learning Styles

LESSON PLAN. See the *Teacher's Manual* for the Chapter 1 lesson plan.

Friends & Family
Activity

TRY THIS!

- List five words that describe you. Then choose five people from different areas of your life. Ask each of them to list five words that tell about you.
- Compare the lists. Which words appear in more than one list? What do the words on others' lists tell you about yourself?

APPLY: Summarize your results in a 50-word paragraph.

Your Interests and Values

Discover...
- what interests you.
- the link between your interests and different careers.
- what you value, or believe is important.

Why Think About Your Interests and Values?

Your interests and values are at the heart of who you are. They will help lead you to a variety of careers that are right for you.

Key Terms...
- interests
- technology
- interest inventory
- values

W ho are you? Don't answer right away. Take some time to think about you. After all, people spend their whole lives discovering who they are. Getting to know yourself is an important part of your journey. In fact, it can be the most exciting journey of your life.

On your way, you'll try new ways of doing things. You'll look at things in different ways. You'll go down many paths. Some will lead to careers. How will you know the way? By exploring and finding who you are.

Discovering Your Interests

How do I like to spend my free time? What am I curious about? What do I find fascinating? These are questions you'll be asking yourself as you explore your interests. Your interests are your favorite activities.

CAPTION ANSWER. Students should offer a brief description of themselves: aspects of their personality, their interests, goals, and dreams.

➤ Before thinking about your future, get to know yourself. Take a look in the mirror. How would you describe the person you see?

People have some interests in common. Look at *Figure 1-1.* Do you share any of these interests? Which ones?

Your Favorite Things

Make a list of your interests. Think about how you spend your time. What school subjects do you enjoy? What are your favorite things to do? Perhaps you like to read, play sports, dance, cook, or build models.

What do you talk about with your friends? What kinds of books and magazines do you read? What kinds of TV shows and movies do you watch? What do you daydream about? Your answers to all of these questions are your interests.

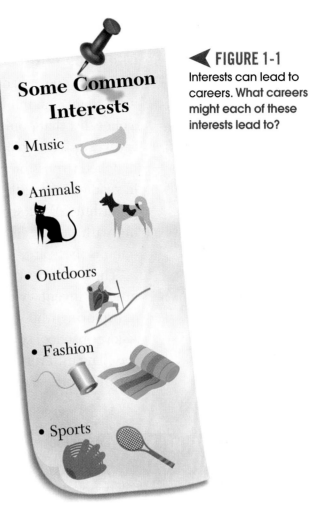

Some Common Interests

- Music
- Animals
- Outdoors
- Fashion
- Sports

◄ **FIGURE 1-1**

Interests can lead to careers. What careers might each of these interests lead to?

Where Do Your Interests Lead?

Now take a close look at your list of interests. You may begin to see patterns. Things you enjoy doing may fall into categories, or groups.

People, Information, or Technology

Do many or most of your interests fall into one of the groups shown in *Figure 1-2* on page 4? Take a look.

The *people* category describes activities involving people. The *information* category has to do with using ideas, facts, words, and figures. The *technology* category involves working with things, such as tools, machines, and other equipment. Technology is the use of ideas, methods, tools, and materials to get things done.

Matching Interests and Careers

So far you've made your own list of interests. You may also want to take an interest inventory. An **interest inventory** is a checklist that points to your strongest interests. You choose interests from groups of items. Then your interests are matched to possible careers. For example, if you're interested in reading and writing, you might be matched to a career in publishing. What careers are right for you if you enjoy working with people? You may be surprised by the number of options there are.

There are no right or wrong answers when you take an interest inventory. An interest inventory is just another way of exploring who you are. It is also a way of exploring careers. Ask your school counselor if you can fill out an interest inventory. The different directions your interests can take you may surprise you.

> ### FIGURE 1-2
PEOPLE, INFORMATION, OR TECHNOLOGY

Many people strongly prefer people, information, or technology. Which interests you?

A

People

If you're interested in people, you may make friends easily. You probably get along well with others. You might enjoy helping your friends solve their problems. You're usually ready to drop everything to be with others. You might enjoy being a salesperson, a fitness trainer, or a police officer. Many careers involve working with people.

B

Information

Maybe you like information. If so, you probably enjoy reading. You may spend hours in the library or exploring sites on the Internet. You might be interested in history and the stories of other people's lives. You may know baseball scores, world records, all kinds of information. Someday you might be a Web site designer, a detective, or a book editor. Many careers are open to people who like information.

C

Technology

Maybe technology really grabs your interest. You may enjoy working with your hands or making or fixing things. You may take things apart just to see how they work. Perhaps you can work on a computer for hours without even noticing the time. One day you might be a video producer, a recording engineer, or a photo lab technician. There are many more career opportunities for people interested in technology.

What Are Values?

Values also give you direction. Your values are what you believe is important. They are the beliefs and ideas you live by.

Like your interests, your values are an important part of who you are. Where do your values come from? You learn them from important people in your life—family members, teachers, religious leaders.

Luis Ramos of Miami, Florida, gives his grandmother credit for many of his values.

> My grandmother taught me to care about others, especially older people. When I was thinking about careers, I knew I wanted to help people.

Luis is a home health aide. He cares for an older man who lives on his own.

Uncovering Your Values

People share many basic values. *Figure 1-3* shows some of them.

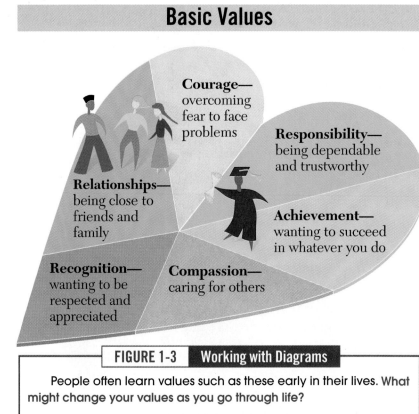

Basic Values

Courage— overcoming fear to face problems

Responsibility— being dependable and trustworthy

Relationships— being close to friends and family

Achievement— wanting to succeed in whatever you do

Recognition— wanting to be respected and appreciated

Compassion— caring for others

| FIGURE 1-3 | Working with Diagrams |

People often learn values such as these early in their lives. What might change your values as you go through life?

Many values are taught by example. If your parents or guardians always make an effort to be truthful with you, you'll probably be truthful, too. If you see them helping others, you'll learn by their example.

EXPLORE Activity !

Do you share any of the values listed in *Figure 1-3?* What other values do you have? Make a chart. In the left-hand column of your chart, list your values. In the right-hand column, tell where these values came from. Compare charts with a partner. Then keep it for later use. Add new values as you discover them.

Your values help you to make all kinds of decisions, from choosing friends to choosing careers. Values can guide you as you make important decisions. They can help you choose wisely.

Investigating Career Clusters on page 18 will help you begin to explore careers that fit you. For more information about particular career areas or clusters, check out the Investigating Career Clusters feature in each chapter. To learn more about career clusters in general, read Chapter 3.

TEACHING CAREER OPPORTUNITIES. Because a Webmaster works with so many different people to set up a Web site, he/she must be able to communicate well orally. Writing skills are also essential for composing and editing text.

CAREER OPPORTUNITIES

CLASSIFIED

THURSDAY, SEPT

Communications and Media

If you love working with computers and surfing the 'net, check out this job in communications.

Critical Thinking

Why would communication skills be important for this job?

Webmaster

Clothing store needs a webmaster to build a Web site and create an online catalog of its merchandise. Requirements: fluency in HTML, a working knowledge of Photoshop and Java, and excellent communication skills. Ability to play a leadership role essential.

LESSON REVIEW AND ACTIVITIES. See the *Teacher's Manual* for answers.

Vocabulary Review

On a separate sheet of paper, write four sentences that use the key terms. In place of the key term in each sentence, draw a blank. Exchange sentences with a partner. See if you can complete each other's sentences with the correct term.

interests   interest inventory
technology   values

Check Your Understanding

Choose the correct answer for each item. Write your answers on a separate sheet of paper.

1. Two things you should consider about yourself when investigating careers are _____.
   a. teamwork and homework
   b. technology and people
   c. interests and values

2. Your values are _____.
   a. the beliefs and ideas you live by
   b. the items you buy at a store for a good price
   c. the things you like doing

Critical Thinking

On a separate sheet of paper, answer the following questions:

1. How do you think you develop interests?
2. Why is it a good idea to think about your interests when making career choices?
3. Who might help you identify your values?
4. Which of your values do you think will be most important to you in a career? Why?

Connecting to the Workplace

Interests and Values

- Interview one of your teachers about his or her interests and values. Ask which interests and values led to his or her career.
- Prepare questions beforehand. Take notes during the interview or tape-record it.
- Write a profile of your teacher based on the interview. Include some of your teacher's own comments in quotes.

Teamwork

What to Do
- Work with two other classmates. Choose one value you all share.
- Think of an idea for putting what you value into practice. For example, your value might be protecting the Earth. Start a recycling program at your school. Perhaps you think caring about other people is important. Collect food or clothing for a homeless shelter.
- Describe to the class your value and idea for putting it into action.

Your Skills and Aptitudes

Now you've got some idea of your interests and values. Don't stop there. You've just gotten to know yourself. What's next? You'll want to take a look at what you can learn to do.

Comparing Skills and Aptitudes

"You can do anything if you put your mind to it." You know, there's some truth to that. You can learn to do almost anything. Once you've learned something, it becomes a skill. A skill is your ability to do something you've learned. You already have many skills. You can read and write. You may know how to play an instrument or a sport. These are skills.

Aptitudes differ from skills. An aptitude is your ability to learn something. Micky Campbell showed an aptitude for building things when she was growing up.

Discover...
- how skills and aptitudes differ.
- what your skills and aptitudes are.
- where your skills and aptitudes might lead you.

Why Find Out What Your Skills and Aptitudes Are?

Your skills and aptitudes are clues to what you can do. They too can point you toward different careers.

Key Terms...
- skill
- aptitude

CAPTION ANSWER. Answers will vary; students should name aptitudes and skills and draw a connection between their aptitudes and skills and specific careers.

◀ You may find a career someday that uses abilities you have now. What is something you do well or know how to do? What careers could it lead to?

"When I was a kid," Micky recalls, "all I wanted to do was put pieces of wood together. I made birdhouses, dollhouses, tree houses—anything I could think of." Today, Micky runs her own construction business near Charlotte, North Carolina. She builds houses—first homes, dream houses, and everything in between. Micky turned her aptitude into a skill by learning carpentry.

What Are *You* Able to Do?

What skills do you have? How can you figure out what your aptitudes are?

EXPLORE Activity

Start by making your own list. Set up a chart like the one in *Figure 1-4*. Group your skills and aptitudes under the headings *Mental, Physical,* and *Social.* Write down your ideas until you can't think of any more.

Show the chart to a friend, a family member, a teacher, or someone else you trust. Ask what he or she thinks your skills and aptitudes are. Add those ideas to the chart.

Keep your chart handy. Add new skills and aptitudes to it as you discover them.

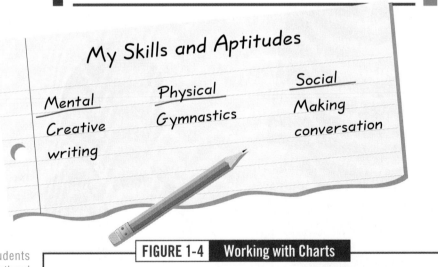

FIGURE 1-4 **Working with Charts**

Discuss your chart with others. Do they agree with the skills and aptitudes you've listed for yourself? How do your ideas differ?

Where Are You Headed?

Do you feel you know yourself any better now? Take a break and take stock. Review your list of skills and aptitudes. Allow yourself to dream a bit about where some of your strengths might lead you.

Your skills and aptitudes are likely to be needed in a variety of careers. Here are a few thoughts to keep in mind as you think about the future.

- Everyone has different skills and aptitudes.
- Certain skills are more important in some careers than in others. For a career in TV or radio, you might need strong language skills, for example. In construction careers, you often have to be able to work well with others. Many health careers call for decision-making and problem-solving skills. City planners, engineers, and technicians need solid math skills.
- You need to develop skills in many areas. You will not have an aptitude for everything you want to learn. Don't let that stop you. Get the skills you want and need.

CAREER Q&A

Finding Out More About a Job

Q: What if I have the skills and aptitudes for a job, but I'm still not sure that I'll like it?

A: Talk to people who work in the job that interests you. Find out what they like about their job. What are the working conditions like? The people who actually work in the jobs that interest you can give you the best idea as to whether you might like the job yourself.

CRITICAL THINKING. Ask students to identify the difference between a *skill* and an *aptitude*.

RESEARCH. Have students look up *aptitudes* as a topic in books or magazine articles. Have them write down the name of at least one book or article mentioning this topic.

CAPTION ANSWER. Answers will vary but may include the following careers: coach, sports broadcaster, sports writer, trainer, sports agent.

◄ Many people dream of being professional athletes. In what other careers might you use your aptitude for a sport?

LESSON REVIEW AND ACTIVITIES. See the *Teacher's Manual* for answers.

Vocabulary Review

In your own words, describe how an aptitude differs from a skill.

skill   aptitude

Check Your Understanding

On a separate sheet of paper, tell whether each statement is true or false. Rewrite any false statements to make them true.

1. Once you've learned something, it becomes an aptitude.
2. An example of a skill is being able to play an instrument.
3. An aptitude is a well-developed skill.
4. Everyone has different skills and aptitudes.

Critical Thinking

On a separate sheet of paper, answer the following questions.

1. How can you turn an aptitude into a skill?
2. What skills do you have now that are not connected to any of your aptitudes?
3. What skills and aptitudes would be useful in a career you dream about?
4. Why is it important to develop skills in more than one area?

Connecting to the Workplace

Why People Work

- Choose five of the following skills:
  - working with special tools
  - typing rapidly
  - solving problems
  - operating machines
  - drawing
  - working with numbers
  - speaking in front of an audience
  - organizing schedules
  - entertaining others
  - writing
- Write them on a sheet of paper. Next to each, list two careers in which the skill might be needed. Compare your list with those of your classmates.

Community Involvement

What to Do

- Look at the list of career clusters on pages 18–19.
- Think of someone in your community who has a career in one of the clusters.
- Write him or her a letter. Ask what skills the person needs for the kind of work he or she does.
- Ask the person to respond by phone or mail to your questions.
- Mail your letter.
- Share the response you receive with the rest of the class.

Your Personality and Learning Styles

"She's got a great personality." "He's got a great personality." How many times have you heard someone say that about someone else? Have you ever thought about what it really meant, though? Your personality is what makes you a special person. By that definition, we all have great personalities.

Exploring Personality

Your personality is what makes you different from everyone else. It is all your characteristics, or qualities. It is your attitudes, or ways of thinking. It is also your behaviors, or ways of acting.

Discover...
- what kind of personality you have.
- your best ways of learning.
- how your personality and learning styles can affect your career choices.

Why Explore Your Personality and Learning Styles?

Both are signs of how you think, act, and feel. They can help direct you to careers that match the kind of person you are.

Key Terms...
- personality
- learning styles

CAPTION ANSWER. Students should describe a specific characteristic of their own personality and of a friend's personality.

◄ Imagine a world in which everyone had the same personality. What special quality of yours would people miss? What special quality of a friend would you miss?

What Is Attitude?

Attitude is a general outlook on life. A positive attitude is achieved when you take a situation and see the good things about it and work on improving any negative things. A positive attitude can make life more enjoyable.

Apply Your Skills!

Write a journal entry: Take one situation in school or in your life that has both positive and negative sides. Write a page explaining the good part of this situation and suggesting what you can do to improve the negative part.

MOTIVIATING STUDENTS. Have students write a brief paragraph describing their own personalities.

DISCUSSION STARTER. Ask students: "Is your personality part of the way you look or the way you feel? What does your personality show?"

TEACHING ACTIVITY. Have students discuss the words in this list in small groups. What specific actions could be described by each word? What other words can be added to the list?

Who Do You Think You Are?

If someone asked you to describe your personality, what would you say? You might start naming some of your characteristics. What are some of the first words that come to mind?

EXPLORE Activity!

Here are a few ideas to get you started. Look at the words below. Which best fit your personality?

outgoing	fun-loving
playful	energetic
caring	loyal
dependable	generous
friendly	quiet
serious	agreeable
confident	cheerful
shy	lively

Write a paragraph about your personality. Include those words from the list above or any other words that describe your personality. Place your description in your Discovery Portfolio.

Looking at Ways You Learn

How you think and learn is another part of your personality. The different ways people naturally think and learn are called **learning styles.** Take a look at the learning styles shown in *Figure 1-5.* Which type of learner are you? What do you like to do? What are the best ways for you to learn? Is there more than one learning style that applies to you?

Eight Styles of Learning

Type of Learner	Likes	Best Ways to Learn
Linguistic 	Likes to read, write, and tell stories; good at memorizing names and dates	Learns best by saying, hearing, and seeing words
Logical/ Mathematical 	Likes to do experiments, work with numbers, explore patterns and relationships; good at math, logic, and problem solving	Learns best by making categories, classifying, and working with patterns
Spatial 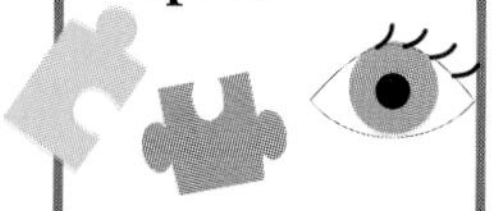	Likes to draw, build, design, and create things; good at imagining, doing puzzles and mazes, and reading maps and charts	Learns best by using the mind's eye and working with colors and pictures
Musical 	Likes to sing, hum, play an instrument, and listen to music; good at remembering melodies, noticing pitches and rhythms, and keeping time	Learns best through rhythm and melody
Bodily/ Kinesthetic 	Likes to touch and move around; good at hands-on activities and crafts	Learns best by interacting with people and objects in a real space
Interpersonal 	Likes having lots of friends, talking to people, and joining groups; good at understanding people, leading, organizing, communicating, and mediating conflicts	Learns best by sharing, comparing, and cooperating
Intrapersonal 	Likes to work alone and pursue interests at own pace; good at self-awareness, focusing on personal feelings, and following instincts to learn what needs to be known	Learns best through independent study
Naturalist 	Likes spending time outdoors and working with plants, animals, and other parts of the natural environment; good at identifying plants and animals and at hearing and seeing connections to nature	Learns best by observing, collecting, identifying, and organizing patterns

FIGURE 1-5 **Working with Charts**

Most people have more than one learning style. Which learning styles would rank as your top two or three?

CAPTION ANSWER. Students should rank their top two or three learning styles, identifying the styles by the labels in the column "Type of Learner."

When you are aware of your own learning styles, you are able to determine the best approach for you to learn something new. You can also determine which career areas are right for you.

Finding Out What Fits You

Why think about your personality? Why figure out what kind of learner you are? Your personality will play an important part in the career you choose one day. It will affect how you work and the people you work with.

Knowing your learning style will help you take the best approach to learning new things. When it's time, you can look for careers that use your strongest learning style. It's a good bet you'll do well in one of them.

What's most important now is that you've made a start. You're getting to know yourself. The better you know yourself, the wiser your choices in life will be. You will be able to better decide what you want to do.

The Global Workplace

Names Must Be Handled Delicately

To start international relations off on the right foot, learn the best way to say your colleague's name. In China and some other Asian countries, the custom is to put the person's first, not last, name after the title Mr. or Mrs. In Korea, a man's first or second name follows Mr., depending on whether he is his father's first or second son. When in doubt, ask "What would you like me to call you?"

Exploration Activity!

Using the Internet or library resources, research the outlook for jobs in China and Korea. What types of jobs are available there?

LESSON REVIEW AND ACTIVITIES. See the *Teacher's Manual* for answers.

Vocabulary Review

Imagine you are a crossword-puzzle writer. Write a clue for each of the key terms.

personality   learning styles

Check Your Understanding

Choose the correct answer for the following items. Write your answers on a separate sheet of paper.

1. Your personality is _____.
   a. all your characteristics, or qualities
   b. the way you think about others
   c. the type of people you know
2. One type of learning style is _____.
   a. tactile
   b. nimble
   c. spatial
3. If you learn best by working alone, your style of learning is _____.
   a. musical
   b. intrapersonal
   c. interpersonal
4. If you're good at doing hands-on activities and crafts, your style of learning is _____.
   a. bodily/kinesthetic
   b. linguistic
   c. spatial

Critical Thinking

On a separate sheet of paper, answer the following questions.

1. How might you discover different sides of your personality?
2. Look at the learning styles chart on page 15. What careers would you match with the different learning styles?
3. Why might you do well in a career that uses your strongest learning style?

Connecting to the Workplace

Your Personality and Careers

- Choose a partner. Write down words that describe his or her personality.
- Think of a career that might fit your partner's personality.
- Write a paragraph that explains why the career would be right for him or her. Begin as follows: You would be a good _____ because you are . . .
- Exchange paragraphs and enjoy them.

Teamwork

What to Do

- Work in a group of eight, one person for each learning style.
- Write a brief skit in which you role-play a person with your assigned learning style.
- If your skit includes other characters, ask other group members to play them.
- Put on your skits for other groups. Have them guess the learning style each skit portrays.

Investigating Career Clusters

The 15 Career Cluster Areas

What Are Career Clusters?

Career clusters are different occupational categories. The 15 clusters that follow are organized by different fields and industries. Most jobs are included in one of the 15 clusters. In each career cluster area, you'll find sample jobs, necessary education and skills, work descriptions, and the job availability through 2005.

Skills Needed

In school, you've already started developing many of the skills you'll need in the working world. Job skill abilities include speaking, listening, writing, reading, math, problem solving, organization, creative thinking, decision making, seeing things in the mind's eye (picturing things in your mind), knowing how to learn, and reasoning. Personal qualities include responsibility, sociability, self-management (self-control), leadership, adaptability, self-esteem, honesty, and friendliness.

THE FACTS	Types of Careers in This Cluster	Work Description	Career Outlook	Education
	Agribusiness and natural resources	Supply consumers with raw materials for food, shelter, and clothing	Slower than average	H.S. diploma, Bachelor's, Master's
	Business and office	Provide management and support services for companies	Good	H.S. diploma, Associate's, Bachelor's
	Communication and the media	Organize information and communicate it to people	Average	H.S. diploma, Associate's, Bachelor's
	Construction	Build, repair, and modernize homes and other kinds of buildings	Average	H.S. diploma, On-the-job training
	Family and consumer services	Develop, produce, and manage goods and services that improve the quality of home life	Average	Voc-Tech diploma, Bachelor's

THE FACTS	Types of Careers in This Cluster	Work Description	Career Outlook	Education
	Environment	Protect natural resources and the best interest of the population	Slower than average	Bachelor's, Master's, Ph.D., On-the-job training
	Fine arts and humanities	Develop, promote, and preserve the arts and social values	Average	Professional training, Bachelor's degree
	Health	Provide services to meet people's physical and mental health needs	Good to excellent	Bachelor's, Master's, Medical degree
	Hospitality and recreation	Help people make travel plans and participate in leisure-time activities	Good	H.S. diploma, On-the-job training, Bachelor's
	Manufacturing	Design and assemble products	Average	H.S. diploma, Voc-Tech diploma, Bachelor's
	Marine science	Discover, develop, improve, and harvest marine life	Good	Bachelor's, Master's, On-the-job training
	Marketing and distribution	Forward goods from manufacturer to consumer; influence consumer to buy products	Good	Associate's, Bachelor's, On-the-job training
	Personal services	Provide services that help people care for themselves and their possessions	Good to excellent	Voc-Tech diploma, On-the-job training, Bachelor's
	Public service	Supply services, many of which are supported by tax money, to the public	Good	H.S. diploma, On-the-job training, Bachelor's, Master's
	Transportation	Move people and goods from one place to another	Good	H.S. diploma, Voc-Tech diploma, Bachelor's

Research Activity Choose one of the 15 clusters that interests you. Research five of the jobs in the cluster and the skills required. Make a chart of your findings. Write a paragraph explaining why this cluster interests you.

Chapter 1 Review

CHAPTER REVIEW. See the *Teacher's Manual* for answers.

Chapter Highlights

- Your interests and values can lead you in many career directions.
- Your skills and aptitudes will be needed in a variety of careers.
- Your personality and learning style may fit some careers better than others.

Recalling Key Concepts

Using complete sentences, answer the following questions on a separate sheet of paper.

1. How can you discover your interests?
2. Where do your values come from?
3. How does an aptitude differ from a skill?
4. What makes up your personality?
5. What are the eight learning styles?

Thinking Critically

Using complete sentences, answer the following questions on a separate sheet of paper.

1. Which of your interests have to do with people? Information? Technology?
2. Why is it important to know what your values are before making career choices?
3. What is something you have an aptitude for? How would you go about developing it into a skill?
4. What do you think the world would be like if everyone had the same skills and aptitudes?
5. What careers do you think might fit your personality?

Building Skills

1. Basic—Mathematics

Take a survey of the learning styles in your class. Ask each student to name his or her main learning style. Record your classmates' responses. Total the number of students for each learning style. Show the number of students for each style in a bar graph. Explain the results of your survey to the class.

2. Personal Qualities—Self-Esteem

Create an award for yourself. Write a short description of the part of your personality you wish to honor. On the award, use wording such as this: *Awarded to* Your Name *on* Date *for His or Her* Description. Decorate the award with drawings that illustrate the part of your personality you are honoring.

Applying Academic Skills

1. Language Arts

Write an essay about yourself. Describe your interests, values, skills, aptitudes, and personality. Tell about goals and dreams you have for your life. Discuss ways you plan to get to know yourself better. If you like, share your essay with a friend or family member.

2. Health and Physical Education

Ask a friend or family member to teach you a new physical activity this week. You might learn a new dance or a new way to play ball, for example. You might experiment with yoga or tai chi. Afterward record your reaction. What did you like about the new activity? What did you dislike? What did it teach you about yourself?

Discovery Portfolio

Begin a Personal Portfolio

- A portfolio is used to hold papers and other items that tell something about you. To begin building your portfolio, find a book, notebook, or folder.
- Put your list of interests, values, skills, and aptitudes in either your book, notebook, or folder.
- Decorate your portfolio with drawings or pictures that reflect your personality.
- Add career activities to your portfolio as you work through this book.

Career Exploration: Career Clusters

Select a career cluster you find interesting from the list of career clusters on page 18. Research a career included in the cluster. Look for information at the library or on the Internet. If possible, talk to someone with a job in the career you have chosen. Find out about the following:

- kinds of work
- working conditions
- skills, training, and education needed
- personal characteristics best for the career
- outlook for the career

Then, using your research, give an oral report to the class about the career.

Chapter 2

Thinking About Work

What You'll Learn...

- You will step inside the world of work.

- You will discover why people work and how work affects their lives.

- You will learn how the world of work is changing—right now.

- You will begin to imagine yourself as part of that exciting world sometime in the future.

- **CAREER CLUSTER** You will explore careers in *agribusiness and natural resources*.

LESSON 2-1
What Is Work All About?

LESSON 2-2
How Work Is Changing

LESSON PLAN. See the *Teacher's Manual* for the Chapter 2 lesson plan.

Friends & Family
Activity

TRY THIS!

Interview three adults you know who work. Ask questions like these:

- What kind of work do you do?
- What do you like most about your job?
- What do you like least?
- If you could do any kind of work, what would you do?

APPLY: Write down the information you collect. What does it tell you about the world of work?

What Is Work All About?

Discover...
● why people work.
● how work affects people's lives.

Why Explore the World of Work?

You'll probably spend part of your life working. You'll want to choose work that is right for you. That will be easier to do if you understand why people work and how work can affect your life.

Key Terms...
● job
● career
● full-time
● lifestyle

Think about your world—your everyday world. Where do you go? What do you do? Who are the people in your life?

You probably spend a lot of time at home and in school. The people around you are mostly family and friends. Your days are full. You have classes and homework. Maybe you take part in after-school activities.

This is the world you know—today. One day, though, your world will be different. Work will be part of your life.

What Is Work?

That's a good question. A quick, easy answer is that work is what people do to earn money. *Figure 2-1* shows that people need money to pay for their needs and wants. Money is not the whole story, though.

CAPTION ANSWER. Answers will vary, but students should observe that people meet other people where they work.

▶ You're with all kinds of people at school each day. Where do you think you'll meet people when you've finished school?

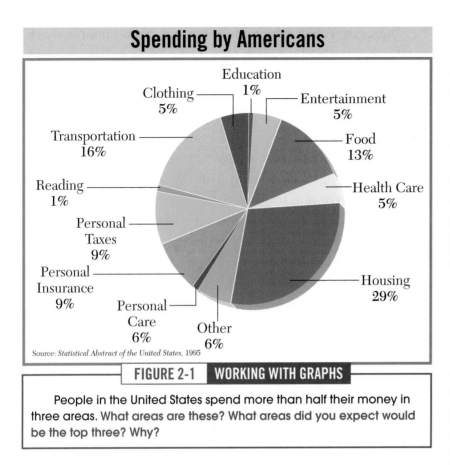

Spending by Americans

- Education 1%
- Entertainment 5%
- Clothing 5%
- Food 13%
- Transportation 16%
- Health Care 5%
- Reading 1%
- Personal Taxes 9%
- Personal Insurance 9%
- Personal Care 6%
- Other 6%
- Housing 29%

Source: *Statistical Abstract of the United States,* 1995

FIGURE 2-1 | **WORKING WITH GRAPHS**

People in the United States spend more than half their money in three areas. **What areas are these? What areas did you expect would be the top three? Why?**

Why Work?

People work for many reasons. Take Roberto Hernandez, a wildlife biologist in Southern California. He has this to say about work.

> *Work isn't just about money. For me, it's about making a difference in the world. I use what I've learned about science to help animals. On the job I also get to meet people who are interested in the same things I am. It's great to work at something you like.*

According to Roberto, there are many reasons for working. People work
- to make a contribution.
- to help others.
- to use skills and talents.
- to meet other people.

There are other reasons for working. Some people work so that they won't be bored. Others think of work as a way to challenge their mind. Work makes many people feel good about themselves. What other reasons for working can you think of?

Jobs and Careers

Everybody would like to enjoy his or her work. Where do you start, though? How do you find work you like? Do you look for a job or aim for a career?

The answer to the last question is "both." Work includes both jobs and careers. A **job** is work that people do for pay. A **career** is one or more jobs in the same area of interest. Each job in a career builds on interest, knowledge, training, and experience from the other jobs. Look at **Figure 2-2** to see how Roberto Hernandez arrived at his career.

➤ FIGURE 2-2

JOBS LEAD TO CAREERS

Roberto Hernandez found jobs doing what he liked. A series of jobs led to his career as a wildlife biologist.

A

Roberto Hernandez began his career as a young child. He fed the wildlife in his neighborhood. Roberto volunteered to keep his neighbor's bird-feeder full.

B

While in high school, Roberto got a job cleaning out animal cages at the local animal shelter. In this job, he learned about animal behavior.

Your Work and Your Life

Like Roberto, you'll want to do work you enjoy. Did you know that you could spend 2,000 hours a year at work? If you work **full-time**, you'll be on the job at least 40 hours a week. Multiply 40 hours by 50 weeks, and you get 2,000 hours. That's time you'll definitely want to spend doing something you enjoy.

Choosing a Way of Life

There are other reasons to think carefully about career choices. For one, the work you do affects your lifestyle. Your **lifestyle** is the way you use your time, energy, and other resources. Many people use much of their time and energy at work.

CRITICAL THINKING. Ask students to explain why lifestyle affects your career choice.

RESEARCH. Ask students to interview someone who has worked for at least 10 years. Ask students to find out about their interviewees' career path. Did he or she ever make a job or career change? If so, why?

EXTENDING THE LESSON. Have students draw a diagram of the lifestyle of a friend, neighbor, or relative and write a paragraph describing how work has influenced that person's lifestyle.

C

In college he worked as a research assistant. This job taught him how to study animals in their natural habitats.

D

Now Roberto works as a wildlife biologist at the San Diego Zoo. His field studies with wildlife help maintain the delicate ecosystem balance.

> Life changes can lead people to change jobs or careers. What are some other reasons people might choose a new job or career?

EXPLORE Activity

Think about the kind of lifestyle you want someday. What do you want to accomplish, or get done, in life? Look at the lists you made of your interests, values, skills, and aptitudes. What clues do they give you about the kind of lifestyle you might like to have?

As you look into the future, leave some room for change. You may need to make changes to have the kind of lifestyle you want or need.

CAREER OPPORTUNITIES

Agribusiness and Natural Resources
Do you love being surrounded by flowers and trees? Then look for this job in your neck of the woods.

Critical Thinking
What are some skills a consulting forester might need in order to do his or her job?

Consulting Forester

Landowner in Vermont is looking for a consulting forester to help prepare to sell trees to a lumber firm. The consulting forester must plan and carry out the planting of trees, mark trees for removal, prepare and negotiate contracts, administer sales of forest products, and make appraisals and inventories.

LESSON REVIEW AND ACTIVITIES. See the *Teacher's Manual* for answers.

Vocabulary Review

Imagine you are a newspaper reporter. You've written articles on each of the following topics: jobs, careers, and lifestyles. All you need now are headlines for your articles. Write four headlines. Each should include one of the key terms. Like all good headlines, each should grab people's attention in as few words as possible.

job   full-time
career   lifestyle

Check Your Understanding

On a separate sheet of paper, tell whether each statement is true or false. Rewrite any false statements to make them true.

1. The difference between a job and a career is that a job is one distinct type of work and a career is a set of many different jobs.

2. Four reasons that people work include to make a contribution, to help others, to use skills and talents, and to meet other people.

3. People in the United States spend more than half their money on housing, food, and clothing.

Critical Thinking

On a separate sheet of paper, answer the following questions.

1. What do you think is the most important reason for working? Explain your answer.

2. How might the kind of work you choose affect your lifestyle?

Connecting to the Workplace

Why People Work

- On a separate sheet of paper, list the reasons people work.
- Make four copies of the list. Then take a survey of five people who work. Give them each a list.
- At the top of the paper, have them write the kind of work they do. Then ask them to check their reasons for working. Share your findings with your classmates.

Community Involvement

What to Do

- Make a list of at least 10 jobs in your community.
- Make a chart. Use these headings: *Make a Contribution, Help Others, Use Skills and Talents, Meet Other People,* and *Challenge the Mind.*
- Under each heading, list the jobs that fit the description. Some jobs may be listed under more than one heading. From the chart, choose a job you might like.
- Explain to the class why you'd like to work at that job.

How Work Is Changing

Discover...

- how the global economy affects jobs.
- how technology is changing the way people work.
- how the working population is changing.
- other recent changes in the workplace.

Why Look at How Work Is Changing?

Changes in the work world will affect the work you do someday. Being aware of these changes will help you make sound decisions about career possibilities.

Key Terms...

- economy
- goods
- services
- global economy
- job market
- workplace

CAPTION ANSWER. By reading labels, comparing prices and brands, and looking at quality.

➤ As part of the global economy, you can buy goods from around the world. How do you decide what to buy?

You know what work is. You understand why people work. You see the link between work and lifestyle. What else would you like to know? How about what's going on in the world of work right now?

The world of work is constantly changing. Some businesses fail. New businesses start. Certain kinds of workers are no longer needed. Other kinds of workers are in demand. The way people work is also changing.

It's important to keep up with these changes. They can affect what jobs are available when you are ready to work.

They can affect the way you do the work you choose. They can also affect who will be working alongside you. There's no doubt about it. The world of work you'll enter one day will be different from the work world today.

Economic Changes

Even today the world of work is different from what it was in the past. One big change is that today the world of work includes the whole world. It's global.

It's a Small World

Have you ever noticed where things you own were made? Check the packaging or labels on things you use every day. That pair of jeans may have been made in Hong Kong. Your radio may be a product of Japan. The shampoo you use may have been made in Mexico or Canada. The label on your backpack may say "Made in U.S.A."

The Global Workplace

Business Cards Are An Essential Tool

Common business practice requires the exchange of business cards. With a card, an associate can remember your company's name and your job title and can contact you. In most of Southeast Asia, Africa, and the Middle East, it is considered rude to present a card with your left hand. In Japan, present cards with both hands. Make sure the words face the recipient and are right side up.

Exploration Activity!

Research business cards. What kind of information is listed on business cards? What do they look like? Make up a business card for a job you would like to have.

MOTIVATING STUDENTS. Ask students to take five minutes to write down as many jobs as they can think of that may be affected by technology.

DISCUSSION STARTER. In the 1970s, people who wanted to learn to operate computers were taught how to operate a keypunch machine. Why don't people learn how to use this machine now?

TEACHING THE GLOBAL WORKPLACE. Explain how business cards are exchanged. Make several different types of business cards available to students for research.

When you buy things that others make, you're taking part in the economy. The term **economy** refers to the ways people make, buy, and sell goods and services. **Goods** are items that people buy. **Services** are activities people do for others for a fee. When you buy goods made in other countries, you are part of the global economy. The **global economy** is all the world's economies and how they are linked. It's a small world—thanks to the global economy.

A World of Jobs

The global economy affects people around the world who buy goods. It also affects jobs around the world. In fact, the global economy affects the job market in each country. The **job market** is the need for workers and the kinds of work available to them.

When you begin looking at the job market, you'll need to know what's happening around the world. Some kinds of work may not be available in the United States. In recent years, some U.S. workers have lost their jobs to workers in other countries. Take the clothing industry, for instance. Many businesses in the United States have hired workers in Asia to make clothing. U.S. businesses hire workers overseas because they will often work for less money than U.S. workers.

The global economy can also create jobs. People around the world want many goods and services U.S. businesses sell. Wheat, trucks, and scientific instruments are just a few U.S. goods sold in other countries. That means jobs for workers in the United States.

Businesses based in other countries sometimes open offices in the United States. They need people here to run them. Today, people in the United States also find work in other countries more easily than they used to.

▲ Today, many jobs are opening up in other countries. In what other country do you think you might like to work? Why?

Changing Technology

Global is one buzzword. *Technology* is another. You hear people talking about technology all the time.

Technology has been part of your life since you were born. Many kinds of technology are part of the world you know. Perhaps you've been using computers since you started school. Fax machines, CD-ROMs, the Internet, laptops, and cellular phones are nothing new to you. These and other forms of technology help people get information and do their work more quickly than before.

Preparing for Change

If you're comfortable with both technology and change, you've got a real head start. Today, workers need to be willing to learn and change. When you enter the work world, you'll learn about new technology. You'll also learn new ways of working. You'll keep learning for as long as you work.

One day, you will use the skills you're learning in school in the workplace. The workplace is another name for the work world. It is any place where work is done.

Every day you're improving basic skills, like reading, writing, mathematics, listening, and speaking. You're developing thinking skills, such as decision making and problem solving. You're also building personal skills, such as honesty and responsibility.

You'll use these skills in all kinds of work later. They'll help you do the best job you can, whatever work you choose. They'll help you adjust to new technology and change. They'll help you compete with others in the world of work.

Social Changes

You'll have a lot of company in the world of work. The number of people in the United States who work continues to increase. There are no signs that this growth is going to stop.

CRITICAL THINKING. Ask students how changes in technology have affected land transportation since the days of the horse and buggy.

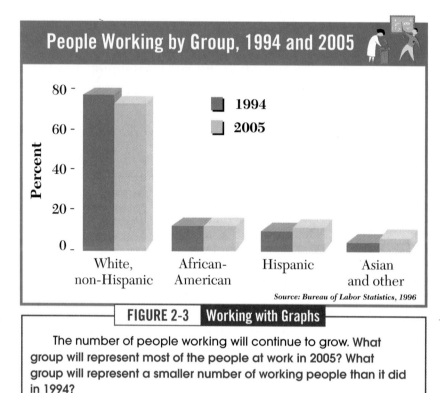

People Working by Group, 1994 and 2005

Percent

- 80
- 60
- 40
- 20
- 0

■ 1994
□ 2005

White, non-Hispanic | African-American | Hispanic | Asian and other

Source: Bureau of Labor Statistics, 1996

FIGURE 2-3 | **Working with Graphs**

The number of people working will continue to grow. What group will represent most of the people at work in 2005? What group will represent a smaller number of working people than it did in 1994?

Who's Working?

One reason there are more people in the workforce today is that more and more women are working. By 2005, there will be almost as many women as men working in the United States.

There will also be more people of different backgrounds working. *Figure 2-3* shows the percentage of different groups in the work world. It also predicts how much each group will grow by the year 2005. The number of Hispanic and Asian workers will increase much faster than the number of workers from other groups.

People will also be staying in the work world longer than people in the past. Some may work longer because they need to. Others will continue working because they want to. You may hear less talk about retiring, or leaving work. People will think of work as something that lasts a lifetime.

A New Workplace

In your lifetime, many changes have taken place in the workplace. People today are working in new ways and places. *Figure 2-4* below shows just some of the things that are new in the work world.

What's Waiting for *You*?

What will the world of work be like when you enter it? You can be sure of a few things. The world of work will include the whole world. You will work in a global workplace. Technology and social changes will keep you on your toes. You'll get to know all kinds of interesting people. The world of work is and will continue to be an exciting place.

Changes in How and Where People Work

Teams	Outsourcing	Telecommuting
People in companies today often work in teams. They set goals and make decisions as a group. They work together to solve problems and put ideas into action.	Work that was once done in one business location is often done in many locations today. Businesses hire other companies and individuals to do work for them. This way of working is called outsourcing.	More people are working at home than ever before. More than 24 million people telecommute, or work at home for a company. Computers, telephones, modems, and fax machines connect them to the company office. Others work for themselves. By 2005, more than 12 million Americans will be their own bosses. Many of them will work at home.

FIGURE 2-4 Working with Charts

Which new ways of working appeal to you? In what careers could you see yourself working in these ways?

The RIGHT Attitude!

Attitude Counts

Success depends on more than hard work. In the recipe for success, in both career and life, attitude is an essential ingredient. You can start cultivating a positive attitude today. What are some positive attitude skills? Enthusiasm, asserting yourself, managing stressful situations, flexibility, self-esteem, and treating people with respect all play a part.

Apply Your Skills!

Brainstorm with a partner, a list of qualities that show a positive attitude. Come up with five or six qualities and share your list with the class. Make a list on the board of all the qualities chosen and pick 10. Write them out on a large sheet of construction paper, and post them in your classroom.

CAPTION ANSWER. Answers will vary; students should demonstrate an understanding of the trends described and should identify careers of interest to them that would lend themselves to the ways of working shown.

LESSON REVIEW AND ACTIVITIES. See the *Teacher's Manual* for answers.

Vocabulary Review

Write a speech about the changing world of work, using all the key terms for this lesson. Read your speech to the class.

economy   global economy

goods   job market

services   workplace

Check Your Understanding

Choose the correct answer for each item below. Write your answers on a separate sheet of paper.

1. Three changes that will affect future careers include _____.
   a. legal, technological, and ethical changes
   b. technological, global, mentor, and social changes
   c. global, technological, and social changes

2. The global economy is _____.
   a. the way the world environment changes the economy
   b. the way the world's economies are linked and managed
   c. the way we manage our world currency

Critical Thinking

On a separate sheet of paper, answer the following questions.

1. What careers interest you? How do you think technology has changed work in one of those careers?

2. In what ways do you think people of different backgrounds are changing the workplace?

3. Which of the following do you think has changed work the most: teams, outsourcing, or telecommuting? Explain your answer.

Connecting to the Workplace

Technology in the Workplace

- In a newspaper, look at the classified ads for jobs. Focus on jobs that interest you.
- Find ads for five jobs that call for knowledge of or experience with technology.
- Look for mention of computers, software, lasers, or robotics, for example.
- Clip, photocopy, or hand copy the ads.
- With the rest of the class, make a bulletin board display of jobs using technology.

Teamwork

What to Do
- In a small group, select a career from the agribusiness and natural resources cluster. Look at "Investigating Career Clusters" on page 37 for ideas.
- Use library resources or the Internet to find out how work in that career is changing.
- Prepare a documentary or factual presentation about the career. Tell about the career and how change will affect it. Make visuals such as charts and graphs to show information.

Investigating Career Clusters

Agribusiness and Natural Resources

What Is the Agribusiness and Natural Resources Cluster?

Occupations in this cluster area involve supplying consumers with raw materials for food, shelter, and clothing. Jobs center around agriculture, land and water management, mining, petroleum production, and agriculture support services.

Skills Needed

Technical communication, mathematics, safety, basic lab, and information

THE FACTS	Types of Careers in This Cluster	Work Description	Career Outlook	Education
	Quality control technician	Supervise the production of agriculture products	Good	H.S. diploma, On-the-job training
	Farm operator	Manage the planting, harvesting, and storing of crops; tend live-stock and poultry	Slower than average	H.S. diploma, On-the-job training, Bachelor's
	Forester	Manage forested lands for a variety of purposes	Average	Bachelor's, Ph.D.
	Petroleum engineer	Explore for and monitor recovery of oil or natural gas	Slower than average	Bachelor's
	Agricultural scientist	Study farm crops and animals and develop ways of improving their quantity and quality	Good	Bachelor's, Ph.D.

Research Activity

Make a list of five agribusiness and natural resources jobs that interest you. Then research the particular skills and tasks required of each job. Also investigate the job outlook and salary range for this particular job. Create a chart that summarizes your findings.

Chapter 2 Review

CHAPTER REVIEW. See the *Teacher's Manual* for answers.

Chapter Highlights

- People work to earn money, to make a contribution, to help others, to use skills and talents, and to meet others.
- People today are working in new ways and places.

Recalling Key Concepts

Using complete sentences, answer the following questions on a separate sheet of paper.

1. Besides to earn money, what are three reasons people work?
2. What is a lifestyle?
3. What is the global economy, and how does it affect jobs?
4. What are three social changes affecting the workplace today?
5. What are some recent changes in how and where people work?

Thinking Critically

Using complete sentences, answer the following questions on a separate sheet of paper.

1. Why would it help to have careers in mind when considering different jobs?
2. Why do you think many people spend much of their time and energy at work?
3. What does it mean to say that thanks to the global economy, it's a small world?
4. Why do you think some people are afraid of technology?
5. Why might an older person choose to continue to work?

Building Skills

1. Basic—Reading

Read a daily newspaper for one week. Look for articles that have to do with the global economy. After reading each article, write one or two sentences summarizing its main idea. Circulate your news digest in class.

2. Personal Qualities—Responsibility

Fold a sheet of paper in thirds. In the left-hand column, list jobs you've had at home, at school, in your neighborhood, and in your community. Include jobs you've done as a volunteer or for money. In the middle column, describe your responsibilities in each job. In the right-hand column, list skills you used in each. Use the lists to tell your classmates about your work experience so far.

Applying Academic Skills

1. Social Studies

Imagine you're in charge of hiring at a large car manufacturer. Sales of cars are down because many people are buying cars made overseas. Your company has to cut jobs. Research agencies that provide people with training or information about new jobs. Make a list of the agencies and what they do. Share your findings with the class.

2. Mathematics

Anita works as a project manager for an export company. The company sells goods to foreign countries. For her projects, Anita hires four people for every $200,000 of goods exported. Her next project involves $900,000 worth of goods for export. How many people will she need to hire for the project?

Discovery Portfolio

Make a Collage
- Make a collage that illustrates the lifestyle you would like to have someday.
- Cut pictures from magazines or draw pictures that show the lifestyle you hope to have. Arrange and paste them on a piece of cardboard the size of a sheet of notebook paper.
- Add words or phrases to the collage that tell about the lifestyle. Look for words or phrases in magazines, or write them yourself. Put your collage in your portfolio.

Career Exploration: Agribusiness and Natural Resources

Select a career from the agribusiness and natural resources career cluster. Use library resources and the Internet to research the career. If possible, also gather information through interviews. Write a report that covers the following:
- kinds of work
- working conditions
- skills, training, and education needed
- personal characteristics best for the career
- outlook for the career
  Include other interesting information.
Read your report to the class.

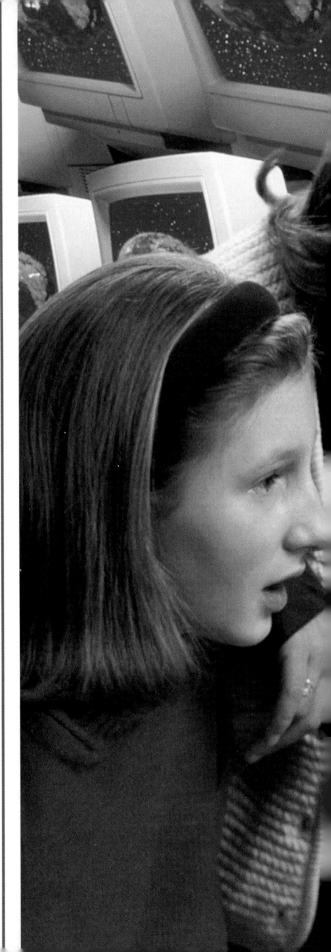

Chapter 3

Researching *Careers*

What You'll Learn...

- You will learn how to research careers.

- You will look at career clusters and kinds of activities people do in many careers.

- You will find out where to get information about careers that interest you.

- **CAREER CLUSTER** You will explore *business and office careers*.

LESSON 3-1
Career Choices

LESSON 3-2
How to Get Information

LESSON PLAN. See the *Teacher's Manual* for the Chapter 3 lesson plan.

Activity

TRY THIS!

Talk to three adult friends or family members about how he or she chose his or her career. Ask questions such as these:

- What kind of education and training did you have?
- What kinds of work do you do?
- What advice would you give someone thinking about entering your career?

APPLY: Listen carefully to each person. Write down what you know now about careers.

Career Choices

Discover...

- which career clusters, or groups of related careers, interest you.
- career interest areas, or kinds of activities, that can direct you toward specific careers.

Why Look at Groups of Careers and Career Activities?

They'll give you an idea of the kinds of careers you might enjoy. Exploring all kinds of career possibilities now will help you make career choices later.

Key Terms...

- career clusters
- career interest areas

When was the last time you went out for ice cream? Did it take you a long time to decide what you wanted? Chances are you had to choose from dozens of flavors. There probably were many flavors you didn't even know existed. How did you ever make up your mind?

Now imagine yourself making a different kind of choice. This time you're considering different types of careers. There are more than 20,000 different careers to choose from. Do you know what you want to do for a living? How will you ever be able to decide?

Why not take a taste? You'd ask for a taste if you weren't sure what flavor of ice cream to get. See what different kinds of careers are available. Explore what types of tasks are involved with each type of career. Then you can start thinking about careers you might like.

CAPTION ANSWER. Answers will vary; entertain all reasonable responses.

➤ It's never too soon to start thinking about careers. You have many choices. What careers do you have in mind?

Career Clusters

MOTIVATING STUDENTS. Ask students to list at least five words or phrases that tell how they feel about making choices.

Of course, tasting all those flavors of ice cream might give you a stomachache. Just thinking about 20,000 careers might make your head ache. Luckily there is an easy way to think about careers. The U.S. Office of Education has organized careers in 15 career clusters. **Career clusters** are groups of careers that have similar job characteristics.

Figure 3-1 on page 44 lists the 15 career clusters. You already know something about the first cluster in the chart. You read about the agribusiness and natural resources career cluster in Chapter 2. You'll learn more about the rest of the clusters in this and later chapters.

The Global Workplace

Dinner Abroad May Not Be the Cuisine You Enjoy

What's for dinner? It may be better not to ask. Frog legs, cow intestines, or sheep eyes are considered delicacies in some countries. Often hosts will offer the country's local cuisine to a foreigner. In the Middle East, sheep eyes may be served, and in Africa, gorilla meat. What to do? Travelers suggest that you try to eat what you can and swallow quickly!

Exploration Activity!

Using library resources, research the special cuisine from a country or region of the world that interests you. What does this culture consider a delicacy? Why do you think this is true?

TEACHING THE GLOBAL WORKPLACE. Explain to students that a country's cuisine develops over time, depending on the culture, climate, and available resources. Give a few examples of types of dishes to help students get started with their research.

The U.S. Office of Education Job Clusters

Career Clusters	Job Examples
Agribusiness and natural resources	Small-animal breeder, horse groom, poultry farmer, forestry technician
Business and office	Receptionist, bookkeeper, computer servicer, claim examiner
Communications and media	Cable television technician, book editor, computer artist, technical writer
Construction	Air-conditioning, heating, and refrigeration mechanic; roofer; building inspector; surveyor
Family and consumer sciences	Child-care worker, pet-care worker, jeweler, floral designer
Environment	Environmental technician, hazardous waste management technician, pollution-control technician, sanitary engineer
Fine arts and humanities	Actor, cartoonist, dancer, musician
Health	Operating-room technician, dental hygienist, nurse's aide, home health aide
Hospitality and recreation	Cruise director, fitness instructor, park ranger, pastry chef, baker
Manufacturing	Industrial laser machine operator, toolmaker, stationary engineer, production supervisor
Marine science	Ocean technician, diver, fish culture technician, marine engineer
Marketing and distribution	Insurance agent, real estate agent, auto sales worker, retail buyer
Personal service	Barber and hairstylist, cosmetologist, massage therapist, bridal consultant
Public service	Teacher, member of the armed services, firefighter, paralegal aide
Transportation	Airline reservations agent, airline pilot, railroad conductor, automotive mechanic

FIGURE 3-1 Working with Charts

People with jobs in the same cluster do similar work. How are the jobs listed for each cluster alike?

CAPTION ANSWER. Point out to students that all the jobs within each cluster involve similar tasks or goals.

Take a look at the 15 career clusters in *Figure 3-1*. Study the job examples for each cluster. Which clusters appeal to you? Why?

Career Interest Areas

Here's another way to discover different kinds of careers. Try matching what you know about yourself to career interest areas. **Career interest areas** are general kinds of activities people do in many different careers.

Figure 3-2 on page 46 shows six career interest areas. Take some time to think about each one.

What's Your Match?

Did you see yourself in any of the career interest areas? You may actually have found more than one interest area that fits you. That's not surprising. There's a little bit of each type in all of us.

Focus on the one or two areas that describe you best. These areas help pinpoint your strongest interests, values, skills, and aptitudes. They will point you to careers you might like.

Careers for All Types!

What careers do you suppose match the different career interest areas? You may be in for a

CAREER OPPORTUNITIES

Business and Office
If you are good at math and the type of person who organizes his or her socks by color, then this job is for you.

Critical Thinking
Why must a bookkeeper be organized and detail oriented?

CLASSIFIED

THURSDAY, SEPT

Bookkeeper

A national real estate company seeks a professional, experienced bookkeeper. Applicants must have accounting experience, excellent organizational and computer skills, and ability to master detail.

surprise. Look at the *Creator*, for example. Creators work in many different careers. Sure, they might be actors, journalists, photographers, or songwriters. They can also be teachers, advertising executives, or plastic surgeons. City planners, robotics engineers, and even Webmasters would also consider themselves Creators.

People in a variety of careers also represent the other career interest areas. *Investigators* include physicians, repair technicians, and librarians. They might design solar energy systems or write computer programs. Lawyers, weather observers, and historians are also Investigators.

Politicians, company presidents, and salespeople are obvious *Influencers*. Influencers also include restaurant managers, TV announcers, and small business owners. Even real estate agents, film producers, and building contractors would call themselves Influencers.

➤ FIGURE 3-2

CAREER INTEREST AREAS

Think of career interest areas as kinds of activities you may or may not like to do. Look again at the lists you made of your interests, values, skills, and aptitudes. Now look at the six career interest areas. Which sound like you?

Creator

You're likely to be a creative thinker. You're also often the independent type. You may need to express your ideas or feelings through some form of art. You may like using materials or machines to make things.

Investigator

You're probably a logical thinker. You may like doing experiments and testing theories. You may enjoy doing research. Discovering new ways of doing things may interest you. Your interests may include science, math, or history.

Organizers are everywhere, too. They're proofreaders, office managers, and reservation agents. They work as magazine editors, laboratory technicians, and food scientists. Financial consultants, word-processing specialists, and printing equipment operators are all Organizers.

Influencer

You're likely to be out in front, in charge, and leading others. You're probably good at making a point. You usually have no problem persuading others to agree with you. You seem to be very sure of yourself. You may be somewhat competitive. You're probably willing to take risks.

Organizer

You probably love working with information or numbers. You may be neat and like everything in its place. Perhaps you find it easy to follow rules and directions. You may thrive on routine. You usually like working as part of a team.

Doer

You always seem busy. You appear to have endless energy. You may like working with your hands. You probably enjoy using tools and machinery. You may find making or fixing things fun. You may love the outdoors.

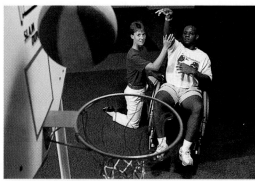

Helper

You tend to think of others before yourself. People may describe you as friendly, fun, or patient. You're always around to lend a hand. You probably work well in groups. You usually communicate well with people.

There are also *Doers* in many careers. Electricians, firefighters, and farmers are a few examples. Dental hygienists, forestry workers, and jewelers are others. Automotive mechanics, hair stylists, and camera operators also are Doers.

Helpers are also all around. Nurses, ministers, and social workers help people every day. Other Helpers include wedding coordinators, travel agents, and environmental engineers. Career counselors, psychiatrists, and child-care workers are also good examples of Helpers.

Think about these careers. Take some time to review the job examples for the career clusters in *Figure 3-1* on page 44. What careers might match the career interest areas that describe you? Which of these careers appeal to you?

LESSON REVIEW AND ACTIVITIES. See the *Teacher's Manual* for answers.

Vocabulary Review

Make two flash cards, one for *career clusters* and one for *career interest areas*. On one side of each flash card, write the term. On the other side, write the term's definition in your own words. Use your flash cards to drill a classmate on the meanings of the key terms below.

career clusters

career interest areas

Check Your Understanding

Choose the correct answer for each item. Write your answers on a separate sheet of paper.

1. One of the 15 career clusters is _____.

   a. financials
   b. economic policies
   c. agribusiness and natural resources

2. One of the six career interest areas is _____.

   a. Business
   b. Creator
   c. Ideals

3. If you tend to think of others before yourself, you are a _____.

   a. Doer
   b. Helper
   c. Creator

Critical Thinking

On a separate sheet of paper, answer the following questions.

1. What do you think the careers in each career cluster have in common?
2. What can career interest areas tell you about yourself?

Connecting to the Workplace

Career Interest Areas

- David is good at researching, organizing his ideas, and writing. He also likes to read and talk to people.
- Which career cluster do you think David might find especially interesting?
- Which career interest area describes him best? Explain your answers.

Teamwork

What to Do
- Work with four other classmates. As a group, choose one of the 15 career clusters.
- Have each member of the group research a career in the cluster.
- Work together to make a brochure that tells about careers in the cluster. Use the information you've gathered. Include visuals in your brochure.
- Present your brochure to the class.

How to Get Information

Discover...

- key questions to ask about careers that interest you.
- where to get information about careers.

Why Research Careers?

You'll want to know as much as you can about careers that interest you. You'll want to use as many resources as possible. The information you gather will help you decide which careers are right for you.

Key Terms...

- research
- exploratory interview
- job shadowing
- volunteering

CAPTION ANSWER. Students will name various resources, including books, encyclopedias, magazines, newspapers, and the Internet.

➤ You won't have any trouble finding career information. You live in the information age, after all. What resources do you use to find information on other topics? Which might also have information about careers?

Which career clusters interest you? Make a short list. Maybe you like helping people. You could do that in a career in the health or personal service cluster. You might also have a talent for acting. Put the fine arts and humanities cluster on your list. You're just curious about the marine science cluster. You should write that one down, too.

Once you identify interesting careers, it's time for some research. When you do research, you investigate a subject and gather information about it. The research you do now will pay off in many ways later.

What Do You Want to Know?

Before you begin, it helps to know what kind of information you're looking for. You'll want to ask a variety of questions about careers that interest you.

The following 10 questions will help you gather basic information about careers.

1. What skills and aptitudes should I have?
2. What education and training would I need?
3. What would my work environment, or surroundings, be like?
4. What hours would I spend on the job?
5. What kinds of work would I do?
6. What responsibilities would I have?
7. Would I be able to move ahead?
8. What will this career be like when I'm ready to work? '
9. What does this career pay?
10. What other rewards would this career provide?

Look for answers to these and other questions in your research on careers. Also be sure to keep your lists of interests, values, skills, and aptitudes handy. Why is it a good idea to refer to those lists as you gather information?

Where Do You Find It?

You know *what* you're looking for. Now you need to know *where* to look for it. Finding out about careers is easier than you might think. You can gather information in many places and ways.

Check Out the Library

Your school or public library is a good place to start. First, see if your library has a job information or career center. If it does, you'll find reference books, magazines, videotapes, and other sources on careers there.

Also search the card catalog or electronic catalog. Look at computer listings under the subject "careers" or "vocations." You'll find all kinds of books on careers. Three books

The RIGHT Attitude!

Flexibility

Ironically, the one constant in business and life is change. Technology, jobs, and the work world are always changing. What's the best method for dealing with change? Welcome it! Flexibility is crucial. Facing change with a positive attitude, in school and/or work, will help you learn new skills and adapt to new challenges.

Apply Your Skills!

Investigate three aspects of your school that have changed in the last 10 years. Ask teachers, sports instructors, and librarians about changes they have noticed or improvements they have made in the recent past. Write a short paragraph about one change and the ways in which students and teachers have had to adapt.

DISCUSSION STARTER. Write on the board: "If you don't know where you're going, you'll probably never get there." Then ask, "How does this statement relate to researching careers?"

TEACHING ACTIVITY. Have students make a list of the career clusters that interest them and add the list to their Discovery Portfolio.

CRITICAL THINKING. Ask students, "Why should you ask these questions about different careers?" Help students understand that the questions allow them to compare different careers.

TEACHING ACTIVITY. If possible, arrange to have current editions of some of these publications available during this class session. Give students time to look through them.

CRITICAL THINKING. What is the most important difference between the *OOH* and the *DOT*? *(OOH* provides general information; *DOT* includes detailed information.)

RESEARCH. Have students look up *occupation* as a topic in books or magazine articles. Have them write down the name of at least one book or article mentioning this topic.

CAPTION ANSWER. Because everyone is part of the global economy, and careers today are affected by developments around the world.

published by the U.S. Department of Labor are especially useful:

- The *Dictionary of Occupational Titles*—a list of 20,000 different kinds of jobs. Find out about jobs you never knew existed. Learn more about jobs that focus on your interests and skills.

- The *Occupational Outlook Handbook*—a general source about hundreds of careers. What do workers in each career do? What education and training do they need? This reference gives vast amounts of career information. It also makes predictions about the future of each career.

- The *Guide for Occupational Exploration*—a collection of careers according to interest areas. Read about the career interest areas in detail. Discover what careers match each career interest area.

Of course, there is more to the library than books. Look in the *Reader's Guide to Periodical Literature* to locate magazine articles on career topics. Skim recent issues of business magazines, such as *Forbes*, *Business Week*, *Entrepreneur*, and *Wired*, for the latest news. Pick up today's newspapers for breaking stories on careers.

► The Internet links you to people and sources of information around the world. Why might career information from around the world be useful?

Don't be afraid to ask a librarian for help. Librarians know exactly where to look and can save you valuable time. A librarian can help you locate government reports, for instance. You'll especially want to find the *Occupational Outlook Quarterly*. It's the place to look for up-to-date information about the work world.

Search the Internet

These days, the hottest place to research anything is the Internet. Computer users can find huge amounts of career information there, especially on the World Wide Web.

EXPLORE Activity

Use a search engine like Yahoo! or Excite to begin your research. Try the same keywords you used in your library search. Before you know it, you'll be linked to Web sites, news groups, and bulletin boards. You can find information about the fastest-growing careers. You can chat with people who have careers you like. You can share ideas, hopes, and dreams with people interested in the same careers as you.

Be careful, though. You can't always trust what you find on the Internet. Anyone can put information on the Web. Very often it's impossible to tell where the information came from. What you take for fact may be nothing more than one person's opinion. What you're reading may be old news, completely out-of-date.

It's important to check any information you gather. It doesn't matter whether you find it in a book, a magazine, a newspaper, or on a Web site. Evaluate its source. Compare it with information from other sources. Check to see how up-to-date it is.

CAREER Q&A

Finding the Best Person to Ask

Q: The *Career Handbook* gives me an idea about a lot of jobs, but how can I find out what people do on the job every day?

A: It's as easy as finding a person who does that job and asking him or her. Ask your friends and family members if they know of anybody who has that job. No luck? Look in the phone book for people who do that job in your community. Write and tell them you are a student who is interested in learning more about their job. Chances are someone will get back in touch with you. Sounds too good to be true? Maybe, but imagine some kid wrote to you and said, "I think that what you do is really cool and could I meet you?" Would you say no?

➤ You'll ask most of the questions at an exploratory interview. Why is it important to gather information before the interview?

CAPTION ANSWER. Gathering information beforehand will enable you to ask informed questions and get the information you want from the interview. It will also help you make good use of the time the person has set aside for you.

Talk to People

Research takes many other forms. You can ask family, friends, and neighbors to help you explore careers. With their help, build a list of people who work in interesting careers. Teachers and school counselors may also be able to add people to your list.

Then do what Michael Klein did. Arrange an exploratory interview. An **exploratory interview** is a short, informal talk with someone in a career that interests you. It's a good way to get an insider's view of a particular career.

Michael had always imagined himself in publishing. He grew up just outside New York City, a center of publishing. When Michael discovered that his mother's friend was a magazine editor, he called the friend. She was more than happy to meet with him. The interview was a real eye-opener for Michael.

> " *I sure learned a lot. My mom's friend was very open with me. She told me about the pluses and minuses of her job. I've got a much better idea of what I'd be getting into now.* "

Michael's interview paid off. His Mom's friend introduced him to the managing editor. The managing editor invited Michael to apply for a part-time job next summer.

Work!

Obviously, the best way to learn about a career from the inside is to work. A job in a particular career area can wait until you're in high school. Right now, though, you can take advantage of a couple of work opportunities.

Try job shadowing, for instance. Job shadowing involves following someone for a few days on the job. You learn about a particular career by watching and listening.

Jana Davies got her first taste of the career she has today by doing just that. Jana is an accountant in Boston. She handles the money matters of many businesses in the city. Mathematics was Jana's favorite subject all through school. When she was in middle school, she spent two days at her uncle's accounting firm. "It was tax season—the most hectic time of year," she recalls. "Everyone in the office was working long hours. I pitched in and did some filing. I remember loving the atmosphere. It was quiet but so busy. Even today I find tax season exciting."

You might also consider volunteering, or working without pay. Volunteering is a great way to explore careers. Hospitals, senior citizen centers, museums, and libraries are always looking for volunteers. Many other businesses may be happy to have a volunteer who is serious about learning. It can't hurt to ask. You'll get valuable experience, whether you choose that career later or not.

EXTENDING THE LESSON. Ask several volunteers to report on volunteer opportunities in the community.

◀ When you volunteer, you give time and energy. In return, you get experience and much more. What career cluster might interest this volunteer?

CAPTION ANSWER. The health career cluster might interest this volunteer.

LESSON REVIEW AND ACTIVITIES. See the *Teacher's Manual* for answers.

Vocabulary Review

Pretend that you're a graphic artist. You've been hired to illustrate entries in a dictionary. Draw illustrations for the key terms below. The terms' meanings should be clear in your drawings. Explain your drawings to your classmates.

research
job shadowing
exploratory interview
volunteering

Check Your Understanding

On a separate sheet of paper, tell whether each statement is true or false. Rewrite any false statements to make them true.

1. When doing research, you should ask some basic questions about the careers that interest you.

2. The library, the Internet, other people, and jobs are all sources of career information.

3. You can always trust information you find on the Internet.

Critical Thinking

On a separate sheet of paper, answer the following questions.

1. What are three things you want to know about a career that interests you?

2. Why is it always important to gather up-to-date information about careers?

3. What, besides experience, might you gain from volunteering?

Connecting to the Workplace

Using the Internet to Research Careers

● Raoul was researching computer careers on the Internet. He found an interesting chat room full of people in computer careers. Several said there was no future in computer careers. Raoul began to think that maybe he should consider a different career.

● Do you think Raoul's source of information is reliable? Why or why not?

Community Involvement

What to Do

● Find out what kind of volunteer work is available locally for someone your age. Look under the heading "Social and Human Services" in the *Yellow Pages*.

● Contact several organizations that sound interesting.

● Make a list of three places.

● Next to the name of each, describe the type of work there.

● Share the list with others.

Investigating Career Clusters

Business and Office

What Is the Business and Office Cluster?

Occupations in the business and office cluster focus on positions providing management and support services for companies. Jobs are in administration, management support, and administrative support.

Skills Needed

Office skills, computer skills, written and oral communication skills, organizational skills, math skills

THE FACTS	Types of Careers in This Cluster	Work Description	Career Outlook	Education
	Accountant	Prepare, analyze, and verify financial reports and taxes for organizations	Good	Bachelor's
	Word processor	Set up and enter reports, letters, and text materials	Slow	H.S. diploma
	Adjuster	Investigate and resolve complaints about merchandise, service, billing, and credit rating	Faster than average	H.S. diploma, Bachelor's
	Chief executive officer	Create policies and direct the operations of corporations	Good	Bachelor's, Master's
	Computer programmer	Write and maintain detailed instructions called programs or software	Faster than average	Bachelor's
	Systems analyst	Study business problems to design new solutions using computers	Faster than average	Bachelor's

Research Activity

Research 10 business and office jobs that interest you. Make a list of computer and office skills required for these jobs. List 10 computer and office skills in the order of their importance.

Chapter 3 Review

◗ Chapter Highlights

- There are more than 20,000 different careers.
- The library, the Internet, other people, and jobs are all sources of career information.

◗ Recalling Key Concepts

Using complete sentences, answer the following questions on a separate sheet of paper.

1. What is the difference between career clusters and career interest areas?
2. What kinds of information might you look for about different careers?
3. What are four places or ways to find career information?

4. How can you make sure that career information you gather is correct?
5. What can you do now to explore working in a particular career?

◗ Thinking Critically

Using complete sentences, answer the following questions on a separate sheet of paper.

1. Why do you think the U.S. Office of Education grouped careers in clusters?
2. Why should you research a career before deciding on it?
3. Why might someone make a career choice without doing research?
4. What kinds of questions might you ask during an exploratory interview?
5. What do you think you can learn about a career by job shadowing?

Building Skills

1. Basic—Writing

Write a letter to someone working in a career that interests you. Describe why you're interested in his or her career. Request an exploratory interview. Include a list of questions for the interview in the letter. Exchange letters with a classmate. Make sure he or she has included everything listed.

2. Information—Acquires and Evaluates Information

At the library and on the Internet, research a question you have about a career. Take notes on the information you find. Also record where you find it. Give a short oral report about how your research went. Compare doing research at the library with searching on the Internet.

Applying Academic Skills

1. The Arts

You have a career in your favorite career cluster. You've been invited to have a booth at a career fair. You want to make buttons for visitors to your booth to wear. The buttons will advertise the career cluster to others. Design a button that tells about the cluster in words or pictures. Hand out paper copies of the button to your classmates.

2. Foreign Language

A career of interest to you requires knowledge of at least one language besides English. Find out about language classes at your school, your local high school, and in your community. Share your findings with the class.

Discovery Portfolio

Make a Career Cluster File

- Make a career cluster file for your portfolio. Organize information you gather about different careers according to career cluster.
- Continue to collect information about careers.
- File what you find under the correct career cluster.
- Include other types of information that might interest your classmates. Circulate your fact sheet in class.

Career Exploration: Business and Office

Research a career from the business and office career cluster.

- Use the library and search the Internet to find information. If possible, also gather information through interviews.
- Make a fact sheet about the career. Include information about the kinds of work, the working conditions, and training and education required. Also include skills needed to do the job and personal characteristics best for the career.
- Explain the outlook for the career.

Chapter 4

Making Career Decisions

What You'll Learn...

- You will discover a way to take charge of your life.

- You will learn how to make major decisions in seven steps.

- You will find out how you can use the seven-step approach to make career decisions.

- **CAREER CLUSTER** You will explore careers in *communications and media.*

Lesson 4-1
Decisions! Decisions!

Lesson 4-2
Important Decisions

LESSON PLAN. See the *Teacher's Manual* for the Chapter 4 lesson plan.

Activity

TRY THIS!

- List five decisions you've made recently.
- Label the decisions with an *E* for *Easy* or an *H* for *Hard*.
- Then ask an adult friend or family member to list and label five recent decisions.

APPLY: Discuss your decisions in class. Why are some decisions harder to make than others? How did you both arrive at the decisions?

Decisions! Decisions!

Discover...

- why decision making is an important skill.
- steps you can follow to make decisions.
- how to deal with things that stand in the way of decisions.
- how to make better decisions.

Why Learn About Making Decisions?

Decisions are an important part of life. The stronger your decision-making skills, the wiser your decisions will be.

Key Terms...

- decision
- obstacle
- outcome
- attitude

Should I go to the mall or study for the test? Should I try out for the school play or go out for a sport? Which movie should I see? Should I tell my friend what someone said about her? Should I do what everyone else is doing?

Every day you make hundreds of decisions. Each **decision** is a choice you make about what action to take. Some decisions are pretty routine. For instance, each morning you decide what to wear. Other decisions take time and thought. You might think carefully about which classes to take, for example.

Your life is full of many choices. The decisions are yours.

Taking Charge

Decision making is an important life skill. When you make a decision, you have a say about some part of your life. You take action, instead of leaving your choices to others or to chance. You take control of where you are and where you're going.

What do you want to do with your life? Whatever you choose, along the way you'll face important decisions. You can't get where you want to go without making decisions.

► You've been making decisions all your life. What decisions have you made already today?

Some decisions are harder to make than others. Try building on each decision you make. Decisions you make every day will give you confidence to face more important decisions. You'll learn to trust yourself. Best of all, you'll feel a sense of freedom. That feeling will come from knowing you're in charge. You're making the decisions that have to do with you.

Reaching a Decision

You may not need much time to make everyday decisions. It's pretty easy to decide what to have for lunch or whether to walk or take the bus home. Routine decisions like these can seem almost automatic. You barely have to think about them.

Major decisions are something completely different, however. They often have a lasting effect on your life. Because of this, you want to take time to think about them carefully.

Breaking It Down

The hardest part about making an important decision may be figuring out where to start. Making a decision is easier if you break the problem into smaller parts.

Figure 4-1 on page 64 shows seven basic steps to follow in making major decisions. You can apply these steps to any important decision you face. If you need to, you can adapt, or change, the steps to fit different situations.

Following the steps may seem awkward at first. Don't worry, though. With each decision, you'll become more familiar with them. Soon you'll see how these steps help you make important decisions.

Overcoming Problems

Of course, nothing is ever as simple as 1-2-3. That's as true of decision making as anything else. Even when you carefully follow the seven basic steps, you can run into obstacles. An obstacle is something that stands in your way.

Meeting Obstacles

Ishiro Nagata ran into several obstacles when he faced an important decision. He had his heart set on a career in

MOTIVATING STUDENTS. Ask students to list the steps they try to take when making important decisions.

DISCUSSION STARTER. Let volunteers read their lists from the Motivating Students activity. Encourage all the students to compare and discuss their ideas.

TEACHING ACTIVITY. Have students suggest an important decision they might be making now or in the near future and explain how other decisions will be affected by it.

CRITICAL THINKING. Ask students to identify people who are good decision makers. What are the signs of good decision making? How has this skill affected the lives of these people?

TEACHING ACTIVITY. Have students compare their decision-making lists from the Motivating Students activity to the Seven Steps to a Decision.

CRITICAL THINKING. Ask students how the way they think of themselves can become an obstacle. What can you do when you are your own obstacle?

communications someday. After careful thought, he signed up to be on the staff of the school newspaper.

Ishiro was excited about the possibility of working on the paper. He was surprised when his friends made fun of the idea. They thought working on the newspaper sounded boring. Ishiro was surprised again when his parents weren't happy with the idea. They were worried he wouldn't have time for his homework.

Ishiro did get a spot on the newspaper's staff. The trouble was he wasn't so sure anymore that he should take it. These thoughts were going through Ishiro's head:

- Maybe my friends are right. It will be boring.
- Maybe my parents are right. I won't have time for my homework.
- Maybe I won't do a good job on the newspaper anyway.

➤ FIGURE 4-1

SEVEN STEPS TO A DECISION

Seven steps can help you make informed decisions.

What should I do for a summer job?

1
Define Your Needs or Wants
Identify the decision you must make. Be as specific as possible. Narrow your ideas so that you can focus on just one decision.

2
Analyze Your Resources
When you analyze something, you carefully study all its parts. You've already spent some time analyzing your personal resources. By now, you should have a good idea of your interests, values, skills, and aptitudes. How will these resources help you make a decision? What other resources can you use?

3

Identify Your Options

Options are possible choices. There are usually at least two options whenever you face a decision. What are your choices in this situation? Think hard. Several options may be open to you.

4

Gather Information

Find out as much as you can about your options. What are the advantages and disadvantages of each? For each option, ask yourself, "What would happen if I...?" Think through all the possibilities.

5

Evaluate Your Options

When you evaluate your choices, you judge their value or importance to you. Review the information you've gathered. Compare your options. Which seems to have the best chance of meeting your needs or wants?

6

Make a Decision

This is the point where you actually decide. Now is the time to choose one of your options.

7

Plan How to Reach Your Goal

A decision is not real until you take action on your choice. When you make a decision, you set a goal for yourself. A goal is something you want to achieve, or carry out. Once you've made a decision, make a plan of action. Figure out how you're going to carry out your decision.

Finding a Way

Ishiro took some time to look at what was standing in the way of his decision. He knew he couldn't change his friends' ideas. That was all right. Working on the newspaper was important to *him*. It made sense for his future plans.

Then he thought about his parents' concerns. Ishiro decided to talk to students who had worked on the newspaper before. He found out how they saved time for their homework. He realized that he could handle his homework too. He just had to manage his time carefully. Ishiro made a plan and shared it with his parents.

Never Give Up!

Ishiro could have let others' ideas stand in his way. He would have given up something important to himself, though.

Friends, family, even the way you feel about yourself can affect decisions you make. If you can identify what stands in your way, you can usually do something about it.

Figure 4-2 shows some common obstacles to decisions and how to handle them. You'll run into these and other obstacles as you face decisions. The important thing is not to give up. Look for a way around the obstacles. Make what is important to you happen.

CAREER OPPORTUNITIES

Communications and Media

People think that majoring in subjects like history and literature in college is a waste of time because subjects like these won't get you a job. To see how wrong they are, look at the job description to the right.

Critical Thinking

Can you think of some stories that a reporter might write about?

CLASSIFIED

THURSDAY, SEP

Reporter

Some experience preferred but willing to consider recent college grad with a B.A. in history or literature for this immediate opening at Georgia newspaper. We are looking for a reporter who can cover it all: state and local government, schools, and our citizens.

What Stands in Your Way?

•**You think you can't do something.** "I can't because I'm not old enough." "I can't because I'm a girl (or a boy)." "I can't because of my race or background."	You may not be able to do everything. For example, your age may keep you from driving or getting a certain kind of job. Make sure that you aren't using who you are as an excuse, though. Don't let an excuse stand in the way of a decision that's right for you.
•**You expect too much of yourself.** "If I can't do it perfectly, I won't do it at all."	It isn't always possible or necessary to do things perfectly. You can always do your best.
•**You expect too little of yourself.** "I won't even try, because I know I can't do it."	If you never try, you'll never know what you can do.
•**Your family expects too much of you.** "What if I let them down?"	Talk to your family members. Ask for their help in making decisions and carrying them out.
•**Your family doesn't have the money to support what you want to do.** "I can't afford it."	You can apply for money for training or education. Find out about scholarships, financial aid, and student loans. You can get a job to pay your expenses. You can find a way to do what you want if you want it badly enough.
•**Your friends or family make fun of what you want to do.** "Maybe they're right. It *is* a stupid idea."	Talk with your friends or family members. Tell them you feel hurt when they make fun of your dreams. Ask them for their support. Give them specific ideas about how they can support you.
•**Your friends pressure you to do what *they* want to do.** "I should go along with them or they won't be my friends anymore."	Trust yourself. You know what is right or not right for you. Your friends aren't really friends if they pressure you into something.
•**You're afraid of failure.** "What if I'm no good at this?"	You fail only if you don't make a decision or don't try.
•**You're afraid of change.** "I don't know what it's going to be like."	Change isn't easy. You can't know exactly what's going to happen, it's true. Think of change as an adventure. Change can open new doors.
•**You don't feel sure of yourself in new situations.** "I don't know how to act or what to say."	With time and experience, you'll feel more comfortable. Don't let fear of a new situation keep you from making a decision.
•**You put things off.** "I'll do that later."	Don't wait around. Make a date with yourself and keep it. If you wait too long, the decision may be made for you.

FIGURE 4-2 **Working with Charts**

We can all think of reasons not to make decisions. Do any of these sound familiar? Why does it help to identify obstacles that get in your way?

CAPTION ANSWER. When you identify obstacles, it's easier to avoid them.

The RIGHT Attitude!

Self-Esteem

Maybe you feel a little awkward talking about your favorite classes, sports, and after-school activities in which you excel. Don't be! As you prepare to investigate possible careers, remember that no one knows your skills better than you do. If you don't speak up and tell people what you're good at, they may never find out.

Apply Your Skills!

Look up the definition of self-esteem in the dictionary. In your own words, describe self-esteem and list three things (school subjects, activities, hobbies) that you are good at and enjoy.

EXTENDING THE LESSON. Ask for volunteers to do more reading about the decision-making process. Is there more than one model? How do the models compare? Ask for volunteers to give brief reports.

Making Better Choices

As you go through life, you'll get better and better at making decisions. As with everything else you do, there's always room for improvement. If you learn something from each decision, you'll make a better choice next time.

Here are some helpful hints for polishing your decision-making skills:

- *Keep practicing the seven basic steps.* The more decisions you make using the seven basic steps, the more skilled you'll become.
- *Pay attention to decisions you make every day.* If a decision doesn't turn out well, try to figure out why. Are you following the steps?
- *Recognize the obstacles that get in your way.* Is there a way around them?
- *Accept the outcome of each decision.* The outcome of your decision is its result or effect. You probably made the best decision you could. Things may not turn out the way you thought. Don't be afraid to start over, though. A new decision may have a different outcome.
- *Be willing to change your decision.* Decisions are not set in stone. You may need to make a new decision if the conditions for a decision change.
- *Check your attitude.* Your attitude is your basic outlook on life. Do you look for good things to happen, or do you expect the worst?
- *Forget about luck.* You don't need to depend on luck for your decision. Take control of your life and what happens to you. Get the facts, make plans, and take action—for yourself!

LESSON REVIEW AND ACTIVITIES. See the *Teacher's Manual* for answers.

Vocabulary Review

Pretend you have to write a one-page article on making decisions for your school newspaper. Use the key terms below in your article. Ask a partner to review your article when you're finished writing.

decision   outcome

obstacle   attitude

Check Your Understanding

Choose the correct answer for each item below. Write your answers on a separate sheet of paper.

1. The third step of the decision-making process is to_____.
   a. make a decision
   b. identify your options
   c. evaluate the information

2. One way to polish your decision-making skills is to_____.
   a. pay attention to the decisions you make every day
   b. identify your options
   c. count on luck

Critical Thinking

On a separate sheet of paper, answer the following questions.

1. Why is it important to learn how to make decisions?
2. Which step in making a decision do you think is easiest? Hardest? Explain your answers.
3. What kinds of obstacles have you faced while making a decision? How did you handle them?
4. How might your attitude make it difficult to learn from a decision?

Connecting to the Workplace

Using Decision-Making Steps

- Imagine you're interested in telecommunications. You'd like to work with satellites or lasers to change how people communicate. You have a choice between a class in computer skills and an advanced math class. You could use both for your dream career. Right now, though, you can take only one.
- Make a chart of the seven steps to show how you come to a decision.

Teamwork

What to Do • In a small group, brainstorm excuses people might give for not making decisions.
- Write down all the ideas you have.
- Then make an attention-grabbing poster. The poster should show the excuses and tell why it's important to make decisions.
- Hang your poster in the classroom for all to see.

Important Decisions

Discover...
- how to make decisions about careers.
- how to check your career decisions.

Why Follow Steps to Make Career Decisions?

Career choices are important decisions. Before making a choice, you'll want to give time and thought to all the possibilities.

Key Term...
- decision-making process

Have you ever taken a hike through a park or the woods? If so, you know there are usually different paths you can take. The path you choose depends on where you want to go.

A career path is like a hiking path. To get to the career you want, you have to make a decision about what path to take.

Taking It Step by Step

Choosing a career is a big decision—one that takes time and thought. You can use the decision-making process to decide on a career path. The decision-making process is the series of steps that help you identify and evaluate choices. It will guide you toward your career goal.

You don't have to make a decision about a career right now. For now, use the decision-making process to explore career paths. You'll have some fun, and it'll be good practice, too. When you're ready to decide on a career, you'll know the steps to follow.

CAPTION ANSWER. You can learn whether it was the right decision for you and whether you need to make a new decision.

► Sometimes making a decision is the only way to do some exploring. What can you learn from exploring a decision?

Step 1. What Do I Need or Want?

The path to a career starts with your hopes and dreams. To begin, think about the lifestyle you want. Where do you want to live? Do you want a career that allows you to travel or to stay at home? How much money do you think you'll need or want to earn? How much time and energy will you want to give to your career? What kind of people do you want to work with?

Think about the big question. What career will give me what I need or want? That's what you'll be deciding.

Step 2. What Resources Will Help Me Decide?

For a career, your resources include yourself. Who are you? What do you have to offer? Get out those lists of interests, values, aptitudes, and skills. Review them and update them. Also consider your personality and learning style. What you know about yourself will help you decide on a career that is right for you.

Step 3. What Careers Seem Interesting?

Here's where you list your options. What are some careers that match your personal goals and resources? Maybe you can't even think of one career you would enjoy. If so, it's time to become more aware of life's possibilities. Open your eyes and ears to what's out there. Consider all the jobs and careers you see around you every day.

Does someone you know have a career that appeals to you? Do you have an idea for a career you're not sure exists? Did a career in one of the career clusters sound interesting? Perhaps a career interest area that describes you points to some careers. These are options to explore.

▲ Family members can help you with career decisions. Who else can give you career advice?

CAPTION ANSWER. Adult friends, guidance counselors, teachers, and people who have careers that interest you can give you advice.

MOTIVATING STUDENTS. Ask students if they have found more than one career cluster that interests them. Then ask how they expect to choose one cluster over the other.

DISCUSSION STARTER. Go over the key terms and objectives with the class. Ask volunteers to share their ideas about the lesson objectives.

Step 4. What Can I Find Out About Them?

Don't hesitate for a moment. You know where to look for information about careers. Go to the library. Search the Internet. Talk to people. Get some experience on the job.

Gather as much information as you can about each career option. Make notes. You may discover other interesting career possibilities during your research. Add them to your list of options. Find out more about them.

Step 5. Which Choice Seems Best for Me?

Now evaluate your choices. Study the information you've gathered. Consider your needs and wants. How does each career match your personal goals and resources?

Compare your choices. Try to zero in on the career that best meets your needs and wants. List the second best, the third, and so on.

Step 6. What's My Decision?

Choose the career that seems best for you. If you're having trouble deciding, take a deep breath and relax. None of the choices may stand out as the right one. The differences between them may be very small. Just make the best decision you can. Use your research and what you know about yourself.

Keep in mind that you can change your mind. No decision has to be final. Still, it's important to make a decision—even if you change your career goal later.

▲ Sometimes it helps to see how your options stack up against each other. What else might you do when you're having trouble making a choice?

Step 7. How Can I Reach My Career Goal?

Don't drop the ball. You've made a decision. Now you have to see it through. Make a plan. Figure out how you're going to get from where you are to where you want to be. Look at Chapter 5 for some help in developing a plan of action.

Using the seven steps listed previously, explore career paths. Write each step on a sheet of paper. Then list your ideas, decisions, and plans after each one.

Checking and Changing Direction

Making a decision and acting on it is not the end of the decision-making process. There is another important step. Once you've put your plan into action, you need to check your decision. Continue to evaluate your decision to make sure it still has meaning for you.

Evaluate, Evaluate!

Evaluation is an ongoing process. You do it all the time. Think about the last time you were with your friends, for

The Global Workplace

Mealtime Customs Differ from Culture to Culture

Different cultures often mean different eating habits. In Italy, Spain, and Latin America, lunch is the biggest meal. A small supper follows late in the evening around eight or nine o'clock. Raw fish is served with many meals in Japan. In Russia, menus list many dishes, but few are actually available. If you are no longer hungry, leave some food on your plate. If you clean your plate, your host will insist on serving you more.

Exploration Activity!

Using the Internet and library resources, research the outlook for jobs in Russia, Italy, and Spain. Will there be many jobs available in these countries in the future? What types of jobs are available there now?

A Decision Is Finally Something You Do on Your Own

Q: How can I be totally sure that I'm making the right decisions?

A: Start by following the decision-making steps in this book. Once you've done that, it's always helpful to ask your friends and family members for advice. In the end, however, the question is rather like a basketball player asking, "How can I be sure that I'll make a basket?" You can't ever be 100 percent sure until after you have done it. That's why making a decision can be so hard.

instance. You might have thought, "This is a lot of fun." Maybe it was more like, "I'd rather be home." You might even have had both of these thoughts. Whatever you thought, you were evaluating the situation.

At each point on your career path, you'll want to stop and evaluate where you are. Right now, take a good look at the information you've gathered about your career choice. Ask yourself, "Is this really what I want to go after? Am I committed to achieving it?" Then continue to evaluate new experiences and information along your career path.

Keep Asking Questions

One way to check your decision along the way is to ask questions. *Figure 4-3* shows some questions that may come to mind.

Career Questions

- Does the work give me a feeling of accomplishment?

- Is the work interesting? Will it always be?

- Am I using my skills in this career?

- Does this career fit my values, lifestyles, and other things that are important to me?

- How am I better off choosing this career over another?

- Do I want to do this kind of work for another 5 or 10 years?

| FIGURE 4-3 | Working with Charts |

Questions are a good way to check a career decision. Some questions will occur to you because of changes in your career field. Others may just show your changing feelings about a career choice. What other questions might you ask about a career decision?

Starting Over

Your answers to these questions will show you the way. You may continue on your career path. You may go back, follow the steps again, and choose a different career.

Never be afraid to start over. Life is about change. That's part of the fun—and the challenge—of being alive.

Mari Lewis of Orlando, Florida, thinks change can be wonderful. She started over when she was about your age. Her family moved to Florida when she was 12. She thought her life was over. She had grown up on a horse farm in Kentucky. All she wanted was to breed horses someday. Suddenly, there was more water all around her than grass. That move changed her life:

> **The more time I spent around the ocean, the more I loved it. It was a natural decision to become a marine botanist. I study ocean plants and how they keep the environment clean. If my family had stayed in Kentucky, I never would have discovered the ocean. I couldn't be happier.**

Change can seem hard at times. It can also open up new opportunities. In some ways, it's all how you look at it. That's up to you.

Starting over can be scary at first. In the end, though, you may discover a path that you didn't even know existed.

CAPTION ANSWER. Answers will vary; students should suggest other questions that explore satisfaction with a career.

TEACHING ACTIVITY. Ask students: How can mistakes help you learn? What may be happening if you never make mistakes? Discuss their responses.

RESEARCH. Have students look up *decision making* as a topic in books or magazine articles. Have them write down the name of at least one book or article mentioning this topic.

EXTENDING THE LESSON. Ask students to write a summary of what they have learned about the way they make decisions. Have them add their summary to the Discovery Portfolio.

LESSON REVIEW AND ACTIVITIES. See the *Teacher's Manual* for answers.

Vocabulary Review

On a separate sheet of paper, write a short how-to paragraph about the decision-making process. Explain how to use the decision-making process to choose and achieve a career goal. Use the key term below at least once in your paragraph.

decision-making process

Check Your Understanding

On a separate sheet of paper, tell whether each statement is true or false. Rewrite any false statements to make them true.

1. A career path is like a hiking path. To get to the career you want, you have to make a decision.
2. The second step in the decision-making process is to decide on your resources.
3. At each point on your career path, don't stop to evaluate where you are, or you will never make a decision.
4. Making a decision and acting on it is the end of the decision-making process.

Critical Thinking

On a separate sheet of paper, answer the following questions.

1. How are career decisions similar to other important decisions you make?
2. Why is it important to use the decision-making steps when choosing a career?
3. When do you think you can stop evaluating a career decision? Explain your answer.

Connecting to the Workplace

Career Plans

- Gaby wanted to be a computer artist. She went to art school to learn to draw on the computer. While in school, she worked as a server to pay her expenses. Gaby found that she liked the restaurant business. She decided to change her career plan.
- Did Gaby waste her time making her first career plan? Why or why not?

Community Involvement

What to Do

- Select a business owner in your community. Interview the owner about the career path he or she has chosen.
- Ask questions like the following during your interview. How did you decide to start a business? What other decisions did you have to make to get the business going?
- Report your findings to the class.

Investigating Career Clusters

Communications and Media

What Is the Communications and Media Cluster?

Occupations in this cluster deal with organizing and communicating information to people. Jobs are found in radio and television broadcasting, journalism, motion pictures, the recording industry, and telecommunications.

Skills Needed

Strong oral and written communication skills, creative skills, technical skills, and an understanding of the communication industry

THE FACTS	Types of Careers in This Cluster	Work Description	Career Outlook	Education
	Telephone operator	Assist with special phone needs	Extremely limited	H.S. diploma
	Radio announcer	Select and introduce recorded music, present news, interview guests on radio	Average	Voc-Tech, Bachelor's
	Technical writer	Gather and organize technical information, put it into words the audience can understand	Faster than average	Bachelor's
	News correspondent	Prepare and report stories that inform the public about events of interest	Slower than average	Bachelor's
	Camera operator	Use cameras to capture the special mood that sells products, provide entertainment, highlight news stories	Slower than average	Voc-Tech, Bachelor's

Research Activity

Traditionally, jobs in communications and the media are competitive. Research 10 communications careers and rank them in order of highest growth rate through 2005. Start with the careers that have the fastest growth and end with those that have the slowest.

CHAPTER REVIEW. See the *Teacher's Manual* for answers.

Chapter Highlights

- When you make a decision, you take charge of some part of your life.
- You can use the seven-step decision-making process to make career decisions.

Recalling Key Concepts

Using complete sentences, answer the following questions on a separate sheet of paper.

1. What are the seven steps in the decision-making process?
2. What should you do if you run into obstacles while making a decision?
3. What can you learn from decisions you've made?
4. What important step follows the decision-making process?

5. What is one way you can check a career decision?

Thinking Critically

Using complete sentences, answer the following questions on a separate sheet of paper.

1. How is making no decision actually a decision?
2. Do you ever say, "I'll go if you go" or "I'll do it if you do"? Why isn't this a good way to make a decision?
3. Do you think it's possible to skip steps in the decision-making process? Would you get the same results?
4. What two steps in the decision-making process make luck unnecessary?
5. Why do you think some people are unhappy in their careers? What might explain why they stay in careers they don't like?

Building Skills

1. Thinking—Decision Making

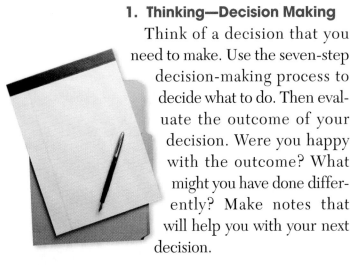

Think of a decision that you need to make. Use the seven-step decision-making process to decide what to do. Then evaluate the outcome of your decision. Were you happy with the outcome? What might you have done differently? Make notes that will help you with your next decision.

2. Interpersonal—Serves Clients/Customers

Carrie sells newspaper advertising space. She spends most of her time working with department and grocery stores because they buy the largest ads. The smaller advertisers say Carrie doesn't spend enough time with them. Use the decision-making process to show how she can give all her customers the attention they need. Show the steps in a chart.

Applying Academic Skills

1. Mathematics

You have to choose between two jobs. A cashier job at a supermarket pays $100.00 for 20 hours a week. A bike repair job pays $5.25 an hour for 16 hours a week. Which job pays more per hour? More each week? What besides money might affect your decision? Which job would you choose, and why?

2. Computer Science

In school, you use two kinds of software—one for word processing, and one for drawing. You'd like to buy some new software to try at home. You've got three choices, but you can't decide which to get. Where could you get the information you need to help you decide? Make a plan for gathering information. Share your plan with a partner.

Discovery Portfolio

Use the Seven-Step Decision-Making Process

- List all seven steps and summarize each step.
- Underneath the summary, make a list of important decisions you think you might face in the future. At the top of the list, write *Use the Seven-Step Decision-Making Process to Make These Important Decisions:...*
- Keep the list in your portfolio. Add to it as you have new ideas.

Career Exploration: Communications and Media

Gather information about a career from the communications and media cluster.

- Look in the library and on the Internet for information.
- If possible, conduct interviews to find out more about the career.
- Write a script for a news broadcast on the career. Include information about the kinds of work, the working conditions, and training and education required. Also include skills needed to do the job.
- Explain the outlook for the career.
- Deliver your broadcast on the career to the class.

Your Career *Plan*

What You'll Learn...

- You will discover how planning can help you reach career goals in the future.

- You will learn what a career plan should include.

- You will set goals and make a plan for a career that interests you.

- **CAREER CLUSTER** You will explore careers in *construction*.

LESSON 5-1
How Planning Helps

LESSON 5-2
Designing a Plan

LESSON PLAN. See the *Teacher's Manual* for the Chapter 5 lesson plan.

TRY THIS!

Invite an adult friend or family member to describe an activity he or she planned. Ask these questions:
- Why did you plan the activity?
- Was the activity a success?
- How did planning make the activity a success?

APPLY: Think of other activities that benefit from careful planning. Why do you think making a plan is important?

How Planning Helps

Discover...
- why planning is important.
- what a career plan should include.

Why Take Time to Plan?

Planning is the surest way to achieve your goals. To reach a career goal, you'll need to make and follow a plan of action.

Key Terms...
- procrastinate
- prioritize
- internship
- part-time job
- temporary job

"I've got a cool idea for…" "Wouldn't it be great if I could…" "If I had the money, I would…"

Everyone has ideas and dreams. Some people, though, go one step further. They make their ideas and dreams a reality. These people usually have something that other people don't. They have a plan of action. They plan how they are going to get what they want. Then they follow their plan.

Why Plan?

Have you ever made a plan? Have you ever set your sights on something and then carefully planned how to get it?

If you answered no, you're not alone. Many people live their entire lives without ever planning anything. They "play it by ear." They take things as they come. They say, "Why bother? No one knows what tomorrow will bring. Just live for today."

CAPTION ANSWER. Students may mention parties, projects, trips, and school events.

▶ Planning helps make activities a success. What kinds of activities have you planned?

The Global Workplace

A Little Knowledge of a Foreign Language Can Make a Big Difference

Many people around the world speak some English. This makes traveling easier for native English speakers. However, before going to a foreign country, learn a few basic phrases of that country's language to help in routine situations. Pocket-size phrase books are easy to carry and usually list many useful words. Learning *thank you* is a good place to start.

- Italy   grazie
- Germany   danke
- Latin America, Spain   gracias
- South Korea   kamsa hamnida

Exploration Activity!

Using library and language resources, learn a few basic phrases in a language that interests you. Learn *hello, good-bye,* and four other terms you think would be helpful.

TEACHING THE GLOBAL WORK-PLACE. Explain to students that learning some words and expressions in another language will help if they travel to a foreign country. Make some language resources available for research.

MOTIVATING STUDENTS. Have each student list at least five different activities that are more successful when they are carefully planned.

DISCUSSION STARTER. Let volunteers read their lists from the Motivating Students activity aloud and discuss the specific benefits of planning.

TEACHING ACTIVITY. Have students outline the lesson using the section heads. (It will look like section I of the chapter outline in the *Teacher's Manual.*) What questions does it answer?

CRITICAL THINKING. Ask students, "If a teacher assigned on a Monday three chapters to be read in a week, when would a procrastinator probably start the assignment? How would a reading plan help?"

You *can* have some control over what tomorrow brings, though. As you learned in Chapter 4, there's a way to have a say about both today and tomorrow. You can take charge of your life by making decisions. Then you can plan how to reach the goals you've set.

Manage Your Time

Planning is important for many reasons. For one, a plan helps you organize your activities and manage your time. That way you don't miss out on anything.

Alice Lonewolf is a seventh grader in Helena, Montana. She wants to be a sports coach someday. A typical school day for Alice includes classes and sports. "I want to be involved in as many sports as I can. Mondays, I play on an intramural baketball team after school. On Tuesdays and Thursdays, I swim at the Y. Friday night and Saturday morning, I have swim

CRITICAL THINKING. Ask students which of their current school courses are helping them prepare for a career. How? What other courses might help them get started toward a career?

team practice. Wednesdays are free for biking or kicking a ball around the yard with my dad.

> " *If I didn't have a plan on paper, this schedule would be impossible. Besides all the sports, I need time to do my homework. With a plan, I have time for everything.* "

Remember Important Events

A plan not only helps you do the things you need or want to do. It also helps you remember when they need to be done. When you have a plan, it's harder to procrastinate. When you **procrastinate,** you put off doing or deciding about something.

John Gikas, a computer student in Cambridge, Massachusetts, learned the importance of a plan the hard way. "I used to procrastinate all the time," John observes. "Last year I missed a chance to go to a once-a-year computer event in Boston. I didn't get my registration form in on time. A lot of my friends who are interested in computers did, though. They got to try out all kinds of new software and hardware. When I get the form this year, I'm going to make a note of the deadline. There's no way I'm going to miss out again."

CAPTION ANSWER. Students may suggest that if you plan what you're going to do and do a little at a time in the time you have, you'll get the project done the way you want and on time.

▼ You'll be amazed at what you can do when you have a plan. What's the best way to do important projects well and on time?

Sort Out What's Important

Rachel Baum of Cleveland, Ohio, found another way planning is useful. She discovered that a plan helps you prioritize. When you **prioritize,** you put tasks in order. You order them from first to last or from most to least important.

Rachel is interested in acting. A family friend told her about a summer theater program for teens. It ran for six days a week, eight hours a day, six weeks of the summer. "Summer was my time for sleeping in, reading, and just having fun," Rachel explains. "Being in a serious theater production is part of my career plan, though. I couldn't pass it up. I figure I'll have plenty of chances to take a vacation later."

Reach Goals

Last but not least, anyone who's ever made a plan and carried it out will tell you the same thing. A plan gives you a feeling of accomplishment. As you complete each part of your plan, you can cross it off. You can say, "I'm that much closer to my goal."

Tilly Ransom of Bedminster, New Jersey, can't remember ever wanting to be anything other than a doctor. When she was about 13, she made a plan. Her plan included science classes and volunteering at the local hospital. It also involved college and medical school. Then she did her residency, or advanced training in a special area, at a hospital.

"I still have that plan," Tilly notes. "It included all the important steps to being a doctor. As the years went by, I completed each one. Now here I am, head of surgery at a big city hospital."

What Goes into a Plan?

You can make a plan for a career that interests you, just as Tilly did when she was about your age. You'll want to include all the important steps. The following steps are part of most career plans.

Education and Training

Most people think of education or training as a first step. *Figure 5-1* on page 86 lists some of your options for education and training. You can get started on this step right now. Work to strengthen your basic skills, such as reading, writing, and mathematics. As you'll learn in Chapter 10, basic skills count in all kinds of careers.

Classes you take now and in high school can help you prepare for a variety of careers. Mathematics classes will give

Deciding on Education and Training

Options	Description	Notes
On-the-Job Training 	Training in a particular job right on the job	• Offered by many companies • Available to new and current workers • Helps workers keep up with changes in their current field
Apprenticeship	Hands-on experience in a job under the guidance of a skilled worker	• Form of training that's been practiced for hundreds of years • Usually for set amount of time
Vocational-Technical Centers	Skills programs in areas such as auto mechanics and computer technology	• Day and evening classes usually available • Relatively inexpensive
Trade Schools 	Training for a particular job, such as hairstyling, truck driving, or cooking	• Often offer more programs than vocational-technical centers • Usually more expensive than vocational-technical centers
Community and Technical Colleges 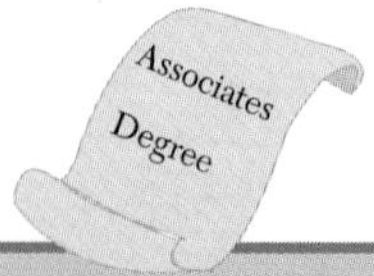	Associate's degree for two-year program in areas such as accounting and desktop publishing or certificate in areas such as court reporting	• Night and weekend classes usually available • Less expensive than trade schools and four-year colleges and universities • May lead to study at a four-year college or university
Four-Year Colleges and Universities 	Bachelor's degree for four years of study and advanced degrees beyond four years	• Preparation for a variety of careers, including teaching, with bachelor's degree • Preparation for careers such as social work, law, architecture, and medicine with advanced degree • Often expensive
Military Service 	Training in more than 200 different jobs, including health technician and air-traffic controller	• Up to six years of active duty required • Possible to attend school before or during service • Education after service sometimes paid for
Continuing Education 	Courses and programs that help adults complete education, brush up on old skills, pursue new paths	• Available at high schools, colleges, and universities • Sometimes leads to a degree

FIGURE 5-1 Working with Charts

You'll have different educational and training needs at different points in a career. Why might you go back to school in the middle of a career?

CAPTION ANSWER. You might go back to school to learn new skills, to improve skills you have, to advance to a different level in your job, or to keep up with developments in your career field.

you skills you might use as a city planner or a computer specialist. Science classes are good preparation for careers in natural resources and agribusiness, health, and marine science. In English, you will develop skills needed in many communications and media careers. Classes in music, art, and dance can lead to careers in the fine arts. Your work in social studies may inspire you to think about careers in travel, law, or government.

Following high school, you may choose to continue your education or get other training. As you think about your options, think about this. Jobs requiring at least four years of college are growing faster than all other jobs. *Figure 5-2* shows that they'll grow almost twice as fast as other jobs by

TEACHING ACTIVITY. As a class, read the eight education and training options in Figure 5-1. Ask which options sound interesting. Discuss the different benefits. Answer any questions students may have.

Growth in Jobs by Level of Education and Training, 1994–2005

Master's degree
Bachelor's degree
Associate's degree
Professional degree
Doctoral degree
Work experience plus bachelor's degree
Work experience
Short-term training and experience
Vocational-training after high school
Long-term training and experience
Moderate-length training and experience

0   5   10   15   20   25   30

Percent

Source: Bureau of Labor Services, 1996

FIGURE 5-2	Working with Graphs

People can earn master's, professional, and doctoral degrees after getting a bachelor's degree. Which will grow faster, jobs requiring a bachelor's degree or jobs requiring a doctoral degree? Why would it be wise to get a bachelor's degree in addition to work experience? Which will grow faster, jobs calling for higher education or jobs calling for training?

CAPTION ANSWER. Jobs requiring a bachelor's degree will grow faster; jobs requiring a bachelor's degree will grow almost twice as fast as jobs calling only for work experience; jobs calling for higher education will grow faster.

the year 2005. They also will usually pay more. College is an important part of many people's career plans.

Jobs Along the Way

Jobs are another step on the way to a career. As you learned in Chapter 3, job shadowing and volunteering are great ways to explore careers. Both can also be an important part of a career plan.

An internship may also be part of your career plan. An **internship** is a temporary, usually unpaid position that provides valuable job skills in a particular career field. It is more formal than a volunteer job and usually requires a bigger commitment of time.

There are internships in teaching, government, and many kinds of businesses. Many college students look for summer internships to get work experience in a career field. You might think about arranging an internship for the summer while you're in high school. An internship can help you find out more about a particular career.

In high school or later, you might decide to take a part-time job related to a possible career choice. In a **part-time job**, you'll work up to 30 hours a week. A part-time job is a good way to learn about a career field that interests you.

TEACHING CAREER OPPORTU-NITIES. A wood-frame estimator cannot build a house alone. He or she must work with an architect, plumber, electrician, and carpenter, among others. As on any team, if one member doesn't want to play, the whole team loses.

CAREER OPPORTUNITIES

CLASSIFIED

THURSDAY, SEPT

Construction
Constructing a building involves a number of people doing different jobs you probably didn't know existed.

Critical Thinking
Why is it important for a wood-frame estimator to be a team player?

Wood-Frame Estimator

Team-oriented estimator is wanted for a growing general contracting business. Must know the amount of wood and number of workers needed to build all types of wood-frame buildings. Knowledge of Microsoft Word and Excel a plus.

A temporary job is another way to try a specific kind of work. It's also a good way to develop job skills you may need. Students and many other people find temporary jobs especially convenient. A **temporary job** usually lasts only a short while. Some temporary jobs are available just for a particular season, for instance. Lifeguarding, golf caddying, and catering—providing food and service for special events— are examples of temporary jobs for young people.

Then, of course, there are full-time jobs. As you have learned, a full-time job amounts to about 40 hours a week. Like most people, you'll probably work at several full-time jobs during your lifetime.

Career Research

Don't forget to include career research as a step in your career plan. Career research does not end when you've identified interesting careers. It doesn't end when you choose a career either. You should continue to do career research as you explore careers. You should do career research as you work toward a career goal. You'll learn about new opportunities and changes in career fields. What you learn could affect your career plan.

Where can you look to find out what's going on? You can use the same resources you would use to research career options. You'll find current information at the library and on the Internet. You can also learn a great deal by talking to people. While you're still in school, discuss with your guidance counselor the job market for different careers. Once you begin working, listen to what you hear on the job about career developments.

Take this advice. Stay informed. That way you can adjust your career plan as needed. When you build research into your career plan, your plan will always be up-to-date.

RESEARCH. Have students investigate college catalogs at your local library or via the Internet and report on what information can be found about the school in the catalog.

EXTENDING THE LESSON. Ask students to interview adults who have gone back to school in mid-career. Have them report why the adult went back and list the problems and benefits.

Working in teams is becoming more important in the global workplace. School requires teamwork, too—in the classroom, in sports, and in after-school activities. The right attitude will make your team a success. Respect your teammates' different skills, backgrounds, and opinions, and you'll find they will do the same for you.

Apply Your Skills!

In groups of four, come up with three important rules for successful teamwork. Share your results with the class. Post a list of the top five teamwork tips in a visible place in the classroom.

Covering All the Bases

Education and training, jobs, and career research are the basic steps included in most career plans. There are other things to keep in mind, though. Money can be an issue. Part of your plan may focus on how you're going to pay for education or training, for instance. Will your family be able to help you? Can you get a scholarship? Maybe you'll have to earn the money yourself. You may need to explore ways to raise money and figure out how long it will take.

Jorge Alvarez of Los Angeles, California, always knew that he wanted to be a lawyer. Being the youngest of six children, however, he was concerned about money.

When he was 14, he volunteered as a law clerk's assistant at a downtown law firm. The next summer, he got an internship as a law clerk at the same office. When he turned 16, he got a paying job—as a part-time law clerk.

Juan continued to work part-time throughout high school. This enabled him to set aside money for his education. When he was ready to enroll in college, he discovered that he was eligible for financial aid. He decided that he could afford to stop working and pour all his efforts into his studies.

Juan worked hard at college and got a scholarship to law school. "My hard work paid off," says Juan. "Now I'm right where I want to be—all because I planned ahead."

Personal responsibilities may also have an effect on your career plan. You may decide to delay a step in your plan until your children go to school, or you may change your plan so you can work at home.

When you sit down to make a plan, you want to try to think of everything that might affect it. Of course, you also need to be prepared for surprises. You can't know the future. You shouldn't let that stop you from making a plan, though. Once you've got a plan, you just need to keep your eye on your goal and be flexible.

LESSON REVIEW AND ACTIVITIES. See the *Teacher's Manual* for answers.

Vocabulary Review

Imagine you are a career counselor who leads workshops on making a career plan. You begin each workshop with a brief speech. Write a speech that includes each of the terms below. Then give your speech to the class.

procrastinate   part-time job
prioritize   temporary job
internship

Check Your Understanding

Choose the correct answer for each item below. Write your answers on a separate sheet of paper.

1. To reach a career goal, you'll need to_____.
   a. know your friends' goals
   b. make and follow a plan of action
   c. have a job offer

2. A career plan includes_____.
   a. a comparison of the career plans of your peers
   b. education and training
   c. how much money you will make

Critical Thinking

On a separate sheet of paper, answer the following questions.

1. What kinds of problems do you run into when you don't make a plan?
2. What do you think is the most important part of a career plan? Explain your answer.
3. Why are temporary jobs a good idea for young people?

Connecting to the Workplace

Making Career Decisions

- Kareem planned to be a master plumber. It would take five years. Besides serving an apprenticeship, he had to take classes, pass some tests, and get a license. As a master plumber, he would make $25 an hour. Kareem found a plumbing apprenticeship at $8 an hour. He later quit to take a factory job that paid him $10.50 an hour.
- Did Kareem make a wise decision? Explain.

Teamwork

What to Do
- As a class, find names and addresses of places of education included in Figure 5-1 on page 86.
- Then form teams of two or three students.
- Each team should select a different school.
- As a team, write a letter requesting information about the school.
- Add the material you receive to a class display about education options.
- Check out the information other teams have received.

Designing a Plan

Discover...

- how to set goals you can reach.
- different kinds of goals that lead to a career goal.
- how to make your own career plan.

Why Make Your Own Career Plan?

You know more than anyone else about your hopes and dreams for the future. A plan will show the steps that lead to one of your career choices.

Key Terms...

- short-term goal
- medium-term goal
- long-term goal
- chronological order

You already know the first step in creating any plan. You need to make a decision. Following the decision-making steps in Chapter 4, you must first set a career goal.

That's really the hardest part. What comes next? Next you need to figure out the steps you must take to reach your goal. You need to create a detailed plan of action.

If that sounds like a lot of work, you're right. It is. You shouldn't let that stop you, though. Everything worthwhile takes time and effort.

How to Reach Your Goals

It will be up to you to set goals to reach your ultimate career goal. What are the secrets to success? Here are a few pointers:

- *Be as specific about each goal as you can.* State exactly what you plan to do. You'll find specific goals easier to aim for and achieve.

▶ Reaching goals now will help you achieve goals throughout your life. What goals have you set for yourself lately?

- *Put your goals in the order that you'll do them.* That way you'll know which to work on first, second, and so on.
- *Make realistic goals.* Aim high, but aim at what's possible. If your goals are too easy, you may lose interest in them. If they're too hard, you may become discouraged and give up.
- *Change your goals as needed.* Check your progress. Think about where you're headed. Don't be afraid to change your mind and take a new direction.

Setting Goals

Right now, a career goal probably seems a long way off. That's partly because you're still thinking about your career options. It's also because a career goal is your ultimate, or final, goal. Before you reach it, you must set and reach other goals. Each will be a stepping stone to your ultimate goal.

Stepping Stones to a Career

The goals between you and a career goal are short-, medium-, and long-term goals. A short-term goal is something you might start right away. Sometimes you can complete it quickly. Say your ultimate goal is to be an editorial director. A short-term goal might be to get practical journalism experience working as an intern at a newspaper.

At the same time or later, you might work on a medium-term goal. **A medium-term goal** is usually more challenging than a short-term goal. It also takes longer to achieve. A medium-term goal might be to earn a bachelor's degree in English.

Beyond your short-term and medium-term goals are long-term goals. A long-term goal may take a long time to reach. Short-term and medium-term goals can sometimes help you achieve a long-term goal. To become an editorial director, you might set a long-term goal of working for a publishing company as an editor or writer. Such an opportunity might be open to you only if you already have some editorial or writing experience.

CAREER Q&A

Goals Are Not Set in Stone

Q: If achieving my goals takes longer than I planned, does that mean my goals are unrealistic?

A: A successful writer once wrote, "Any goal you set will take 7 to 12 years longer to complete than you dreamed it would…." Her answer: No, your goals almost always take longer than planned. Figure out why your goals are taking so long. Did you need more money? Did you forget to include the hours spent on chores? Don't be afraid to adjust your future goals to include the things you missed.

MOTIVATING STUDENTS. Have students write down at least five of their own goals.

CAPTION ANSWER. Answers will vary but may include both academic goals such as earning a higher grade in a class, completing a project, or improving or mastering a skill and personal goals such as making new friends, saving money to buy something, or changing behaviors or attitudes.

DISCUSSION STARTER. Discuss the importance of setting your own goals. Why should your goals be based on what *you* want? What might happen if you allow other people to set your goals for you?

TEACHING ACTIVITY. Have students take turns reading "Stepping Stones to a Career," Figure 5-3. Discuss how Bill Mann's jobs, experiences, and education led him to his ultimate goal.

To get a clearer picture of the goals on the way to a career goal, look at *Figure 5-3.* Bill Mann followed these stepping stones to his ultimate goal as a landscape architect.

Now You Do It

As you can see, making a career plan is a big job. Why not give it a try right now? Design a plan for one of your career choices. It's a good way to prepare for future career decisions. You won't waste energy worrying later. You won't procrastinate either. You'll know what's involved, and you'll be able to sit down and do it.

► FIGURE 5-3

STEPPING STONES TO A CAREER

Short-, medium-, and long-term goals can help you reach your ultimate career goals in stages.

A
List the Steps

Bill Mann's career decision began with a summer job. Every summer during school Bill worked as a landscaper. He mowed lawns and planted shrubs and trees. A neighbor suggested Bill think about becoming a landscape architect. Bill did some research and decided the career was made for him. He listed the steps he would take to reach his career goal.

B

Short-Term Goal

One of Bill's short-term goals was to go to college. Bill wanted to get a well-rounded education that would help him in any career. He also wanted to take courses that would be useful to a landscape architect. Bill majored in ecology. His studies focused on living things and how they relate to each other and the environment. He also took a drafting course so he could learn how to draw plans. Bill finished college with a bachelor's degree.

C

Medium-Term Goal

Bill's first medium-term goal was to get an advanced degree in landscape architecture. Bill applied to take part in a three-year master's degree program at a university. While a student, he set a short-term goal of working on a surveying crew. As a surveyor, he measured land and set boundaries. He could use these practical skills in his career.

D

Additional Medium-Term Goals

Another of Bill's medium-term goals was to get a license as a landscape architect. Bill was able to do this in his first job in the field. Bill's first job was with the department of transportation. He worked as an apprentice under a licensed landscape architect at the department of transportation. After two years, he took and passed the licensing exam.

E

Long-Term Goal

Bill's long-term goal was to work as a landscape architect for the National Park Service. He thought national parks could be made more people-friendly and still respect the environment. Bill reached his long-term goal and saw some of his ideas become reality. Working for the park service, he designed a new visitor center for a major Civil War battlefield.

EXPLORE Activity

Get started with your own career. First, write your ultimate goal at the top of a sheet of paper. Then make three lists.

In the first, list classes and activities now and in high school that are related to the career goal. Also make notes about career research you might do.

In the second list, write the education or training you'll need after high school. Be specific. List courses you might take and degrees you must earn. Write down where you can get the training you need.

In the third list, put jobs that will lead to your ultimate goal. Include all kinds of work experience. Don't forget internships or apprenticeships and volunteer, part-time, and temporary jobs.

You may need to do some research to put these lists together. Check out the usual sources in the library and on the Internet. Go to your guidance counselor or a teacher for help. Ask adult family members or friends for advice.

Mapping It Out

Once your lists are complete, you're ready for the next step. Figure out whether each of the items you've listed is a short-, medium-, or long-term goal. Think about when you might start and complete each one. What can you do now? What will you do, say, one, three, and five years from now? How long will it take you to reach your ultimate goal?

Design a career plan like the one shown in *Figure 5-4.* Chart your goals in chronological order, or the order in which they will happen.

If you're not working on a computer, use a pencil. Remember, your

A Career Plan

	Now 1 Year 2 Year 3 Year 4 Year
Short-term goal	Work at a newspaper as an intern and get practical journalism experience.
Medium-term goal	Earn Bachelor of Arts degree in English from a college.
Long-term goal	Work for a publishing company as an editor or writer.
Ultimate goal	Become an editorial director.

FIGURE 5-4 Working with Charts

Chronological order makes it easy to see the steps to a career goal. **Which goals will this person need to work on at the same time for a while?**

CAPTION ANSWER. This person will need to work on the short-term goal of getting journalism experience and the medium-term goal of earning a B.A. at the same time.

plan is never set in stone. Your goals and the time you spend on them may change over time. You must face your future with an open mind. Think of it as an athletic contest. Your plans might change with every step of the game. That's what makes it exciting.

The important thing is to have a plan. Without one, you've just got an idea or a dream. With a plan, you're moving toward your ultimate career goal, step by step. You'll keep moving forward until you find the career that's right for you.

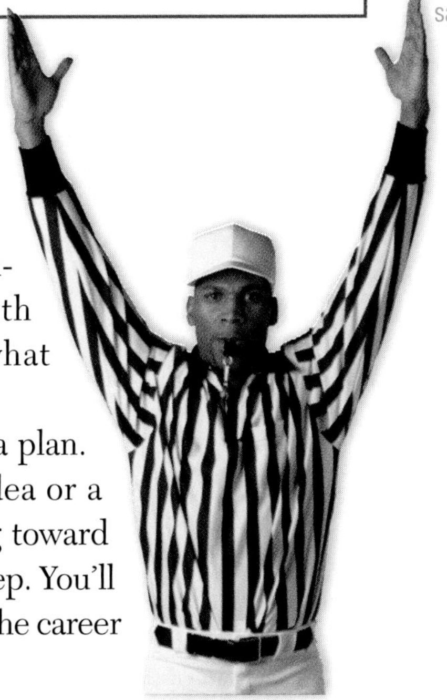

LESSON REVIEW AND ACTIVITIES. See the *Teacher's Manual* for answers.

Vocabulary Review

Write a paragraph about the different kinds of goals that lead to meeting a career goal. Compare and contrast the goals. Use in your paragraph each of the terms below.

short-term goal
medium-term goal
long-term goal
chronological order

Check Your Understanding

On a separate sheet of paper, tell whether each statement is true or false. Rewrite any false statements to make them true.

1. The first step in creating any plan is to make a decision.
2. If the goals you set are too easy to achieve, you may lose interest in working on them.
3. The goals between you and your career goal include short-, medium-, and long-term goals.
4. Meeting a medium-term goal is usually less challenging than meeting a short-term goal.

Critical Thinking

On a separate sheet of paper, answer the following questions.

1. How do short-, medium-, and long-term goals help you reach your ultimate career goal?
2. Why is it important to be specific when you set goals?
3. Why is it okay to change your goals as needed?
4. Why do you think you should write down your career plan?

Connecting to the Workplace

Career Goals

- Work with a classmate. Select several careers that you each find interesting.
- Then help each other research and make a list of goals to reach each career goal.
- Trade lists with another pair of classmates.
- Study the career plans your classmates have drawn up.

Community Involvement

What to Do

- Identify a group that is active in your community.
- Look through the Yellow Pages of your phone book to find names of groups and their phone numbers.
- Contact the group.
- Ask to interview the group's leader or a member of the group about the group's goals.
- Ask how the group plans to meet its goals.
- Share your findings with the class in a brief oral report.

Investigating Career Clusters

Construction

What Is the Construction Cluster?

Occupations in the construction cluster involve building, repairing, and modernizing homes and other kinds of buildings. Construction workers are grouped into three general areas: structural, finishing, and mechanical.

Skills Needed

Mathematics skills, mechanical drawing skills, building skills, physical strength and stamina, manual dexterity, and ability to read blueprints.

THE FACTS	Types of Careers in This Cluster	Work Description	Career Outlook	Education
	Stonemason	Build stone walls, set stone exteriors and floors for buildings	Good	Voc-Tech, On-the-job
	Carpenter	Cut, fit, and assemble materials in the construction of structures	Good	Voc-Tech, On-the-job
	Electrician	Install, connect, test, and maintain electrical systems	Slower than average	H.S. diploma, Apprenticeship
	Sheet-metal worker	Make, install, and maintain air-conditioning, ventilation, roofs, siding, and other building parts	Good	Apprenticeship
	Construction inspector	Examine the construction of structures to ensure compliance with regulations	Faster than average	H.S. diploma, Construction experience

Research Activity   Make a list of five construction jobs that interest you. Research the tasks involved for each position. Make a chart of your findings, and write a few sentences about why one of the jobs interests you.

Chapter 5 Review

CHAPTER REVIEW. See the *Teacher's Manual* for answers.

▶ Chapter Highlights

- Planning helps you do what you need or want to do when it needs to be done. It helps you prioritize. It also gives you a feeling of accomplishment when you reach a goal.
- You need to set realistic goals on the way to your career goal. It helps to be specific, put your goals in order, and make changes as needed.

▶ Recalling Key Concepts

Using complete sentences, answer the following questions on a separate sheet of paper.

1. Why is planning important? Give four reasons.
2. What basic steps are included in most career plans?
3. What three kinds of goals do you set and meet on the way to your ultimate career goal?
4. Why do you need a career plan?

▶ Thinking Critically

Using complete sentences, answer the following questions on a separate sheet of paper.

1. Why is it important to plan time for rest and relaxation?
2. How might achieving an important goal affect your attitude toward other goals?
3. Why might you take a part-time job instead of a full-time job while you're a student?
4. How can you tell if your goals are realistic, or reachable?

Building Skills

1. Basic—Listening

Invite a friend to share with you his or her goals and plans for achieving them. Listen carefully. Then draw a picture that illustrates how your friend plans to reach his or her goal. Title the picture "Go for Your Goal!" Present it to your friend, and ask whether it accurately represents the plan.

2. Interpersonal—Participates as a Member of a Team

In a small group, decide on a project for your school. You might plant flowers on school grounds or start a club after school. Maybe you'd like to organize activities during recess. Plan the short-, medium-, and long-term goals needed to reach your goal. Put your plan into action. Report on the project's progress.

Applying Academic Skills

1. Mathematics

Kareem gave up his career plan to become a master plumber to take a factory job. After five years, his wages rose from $10.50 to $12 an hour. He could have become a master plumber in five years and earned $25 an hour. Kareem works 40 hours a week. How much does he earn a week at the factory? How much more would he have made each week as a master plumber?

2. Science

Imagine you make videos about the steps people can take to different careers. Your next video is about becoming a physical therapist. Research the basic steps in reaching that career goal. Break them into short-, medium-, and long-term goals. Then explain the career plan, as if you were advising someone to follow it.

Discovery Portfolio

Determine Your Career Goals

- Focus on two careers that interest you. List what you can do to reach each career goal. Then list in chronological order the goals for each career. Keep these lists in your portfolio.

- Write a brief essay about a goal you achieved. Describe the goal and the steps you took to reach it. Explain how you felt when you accomplished the goal.
- File the career plan you made in this chapter in your portfolio.

Career Exploration: Construction

Research a career in the construction career cluster.

- Search for information in library resources and on the Internet.
- If practical, interview someone about the career.
- Include information about the kinds of work, the working conditions, and training and education required. Also include skills needed to do the job.
- Explain the outlook for the career.
- Using only visuals, share with the class what you've discovered.

Finding a Job

What You'll Learn...

- You will learn how to go about finding a job.

- You will identify sources of information about job openings.

- You will discover how to use information you gather to get the job you want.

- **CAREER CLUSTER** You will explore careers in **family and consumer services**.

LESSON 6-1
Gathering Leads

LESSON 6-2
Organizing Your Job Search

LESSON PLAN. See the *Teacher's Manual* for the Chapter 6 lesson plan.

Friends & Family Activity

TRY THIS!

- Have a "roundtable" discussion with a group of friends or family members about finding jobs.
- Gather in a circle.
- Go around the group. Each person should name a job he or she is interested in and explain why.

APPLY: After each person describes a job, as a group brainstorm ways to find out about openings for the job. Where would you start?

Gathering Leads

Discover...
- what is involved in a job search.
- how talking with people can turn up job leads.
- other ways to find out about job openings.

Why Learn About How People Find Jobs?

One day, you will be looking for a job. You'll want to know where to look for information about job openings. You'll want to find the right job—one you'll enjoy and do well at.

Key Terms...
- work permit
- job lead
- networking
- contact list
- referral
- classifieds
- school-to-work program

You've got an idea for a job. Maybe you'd like to work as a party helper or a pet sitter. You want to do lawn or garden care. Perhaps you'd like to volunteer your time at your local hospital or recycling center.

Many part-time and volunteer job opportunities are open to you right now. There'll be more jobs to choose from when you reach age 14. By the time you reach high school, you'll have an even greater variety of job choices. To apply for some jobs, you'll need a work permit if you're under 16. In some states you'll need one if you're under 18. A **work permit** is a document that shows you know that the number of hours young people can work is limited. It also shows that you are aware that the kinds of jobs young people can hold are limited.

The main thing you need to start moving toward a job at any age, however, is an idea of what you want to do. Then you can take the next step. You can start your job search.

▶ Talking to people is an important part of every job search. What do you think you can learn by talking with people? What can they learn from you?

Starting Your Search

What kind of detective do you think you'd make? It's a detective's job to track down information. They search for leads—clues and evidence that will help them solve a case.

You'll have a chance to develop your detective skills when you begin looking for a job. A large part of a job search is detective work. Your search for the right job will begin with a job lead. A job lead is information about a job opening.

Once you get a job lead, you'll follow it. You'll gather more information. You'll chase job leads until you land the job you want.

Networking

How do you go about finding job leads? One of the best ways is by networking. Networking is communicating with people you know or can get to know. When you network, you share information and advice with others.

You've probably already done some networking. Remember that summer art class or softball league you heard about? How about the after-school teen center that just opened? You talked with teachers, friends, neighbors—anyone who might

CAREER OPPORTUNITIES

CLASSIFIED

THURSDAY, SEP

Child-Care Worker

Help the houseparent at our group foster home for children ages newborn to 12 years old. Help meet the physical, social, and emotional needs of our foster children. Bachelor's degree and two years' similar work experience required.

Family and Consumer Services

Do people often ask you for advice? Are you a good listener? Do you like kids? Yes, yes, yes? Then check out this job.

Critical Thinking

Why do you think a college degree is needed to take care of kids? What kind of subjects do you think a child-care worker needs to study?

know something about it. You got the information you needed. You found out whom to call. Networking led where you wanted to go. It can also lead to a job.

How It Works

It's easy to start networking to find a job. You can begin by just talking with people about what you're interested in. Spread the word. Ask people you know to spread the word to others for you.

Your network will grow quickly. You'll get to know more people, and more people will get to know you. That's what networking is all about. Someone you know will know someone else. That person will know someone else—who knows a person you need to talk to. To get the ball rolling, all you have to do is talk to people you know.

Figure 6-1 shows that networking works. In fact, more people get their jobs through networking than any other way. It's one of the best ways to find out about job openings.

Tony Demetriou knows that from experience. He used networking to find a job mowing lawns in the summer and shoveling snow in the winter. Tony talked to his next-door neighbors about lawn mowing and snow shoveling. One said he did the work himself. The other had older children who did the work.

Although neither neighbor had work for him, Tony was able to add both neighbors to his network. A few days later, one of the neighbors telephoned Tony with a job lead. She had several older friends in the neighborhood who needed someone to do the work Tony was interested in. She gave their names and phone numbers to Tony. Tony called them. They were happy to hear about the services he had to offer. Tony now has a busy schedule year-round mowing lawns and shoveling snow.

▲ You can begin networking with any-one you know. **How might friends and family members be able to help you find a job?**

CAPTION ANSWER. They might know people who know something about or do the kind of work you're looking for.

RESEARCH. Have volunteers research the age requirements for working in your state and report their findings to the class.

How to Get Started

Start building your own network now. It's never too soon. Talk to people about jobs and careers that interest you. School clubs and events such as career fairs are great places to network. As you gather information about interesting careers, you can also share information about your interests and skills. When you start looking for a job, your networking may bring you job leads.

The steps in networking are simple. First, it helps to make a contact list. A **contact list** is simply a list of people you know.

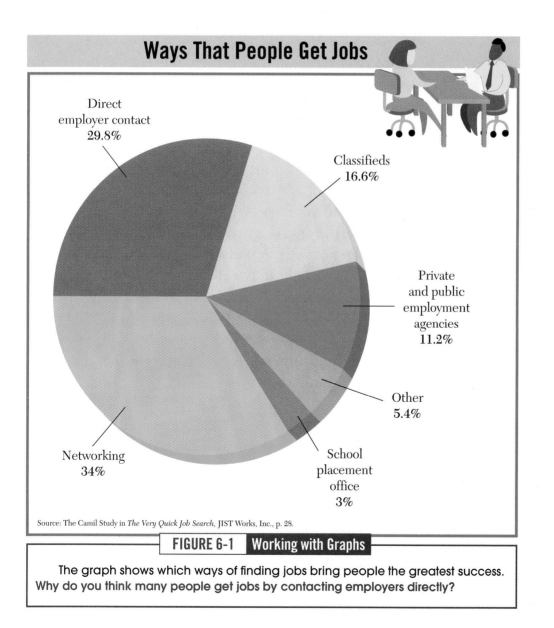

Ways That People Get Jobs

Direct employer contact 29.8%

Classifieds 16.6%

Private and public employment agencies 11.2%

Other 5.4%

School placement office 3%

Networking 34%

Source: The Camil Study in *The Very Quick Job Search*, JIST Works, Inc., p. 28.

FIGURE 6-1 | Working with Graphs

The graph shows which ways of finding jobs bring people the greatest success. Why do you think many people get jobs by contacting employers directly?

TEACHING ACTIVITY. After students make a list of their resources, have them share their list with a partner. Allow them to revise their lists, based on what they learned from their partners.

EXPLORE Activity

Why not get a list going now? Include everyone—family members, family friends, neighbors, teachers, classmates, friends of friends. People who are just acquaintances also belong on your list. Keep your list up-to-date by adding new people you meet or get to know.

You can take this exercise one more step by thinking of a job you'd like, such as baby-sitting or doing office work such as filing. Make a contact list for that job. Write down the names of everyone you know who might give you a lead for the job.

Once you have a list, the next step is to contact the people listed. Make contact when you're ready to look for a job. You can also make contact when you're still thinking over a job idea. Talk to each person on your list about your job idea. Ask for any information that might lead to a job.

Some people on your list may not know anything about job openings. A neighbor or friend of theirs might, though. Don't cross people off your list. Ask whether they know someone who works in the area you're interested in.

CAPTION ANSWER. Answers will vary; students may name friends, family members, teachers, and others.

That's the next step in networking. Get a referral from each person you talk to. A **referral** is someone to whom you are referred, or directed. That person may have the information about a job or job opening that your contact did not. Your contact list will grow with each referral. By contacting referrals, you'll build your network.

▶ Contacts are anyone you know. Who would be the first five people on your contact list?

Networking will come in handy as you plan and build a career. By talking with people, you can learn a lot about your career field. You can also share what you know with other people. You never know where networking will lead. The networking you do today may lead to a job in the future.

Telephone Tips

- **Write a script for your call.** Write down who you are and why you're calling. Jot down important questions. A script will help you remember what you want to say. It will also help you feel more relaxed.

- **Ask to speak with someone who can answer your questions.** The person who answers the phone may not be that person. Go to the top. Ask to speak with the head of the household or the head of a department.

- **Get the information you want.** Ask about job openings. Don't forget to ask for referrals.

FIGURE 6-2	Working with Checklists

The telephone is a useful job-hunting tool. How else can you contact businesses you'd like to work for? Why might a phone call be a better job-hunting tool than other methods?

CRITICAL THINKING. Ask students how they could use phone calls with other methods of finding job leads. (They can be used as a follow-up or to find out to whom to send an inquiry.)

CAPTION ANSWER. You can write letters or send E-mail messages. A phone call gets someone's attention right away, and you get a response right away instead of no response or a response after some time has passed.

Other Ways to Get Information

Although networking is one of the best ways to find a job, it isn't the only way. *Figure 6-1* on page 107 shows that people have success finding jobs in other ways.

Get on the Phone

One of the first things many job seekers do is call businesses they might like to work for. They ask for general information. They also ask about job openings and whom they can talk to about them.

Calls like these are known as cold calls. The person on the other end of the line doesn't know you. You don't know them. After making a few cold calls, you, may understand the term in a different way. You may get a cold response. Your call may get you nowhere.

Cold calls don't have to work that way. The secret is careful planning. Look at *Figure 6-2* for some tips on using the telephone to get job leads. Give them a try. They may help you locate the job you want—whether it's cleaning pools, watering plants, or washing cars.

Using the Internet

Q: Can I use the Internet to find a job?

A: Yes. Many businesses list job openings on their Web sites. First, go to any Internet search engine (Yahoo!, Infoseek…) and type in the job you are looking for. If that doesn't work, figure out what cluster your job belongs to and type it in. Click onto the home page of any company, and chances are you will see something that reads "job opportunities." Not only is it easy, but your hands and clothes don't get dirtied by newsprint.

The more calls you make, the more comfortable you'll feel on the phone. Just remember, the first cold call is often the hardest. You'll warm up in no time.

Check the Classifieds and Job Postings

Many job hunters go straight to newspaper classifieds. The **classifieds** are advertisements organized in classes, or groups. One group of ads might list things for sale. Another might list places for rent. Another usually lists job openings. The jobs listed are often available in the community or region the newspaper serves.

The classifieds seem like a natural place to look for job leads. The truth is, though, that only a small number of people find jobs through ads. Many job openings never make it to the classifieds. People fill the openings through networking.

You may also want to check job postings in your community. Many businesses post "Help Wanted" signs when they have job openings. A local day-care center may have a bulletin board on which parents post ads for baby-sitters and other jobs, for example.

Take Your Search to the Internet

Today, of course, there's a brand-new place to look for job ads. That place is the Internet. On the Internet, you can find jobs far beyond your own community. You'll be looking at job openings in the worldwide community. When you begin a search one day for a full-time job, you'll probably check the Internet for listings.

CRITICAL THINKING. Ask students to evaluate the use of words such as *bright*, *personable*, and *mature* in posted job ads. What are employers trying to accomplish by using these words?

EXTENDING THE LESSON. Have students use the "Government Listings" section of the phone book and make a list of the government agencies that could offer information about jobs or job placement.

EXPLORE Activity

Just for fun, locate some job listings on the Internet. You may be able to log on to the Internet on a computer at home, school, or your local library. Many public libraries have computers connected to the Internet.

Use a search engine such as Yahoo! or Excite! To find links to job sites, type in keywords such as *careers* or *employment opportunities*. You might visit Monster Board, America's Job Bank, or USAJobs, for example.

You can also go to company sites. Use the name of a company whose products you like as the keyword for your search. When you reach the company's site, click on the link to employment opportunities.

Take notes on three interesting job openings you find on the Internet. Record where you found the posting, what the job is, and why it interests you.

TEACHING ACTIVITY. Bring to class the classified ads from several local newspapers. Discuss what students already know about classifieds and how classifieds are organized.

Get Help and Advice

Another place to look for help or advice about jobs is your school. Most schools have a counselor or teacher who helps students with career plans. Some schools even have a placement office to help students find jobs.

Make your school counselor part of your network. Tell him or her about careers you'd like to explore. Ask about student organizations related to careers. Your counselor may be able to set up an appointment for you to do some job shadowing. He or she may also know about volunteering opportunities in your community and special events such as career fairs.

In high school, your school counselor may be able to help you get into a school-to-work program. A school-to-work program brings schools and businesses together. If you take part, you will gain work experience and training at a local business. When you graduate from high school, you might be the first one called when there is a job opening at the business.

CAPTION ANSWER. Answers will vary according to students' career interests; students should suggest keywords that narrow their search to specific careers of interest to them.

◄ Thousands of jobs are posted on the Internet. What keywords would you use to find job listings for careers of interest to you?

LESSON REVIEW AND ACTIVITIES. See the *Teacher's Manual* for answers.

Vocabulary Review

Imagine that after a long job search you've just gotten the job you wanted. A friend has written you asking for job-hunting advice. Write a letter to your friend explaining how to find a job. In your letter, use each of the key terms below. Exchange letters with a classmate, and read his or her advice.

work permit	referral
job lead	classifieds
networking	school-to-work
contact list	program

Check Your Understanding

Choose the correct answer for each of the following items. Write your answers on a separate sheet of paper.

1. Your search for _____ will begin with a job lead.
   a. how to perform on the job
   b. the right job
   c. a network
2. You can build a network by_____.
   a. giving people your phone number
   b. making a contact list
   c. asking people to look for jobs for you

Critical Thinking

On a separate sheet of paper, answer the following questions.

1. What do you need before you can begin a job search?
2. Why do you think most people get their jobs through networking?
3. Why is it important to use more than one way to find a job?

Connecting to the Workplace

Researching Job Ads

- Look at the classifieds section in your local newspaper. Study the job ads carefully. Then write an eight-line classified ad for a job that interests you.
- Model your ad after the job ads in the newspaper. Use abbreviations to save space.
- Post your ad on a classroom bulletin board.
- Look at the ads your classmates have posted. Which jobs interest you? Explain why in a 50-word paragraph.

Teamwork

What to Do
- Work with a partner. As a team, choose a job in the family and consumer services career cluster. For a description of this cluster, see page 121.
- Research openings for the job you selected. Use at least two methods for researching job openings described in the lesson.
- Present your findings to the class in an oral report.

Organizing Your Job Search

You've got some good ideas about where to look for job leads. Now you need something else every good detective has. You need a way to keep track of the information you gather. Being organized is the key to a successful job search. It's the best way to make sure your leads go somewhere.

Keeping Track

You'll talk to many people during a job search. You'll discover job leads in many places. It's easy to forget people's names and what they said. Don't rely on your memory. Don't make notes on scraps of paper. You need a well-organized system for remembering.

Setting Up a System

Once you have started your job search, don't let it get away from you. Organize it from the beginning. That way you'll know where you started, and you'll see where you're going.

A simple way to do this is to record job leads on index cards or sheets of paper. Put each lead on its own card or sheet of paper.

Discover . . .
- how to keep track of job leads.
- how to gather information about jobs and businesses.

Why Bother Organizing Your Job Search?

Organization helps you stay on top of the information you've gathered. When you're organized, it's easier to use the information to get the job you want.

Key Terms . . .
- database
- employer
- annual report

CAPTION ANSWER. Answers will vary. Students should name specific school or personal projects or activities and describe how they organized them. Students should also comment on the effectiveness of the systems of organization they used and discuss how they might handle future projects or activities differently.

◄ Organizing your job search is a good idea. Think of some other projects or activities you have organized. What kind of system did you use for each? How did it work? What could you have done differently?

Starting a new job is hard for anyone. You may not know your coworkers' names, where to eat lunch, or even where to find the bathroom. What's the best thing to do? Relax! Realize that your employer doesn't expect you to know everything right away. If you're willing to learn and have a sense of humor, your first few weeks will not be too difficult.

Apply Your Skills!

Brainstorm (with one other person) answers to this question: What are 10 things you can do to prepare for your first day at a new job?

If you like working with computers, you can organize your job leads another way. You can create a database. A **database** can store data, or information, in different ways. To create a database, you make an entry for each item. Later, you'll be able to search, sort, and reorganize the information you enter.

Getting the Details Down

The place to begin organizing is your contact list, the list of people you know. In addition to this list, you may have written down names of businesses you'd like to work for. You may also have found job openings advertised in the classifieds or posted in your community. Your school counselor or placement office may also have given you some leads. Each contact or lead should be entered on a card or in your database.

Whether you use cards or a database, you'll want to record the same information. Include the following for each lead:

- name and title of person or business
- if a person, name of his or her department and company
- address and telephone number
- additional information

Figure 6-3 shows how to list all of this information on a job-lead card.

How the System Works

Now here's how to use your system. Let's say you have decided to use job-lead cards. After you've made a card for

> **FIGURE 6-3**
> You'll need to keep detailed information on your job-lead cards in order to make a contact. How would you open a conversation with Mrs. Goldbaum, using this information?

CAPTION ANSWER. Students should relate what they would say if they called Mrs. Goldbaum.

Mrs. Goldbaum
335 Prospect Street
206-345-9278
She needs someone to help with grocery shopping once a week. Aunt Elaine suggested I call her.

each contact or lead, make contact. After contacting the person or business, make notes on the card. Keep your cards handy. If someone you've talked to calls you, get out his or her card. Use it to refresh your memory. Update the card with new information.

The time you take to get organized and stay organized will be worth it. As *Figure 6-4* on page 116 shows, a well-organized job search helped Jason Lee locate a job. Organization can work for you too.

More Detective Work

Getting a job lead is exciting. Getting a job is even more so. In between, though, you have another job to do. You need to do some investigating.

What You Are After and Why

You want to find out as much as you can about possible jobs. You also want to find out about employers you might work for. An **employer** is a person or business that pays a person or group of people to work.

The information you gather will help you in a couple of ways. First, you'll make a good impression. Knowing about a job or business will give you self-confidence. That will make you feel more comfortable talking to your contact. You'll also be able to ask intelligent questions about a job opening. The person you talk to will notice that you took the time to do some research. He or she will know that you are interested and serious.

What you learn will also help you decide whether a particular job is right for you. You want to be happy and successful where you work. It helps to know what kind of situation you'll be working in. You'll also want to find out what you can about the people you'll be working with. You'll want to know as much as possible about the kind of work you'll do. Then you can match what you learn with what's important to you.

MOTIVATING STUDENTS. Have students write a paragraph explaining the value of being organized in certain areas of their lives. When is it important to be organized?

DISCUSSION STARTER. Guide students in discussing why they may come up with a number of job leads. Ask, "Why might many people want to help you find a job?"

TEACHING ACTIVITY. Prepare two sample job-lead cards on the board. Answer any questions students may have.

CRITICAL THINKING. Ask students what might happen if a potential employer called and their database or lead cards were not handy.

TEACHING ACTIVITY. After students have read this section ["What You Are After and Why"], ask them the two reasons for finding out as much as possible about potential employers. Write the reasons on the board.

CRITICAL THINKING. Ask students to what lengths a person should go to find out about a possible place of employment. Have them explain their answers.

Asking Questions

Much of what you'll want to know about possible jobs and employers will depend on the jobs themselves. If you're interested in cleaning garages around your neighborhood, you probably won't need to do much research. You may just ask around to see who knows various neighbors. Then you might ask whether they are pleasant and safe people. If you discover an opening at a local business, however, you'll probably want to gather more information.

You can get some basic facts about a business by asking questions like these:

- What kinds of goods or services does the business offer?
- What kind of reputation does the business have with its workers and customers?
- What types of work do people do there?
- Is the business growing and expanding?
- Is it possible to move up in the business?

> **FIGURE 6-4**

ORGANIZING JOB LEADS

Jason Lee of Roanoke, Virginia, wants to be a veterinarian someday. After his first year of college, he took a summer job at a small animal clinic. Jason's job lead cards show how networking got him the job he wanted.

Liz Sherman, Neighbor
134 Dogwood Street
Roanoke   724-5367

Suggested I call the following people:
• Dr. Alda Stone, veterinarian
  Roanoke Dog and Cat Hospital, Roanoke
• Winnie Scott, office manager
  Vinton Pet Care, Vinton

A
While home on break, Jason talked to his neighbor Liz Sherman about her new puppy. He mentioned that he wanted to work with animals. Liz gave him the name of her vet. She also gave him the name of the office manager at an animal clinic. Jason made a card with Liz's name that included the two referrals.

Of course, these aren't the only questions you'll want to ask. You can add other, more specific questions as you think of them.

RESEARCH. Have each student acquire an annual report for a business that interests them. They can request them by mail or download them via the Internet.

B

Then Jason made cards for each of Liz's referrals—Alda Stone and Winnie Scott. He followed up by calling them. Dr. Stone wasn't sure she would need help. Jason made note of this on Dr. Stone's card. Winnie Scott connected Jason to Dr. Ainsley, the vet at the other clinic. Dr. Ainsley said he was thinking of hiring someone. He promised to give Jason a call in a couple of months.

Dr. Alda Stone, veterinarian
Roanoke Dog and Cat Hospital
150 Main Street, Roanoke
724-2300

• Called 2/23
Not sure she'll be hiring
for this summer

Winnie Scott, Office Manager
Vinton Pet Care, Vinton
564-8907

• Called 2/23

Connected me with Dr. Ainsley,
the vet at the clinic

Dr. Jim Ainsley, veterinarian
Vinton Pet Care, Vinton   564-8907

• Spoke on 2/23 May be hiring for summer.
Won't decide for a couple of months • Took
my phone number and promised to call me
• Called me 4/15 and set up an interview for
4/20 at 1:30 pm • Interview on 4/20 went well,
will call me by 4/30 at the latest
        — 4/27 GOT THE JOB!

C

Jason made a card for Dr. Ainsley. On it, he made notes about their conversation. Dr. Ainsley called Jason back in the spring. Jason looked at his notes to recall their earlier conversation. Dr. Ainsley told Jason there was a job opening at the clinic for the summer. He invited Jason for an interview. A week later, he offered Jason the job.

Getting Answers

How do you get answers to your questions? Here are a few suggestions. People who work at the business are a good source of information. If you know someone who works at the business you're interested in, ask him or her about it. Also talk to customers of the business. Ask why they use it and what they like about it. Ask them how it is different from other businesses that do the same thing.

You might even visit the business. Judy Johnson thought that would be a good idea. She had her eye on a part-time job at a bakery in town. Before calling about the job, she stopped by the bakery to check it out. "My best friend came with me," Judy explains.

> **" We bought a few cookies to see what the baked goods were like. There were lots of other customers. The woman behind the counter was very friendly and helpful. It looked like a great place to work to me. "**

Do what Judy did if you can. Visit before you make contact. Take a friend or family member along. Pay attention to what you see. Does the business have a good atmosphere? Does it look like a safe place to work? Do the people who work there look happy? Are they courteous and ready to help? Are the customers happy? Ask yourself, "Is this a place I'd like to work?"

Other Paths to Information

Chances are you won't have to go too far right now and in high school to get the information you want about a business. The jobs that interest you are likely to be nearby.

Later on, though, you may get job leads in other places. You'll need to gather information in other ways. One way to find out about a business is to call or write and ask for its magazine, newsletter, or annual report. An **annual report** is a summary of a company's business for the year. It will tell you a lot about a business, including how well it is doing.

You might also check out the Web site of the business, if it has one. There you'll find a lot of general information.

▲ There are many ways to gather information about places where you might work. Where would you get information about a business or organization you'd like to work for?

You'll get up-to-the-minute news about the business. You'll learn about its latest products or projects.

However you gather information about a business, take time to review it carefully. Then ask yourself, "Is this a place I'd like to work?"

Gather Your Facts

All your detective work will pay off. You'll know more than you did before you started. Don't worry if other questions come to mind. You'll have a chance to ask them when you talk to your contact.

Be prepared, though. You won't be the only one asking questions. A possible employer will want to know about you. Employers want to know about your education, skills, and interests. They're also interested in other jobs you've held, including both part-time and volunteer work.

The next step is to gather the facts about yourself. Presenting yourself is an important part of your job search. You'll learn about this important step in Chapter 7.

EXTENDING THE LESSON. Divide the class into small groups. Ask each group to select a local company and gather facts about it.

The Global Workplace

Dress Should Be Appropriate

Professional dress varies in cultures around the world. Many places are more formal in their way of dressing than the United States. When visiting or working in a foreign country, wear a conservative outfit. Suits and conservative dresses work well in many situations. Jeans, tennis shoes, and casual outfits are better left at home. When in doubt, see what everyone else is wearing and dress with equal formality.

Exploration Activity!

Using library resources, research the formal wear of a country of your choice. What is the tradition behind the clothes this country considers formal?

TEACHING THE GLOBAL WORK-PLACE. Point out to students that many countries have clothing traditions that are different from our own. Explain that clothing styles have developed over time and often depend on cultural norms and the climate of the country involved. Offer students methods for finding out more information about clothing around the world.

LESSON REVIEW AND ACTIVITIES. See the *Teacher's Manual* for answers.

Vocabulary Review

Write a glossary entry for each of the terms below. First write the definition of the term. Compare your entries with those of your classmates.

database   annual report

employer

Check Your Understanding

On a separate sheet of paper, tell whether each statement is true or false. Rewrite any false statements to make them true.

1. The best way to keep track of job leads is to memorize the company information you uncover.
2. The place to begin organizing your job search is your contact list.

3. One way to find information about a company is to write or call for its annual report.

Critical Thinking

On a separate sheet of paper, answer the following questions.

1. Why do you think it's important to organize your job search from the beginning?
2. What would you especially want to know about a business you might work for? Explain your answer.
3. What would be convenient about using a database instead of cards to organize job leads? How might a database not be practical?

Connecting to the Workplace

Developing a Contact List and Card System

- Think of a part-time or volunteer job you'd like to have. Possible jobs include tutoring, baby-sitting, dog walking, newspaper delivery, helping older people shop.
- Put together a contact list that will help you get the job.
- Use a card system to organize your search for work.
- Share your system and search results with your classmates.

Community Involvement

What to Do

- Select a business in your community that offers family or consumer services.
- List questions you have about the business. Then gather information to answer your questions.
- Ask friends and family members what they know about the business. Do some networking to get more information.
- If it's possible, visit the business. Then write a brief report on the business, based on your research. Read your report to the class.

Investigating Career Clusters

Family and Consumer Services

What Is the Family and Consumer Services Cluster?

Occupations in family and consumer services involve developing, producing, and managing goods and services for consumers and life in the home. Jobs center around food, housing, clothing, textiles, and child development.

Skills Needed

Science skills, artistic skills, communication skills, interpersonal skills

THE FACTS	Types of Careers in This Cluster	Work Description	Career Outlook	Education
	Child-care worker	Nurturing and teaching preschool children	Faster than average	H.S. diploma, Bachelor's
	Interior decorator	Plan the space and furnish the interiors of homes and commercial establishments	Faster than average	Bachelor's
	Fashion coordinator	Work for department stores to organize displays and present fashion shows	Slower than average	Voc-Tech, Bachelor's
	Dietitian	Plan nutrition programs and supervise preparation of food	Average	Bachelor's
	Food journalist	Research and report on food and nutrition for magazines, newspapers, TV, or radio	Slower than average	Bachelor's

Research Activity Make a list of five family and consumer service jobs that interest you. Then research the particular skills and tasks required of each job. Also investigate the job outlook and salary range for each job. Create a chart that summarizes your findings.

Chapter 6 Review

▶ Chapter Highlights

- Networking is one of the best ways to get job leads. You can gather leads by telephoning businesses directly, checking the classifieds, and searching the Internet. You can also ask a school counselor or teacher for help.
- Being organized is the key to a successful job search.

▶ Recalling Key Concepts

Using complete sentences, answer the following questions on a separate sheet of paper.
1. What is networking?
2. How is networking useful in developing job leads?

3. What are some other sources of job leads besides networking?
4. What are two ways you can keep track of job leads?
5. How can you gather information about jobs and businesses?

▶ Thinking Critically

Using complete sentences, answer the following questions on a separate sheet of paper.
1. Why might employers like to hire people referred to them through a network?
2. Which source for job leads would you use first in job hunting? Why?
3. Which source for job leads would give you the most control over your job search? Explain.

Building Skills

1. Basic—Speaking

Role-play telephone conversations. Pose as someone looking for a job. Explain what you are looking for and why. Have a partner pose as a friend. He or she should respond with interest and give you a referral. Role-play a second conversation with the referral. Then switch roles with your partner. Afterward, discuss how you could improve your telephone skills.

2. Information—Uses Computers to Process Information

Explore job listings on the Internet. Then create a computer file for people to read before job hunting on-line. In the file, give advice for conducting an on-line job search. Suggest keywords other than *careers* and *employment opportunities* to use for a job search. List Web sites that provide job listings. Include other advice that will help someone search the Internet for job leads.

Applying Academic Skills

1. Mathematics

Steve has 20 people on his first contact list. Each person refers him to 2 more people. Each of those people refers him to 1 more person. How many people will be on Steve's list after these referrals?

2. Language Arts

Review the classifieds for job openings. Make a list of abbreviations used in the ads. Find out what each stands for. Make a master list with your classmates that includes all the abbreviations you've found. Then write a classified ad for a job using as many abbreviations as possible.

Discovery Portfolio

Building Your Own Network

- After you've put together a basic contact list, store it in your portfolio. Add to it new names as you think of them. Contact people on your list to discuss your career ideas and goals. Ask your contacts to refer you to other contacts.

- Assemble a job-hunting file, and keep it in your portfolio. Clip jobs that interest you. Gather articles about networking and other ways of getting job leads. Organize the materials for easy reference when you're ready to look for a job.

Career Exploration: Family and Consumer Services

Gather information about a career in the family and consumer services career cluster.

- Use library resources and the Internet to find information. If possible, interview someone to find out more about the career. Then make a brochure. Include information about the kinds of work, the working conditions, and training and education required. Also include skills needed to do the job.
- Explain the outlook for the career.
- Share your brochure with your classmates.

Applying for a Job

What You'll Learn...

- You will find out what is involved in applying for a job.

- You will discover ways to present yourself to an employer.

- You will learn what to do before, during, and after an interview.

- **CAREER CLUSTER** You will explore careers in the **environment.**

LESSON 7-1
Presenting Yourself

LESSON 7-2
Putting Your
Best Foot Forward

LESSON PLAN. See the *Teacher's Manual* for the Chapter 7 lesson plans.

Friends & Family Activity

TRY THIS!

Give three adult friends and family members a questionnaire about their first job. Include questions such as these:

- What was your first job?
- How did you find out about it?
- How did you persuade someone to hire you?
- What advice do you have for someone applying for a job?

APPLY: Compare and contrast your findings with those of your classmates. What have you learned about applying for a job?

Presenting Yourself

Discover...

- how to organize information about yourself in a résumé.
- what a cover letter is and why it is important.
- tips for filling out job applications.

Why Learn How to Present Yourself to an Employer?

You may be thinking about a part-time or volunteer job now. One day, you'll apply for a full-time job. Whether or not you get the job may depend on how you present yourself.

Key Terms...

- résumé
- format
- cover letter
- job application
- references

Life is full of wonderful surprises. On your birthday you open a small present with only a note inside. It tells you to look outdoors. You do, and there's the new bike you wanted. You finally read that book with the boring cover. To your surprise, it turns out to be your all-time favorite. You take time to get to know someone who seems different from you. You're surprised later to find how much you have in common.

Many of life's surprises are pleasant. Even so, people don't always welcome surprises. Employers, as a rule, aren't looking for surprises. They don't have time. In the world of work, first impressions count.

➤ First impressions can be powerful. **What were your first impressions of some of your close friends?** Of middle school? What do you think of both now?

Putting a Résumé Together

Employers want to find the best person to fill a job. Whether it is a part-time job after school or a full-time job, most job openings attract many applicants. Employers have to pick and choose among them. They don't have time to get to know people well. They can't take time to talk to everyone. They look for people who stand out from the crowd. They choose people who make a good impression on them in some way.

How can you make a good impression? It all comes down to how you present yourself.

Wanted: Information about You

By the time you apply for a job, you've gathered some information about the employer or business. Gathering information about yourself is also an important part of your job search. Information you give employers will help them get to know you. It will help them decide if you're the right person for a job.

You've already taken some steps to gather information about yourself. You've done some thinking about your interests. You've also identified some of your skills and aptitudes. Those are just some of the things you'll want to include in a personal summary for an employer.

Two Different Formats

In the work world, a summary of personal information is known as a résumé. A résumé describes your education, skills, work experience, activities, and interests.

There are two basic kinds of résumés—a chronological résumé and a skills résumé. A chronological résumé presents information in order of time—reverse time order, to be exact. For an example of a chronological résumé, look at *Figure 7-1* on page 128. Kira Franklin has listed her work experience in reverse time order. Her current job appears first, then the job before that, and so on.

CAPTION ANSWER. Answers will vary, but students may comment that their first impressions were not accurate or may have been exaggerated. Students may observe that they have a completely different view of both their friends and school now.

MOTIVATING STUDENTS. Ask students to raise their hands if they have ever applied for a job. Ask volunteers to discuss their experiences.

DISCUSSION STARTER. Ask students, "What makes applying for a job interesting? stressful? What could you do to make it easier?"

TEACHING ACTIVITY. If you have copies of résumés prepared by previous students, let the class read and discuss them.

Chronological Résumé

1 Name and Address. Give your name, full address, and telephone number (with area code) at the top of your résumé.

2 Job Objective. State the job you are applying for. You can change your job objective for different jobs. Also describe your career goal if you have one.

3 Work Experience. List your work experience, beginning with your most recent job. Include volunteer work if it relates to the job you're applying for.

4 Education. List the schools you have attended or are currently attending. Also include any subjects or programs you specialized in.

5 Honors and Activities. List any honors or awards you have received. Name activities you have participated in that relate to the job you want.

6 Special Skills and Abilities. Identify any business or other skills and abilities you have gained in school, on a job, or in other situations.

Kira Franklin
87 Southwest Eighth Avenue
Morgantown, OR 93072
(219) 760-3801

JOB OBJECTIVE: Seeking a challenging full-time summer position working with children and ecology. Goal is a career in environmental education.

EXPERIENCE:

August 1999	**Camp Counselor, WISTEC Science Camp, McKenzie River, Oregon** Responsible for twelve campers ages 8 to 10 during three one-week sessions. Helped plan science activities and outdoor projects having to do with the environment and ecology issues.
June-July 1999	**Science Club Teaching Assistant, WISTEC Science Center, Morgantown, Oregon** Organized and taught weekly science activity classes for children ages 5 to 7.
Summer 1998	**Experiment Tester, Franklin Publishing Group, Eugene, Oregon** Tested science experiments for students ages 8 to 11.
Summer 1997	**Volunteer, Parks Conservation Project, Eugene, Oregon** Helped care for recreation walkways throughout the city by picking up litter, pruning trees and shrubs, and installing benches. Led group of young volunteer workers.
1997-1999	**Flute instructor to beginning and intermediate students.**

EDUCATION: Currently a senior, Morgantown High School, Morgantown, Oregon

HONORS AND ACTIVITIES: Dean's Honor List, Biology Award, student delegate to Morgantown's "Science in the City Project," Most Valuable Musician Award 1999, Food Rescue volunteer

SPECIAL SKILLS AND ABILITIES: Experience with Macintosh and DOS computers, Microsoft Word, Windows 95, Internet searches. Creative thinker. Like to solve problems. Work well with people and as member of a team.

▲ FIGURE 7-1

There are different formats for organizing information in a résumé. Most résumés, however, include the same basic information. Headings and spacing are used to show major categories of information. **How do the headings in the chronological résumé compare with those in the skills résumé?**

CAPTION ANSWER.
Students should note similarities and differences between the headings used in the chronological résumé and those used in the skills résumé.

The skills résumé in *Figure 7-2* below, shows the same information about Kira in a different format, or arrangement. A skills résumé highlights skills and accomplishments. Each heading identifies a skill or strength. After each heading is a description of the skill and the experience related to it.

Skills Résumé

Kira Franklin
87 Southwest Eighth Avenue
Morgantown, OR 93072
(219) 760-3801

JOB OBJECTIVE:
Seeking a challenging full-time summer position working with children and ecology. Goal is a career in environmental education.

SKILLS AND ABILITIES:

Science Work with Children:
Worked with children as a teacher aide and camp counselor in two WISTEC summer science programs in the summer of 1999. Responsible for creating and carrying out science projects and outdoor ecology experiences for children ages 5 to 10 in classroom and camp environments. Also taught flute lessons, which at times involved scientific explanations of breathing!

Computer Skills:
Experience with Macintosh and DOS computers, Microsoft Word, Windows 95. Used knowledge of computers and the Internet to gather information for science experiments in the summer of 1998.

Teamwork:
All my experience has involved working with other people to create and carry out activities, projects, and programs. I am an enthusiastic team player. On the Parks Conservation Project in 1997, I was leader of a group of young volunteers.

Responsible Worker:
I take the quality of my work very seriously. I can be counted on to do more than is required and to meet all deadlines. I particularly like the challenge of organizing complex tasks!

EDUCATION:
Currently a senior, Morgantown High School, Morgantown, Oregon

HONORS AND ACTIVITIES:
Dean's Honor List, Biology award, student delegate to Morgantown's "Science in the City Project," Most Valuable Musician Award 1999, Food Rescue volunteer

◀ **FIGURE 7-2**
A skills résumé lets you highlight your areas of strength. What skills has Kira Franklin listed? Under what heading can you find information about Kira's work experience?

CAPTION ANSWER. Science work with children, computer skills, teamwork, responsible worker; *Skills and Abilities*

How to Fill Out an Application

Q: When I'm filling out a job application, should I use a pencil or pen?

A: Always use a pen because pencil can smudge and may be hard to read. Afraid of making mistakes? Write your answers out in pencil first and then go over it with a pen. (Don't forget to wait for the ink to dry before you erase the pencil marks!)

If you have the kind of handwriting that people complain about, take the application home and type in the answers.

CRITICAL THINKING. Ask students why a résumé should be only one page. Also ask what a résumé with misspellings or improper grammar tells a prospective employer about the applicant.

RESEARCH. Have students research résumés and cover letters and bring in a sample copy of each to class.

Which Format Is Better?

The kind of résumé you choose may depend on the job you're looking for. It can also depend on what you want to emphasize: work experience or skills. People who've had a series of jobs in one career field often use a chronological résumé. Time order is an excellent way to show growth from job to job.

A skills résumé is often a good choice for first-timers in the job market. That's because it focuses on strengths instead of work experience.

EXPLORE Activity

Take steps now to gather information for a skills résumé. Identify your strengths. Think of skills you've learned at home, at school, or over the summer. Think of skills you've used in a hobby, a project, a class, or on a team. List these skills and how you used them. Add to your list as you develop new skills. When you're ready to create a skills résumé, you can refer to your list of skills.

Whatever format you finally use, don't be shy. Make yourself look good! That's the first rule in putting together a résumé. Remember, your résumé is a personal introduction. It may be the first picture an employer has of you. It should shine a positive light on your experience, skills, and interests.

Don't Forget the Details!

Once you've put your résumé together, follow these basic tips. They'll add to the good impression you want to make.
- Keep your résumé short. One page is usually plenty.
- Make sure your résumé is neat and easy to read.
- Check for errors. Have you made mistakes while typing? Is everything spelled correctly? Have you used proper grammar?

Electronic Résumés

If you can, create your résumé on a computer. That way, keeping information up-to-date will be easy. As you develop new interests and skills, you can quickly add them to your résumé. You can keep track of your work experience as it grows. You'll also be able to change your job objective quickly, for different jobs. Switching formats will be quick and easy, too.

There are many other good reasons to use a computer to create a résumé. Most large businesses today scan into their computers résumés they receive. They store the résumés in a database. When there's a job opening, it's easy for them to do a search. They use keywords describing skills or work experience. Typical keywords include *creative thinker, computer skills,* and *team worker.* The keywords quickly locate people who might be right for a job.

Smart job seekers today know it's important to create a résumé that's computer-friendly. They keep it simple. They usually use black ink on white paper. They avoid boldface, italic, and other fancy type. They type headings in capital letters. They indent or use bullets for items under headings. Most important, they include keywords so that a computer search will find their résumé.

These are also good tips for any kind of on-line résumé. One day, you may send your résumé by E-mail. You may even post it on a jobs site on the Internet or on a personal Web page. You'll want your résumé to look its best on whatever computer screen it appears.

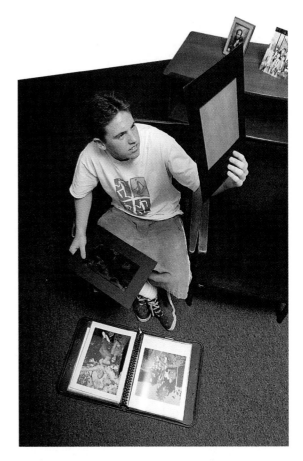

▲ Depending on the job, an employer may also be interested in examples of your work. You might prepare a portfolio, or collection of work samples. You might also share a recording or videotape. **For what kinds of jobs might an employer expect each?**

CAPTION ANSWER. Answers will vary but may include the following: portfolio—graphic artist, painter, photographer; recording—songwriter, musician, singer, conductor; videotape—actor, dancer.

Covering Yourself

No résumé should go anywhere without a cover letter. A cover letter is a one-page letter telling who you are and why you're sending a résumé. *Figure 7-3* on page 132 shows a sample cover letter.

A cover letter is another opportunity to make a good impression on an employer. Let your personality come

Cover Letter

❶ Opening. Introduce yourself. State the job you are applying for and how you found out about it.

❷ Body. Sell yourself. Describe the skills and experience you have that make you right for the job. Mention that you are sending a résumé. Include information that is not in your résumé.

Kira Franklin
87 Southwest Eighth Avenue
Morgantown, OR 93072
(219) 760-3801

April 3, 2000

Dr. Derek McDermott
Director
Oregon State Department of Science Education
Salem, OR 97310

Dear Dr. McDermott:

Ms. Gina Alvarez, my biology teacher at Morgantown High School, suggested that I contact you about a full-time summer intern position in your Summer Science Institute program for children. Please consider me as an applicant for an intern position.

As my résumé shows, I have a great deal of science experience. I learned a lot working with WISTEC the last two summers. I also discovered how much I like working with children. It was fun coming up with interesting science activities for all of us to do together!

With my science skills and experience working with children, I think I would have a lot to offer to the Summer Science Institute. I am very interested in pursuing a career in environmental education.

I would be happy to meet with you for an interview at your convenience. My phone number is (219) 760-3801. Thank you for your consideration. I look forward to meeting with you.

Sincerely

Kira Franklin
Kira Franklin

❸ Closing. Describe how you plan to follow up. Ask for an interview. Include your phone number so the employer can contact you. Thank the person you are writing to for his or her time and interest.

▲ FIGURE 7-3

Every good cover letter has three parts. Each part has a specific purpose. **What part of the letter is the best place to let your personality come through?**

through. You want to catch the interest of the person you are writing to. A cover letter is a good place to highlight interesting details about yourself that do not appear in your résumé. What you say in a cover letter will persuade the reader to turn to your résumé. It may even get you the job.

Tackling Job Applications

EXTENDING THE LESSON. Have students gather two job references that include name, phone number, and relationship to student. They must also get permission to use that person's name.

Some employers consider a cover letter with résumé a letter of application. Others do not. These businesses may have you fill out a job application. A job application is a form that asks questions about your skills, work experience, education, and interests.

Here are some helpful hints for filling out job applications:

- Don't begin writing until you've read the entire application.
- Follow directions carefully.
- Be neat.
- Answer all questions truthfully. If a question doesn't apply to you, write *NA* for *Not Applicable.* This will show that you haven't missed part of the application.
- Check your work when finished.

When you're asked to complete a job application, ask to take it home. It will be easier to concentrate. You'll have the information you need at your fingertips. You'll also be able to practice first in pencil or on a copy of the application. If you can't take a job application home, be sure to have your personal facts with you.

You may also have to supply references on a job application. References are people who will recommend you to an employer. Choose references carefully. Ask people who know you well and who think highly of you to be your references. Teachers, neighbors, and anyone you've worked for make good references. Always ask permission to use someone as a reference. You usually have to supply names, addresses, and phone numbers for all your references.

A job application deserves just as much attention as a résumé and a cover letter. Follow directions. Be truthful, neat, and complete. Just as important, don't forget to let "who you are" shine through.

LESSON REVIEW AND ACTIVITIES. See the *Teacher's Manual* for answers.

Vocabulary Review

Make a poster about presenting yourself to an employer. The poster should feature the key terms below. Use both captions and images to explain the terms. Display your poster in the classroom.

résumé   job application
format   references
cover letter

Check Your Understanding

Choose the correct answer for each item below. Write your answers on a separate sheet of paper.

1. Two types of résumés include chronological résumés and
   _____.

   a. name résumés
   b. skills résumés
   c. job résumés

2. A form that asks questions about your skills, work experience, education, and interests is a _____.

   a. résumé
   b. cover letter
   c. job application

Critical Thinking

On a separate sheet of paper, answer the following questions:

1. What skills and abilities would you include in a chronological résumé? Why?
2. Why do you think you should always send a cover letter with a résumé when applying for a job?
3. What can an employer learn about someone from the look of his or her job application?

Connecting to the Workplace

Creating a Résumé

- Put together your own skills résumé. Start with your job objective.
- Think of a part-time or volunteer job you'd like to have. Then summarize your personal information for that job.
- Describe your strengths under the heading *Skills and Abilities*. Also include information under the headings *Education* and *Activities and Awards*.
- Ask a teacher or someone you know in business to give you feedback.

Teamwork

What to Do
- Form a group with some of your classmates.
- Together, make a guide for young teens that tells how to apply for a job.
- Explain how to put together a résumé.
- Describe how to write a cover letter.
- Give instructions for filling out job applications. Gear all the information and any examples to part-time or volunteer work.
- Compare your guide with those of other groups.

Putting Your Best Foot Forward

What happens next? What you want when you send a résumé or complete an application is an interview. An **interview** is a formal meeting about a possible job between a job seeker and an employer. It is the employer's chance to meet you and decide if you're right for the job. It is your chance to convince an employer that you *are* the right person for the job.

Getting Ready for an Interview

What you do *before* an interview is as important as what you do *during* the interview. Would it surprise you to know that you're already preparing for your first job interview? Have you ever tried out for a team, a play, or the school orchestra

Discover...
- how to prepare for an interview.
- what happens in an interview.
- how to follow up after an interview.

Why Become Familiar with the Interview Process?

Interviews are an important part of applying for a job. The more practice you get, the more confident you'll be in future interviews.

> ### Key Terms...
> - interview
> - body language

CAPTION ANSWER. Speaking skills, listening skills, and courteousness are everyday skills you can bring to an interview.

◀ Many everyday situations will help prepare you for a job interview. What kinds of everyday skills can you bring to an interview?

or band? Have you ever run for school office? In each case, you had to show that you were ready and able to do the job.

Maybe you've had a talk with adult family members about something you really wanted. Perhaps you tried to persuade them to give you more responsibility or independence. Maybe you stopped by next door to meet your new neighbors. While talking, you found out they sometimes need someone to walk their dog. You spent some more time talking and patting the dog. Before you knew it, you were hired.

These situations help build your confidence. They also involve skills that you'll use one day in a job interview.

Know Before You Go

When you finally get an interview, you've got some work to do. Review your personal information. Know yourself inside and out. Be prepared to answer questions about your interests, skills, work experience, education, and career goals. An interview is your best opportunity to sell yourself. If you're prepared, you can use it to full advantage.

Also get to know the business or organization that has the job opening. Chapter 6 tells where to look for information and what information to look for. What you know about a possible employer will help you answer most questions you're asked. You'll also be prepared to ask intelligent questions.

Know the job you want. If you saw the job in an ad, study the ad carefully. If you got the job lead by networking, talk to your contact. Find out as much as you can about the job before the interview.

▼ Rehearsing before an interview will help you be more relaxed. What should you practice?

Practice Makes a Difference

You can't know exactly how an interview will go. You can imagine what it might be like, though, and you can practice. The more practice you have, the more comfortable you'll feel during a real interview.

One way to practice is to ask a friend or family member to role-play an interview with you. Practice right now to prepare for that part-time or volunteer job. Role-playing is creative and fun. It can make you think hard about different situations.

CRITICAL THINKING. Ask students how excessive worrying might actually contribute to interview problems.

TEACHING ACTIVITY. Encourage students to do practice interviews, first with each other and then with experienced adults—parents, teachers, parents of friends, counselors.

EXPLORE Activity

Give your partner a copy of your résumé and a description of the job you have in mind. Have your partner ask you typical questions. Practice answering them.

Tape-record or videotape the interview if you can. Then listen to yourself. Look at yourself. Are you speaking clearly? Do you sound confident? Are you sitting up straight? Do you look interested and relaxed? Do you look directly at the interviewer? Keep practicing until you get it right.

There are other things you can do to practice, in addition to role-playing. Make a list of questions you might be asked. Prepare answers to them. Questions such as "Why are you the best person for this job?" can be challenging to answer on the spot. They will be easier to answer if you've thought about them ahead of time. Also make a list of questions you want to ask about the job.

Dress the Part

Last but not least, give some thought to what you are going to wear. Remember, first impressions count. The first thing an employer will notice when you meet is your appearance.

Sometimes it's hard to know what to wear to a particular event. When there's a dance or a party, you ask your friends

what they're planning to wear. You want to fit in with everyone else. That's a good rule to follow when dressing for an interview. Find out what others in the same job would wear.

Dress a bit better than you would on an actual day on the job. Make sure you're neat, clean, and well groomed from head to toe. Let your skills and personality stand out, not your clothes, jewelry, perfume, or makeup.

The Interview Itself

In many ways an interview is no different from a big test or a big game. If you've put effort into preparing, it's likely to go well for you. Knowing you've done all you can to get ready is reassuring. You'll feel confident and relaxed.

A Winning Attitude

The biggest boost you can have going into an interview is a positive attitude. If you feel positive, you'll have just the attitude employers are looking for. When you have a positive attitude, you feel good about yourself. You're also excited about the job. According to Bev Curtis of Environment First in Portland, Maine,

> **Attitude is everything.**

Environment First educates the public about protecting the environment. Bev runs its volunteer program. "What I'm looking for," Bev explains, "is more than interest in the environment. I'm looking for energetic people. We need people whose enthusiasm will rub off on others. If the person I interview is enthusiastic, the job is theirs."

So go ahead. Communicate your positive attitude to an employer! You'll show you can be counted on to do your best. Start building a positive attitude right now. How would a positive attitude change how you feel about yourself? How would it change how you feel about what you can do in school and other activities?

A Good Conversation

There are many ways to communicate a positive attitude during an interview. An employer will listen carefully to how you answer questions. Your answers will show whether you are hardworking, dependable, and skilled. They'll also show how you feel about the job and yourself.

Be ready to answer questions like the following:
- What can you tell me about yourself?
- What are your greatest strengths? What are your greatest weaknesses?
- Do you prefer to work with others or on your own?
- Why do you want this job?
- What are your career goals?

Your answers should be honest and specific. What's your dream job? How might you answer each of these questions for that job?

A good interview is like a good conversation. Each person should have a chance to speak and ask questions. Each should listen carefully and pay attention to the other. You'll have a turn to ask questions. The questions you ask should focus on

Stress

Do you ever feel as if you have too much to do? Does this feeling make you tense and maybe keep you awake at night? If you have experienced this feeling, you know what stress is.

Coping with stress is an important part of having a good attitude. Remember to rest, exercise, and eat well. Break large tasks into smaller parts and find someone to help you. Discussing your feelings with someone you trust can also do wonders to lessen stress.

Apply Your Skills!

Role-play with a partner these "stressful" situations.
- You just got a big part in the play. You have two weeks to learn your lines.
- You are organizing a school dance. You have to organize the music, decorations, food, and invitations.
- You have three important tests in one week of school.

CRITICAL THINKING. Ask students what a smile and a firm handshake tells an employer about a prospective employee.

the business and job, not yourself. They should show your enthusiasm and interest.

Watch Your Body Language

What you do and how you act in an interview can also say a lot. In fact, sometimes your actions can speak louder than your words.

Body language can communicate many things. **Body language** is the gestures, posture, and eye contact you use to express yourself. For better or worse, body language plays an important part in an interview. *Figure 7-4* below shows some of the positive messages you can send with body language. In what everyday situations might you practice positive body language?

After You Say Good-Bye

At the end of the interview, you may be offered the job on the spot. More often than not, however, you'll have to wait.

> ### FIGURE 7-4

BODY LANGUAGE

Make sure your body language sends the right message at an interview. Your gestures, posture, and eye contact should say you're a positive, confident person.

A

Introduce Yourself

Make eye contact right away. Be sure to smile as you introduce yourself to the interviewer. Extend your hand, and shake hands firmly. Try practicing your handshake with others before the interview. Your handshake shouldn't be limp or crushing.

You won't have time just to sit by the telephone, though. There are some important things you should do following an interview.

B

Maintain Good Posture

Sit down when the interviewer invites you to. Then check your posture. Don't slouch. Sit up straight, leaning forward slightly in your chair. Look directly at the interviewer. Then the interviewer will know you're interested in what he or she has to say. Nod your head occasionally as you listen to show you're paying attention.

C

Think About Body Language

Think about your hands whether you're listening or speaking. Don't clench your fists or bite your nails. Don't play with your hair or clothing. These are all signs that you're nervous or unsure of yourself. When speaking, use your hands in a relaxed, confident way.

D

Leave a Positive Impression

Be friendly as the interview comes to an end. Stand up straight. Shake the interviewer's hand. Smile and make eye contact as you do.

Take Time to Say Thanks

First, write a short thank-you letter to the person who interviewed you. Don't put this off. A letter of thanks should go out no later than the day after the interview. The interview will still be fresh in your mind. You will also be fresh in the mind of the employer.

In your letter, thank the interviewer for his or her time. Then express your enthusiasm for the job. Stress the skills and other experience you have that match the job. Say how much you'd like to work for the company.

Mention something you discussed in the interview. If you forgot to tell the interviewer something about yourself, include it in your letter. Ask questions if you still have some.

Write a letter of thanks no matter how the interview went. The interviewer is a new contact. He or she may give you a referral if you ask. You may even be considered for a different job if you follow up.

3827 Elmdale Drive
Sumner, Pennsylvania 19372

April 21, 1999

Mr. Emilio Alvarez
Editorial Director
Jarod Publishing Company
163 Pelton Avenue
Sumner, Pennsylvania 19372

Dear Mr. Alvarez:

Thank you for meeting with me yesterday to talk about a summer internship at Jarod Publishing.

The internship sounds interesting and challenging. It would also make good use of the skills I have developed working on my school newspaper. As noted in my résumé, I have served as a reporter and editor for the school paper for the past two years.

I hope that you will consider me for an internship this summer. As I mentioned to you yesterday, I am very interested in a career in communications. I know that I could learn a great deal at Jarod Publishing. With my experience on the school newspaper, I think I could contribute a great deal, too.

Thank you again for taking the time to meet with me. I look forward to hearing from you.

Sincerely,

Amy Bloomfield
Amy Bloomfield

▲ Everyone likes to be thanked. Write a thank-you letter right after your interview. What might you mention about the interview in your letter?

CAREER OPPORTUNITIES

Environment
These days you hear politicians, movie stars, and even ordinary people talking about saving the environment; but who's doing the work? It could be you. Take a look at this job.

Critical Thinking
Think of a list of problems that an environmental specialist might have to fix at a factory?

CLASSIFIED

THURSDAY, SEP

Senior Environmental Specialist

Developer of electronic products is seeking a specialist to:
• Ensure that the employees and machines in our factory conform to environmental laws.
• Look into environmental problems and make corrections.
Requirements: degree in environmental, chemical, or mechanical engineering, five years' experience, and knowledge of the EPA and environmental laws.

The Global Workplace

Shoe Customs Vary from Country to Country

Taking shoes off in the United States can be rude, not to mention unpleasant. But in Buddhist temples, shoes are always taken off as a sign of respect. The same is true in Muslim mosques. In Japanese and Indonesian homes, shoes are usually left by the door. The entire visit will take place in bare feet. What to do when in doubt? See what the host does and follow his or her lead.

Exploration Activity!

Research religion and signs of respect in Asia. What different religions are found in China, Japan, Indonesia, Korea, and Vietnam?

Take Stock

You should also make some notes for yourself while the interview is still fresh in your mind. Write a summary of the interview. What went well? What could you improve? Note questions that you had trouble answering. Jot down anything you'd do differently next time.

Look at every interview as a learning experience. That includes interviews you may have for part-time or volunteer work. Each interview will go more smoothly than the last. You'll know better what to expect. You'll also know better how to present yourself as the best person for the job.

Take It in Stride

You may get the job. You may not. If you don't, don't give up. Rejection is part of life and part of the learning process.

If you don't get the job, contact the employer and ask why, if it's convenient. Use that information to prepare for your next application and interview.

Above all, don't put yourself down. The right job is out there waiting for you. You just have to keep moving toward your goal.

LESSON REVIEW AND ACTIVITIES. See the *Teacher's Manual* for answers.

Vocabulary Review

In a paragraph of 200 words or less, explain the part body language plays in an interview.

interview

body language

Check Your Understanding

On a separate sheet of paper, tell whether each statement is true or false. Rewrite any false statements to make them true.

1. What you do *before* an interview is not as important as what you do *during* the interview.

2. At an interview, attitude and body language count as much as what you say.

3. It is important to follow up after an interview.

Critical Thinking

On a separate sheet of paper, answer the following questions.

1. What would you wear to an interview for a job in an office? For a baby-sitting job? For a volunteer job at a home for senior citizens? For a job delivering newspapers?

2. Imagine that you have an interview for a baby-sitting job. What questions should you be prepared to answer?

3. What questions would you ask an employer at a job interview?

4. What would you do if you did not hear from an employer after an interview?

Connecting to the Workplace

Interview Practice

- Put yourself in the place of an employer.
- Interview an adult you know for the job he or she currently holds.
- Ask typical questions like those listed in the lesson.
- Listen carefully to the person's answers. Also allow time for him or her to ask questions.
- Afterward, discuss the questions and answers and other aspects of the interview.
- Make notes about what this activity taught you about interviewing.

Community Involvement

What to Do

- Select a volunteer job in your community.
- Call to set up an informational interview to find out more about it.
- Use what you have learned in this lesson to prepare for, carry out, and follow up the interview.
- Describe to the class how the interview went.
- Include several ideas about what you would do differently in a future interview.

Investigating Career Clusters

Environment

What Is the Environment Cluster?

Occupations in the environment cluster involve the protection of natural resources and guarding the best interests of the population. Jobs center around pollution prevention and control, disease prevention, environmental planning, and resource control.

Skills Needed

Science skills, communication skills, drawing skills, math skills, physical strength, and knowledge of the environment

THE FACTS	Types of Careers in This Cluster	Work Description	Career Outlook	Education
	Environmental technician	Use principles of science and math to solve problems in the environment	Average	Associate's
	Urban planner	Plan to provide for growth and revitalization of communities	Faster than average	Master's
	Landscape architect	Design residential areas, public parks, college campuses, and shopping centers to be functional, beautiful, and in keeping with the environment	Average	Bachelor's
	Conservation scientist	Manage, improve, and protect rangelands for livestock	Average	Bachelor's
	Zoologist	Study animals—how they grow and where they live	Fast growing	Master's

Research Activity   Investigate environmental careers in your community. Make a list of five of these occupations, and research the job duties and working conditions. Pick one that interests you and write one page about that job. Include job duties, working conditions, employment outlook and the reason it interests you.

Chapter 7 Review

◉ Chapter Highlights

- Résumés, cover letters, and job applications are ways of applying for a job. They are also opportunities for making a good impression on an employer.
- Preparing well helps an interview go well. Know yourself, the business or organization, and the job you're applying for. Practice. Dress appropriately.

◉ Recalling Key Concepts

Using complete sentences, answer these questions on a separate sheet of paper.

1. How do you decide what résumé format to use?
2. What are the three main parts of a cover letter? What is the purpose of each?
3. Why do you need to line up references before filling out a job application?
4. What does your attitude tell an employer?
5. Why should you make notes about an interview afterward?

◉ Thinking Critically

Using complete sentences, answer these questions on a separate sheet of paper.

1. What skills that might be included in a résumé have you learned in school?
2. Whom besides teachers, neighbors, and people you've worked for might you ask to be a reference?
3. Why shouldn't you ask questions that focus on yourself in an interview?
4. What might an interviewer think if you do not make eye contact?

Building Skills

1. Personal Qualities— Integrity/Honesty

Imagine that your friend is putting together a résumé. She has never held a job before. She is thinking about making up some work experience to include on her résumé. What would you advise her to do?

2. Technology—Applies Technology to the Task

With a partner, create a scannable résumé. Follow the tips for computer-friendly résumés. Use either the chronological or the skills format. Include keywords. When the résumé is complete, print it and scan the copy into a computer. Discuss how it looks on the computer screen. What needs to be changed or corrected?

Applying Academic Skills

1. Mathematics

Put your work experience in time order for a chronological résumé. Arrange the following dates in correct reverse time order: June–August 1997, June–August 1999, December 1998–January 1999, July–September 1998, September 1999–present, January–June 1998, October–December 1997.

2. Social Studies

Create a time line of personal growth. Plot events that have contributed to your career skills or work experience. Include classes, assignments, activities, hobbies, and projects. Also include part-time, weekend, volunteer, and summer jobs. Write the date for each event. Share the time line with your family and classmates.

Discovery Portfolio

Preparing for the Interview

- File information about yourself in a special section of your portfolio.
- Keep a record of your interests, talents, skills, and achievements in the file.
- Collect information about part-time or volunteer jobs you've had.
- Ask people who know you well to write a general letter of recommendation for you. Keep the originals of their letters in your portfolio.

Career Exploration: Environment

Research a career from the environment career cluster.
- Use the library and search the Internet to find information.
- If possible, also gather information by interviewing someone with the career.
- Make a pamphlet about the career.

- Include information about the kinds of work, the working conditions, and training and education required. Also include skills needed to do the job.
- Explain the job outlook.
- Include other information that is interesting.
- Share your pamphlet with the class.

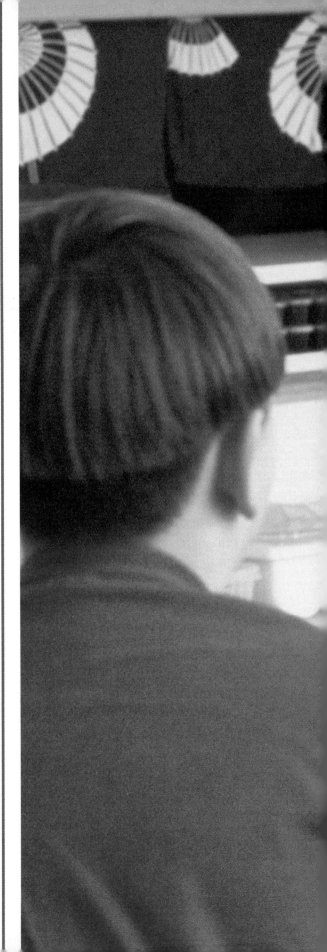

Chapter 8

On the Job

What You'll Learn...

- You will find out more about life in the workplace.

- You will learn what to expect on your first day at a new job.

- You will discover what an employer will expect of you.

- **CAREER CLUSTER** You will explore careers in the *fine arts and humanities.*

LESSON 8-1
What You Can Expect

LESSON 8-2
What an Employer
Expects of You

LESSON PLAN. See the *Teacher's Manual* for the Chapter 8 lesson plans.

Friends & Family Activity

TRY THIS!

Think of a time when you did something new. Maybe you went to a new school or went camping for the first time. Maybe you went to your first dance, traveled on your own, or stayed home alone. Recall how you felt at the time. List five words that describe your feelings. Then ask two friends to do the same thing.

APPLY: Compare your lists. What feelings did you share? Which feelings might you also have on the first day at a new job?

What You Can Expect

Discover...
- how to handle your first day at a job.
- ways you may be paid and benefits you may receive.
- how you can expect to be treated at work.

Why Learn About What to Expect on the Job?

What you learn about the workplace will help you prepare for your first full-time job.

Key Terms...
- employee
- orientation
- coworkers
- supervisor
- wages
- entry-level
- overtime
- salary
- commission
- benefits
- minimum wage
- discriminate
- disability

Where do you imagine yourself working someday? Do you picture yourself indoors or outdoors? Are you in an office building or a home office? Perhaps you work in a studio, a theater, or a lab. Maybe your work involves a lot of traveling. What you do, where you do it—your options are as big as your imagination.

You may wonder, though, what being in the workplace will really be like. What can you expect as an employee, someone who works for a person or business for pay?

Your First Day on the Job

Remember that first day in a new class? How about the day you moved to a new home or neighborhood? As with anything new, you probably had mixed feelings. You may have felt excited, unsure, and

▶ When you go to work at a company, you become part of a team. Why is it important to get to know people at work?

nervous at the same time. You may have been happy to be there one moment and scared or sad the next moment.

On your first day at a job, you'll have many of the same feelings. Beginning a new job is an adventure like other new experiences. It can be stressful—but you can enjoy it—especially if you're prepared.

Getting Ready

There are several things you can do to make sure you have a good first day. Start by calling your employer a day or two before you begin work. Ask when you should arrive and where you should go first. If you're uncertain about how to dress, ask what you should wear. Find out if you need to bring any tools, supplies, or special equipment. Also ask what personal information you may need to supply the first day.

Then get everything together. Decide what you're going to wear. Gather the personal information you need. Also take some time to figure out how long it will take to get ready and get to work. On the big day, allow plenty of time so you won't have to hurry.

What's Waiting for You

While you're preparing to report to work, your employer will also be preparing—for you. Many companies provide orientation for new employees. An **orientation** introduces you to a company. It explains the company's policies and procedures, or ways of doing things. As part of an orientation, you often get a tour of your new work environment. You also meet many of your **coworkers**, the people you will work with.

You may find orientation on the first day of work familiar. Many middle schools and high schools hold orientation days for entering students. Orientations are also sometimes held for special activities and for volunteer jobs.

You'll notice some similarities, but orientations will differ from one place of work to the next. At a large company, you may receive an employee handbook. You'll find answers to many of your questions there. Throughout the day you may have a chance to hear many people talk about the company. At a smaller company, your supervisor may meet with you and

CAREER Q&A

How to Approach Starting a Job

Q: What are the most important things to remember when starting my first job?

A: Show up to work on time and do what you are assigned. When your boss plans out the day, he or she plans on your being there and doing your job. If you're late, or just don't show up, then you ruin his or her workday. How do you feel about someone who ruins your day? Well, your boss is human, too!

CAPTION ANSWER. Workers may be able to teach each other about the job and about how things are done at the company.

MOTIVATING STUDENTS. Ask students to make short lists of the benefits and problems they expect when they start working. Discuss their lists.

give you the information you need. Your **supervisor** is the person who checks and evaluates your work.

For a part-time job such as baby-sitting, house-sitting, or yardwork, orientation may be even more informal. The person who has hired you may quickly explain what you need to do. Then he or she may show you where to find keys, tools, and other supplies.

Whatever introduction you receive at a new job, pay close attention. Listen carefully, make notes, take materials home to read. All in all, it won't be unlike the first day in a new class.

▲ Don't be afraid to ask questions when you're new to a job. What should you do if you still do not understand something after receiving an answer?

Getting It Right

However warm a welcome you receive, the first day on the job may seem overwhelming. You'll meet new people. You'll receive all kinds of new information. You'll want to feel a part of things, but you just won't feel that you are—at least not for a while.

The secret is to be patient; take things one step at a time. For instance, don't worry if you forget people's names. You can't be expected to remember everyone's name at first. Just ask again. Repeat the name out loud as you're introduced. Then use the name again when talking to the person.

If you don't understand an employer's policies, or rules, ask your supervisor to explain them. If you're not sure what to do or how to do something, your supervisor is there to help.

Use your first few days on the job to get a clear idea of your job responsibilities. Ask your supervisor to explain exactly what is involved in your job. What should you do first? Next? Take your time. You won't be expected to learn everything the first few days. You won't do it all right the first time either.

In good time, you'll feel part of the group, and you'll know what you're doing. Just be friendly, and don't be afraid to ask questions. Remember, your coworkers started out the same way you did. They all had a first day, too.

How Will You Be Paid?

Everyone works for a reason. What do you think yours will be? As you read in Chapter 2, one of the main reasons most people work is to earn money.

Forms of Payment

Being paid for your hard work is a big part of having a job. The money you earn is called wages, salary, or commission.

Wages are a fixed amount of money paid for each hour worked. Many people with part-time jobs earn wages. If you baby-sit, for example, you probably receive wages. Say your wages for baby-sitting are $5 an hour. If you work four hours, you earn $20.

> Many workers who earn wages must "clock in" at a time clock. Why is it important for these workers to keep track of their work time?

You may also earn wages at your first full-time job. Wages are the form of payment for many **entry-level**, or lower-level, full-time jobs. At the end of each week, your employer will figure the number of hours you've worked. The number of hours will be multiplied by the hourly rate for your job.

EXPLORE Activity

Take this example. Jim Moore has a full-time job at a guitar shop in Ithaca, New York. He works 40 hours a week and is paid $6 an hour. How much does Jim earn each week?

Obviously, with hourly wages, the more hours you work, the more money you make. Many people who earn wages are also paid overtime. They receive **overtime** when they work more than 40 hours a week. Overtime pay is usually one and one-half times regular pay for each hour worked beyond the 40 scheduled hours.

EXPLORE Activity

One week a month, Jim Moore also works 4 hours on Saturdays for a total of 44 hours. That week he receives his regular pay for the first 40 hours. In addition, he earns $36 for 4 hours of overtime. How does his employer arrive at $36 for Jim's overtime pay? What are Jim's total earnings for the week?

Unlike wage earners, most people on salary do not get paid overtime. They receive the same amount of pay no matter how many hours they work. A salary is a fixed amount of money for a certain period of time. Salaries are usually figured by the year and paid each month or every two weeks.

EXPLORE Activity

If your salary is $12,000 a year, for instance, you would be paid $1,000 a month. How much would you be paid if you received your pay every two weeks?

Some workers are paid a commission. The earnings of people who make a commission are based on how much they sell. Tamara Peterson is a salesperson in a clothing store. She receives a 10 percent commission on the clothing she sells. In other words, for every $10 of clothing she sells, she earns $1. "The more I sell," Tamara explains, "the more I make."

There's no limit to what I can earn on commission. That inspires me to get out there and make one sale after another.

Kinds of Benefits

Whatever the job, whatever the form of payment, everyone looks forward to payday. The rewards for working aren't limited to a paycheck, however. Many jobs come with benefits. Benefits are the "extras" an employer provides in addition to pay.

Can you think of any benefits you have at your part-time job? If you do yardwork for the family next door, maybe you

RESEARCH. Have students research one of the following: the minimum wage, the Fair Labor Standards Act, or the Americans with Disabilities Act of 1990.

get to swim in their pool. If you work in a store, you might get a discount, or money off, what you buy there. As a baby-sitter, you may get to watch as much TV as you want after you've put the children to bed.

The kinds and value of benefits for full-time workers vary from employer to employer. *Figure 8-1* below shows benefits many employers offer.

Honest and Fair Treatment

A paycheck, benefits—what more could you ask for? The answer is "much more." You have rights in the workplace, too. Under the law, your employer must respect these rights.

You have a right to expect your employer to be honest with you. You should be paid the agreed amount regularly and on time. You must be paid at least the minimum wage—the lowest hourly wage an employer can legally pay for a worker's

> ### FIGURE 8-1

BENEFITS

For many people, benefits are an important reason for working. Which benefits do you think will be most important to you in your first full-time job?

A

Health Insurance
With health-care costs rising rapidly, many workers consider health insurance the most valu-able benefit. Health insurance helps pay doctor and hospital expenses. Today, workers often share the cost of health insur-ance with their employer.

B

Paid Time Off

A company or organization may name holidays on which workers do not have to work. At many businesses, workers receive pay for these holidays. Employees may also receive pay for time off for illness and vacation.

C

Retirement Plan

To help workers save for when they no longer work, some employers set up a retirement fund. Usually you must contribute at least a certain percentage of your pay to the fund. Your employer may match your contribution by depositing an equal amount in the fund.

D

Child Care

Some people with families are lucky enough to work for companies that offer child care. Such child care is usually low-cost and convenient. Workers drop off their children at a company-run day-care center when they arrive for work. They may visit their children during lunch or break. At the end of the workday, they stop in to pick up their children.

E

Education Assistance

Your employer may be willing to help you pay for further education. Some employers, for instance, cover all or part of college or technical school costs if you are working for a degree. Others cover the cost of classes or workshops that will help you do your job better.

services. You should receive all the benefits that were promised when you got the job. If your work situation changes, you should be told as soon as possible.

You also have a right to be treated fairly by your employer. Under the law, your employer cannot **discriminate** against you. That is, you cannot be treated unfairly because of your race or age. Your gender—whether you are male or female—cannot be used as a reason for unfair treatment. You must be treated the same as others—no matter what your religious beliefs or nationality (where you were born). Your employer cannot treat you unfairly because of your physical appearance or disability. A **disability** is a condition such as a visual or hearing impairment or paralysis.

Many state and federal laws protect workers against unfair treatment. If you feel you have been treated unfairly, discuss it first with your supervisor. Try to resolve the problem with him or her. If the problem continues, you may need to talk to the person above your supervisor. If the company does not correct the problem, the next step is to file a complaint. To do that, you would contact the government agency that carries out the law.

The issue of honest and fair treatment may not seem important to you right now. It may not be an issue in your work for friends, family, or neighbors. It doesn't hurt, though, to know your rights. You'll know what you can expect. If you have a problem, now or in the future, you can do something about it.

Most employers do what they must under the law. Many do much more to create a positive working environment for employees. You have something to contribute to the working environment, too. Read on to find out what.

Vocabulary Review

Imagine that it is your job to write the employee handbook. The first two pages of the handbook tell what a new employee can expect on the job. Write those two pages, using each of the terms below.

employee
orientation
coworkers
supervisor
wages
entry-level
overtime

salary
commission
benefits
minimum wage
discriminate
disability

Check Your Understanding

1. To make the first day on the job easier, you can_____.
   a. bring a friend with you
   b. prepare for it by calling ahead
   c. show up a little late so everyone is there when you get there

2. Employees have a right to_____.
   a. honest and fair treatment
   b. determine the hours they work
   c. create job tasks

Critical Thinking

On a separate sheet of paper, answer the following questions.

1. Do you think orientation programs are helpful? Why or why not?
2. Why is it a good idea to ask questions when you're new to a job?
3. What kind of person might do well at a job that earns a commission?
4. What types of benefits would you expect to earn in a full-time sales job?
5. Why do you think laws have been passed to make sure employers do not discriminate against people?

Connecting to the Workplace

Beginning a New Job

- It's Tyrone's first day on the job as a recreation aide. At a short orientation, the head of recreation explains the responsibilities of a recreation aide. Then she asks if anyone has questions. Tyrone has several questions, but none of the other aides do. He doesn't want to look stupid, so he does not ask his questions.
- What problems might he have because he didn't ask questions?

Teamwork

What to Do
- Form a group with several classmates.
- Together, prepare an orientation program for a company. You may make up the company or choose a real company.
- Design an informative presentation. Use skits, talks, and written or audiovisual materials to welcome new employees to their new jobs.
- Hold the orientation for your classmates.

What an Employer Expects of You

Discover...

- qualities employers look for in employees.
- how to behave in the workplace.
- how your work is evaluated.

Do your teachers discuss their expectations of students at the beginning of the year? If so, listen carefully. You may pick up pointers that will help you be successful when you have a job. Many employers expect the same things of employees that teachers expect of students in the classroom.

Why Find Out What Employers Will Expect from You?

When you start working full-time, you'll want to fit in and do well. You can get ready now by developing certain qualities and learning right ways to behave.

Key Terms...

- cooperate
- initiative
- ethics
- performance reviews

What Employers Want

These days, employers have great expectations of their employees. It used to be that employers looked for workers with specific skills. As you know, though, the workplace is changing rapidly. Employers today

CAPTION ANSWER. Do it and do the best job possible without complaining, to show cooperation.

➤ You can show your willingness to cooperate by doing whatever task you're assigned. What should you do if the task is boring?

aren't just looking for people with skills to do a particular job. They want people who can do many things well. They also want people who fit in and adapt to the changing workplace.

What can you do now to be the kind of employee employers are looking for? You can strengthen your basic skills—reading, writing, mathematics, speaking, and listening. You'll learn more about how to do that in Chapter 10. You can work on your thinking skills—reasoning, making decisions, and solving problems. You can also develop the personal qualities that employers value most.

Working Well with Others

Employers prize employees who know how to cooperate. When you **cooperate**, you work with others on the job to reach a common goal.

You have many opportunities right now to learn how to cooperate with others. Here are just a few ways.

- Do tasks you don't like without complaining or trying to avoid them.
- Do your fair share of a job when working with others.
- Pitch in to help someone who has a tough job or has fallen behind.
- Volunteer to help others meet a deadline or reach a goal.

People who can cooperate with others are valued. They're needed in all kinds of jobs.

Following Directions

Think about it. How many times a day do you get directions for doing something? Almost every assignment at school comes with its own set of directions.

What is your strategy or approach to following directions? Do you stop everything you're doing and listen carefully? Do you take notes? Do you ask questions when you don't understand what you're supposed to do? These are all excellent ways to make sure you get the directions right.

On the job, you'll be asked to do many things. To complete each task, you must first follow directions. The ability to follow directions is a useful skill—at home, at school, and on the job.

The RIGHT Attitude!

I Think I Can…

You would probably choose teammates who have a positive attitude for new projects in school. Employers are the same. They want "can-do" people to work for them. Can-do people are usually able to come up with new ideas to complete a project. They work well in groups and ask for help when they need it.

Apply Your Skills!

Write a list of fresh ways to improve and finish a school or work project. Use at least one of these ideas to complete your project.

MOTIVATING STUDENTS. Have students brainstorm the qualities employers might look for in employees. Write their ideas on the board.

Doing What Needs to Be Done

Doing what you are told is important. Why stop there, though? Employers also value employees who show initiative. When you show **initiative**, you do what needs to be done without being told to do it.

Jolene Anderson showed initiative at her after-school job as a supermarket cashier. When she saw a customer accidentally drop a jar, she alerted the manager. Someone was able to clean up the broken glass and wet floor before anyone was hurt. "The manager said that I've got what it takes to be an assistant manager someday. What it takes is a lot of initiative," explains Jolene.

You've probably shown initiative on many occasions at home or at school, maybe even at a part-time job. Can you think of a time when you did something above and beyond what you were told to do? What was the result of your initiative? Did you get a special thank-you or a higher grade?

Taking on More Responsibility

Responsibility is the willingness to accept a task, carry it out, and be accountable for it. Employers are on the lookout for people who are willing to take on more responsibility. Employees with this quality help make better products and provide better service.

How do you react to more responsibility? Would you rather stick with what's familiar and easy? The next time your teacher asks for volunteers, raise your hand. It may seem scary at first, but then you'll be pleasantly surprised. The more responsibility you take on, the more confident you'll feel. The more confident you are, the better job you'll do.

Continuing to Learn

Have you ever heard someone say, "You learn something new every day." Do you? If you don't, start to right now. Learning makes all of life more interesting.

▲ People with initiative look for work that needs to be done. How have you shown initiative this week?

Try it out at school. Look to learn something from everything you do. Challenge yourself to learn something from activities or classes that you don't find particularly interesting. Then take your curiosity and willingness to learn to your job. Continue to learn there. Learn everything you can about your job. Learn your employer's or company's ways of doing things. Learn to work with your coworkers.

Employees who have good learning skills are valuable in today's changing workplace. Survey after survey has shown that employers want one thing more than anything else. They want employees who are willing to learn.

CRITICAL THINKING. Ask students, "How would you respond if a coworker was behind because of poor work habits or because of an illness?"

CRITICAL THINKING. Ask students, "Why do you think some people avoid learning new skills?"

Working by the Rules

It's not enough to have the skills to do a job and the personal qualities described above. Employers also expect their employees to have ethics. Ethics are the rules of behavior that govern a group or society.

Right Ways to Behave

Employees who behave ethically do not lie, cheat, or steal. They are honest and fair in their dealings with others. They can be trusted. *Figure 8-2* on page 164 shows different areas and examples of ethical and unethical behavior on the job.

Why Is Ethics Important?

Employees who act ethically build a good reputation, or name, for themselves. They are known to be dependable and trustworthy. They also contribute to their employer's or company's reputation.

Unethical behavior can have a spiraling effect. A single act can do a lot of damage. Here's just one example. Jill baby-sat all day on weekends for a young boy across the street. She was paid the usual hourly wages for baby-sitters in her neighborhood. The boy's mother also left $20 spending money for expenses during the day. She trusted Jill to use it wisely.

After a few weekends, Jill felt that she was not paid enough for taking care of the little boy. She was afraid to

Workplace Ethics

Areas of Concern	Ethical Behavior	Unethical Behavior
Time	Working the hours you say you will 	Taking longer breaks than allowed, coming to work late or leaving early, talking on the telephone with friends and family members while at work, doing personal business using office equipment
Money 	Using company money wisely and only for company business	Taking money from cash register, taking goods from a store without paying for them, using company money to pay for personal items or entertainment on a business trip
Employer's Property	Using company property carefully and only for company business 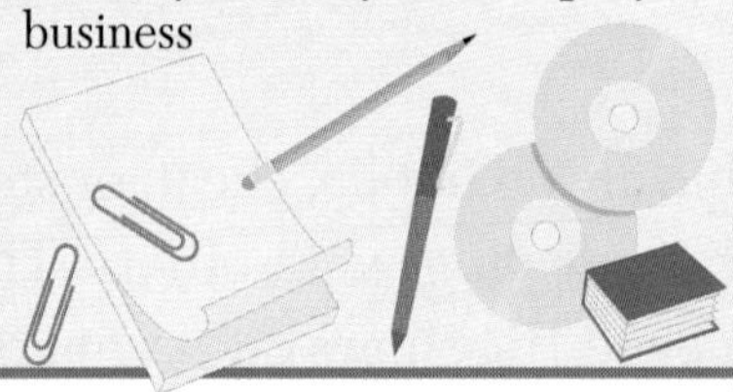	Taking office supplies home, copying company software for your own use, using the company copy machine to make photocopies for personal use, making personal long-distance phone calls on office phones
Information	Keeping company information secret from people outside the company 	Telling people who do not work for the company about new products or services, expansion plans, and ongoing projects; sharing information about employees and customers with people outside the company
Treatment of Others 	Treating your employer, coworkers, and customers fairly, openly, and honestly	Having a negative attitude toward people of different backgrounds, calling people names, making racist or sexist comments, making generalizations about groups of people

FIGURE 8-2 | **Working with Charts**

When you behave ethically, you do the right thing. **How do you learn ethical behavior?**

CAPTION ANSWER. You learn how to behave ethically as you grow up; you follow role models such as parents, other family members, religious leaders, and teachers.

ask for higher wages, though. Her neighbor might get a different baby-sitter. Instead, Jill began to take $10 a week for herself from the spending money. After all, her employer never asked how she used the money.

Jill's employer did notice that the spending money was being used, though. She asked her son where Jill and he had gone during the day. He told her they never left the house. Then the boy's mother asked Jill how she used the money. Jill lied to cover up what she had done. Her employer knew she was lying. She told Jill she was going to look for another baby-sitter. She also told other parents in the neighborhood what had happened. No one would hire Jill because she had been dishonest.

TEACHING ACTIVITY. Have students cover up the Unethical Behavior column for Figure 8-2. As a class, read columns 1 and 2 of each row and fill in an example for column 3. Compare with the text.

Ethics and You

How will you know the right way to behave on a job? Even if you haven't held a job yet, you've got experience with ethical problems. Like everyone else, you face ethical decisions every day. You decide how to behave in many difficult situations.

EXPLORE Activity

Think of a time when you acted ethically at home, at school, with your friends, or in your community. What rule of behavior did you follow? To be honest? To show respect for people or property? To keep secrets from people who are not supposed to know them?

You don't have to wait until you have a job. You have many opportunities to behave ethically every day. Do the right thing when faced with a decision. The ethics you practice in areas of your life now will carry over to the workplace.

How Are You Doing?

Progress reports, report cards, test scores, conferences—all tell you how you are doing in school. Each is a way of evaluating your work.

Your work at a job will also be evaluated from time to time. Many companies schedule performance reviews on a regular basis. **Performance reviews** are meetings between you and your supervisor to evaluate how well you're doing your job.

Reviews are important to both you and your employer. They let you know how you're doing. They help you become better at what you do. They also help you build your career.

A performance review is a good time to set goals. Your employer may set some for you. You should also set some for yourself. You may discuss your future with the company. Your review may lead to a pay increase and new responsibilities. You'll learn more about growing on the job in Chapter 12.

EXPLORE Activity

Imagine that your performance review for your part-time cashier's job is scheduled for tomorrow. Make a list of your accomplishments. What could you do better? What are your goals?

What should you do if you don't get feedback? You may go to work for a company that does not hold performance reviews. Your work at a part-time or volunteer job may not be

CAREER OPPORTUNITIES

Fine Arts and Humanities

Almost every image you see around you has the artist's touch. Being good at art can get you a job like this.

Critical Thinking

Look at some images around you, and list the skills a graphic designer needs to make them.

CLASSIFIED

THURSDAY, SEPT

Graphic Designer

Newspaper is seeking an experienced graphic designer to join our computer graphics department and help make advertisements and create art for brochures and newsletters (B/W + 4/C). Requires at least 3 years' experience using Quark Xpress and Photoshop.

Some employers evaluate workers informally. Which type of evaluation—formal or informal—do you think you would prefer? Why?

CAPTION ANSWER. Answers will vary. Remind students that an employee who knows he or she is doing the best job he or she can, will face either type of evaluation without fear.

EXTENDING THE LESSON. Ask students to evaluate how they are doing in each subject in school and to write a one-page evaluation.

evaluated. Your teachers may give you nothing more than a grade. If that's the case, schedule a meeting to discuss your performance. There's nothing wrong with asking how you're doing. It will show that you take an interest in your work. In addition, you'll get useful ideas that will help you improve your performance.

It's also a good idea to take time now and then to evaluate yourself. What do you think and feel about the different things you do? Evaluate yourself as a member of your family. Evaluate yourself as a friend. Look at your performance at school and in other activities. What do you do well? What could you do better? What would you like to do that you're not doing?

Before you know it, evaluation will be a habit. It will be a good habit, too. Why? Evaluation by yourself and others will help you grow—whether you're at home, at school, or on the job.

LESSON REVIEW AND ACTIVITIES. See the Teacher's Manual for answers.

Vocabulary Review

Pretend you are head of a company. You always write a letter to welcome new employees to the company. In the letter, describe the qualities you seek in employees. Use each of the key terms below.

cooperate

initiative

ethics

performance reviews

Check Your Understanding

On a separate sheet of paper, tell whether each statement is true or false. Rewrite any false statements to make them true.

1. Employers want employees who can cooperate and follow directions.
2. Employers don't have the right to expect employees to act ethically.

Critical Thinking

On a separate sheet of paper, answer the following questions.

1. Which qualities wanted by employers do you have already? Which would you have to work to develop?
2. What are two ways you can show initiative at home? At school?
3. Of the different kinds of ethical behavior, which do you think will be your biggest challenge? Why?
4. Why are performance reviews as important to workers as to their employers?
5. How can self-evaluation help you grow?
6. Why might it be hard to ask for an evaluation of your work?

Connecting to the Workplace

Problem Solving

- You have a job on weekends. That means that you usually miss school activities scheduled for Saturdays.
- One Saturday, you ask to leave work an hour early so that you can try out for the school play.
- Your employer agrees.
- On your weekly paycheck, however, you notice you've been paid for the hour.
- What should you do?

Community Involvement

What to Do

- With a group of friends or classmates, identify a need in your community.
- Figure out a way to fill it.
- Cooperate with the members of your group to do a community service project.
- Report to the class about what you did. Tell about the qualities you needed for the project.
- Compare these qualities with those that employers look for in employees.

Investigating Career Clusters

Fine Arts and Humanities

What Is the Fine Arts and Humanities Cluster?

Occupations in the fine arts and humanities cluster involve promoting and preserving the arts and social values. Jobs center around areas like the performing arts, visual arts, writing, religion, history, and museum work.

Skills Needed

Creative skills, artistic skills, communication skills, understanding of the arts, talent in a chosen area, perseverance

THE FACTS	Types of Careers in This Cluster	Work Description	Career Outlook	Education
	Actor	Entertain and communicate through the interpretation of dramatic roles	Faster than average	Professional training
	Dancer	Express ideas, stories, rhythm, and sound with movements of the body	Faster than average	Professional training
	Designer	Organize and design products to serve various purposes and to be visually pleasing	Faster than average	Associate's, Bachelor's
	Musician	Play instruments, sing, compose, arrange, or conduct groups in performance	Faster than average	Professional training
	Museum curator	Search for, acquire, arrange, restore, and exhibit items of lasting value	Average	Master's

Research Activity

Research five fine arts and humanities careers. Make a chart with the projected growth rate from now until 2005. Although they are still highly competitive, many of these careers have a good outlook. Add another column to your chart that states the level of competition in this field.

CHAPTER REVIEW. See the Teacher's Manual for answers.

▶Chapter Highlights

- Employers today want employees who can cooperate, follow directions, and show initiative. Employers also prize employees who are willing to take on more responsibility and to learn.

- Employees are paid wages, salary, or commission. They may also receive benefits, such as health insurance and paid time off.

▶Recalling Key Concepts

Using complete sentences, answer the following questions on a separate sheet of paper.

1. Why do companies provide orientation for new employees?

2. How do wages differ from a salary?
3. What is initiative?
4. What are three areas of ethical behavior in the workplace?
5. What is the purpose of a performance review?

▶Thinking Critically

Using complete sentences, answer the following questions on a separate sheet of paper.

1. What do you think will be the main thing on your mind the first day at a new job? Explain.
2. Why do you think benefits are important to many workers?
3. Why are honesty and fairness important in the workplace?

Building Skills

1. Thinking—Knowing How to Learn

Think of a part-time job you'd like to have. With a partner, role-play a phone conversation with your employer. The employer has called to answer questions you may have about your first day. What questions would you ask? Switch roles, and role-play a second conversation.

2. Personal—Sociability

Make a list of ways to get to know coworkers. Keep writing until you've run out of ideas. Compare lists with a classmate. How many ways of getting acquainted have the two of you identified?

3. Interpersonal—Works with Cultural Diversity

Write a description of yourself. Tell about your appearance and personality. List some of your interests and values. Trade papers with a classmate. Then explain to your classmates why your partner is an important member of the class. Discuss what different people contribute to both the classroom and the workplace.

Applying Academic Skills

1. The Arts

Make a collage that celebrates at least five careers in the fine arts and humanities. Review "Investigating Career Clusters" on page 169 for ideas of careers to include. Use pictures and words to illustrate the careers. Cut pictures and words out of old magazines or newspapers. You can also make your own drawings and labels. Display your collage in the classroom.

2. Mathematics

Tamika has just completed her first month in television advertising sales. The monthly base salary is $2,400. In addition to the salary, Tamara makes a commission of 15 percent on what she sells. Tamika worked hard and sold $8,000 worth of advertising this month. How much is her commission? What are her total earnings for the month?

Discovery Portfolio

Enhancing Work Performance

- Parent-teacher-student conferences and report cards provide a "performance review" of your work at school.
- Using information collected from these sources, list some goals for improving your work performance.
- Keep a copy of your list of goals in your portfolio. Use it to measure your progress.

Career Exploration: Fine Arts and Humanities

Research a career in the fine arts and humanities career cluster.

- Look for information in the library and on the Internet.
- If possible, interview someone with a job in this career cluster.
- Create a display about the career.
- Include information about the kinds of work, the working conditions, and training and education required. Also, include skills needed to do the job.
- Explain the career outlook.
- Set up your display at a class career fair.

Working with Others

What You'll Learn...

- You will learn the basics of working well with others.

- You will find out how to build relationships and deal with conflicts when they arise.

- You will discover why being able to work as part of a team is important.

- You will take a look at how teams work.

- **CAREER CLUSTER** You will explore careers in *health*.

LESSON 9-1
Building Relationships

LESSON 9-2
Teamwork

LESSON PLAN. See the *Teacher's Manual* for the Chapter 9 lesson plan.

Friends & Family Activity

TRY THIS!

Ask two adult friends or family members to think of a time when they worked closely with people different from themselves. Use these questions:

- What did you have in common? How did you differ?
- What did you each contribute to what you were doing?
- What did you learn about yourself by working with other people? About others?

APPLY: Write a newspaper article based on the interviews, using the five *W*s—Who, What, When, Where, and Why.

Building Relationships

Discover...
- the key to getting along with others.
- how to build relationships with other people.
- the part self-esteem plays in relationships.
- how to deal with conflicts between people.

Why Is Getting Along with Others Important?

Getting along with others will help you at home, at school, and on the job.

Key Terms...
- relationships
- respect
- empathize
- self-esteem
- conflict
- prejudice
- mediator
- compromise
- conflict resolution

How well do you get along with others? Think about all your relationships—your connections or dealings with people. You have relationships with your friends and family. You also have relationships with teachers and others each day at school. Then there are the people in your community, such as neighbors and shopkeepers. How do you treat all of these people? How do you behave toward them?

You may act differently with different people, depending on how well you know them. You don't have to know people well to get along with them, though. The key to getting along with people is quite simple. It's the same no matter who's involved. The key is respect, or consideration, for others.

Respect Is the Key

Remember your report cards in elementary school? In addition to grading your schoolwork, your teacher also commented

➤ Learning how to build strong relationships is a skill that will help you throughout your life. Why do you think that this is so?

on your social skills. Maybe your teacher wrote, "Works well with others." Maybe he or she made these notes: "Respects other people's opinions," "Always willing to help others."

All of these skills showed how well you got along with others. These skills were important on the playground and in the classroom then. They are also important now—at school and in all your activities.

Employers take these skills seriously. They know that employees who have these skills have the key to good relationships in the workplace. Employees who have these skills show respect for other people.

Getting Along with Others

Show other people respect. It sounds easy, but it can be hard work sometimes. You already have a lot of experience building relationships at home and at school. As you know from experience, it's impossible to get along with everyone all the time.

We've all known someone who made our surroundings at home or school unpleasant or difficult. The workplace is no different. There will be people you don't like. Not everyone will like you. Some people will just be easier to be with than others.

You'll want to do everything you can to build and keep good relationships with people at work. When you get along with coworkers and others at work, you will do a better job. You will also enjoy your work more.

Ways to Build Relationships

Here are some pointers for getting along with others. You can use them right now in your relationships at home, at school, anywhere you are with people. You can also use them on the job.

▲ You can show respect, or consideration, for others in many ways. **How is this person being considerate of someone else?**

CAPTION ANSWER. She's lending a hand to someone who needs her.

MOTIVATING STUDENTS. Ask students how they would rate the importance of getting along with others on the job. Is it a big consideration for them?

CAPTION ANSWER. In your life you will have relationships with many different people in many different settings, and these relationships will have an impact on how you live and work and on your happiness and the happiness of others.

- *Treat people as you would like to be treated.* Be thoughtful and considerate.
- *Try to understand the other person's side.* Be open-minded. **Empathize**—try to see things from the other person's point of view and understand his or her situation.
- *Speak carefully.* Think of the way others will feel when they hear what you have to say. Share information clearly and thoughtfully so that others understand you.
- *Listen when others talk.* Let other people know you're interested in them. Pay attention to what they say. Ask for and listen to their opinions and ideas.

▲ When family members help each other, they build strong relationships. In what ways do you help members of your family? In what ways do members of your family help you?

- *Help others.* Lend a hand if you see someone having trouble doing something. If you finish what you have to do, help someone else.
- *Be friendly.* Be pleasant and smile. Greet people. Invite newcomers to join you.
- *Have a sense of humor.* Find ways to see the light side of a situation. Let your sense of humor carry you and others through difficult times.

EXPLORE Activity

Choose one of the pointers for getting along with others. Put it into practice tomorrow. Observe what happens. Note people's reactions. Think about how you feel. Think about how others feel. Do the results surprise you?

Continue to practice the behavior you selected. Choose another pointer. Practice it.

Getting Along with Yourself

Some of the pointers for getting along with people may be easier to follow than others. Some may come more naturally to you. Why? Think about this. You treat other people the way you treat yourself. If you respect and like yourself, chances are you will feel the same way about others.

Here's an example. Say you make a mistake. Do you put yourself down? Do you think to yourself, "I'm really stupid" or "I never do anything right"? If you do, you may put others down when they make mistakes.

On the other hand, you might say, "I made a mistake, but I'll get it right next time." When you do, you give yourself a break. You're realistic about your expectations for yourself. You understand that nobody's perfect. You will probably forgive others when they make mistakes.

How you feel about yourself—your self-esteem—affects how you get along with others. Self-esteem is your recognition and regard for yourself and your abilities. When you have high self-esteem, you are confident about yourself and what you can do. You have a positive image of yourself. When you are positive about yourself, you are likely to have positive feelings toward other people.

Dealing with Conflict

Even when people do their best to get along, conflicts can arise. A conflict is a strong disagreement. It often occurs when people have different needs or wishes. Conflicts can occur in families and among friends and neighbors. Employees, employers, and customers may also have conflicts with each other from time to time.

▼ Learning a new skill or reaching a goal you've set can boost your self-esteem. What activities do you do well? What activities would you like to try?

Everyone experiences conflicts with others. How have you handled recent conflicts? What would you do differently?

Causes of Conflicts

People disagree for many reasons. Think about the last time you had a disagreement. Can you remember the cause? Maybe you felt that someone wasn't respecting your feelings. Did someone say something unkind about you? Perhaps you and the other person wanted two different things. For example, did you and your best friend disagree about what you wanted to do? Maybe you wanted the same thing.

Conflicts have a variety of causes. Some are based on misunderstandings. These misunderstandings often occur when people don't communicate clearly. Other conflicts come about because people have different beliefs or opinions from each other. Gossip and teasing can also lead to conflict. Jealousy—when one person wants something another has—can result in conflict, too.

Prejudice is another cause of conflict. **Prejudice** is a negative attitude toward a person or group that is not based on facts or reason. Prejudice causes people to judge others without taking the time to get to know them. It often leads to heated arguments and angry clashes.

Resolving Conflicts

No matter what its cause, a conflict is like any other problem. To deal with a conflict, you need good problem-solving skills. Some conflicts can be solved by the people involved. You may disagree with your brother or sister about what television program to watch, for instance. After talking it over, though, you may be able to agree on a solution.

If you can't agree, you may need to ask a family member to help you find a solution. As a third person who is not involved, he or she may be able to act as a mediator. A **mediator** is someone who helps opposing people or groups compromise or reach an agreement. When opposing sides **compromise,** they each give up something to settle a disagreement. They consider each side's feelings.

Did you know that the skills you're practicing now will serve you well when you're an adult? Disagreements among people in the workplace can be handled in much the same way as conflicts at home and school. At work, however, a step-by-step process called **conflict resolution** may be used to settle disagreements. *Figure 9-1* on page 180 shows how conflict resolution works.

TEACHING ACTIVITY. Introduce this section about conflict by helping students discuss the importance of resolving disagreements. Have students describe some disagreements in their experience that could have been resolved through better communication.

CRITICAL THINKING. Ask students to explain why prejudice is destructive in the workplace.

TEACHING CAREER OPPORTUNITIES. A coordinator of youth services can help reduce the number of teenage pregnancies in a neighborhood. A coordinator of youth services can also plan activities that educate teenagers, helping keep them off the streets and out of trouble.

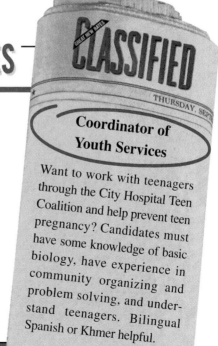

CAREER OPPORTUNITIES

Health

Teaching people about health concerns can be just as important as curing sick people.

Critical Thinking

How can a coordinator of youth services help change a teenager's life and improve a community?

CLASSIFIED

THURSDAY, SEP

Coordinator of Youth Services

Want to work with teenagers through the City Hospital Teen Coalition and help prevent teen pregnancy? Candidates must have some knowledge of basic biology, have experience in community organizing and problem solving, and understand teenagers. Bilingual Spanish or Khmer helpful.

RESEARCH. Ask students to find out about mediators and the job that they do. Can students name any famous business cases in which a mediator was required?

EXTENDING THE LESSON. Have artistic students draw a cartoon of a conflict or problem in the workplace. Other students may write a short paragraph or draw a picture coming up with possible solutions to the problem.

Preventing Conflicts

How can you best prepare yourself to deal with conflicts in the workplace? You can practice your problem-solving skills right now at school, at home, and with your friends. You can also work on your communication skills. Good communication can help you avoid conflicts.

Learning to control your anger is another way to prevent conflicts. Controlling anger is not always easy and takes a great deal of practice. When you feel yourself getting angry, try these ways of cooling off.

- Take a deep breath and count to 10.
- Go for a walk or do something else that is physical.
- Laugh it off and walk away.

> **FIGURE 9-1**

STEPS IN CONFLICT RESOLUTION

Conflict resolution is a way to work out a solution to a problem. The people involved in a disagreement work together to bring the conflict to an end. Where besides work might you use these steps to resolve a conflict?

1

Define the Problem
Take turns describing the problem from your point of view. As you speak and listen, show respect for each other.

2

Suggest Solutions
Offer solutions to the problem.

3

Evaluate the Solutions
Discuss the suggested solutions. Explain the part of each suggestion that you agree with. Also explain the part you cannot accept. Listen carefully as the other person does the same.

- Take a few minutes to have a "talk" with yourself.
- Remind yourself of the reasons you don't want to act angry.

It's always best to head off conflicts before they even start. The best way to do this is to pay attention to your own behavior toward others. By exploring your actions, you may find qualities in yourself that you can improve. Perhaps you need to work on accepting other people as they are. Maybe you need to try looking at situations from another person's point of view.

Go back to the pointers for getting along with others. See what you can improve. After all, your relationships with others begin with you.

4a

Compromise

If you are close to agreeing, compromise. In other words, give up something to settle the disagreement.

6

Ask Someone Else to Decide

You both may want a solution but cannot agree on what it should be. Your only choice may be to hand the conflict over to a mediator. Agree that you will go along with the decision that person makes. Then ask the mediator to make the final decision.

5

Get Another Point of View

If you can't reach a solution, invite a third person to help. Ask that person to listen and make suggestions for a solution.

4b

Think Creatively

If you can't compromise, brainstorm solutions. Think of as many ways as you can to approach the problem. Then try again to compromise.

LESSON REVIEW AND ACTIVITIES. See the *Teacher's Manual* for answers.

Vocabulary Review

Use each of the key terms below in a sentence. Each sentence should tell something about your own experience getting along with others. Share one of your sentences with the class.

relationships   prejudice

respect   mediator

empathize   compromise

self-esteem   conflict

conflict   resolution

Check Your Understanding

Choose the correct answer for each item. Write your answers on a separate sheet of paper.

1. When you are positive about yourself, you are likely to _____.
   a. lose the respect of others
   b. gain control of others
   c. get along with other people

2. The first step to resolve a conflict is to _____.
   a. explain your solution
   b. define the problem
   c. ask the other person to listen

Critical Thinking

On a separate sheet of paper, answer the following questions.

1. How do you feel when someone does not show respect for your feelings and ideas?

2. Which of the pointers for getting along with others do you think is most important? Why?

3. How does learning to do something new help increase your self-esteem?

4. What do you do to avoid a conflict?

Connecting to the Workplace

People Skills Needed on the Job

- In a newspaper, look for a classified ad for a job in the health career cluster.
- Clip or copy the ad.
- Write a summary of the job. Include a description of the job and the people skills needed for it. Use the ad and your own ideas to identify the people skills needed for the job.

∱∱∱ Teamwork

What to Do
- Many schools use peer mediation to deal with conflicts. In peer mediation, specially trained students help resolve conflicts among their peers, or people their age. Form a committee with others interested in conflict resolution at school.
- Ask a teacher or guidance counselor how you can find out about peer mediation.
- Organize a meeting to share information.
- Make a plan for creating a peer mediation program at your school.

Teamwork

Think of all the ways you work with others to get something done. Perhaps you pitch in at home to help your family do chores. Maybe you and your classmates have put on a performance or held a fund-raiser. You might be a member of the student council, making decisions with others about school issues and activities. Don't forget all the projects you've completed in cooperative learning groups.

Working as a team member is already an important part of your everyday experience. It will continue to be important when you enter the world of work.

Why Work as a Team?

What do wolves, the organs in your body, musicians, and soccer players all have in common? They all work as a team!

Wolves are just one of many types of animals that band together. Wolves live in packs because they have a better chance of surviving that way. They may also feel a need to be part of a group, just as we do.

The human body functions smoothly, with each organ doing a different task. It takes all the organs working together, though, to keep us alive and healthy.

Discover . . .
- why teamwork is important.
- the steps involved in teamwork.
- problems teams face and how to handle them.

Why Is It Important to Learn to Be a Member of a Team?

People work together to complete all kinds of projects successfully. You'll be able to use team skills in school and in the work you do someday.

Key Terms . . .
- team planning
- assess

CAPTION ANSWER. Students should describe goals they have shared with others on a team and responsibilities they had as a team member.

◄ Sharing goals and responsibilities as part of a team is an experience that is valuable to everyone. What goals have you shared with others on a team? How did you contribute to meeting your team's goal?

Why do musicians work together? "There's nothing like being in the middle of an orchestra and hearing that sound wrapping around you." That's how one young flute player put it. Musicians work together to create a certain sound, but they also enjoy playing the music. As for soccer players, a good team offense and defense are hard to beat.

Teams in the Work World

As you learned in Chapter 2, businesses today rely more and more on teams of workers to get jobs done. There are hospital surgical teams, software design teams, and book sales teams, to name only a few. In each case, the members of the group work together for a common purpose. The purpose may be to plan and complete a difficult operation. It may be to create a new computer game. It may be to break the record for number of children's books sold in a year. Members of teams share the responsibilities and rewards of their efforts.

"Two heads are better than one." That's what they say. More people on a particular job or problem means more chances for creative solutions.

Businesses also find that teams can get more done than the same number of people working separately. The goods teams make and the services they offer are higher quality. Fewer supervisors are needed when people work in teams.

What's in it for the team? Team players tend to feel good about their work. They stay interested in what they're doing because they often have different tasks on a team.

EXPLORE Activity

Test it out for yourself. Think of a problem at school. Write down as many ways to solve the problem as you can in one minute.

Then ask three friends to do the same. Put all of your ideas together. Is the list longer than when you started it? What ideas did your friends have that you didn't think of? Did any of your friends' ideas give you new ideas? A variety of ideas and points of view is one of the best reasons for working as a team.

High self-esteem is common among team players. Team members are usually in charge of their own work and help make and carry out decisions. As a result, they feel good about themselves and what they can do.

As an extra bonus, people who work on teams usually get along well with each other. That's because they have a chance to get to know each other. Team members learn about each other's behaviors, attitudes, and ways of thinking. They're not so quick to judge one another. That means cooperation instead of conflict in the workplace.

CAPTION ANSWER. Answers will vary; students may observe that they learned how to focus on a specific task, to cooperate with others, to share responsibilities, or to be flexible.

◄ Think of a group project you've worked on. What did you learn from the experience that might help you in a future career?

DISCUSSION STARTER. Ask students to think about a school committee they have been on. Who was the team leader? What special skills did that person need to help the team set and meet its goals?

TEACHING ACTIVITY. Ask students if a team can operate without a leader. Have the students list advantages and disadvantages of shared responsibility.

Team Planning

Imagine that you and your friends have decided to throw a surprise birthday party. What will happen if you each go ahead and do what you think should be done? You may take care of some things, but you may forget others.

If you plan the party together, you will have much better results. One person can send invitations. Another can decorate. One can be in charge of music, and another can buy the food. The end result will be a great party.

The same goes for running any successful team project. Before you start, you should make a plan. Since you will be working as a team, plan as a team. **Team planning** involves working with others to set goals and assign tasks. It also involves communicating regularly about how things are going.

Setting Goals

Taking time to set goals helps everyone understand the purpose of the group. When you set goals as a team, you will all be moving in the same direction.

Take it from Nate. He thought it would be fun to form a basketball team and join the summer league. "Most of us just wanted to shoot some hoops and have fun," Nate explains. "There were a couple of guys, though, who were out to win the city championship. I figured that out pretty quickly. They got really angry every time we lost a game. After a few losses, it was no fun playing together anymore."

CAPTION ANSWER. Answers will vary; students should name specific roles in a group, such as researcher, writer, or presenter, and support their choices.

▼ You probably have many opportunities in group projects at school to play a role that's new to you. What new role would you like to have in your next group project? Why?

The Global Workplace

Greetings in Other Cultures May Differ Considerably

Handshakes are not always the norm in greetings. In Europe, people use a limp handshake. They never use two hands or shoulder slapping in greetings. A handshake or a kiss on both cheeks is normal practice in the Middle East. When two people meet in certain parts of the Far East, hands are put together in a prayer position with a subtle bow. This is also true in India.

Exploration Activity!

Using library resources, research the bow. What does it signify in Japan? India? What do the different kinds of bows mean?

TEACHING THE GLOBAL WORK-PLACE. Point out to students that bowing and other greetings often show something specific about the relationship of the two people involved. Offer methods for finding out more information about greetings around the world.

Can you think of times when you've been in a group in which people had different goals? It probably was not a good team experience.

Sometimes the best way to approach a large project is to use "stepping-stone goals." Short-term, medium-term, and long-term goals can be stepping stones to your final goal. These in-between goals, which you read about in Chapter 5, work as well for groups as for individuals.

Assigning Roles and Tasks

You can set short-term, medium-term, and long-term goals by breaking a project into smaller tasks. Different people on the team can work on different parts of the project.

It's important for each team member to have a role, or part to play. Sometimes a person's role is a task, such as "buy the food." More often, your role as a team member will take advantage of your interests and skills.

Remember that party you were planning? You might choose the person with the best computer skills to create party invitations. The artist in the group might be in charge of

CRITICAL THINKING. Ask students what they feel are the most valuable contributions a team player or worker can make when setting goals. Have them explain their answers.

TEACHING ACTIVITY. Have students make a list of possible roles in team activities. Have them share their lists with a partner.

decorations. The one who always has the latest CDs would probably do a good job handling the music. On a team, no one has to be good at everything. You all can take advantage of each other's interests and skills.

Working with others has additional benefits. People in the group may share their expertise or know-how with you. If you want to learn more about computer graphic design, for instance, this may be your chance. Ask the person who knows all about computers to share his or her knowledge with you.

No matter what your role, the other members of the team will count on you. If you do not do your job, everyone loses. Say you're planning that surprise birthday party with three other friends. Since there are four people, you divide the work into four tasks. The tasks are invitations, decorations, music, and food. If all four do their part, the party will be a success. What happens if the person in charge of food doesn't do his or her job? No one gets a slice of birthday cake, that's what!

EXPLORE Activity

Now is a good time to explore different roles in a group. Be the researcher in your next group project in social studies or science. You may discover you're good at it. Another time, volunteer to be the main presenter. After you've done it once or twice, you'll feel at ease in front of the class. Even if you don't think of yourself as artistic, work on the maps, graphs, displays, or charts needed. You'll enjoy doing something different.

Find ways now to explore various roles in all your team activities. Later, in the workplace, your role on a team will often be linked to your job responsibilities. You will be asked to bring your special skills and knowledge to the group. You can identify and develop those strengths by experimenting with different roles now.

Assessing

No birthday cake at a birthday party is a problem. Problems are less likely to crop up if team members meet from time to time to **assess,** or judge, their progress.

Communication is important. When team members gather regularly, they can share difficulties they are having. If necessary, they can reassign roles and tasks. Sometimes the team may even decide to rethink its goals.

It's also a good idea to assess a project when it is over. Frequently, someone "higher up" will evaluate the outcome of a project. That person may be a parent, a teacher, or a supervisor.

CAREER Q&A

What If I'm Shy?

Q: I'm shy around people I barely know and have a hard time talking to them. What can I do?

A: The problem with being shy is that people may think that you're stuck up. If it's hard for you to talk in a group, use body language to show that you are friendly. Smiling a lot is a good start, or nodding to show that you are listening. Also, ask questions to start a conversation or to keep one going.

CRITICAL THINKING. Which do students feel is more important to an assessment of a team project: a self-evaluation by the team or an evaluation by others?

CAPTION ANSWER. It depends on the project. Team members should meet on a regular basis—daily, weekly, monthly—as the project demands.

◄ Teams need to talk about how they're doing and where they're headed. **How often do you think a team should meet to assess its progress?**

Customers and others can also help assess a team's work. Listen carefully to their comments.

> **The design team was very creative, but the people were not easy to work with.**

> **We couldn't have asked for better service and food at our party.**

> **My hospital stay went so smoothly. I had great care, from the admitting nurse to the surgeon to the young volunteers.**

Comments like these tell a team what kind of job it has done. They point out strengths and weaknesses.

The team itself should also assess what it has accomplished. The team as a whole and individual team members might check their work by asking questions such as these:

- How well did I do my job?
- How well did other members of the team do their jobs?
- How well did we work together?
- What could we do differently next time?

This kind of self-assessment helps. It can make each group experience better than the last.

Dealing with Problems

Teams face their share of problems no matter how well organized they are. Think of the groups you've been a part of. How about the last cooperative learning group you took part in at school, for instance? What was that experience like? What did you find frustrating? Did you end up doing all the work? Did one member of the group boss everyone around? Did someone try to take credit for everything? Were you all working toward the same goal? Maybe no one listened to your ideas.

Figure 9-2 at right shows some common problems teams face. Most of these problems can be avoided. How? Team members must set clear goals, take action promptly, and most important, keep communicating.

If you've had a bad experience working in a group, don't give up. Groups differ, just as individuals do. As Aimee Fontainbleu of Waynesburg, West Virginia, discovered during her first seventh-grade project, some groups simply work better than others.

"When I heard the dreaded words 'Choose three people to work with,' " Aimee recalls, "I just wanted to run. After my experience with groups in sixth grade, I wanted to work by myself. It was the first project of the year. I wanted to get off to a good start.

"As it turned out, this group was different. I couldn't believe the ideas we came up with. The others thought of things I *never* would have thought of. When we put our heads together, we were awesome. Our project really came together.

"Our group worked well because we all listened to each other. We all did our share of the work. Nobody tried to take over or take all the credit. We all felt like we had something important to contribute. It was so much fun. We can't wait to do another project together."

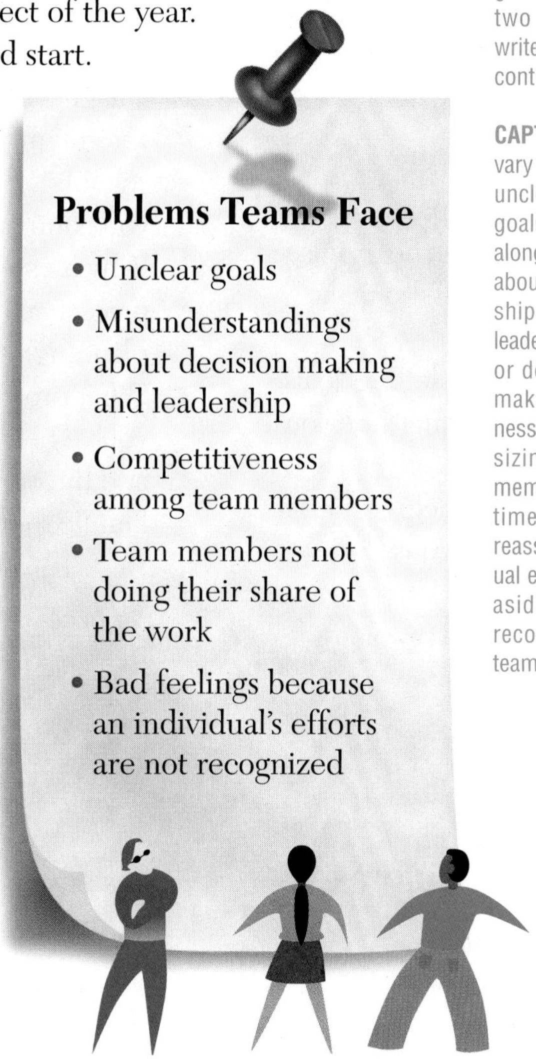

Problems Teams Face

- Unclear goals
- Misunderstandings about decision making and leadership
- Competitiveness among team members
- Team members not doing their share of the work
- Bad feelings because an individual's efforts are not recognized

Teamwork is challenging, but it can also be fun. As with many other skills, the secret is practice. Practice now while you're in school. Put your team skills to work wherever you can. Today's workplace needs people who can be part of a team. If you practice, you'll have what it takes.

RESEARCH. Have each student find and read a current article on teamwork used by a specific business. Tell students to explain in a paragraph how the team improved the work of the business.

EXTENDING THE LESSON. Ask students to look for a team in their own experience whose members have a variety of ethnic backgrounds. Have the students choose two members of the team and write a short report on the special contribution of these two people.

CAPTION ANSWER. Answers will vary but may include the following: unclear goals: taking time to set goals at outset and assess them along the way; misunderstandings about decision making and leadership: selecting leader(s), giving leader(s) power to make decisions, or devising a group process for making decisions; competitiveness: building team spirit, emphasizing common goals; team members not doing work: taking time to assess progress and reassign roles and tasks; individual efforts not recognized: setting aside time at end of project to recognize contributions of each team member.

▲ **FIGURE 9-2**
Working on a team can be hard work. What solution can you suggest for one of the problems teams face?

LESSON REVIEW AND ACTIVITIES. See the *Teacher's Manual* for answers.

Vocabulary Review

Make a poster that tells about team planning. Your poster should show the three main steps in team planning. Explain your poster to the class in an oral presentation. Use each of the key terms in your presentation.

team planning   assess

Check Your Understanding

On a separate sheet of paper, tell whether each statement is true or false. Rewrite any false statements to make them true.

1. Team planning involves setting goals, assigning tasks, and making sure you are in charge.
2. Setting goals as a team helps everyone move in different directions.
3. Team members need to keep communicating to avoid problems.

Critical Thinking

On a separate sheet of paper, answer the following questions.

1. Why is teamwork important in school? How will knowing how to work on a team be important to you in the future?
2. Imagine that you've been asked to be a member of a leadership team at school. What interests and skills could you contribute?
3. Why is assessing the outcome of a project an important part of team planning?
4. What problems have arisen in groups you've been part of? How did you and the other members of the group handle them?

Connecting to the Workplace

Teamwork in Health Careers

- Research the use of teams in a health career of interest to you.
- Use library resources and the Internet to gather information.
- If you have time, write a letter or interview someone with a job in the career, in person or by telephone.
- Write a one-page report about what you have discovered.

Community Involvement

What to Do

- For one week, check your local newspaper for articles about teams at work in your community.
- Write a summary of each article you find.
- In each summary, describe who made up the team, its purpose, and the outcome of its project.
- Select the example of teamwork that you find most interesting. Tell your classmates about it.

Investigating Career Clusters

Health

What Is the Health Cluster?

Occupations in the health cluster provide services to meet people's physical and mental health needs. Careers include physicians, nurses, pharmacists, therapists, health technologists, and technicians.

Skills Needed

Science skills, physical and emotional stamina, decision-making skills, math skills, and a desire to help the sick and injured

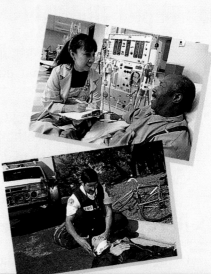

THE FACTS	Types of Careers in This Cluster	Work Description	Career Outlook	Education
	Chiropractor	Treat people by massaging muscles and manipulating bones, especially in the spine	Faster than average	Chiropractic program, State license
	Pharmacist	Provide drugs and medicines that are ordered by doctors	Good	Pharmacist program
	Dental hygienist	Clean teeth, take and develop X rays, and explain care of the mouth to patients	Much faster than average	Dental hygiene program, State license
	Radiological technologist	Operate machines that produce X rays of the brain and other parts of the body	Faster than average	Associate's
	Physician	Perform medical examinations, diagnose illnesses, and treat people who are sick	Faster than average	Medical school degree, Three-year residency

---

Research Activity

In general, health occupations will grow at a faster than average rate through 2005. Research health careers.

List 10 of the fastest growing professions in this career cluster.

Chapter 9 Review

▶ Chapter Highlights

- Respect and a positive attitude about yourself are keys to getting along with others.
- People who work on teams generally get along well with each other. On a team, they have a chance to get to know each other.

▶ Recalling Key Concepts

Using complete sentences, answer the following questions on a separate sheet of paper.

1. What is respect?
2. What are five causes of conflict?
3. When might you ask a third party to make a decision to end a conflict?
4. What is involved in team planning?

5. What kinds of problems do teams often face?

▶ Thinking Critically

Using complete sentences, answer the following questions on a separate sheet of paper.

1. Why is a sense of humor helpful in getting along with others?
2. Do you think you have a positive attitude toward yourself? Why or why not? How could you develop one?
3. Why might close friends have conflicts?
4. What kinds of things have you done with a team that you could not have done alone?
5. What would you do if someone on your team wouldn't do any of the work?

Building Skills

1. Thinking—Problem Solving

Matt shares a bedroom with his brother, Josh. They argue constantly. Josh never finishes his homework early enough for Matt to listen to music before bed. Matt's light bothers Josh when he is trying to sleep. List two possible solutions that are fair to both Matt and Josh. Compare your ideas with those of a friend.

2. Interpersonal—Participates as a Member of a Team

Work together with five or six other students to prepare a newscast. Cover recent events at school and in your community, including sports and weather. Choose a director, writers, researchers, reporters, and an anchorperson. Take some time to rehearse. Then present your newscast to the class.

Applying Academic Skills

1. Social Studies

Read a daily newspaper for one week. Collect examples of conflicts. Look in all the sections of the paper: front page, sports, features, even the comics and advice columns. In each case, identify the conflict, the people involved, and its outcome. Choose one example. Write an imaginary letter to the people involved. Tell them what you recommend and why.

2. The Arts

Look at the light side of getting along with others. Draw a comic strip about building relationships. Paste it at the top of a sheet of paper. Circulate your comic strip among your classmates. Ask them to comment on your comic. How did they interpret it? Did they find it funny? What did it teach them?

Discovery Portfolio

Write a Short Story, Poem, or Song About Building Relationships

- Your short story, poem, or song might tell how you feel about a relationship. It might describe relationships in an entertaining or thought-provoking way.
- Store your composition in your portfolio. After you read it, write a short story, poem, or song on another topic.

Career Exploration: Health

Research a career that you find interesting in the health career cluster.

- Look for information in the library and on the Internet.
- If possible, interview someone with a job in the career you've selected.
- Write a classified ad for a job in the career. Include information about the kinds of work, the working conditions, and training and education required. Also include skills needed to do the job.
- Explain the job outlook for the future.
- Post your ad in the classroom.
- Encourage interested students to respond.

Chapter 10

Basic Skills *Count*

What You'll Learn...

- You will discover why basic skills are important.

- You will gather tips for improving your communication skills.

- You will learn how to build your math, science, and computer skills.

- **CAREER CLUSTER** You will explore careers in *hospitality and recreation*.

LESSON 10-1
Getting Your Message Across

LESSON 10-2
Applying Other Skills

LESSON PLAN. See the *Teacher's Manual* for the Chapter 10 lesson plan.

Friends & Family Activity

TRY THIS!

Make a chart with eight columns. Select three adult family members or friends with different jobs. Write the name and job of each in the first column. Add these other column heads: Speaking, Listening, Reading, Writing, Math, Science, Computers. Ask the people listed how they use the skills on the chart in their jobs.

APPLY: Make notes for each person in the appropriate columns. Then study the information. What does it tell you about the importance of basic skills?

197

Getting Your Message Across

Discover...
- how to apply the basics of speaking.
- how to listen effectively.
- how to improve your reading and writing skills.
- how to use images, or pictures, to present ideas.

Why Are Basic Skills Important Skills?

All are tools for getting information and sharing ideas.

Key Terms...
- communication
- purpose
- audience
- subject
- active listening
- previewing
- skimming
- context clues
- images

Let's play telephone. Do you remember that game? One person whispers a message in another person's ear. That person whispers it to the next person and so on. By the time it reaches the last person, the message is usually very different from what it was at the start. Why? People along the way may not have heard or repeated the message correctly. That may be because they didn't speak or listen carefully.

You may laugh when you hear a garbled message at the end of a game of telephone. It's no laughing matter, though, when a real message you are sending or receiving is confused. The exchange of information between senders and receivers is called communication. Communication skills—speaking, listening, reading, and writing—are among the most important basic skills you can have. They will play a big part in your success at school and in the world of work.

► Being able to communicate is a basic skill. In what ways do you communicate each day?

Speaking

What do you like to do with your friends? There may be times when you plan something special. Chances are, though, that you like to spend most of your time together just talking. You talk with each other at school. You talk on the telephone after school. You get together on the weekend and just talk.

Talking is an important part of relationships. It is also an important part of nearly every kind of work. In the work world, speaking is one of the main ways of sharing information.

Having a Purpose

Whether you're speaking to one person or to a group, you want your listeners to get your point. To make a point, you need to have a clear idea of your purpose, audience, and subject.

Most people have a **purpose,** or overall goal or reason, for speaking. Think of the last time you spoke to someone. What was your reason for speaking? You may have needed help or information. Perhaps you wanted to share an idea, a point of view, or your feelings about something. Maybe you just wanted to say hello. You may have had more than one purpose.

It is important to have a clear purpose in mind when speaking. After all, when you know what your goal is, you are more likely to reach it.

Who's Listening?

Knowing your audience can help you achieve your purpose in speaking. When you think of an audience, you may imagine people seated in a theater or stadium. An **audience** is actually anyone who receives information. When you speak, your listeners are your audience.

It helps to know who your listeners are. Then you can choose the best way to reach them with your words and ideas. You wouldn't talk to a teacher in the same way you talk to your best friend. You wouldn't use the same tone of voice with a baby as you would to present a report. You use different ways of speaking with different audiences.

The RIGHT Attitude!

Learning from Mistakes

It's easy to learn from successes, but what about mistakes? Part of becoming a successful worker is learning how to have a sense of humor about your own mistakes. Put your mistakes to work for you! Just ask, "What have I learned from this experience, and what can I do differently next time?"

Apply Your Skills!

Write a paragraph about a mistake you have made. What did you learn? What will you do differently next time?

What's Your Subject?

It also helps to know your subject—your main topic or key idea—when speaking. Getting to know your subject may require some preparation. It's well worth the time, though.

Think of a speaker who completely captured your attention. That speaker probably knew his or her subject very well. He or she probably shared specific facts and examples that made the subject come alive for you.

Planning Ahead

To know your purpose, audience, and subject, you need to plan ahead. Think about what you're going to say before you speak. You won't need a plan every time you talk to someone, but planning can be useful in many situations. Planning can improve your oral reports. Planning can also make talking to someone or leaving a clear phone message easier.

Tawana Johnson knows the importance of planning. She often makes a plan before talking to her mother. "When I want to ask my mom something important, I think about what I'm going to say," Tawana explains.

" I also try to figure out in advance how she will react. My mom is much more open to my ideas when I've planned ahead. That's because I know what I want to say and why I want to say it. All it takes is a little preparation. "

Good Speaking Habits

Of course, what you have to say doesn't matter if no one can understand you. You might be running for school office, sharing a project, or calling about a job opening. No matter what the situation, *how* you say something will be just as important as *what* you have to say. For some tips on improving your speaking skills, look at ***Figure 10-1*** at right.

Listening

The other side of speaking is listening. Like speaking, listening takes practice. Listening is not just being quiet when

Good Speaking Habits

- **Connect with your audience.** Make eye contact with your listeners. Address people by name if possible.

- **Match your body language to your message.** Check your posture and facial expressions. Use appropriate gestures.

- **Avoid nonwords.** Avoid words such as *uh* and *um* and "empty" words such as *well, sort of, like,* and *kind of.*

- **Stress key ideas with inflection.** Inflection is the pitch or loudness of your voice.

- **Use correct pronunciation.** Pronunciation is how you say the sounds and stresses of a word.

- **Practice enunciation.** Enunciation is speaking each syllable clearly and separately.

- **Be enthusiastic and positive.** Remember, attitude counts!

someone talks. It's not the same as hearing. Listening is a conscious action. When you listen, you use your brain to interpret, or make sense of, what you hear.

Active Listening

Many people don't know the first thing about listening. They think about other things while you're talking to them. They plan what they're going to say. They look away instead of making eye contact. They interrupt. They may even finish your sentences. Talking to a poor listener can be frustrating, even aggravating.

Name some people you like talking with. The people who come to mind are probably good listeners. Good listeners show that they care about what someone is saying. They practice active listening. **Active listening** is listening and responding with full attention to what's being said.

CRITICAL THINKING. Have students think about body language. How does it provide clues as to whether or not a person is listening?

Active listeners focus on the main ideas a speaker is communicating. They use body language and facial expressions to respond. They might sit up straight, lean forward, smile, or nod, for example, to show their interest. Active listeners also react by making comments and asking questions. They encourage whoever's speaking to tell more.

EXPLORE Activity

Try active listening with your friends, family members, and teachers. Don't tell them what you're up to. Just practice being an active listener whenever you talk together.

Note how people react when you pay attention to what they're saying. Think about what you learn by being a good listener. Also identify ways you can continue to improve your listening skills. As *Figure 10-2* at right shows, listening will be one of your main activities in the workplace.

Taking Notes

Active listening can be a very useful tool in class. In some cases, you will want to go a step further and take notes as you listen. Taking notes helps you remember facts and keeps your attention focused. When you take notes, both your mind and your hands are involved in listening.

Practice these skills as you take notes in class. You'll find a use for the same skills one day in the workplace and in many other situations.

- Jot down summaries in your own words. Focus on keywords and main ideas. Don't try to write down everything a speaker says.
- Note actions you need to take.
- Use bullets (•), asterisks (*), and arrows (→) to show how ideas are related or connected.
- Review your notes fairly soon after you take them to be sure you understand the information.
- If you can't take written notes, make mental notes of important points.

Time Spent Speaking and Listening on the Job

Speaking
23%

Listening
55%

Other Activities
22%

FIGURE 10-2 Working with Graphs

The average employee spends more than half the workday listening. Speaking takes up nearly a quarter of the workday. What do you suppose the other activities in an average workday include?

Reading and Writing

Reading, writing—not a day in school goes by without them. Schools spend a lot of time teaching students how to read and write well. They do this for a very good reason. It's hard to get along in the world today without these basic skills.

Right now, you need strong reading and writing skills to do well in school. In the near future, you may use these skills to get a driver's license and complete applications for college. You'll also need reading and writing skills to apply for a job.

Reading and writing are also important *on* the job. Can you name a job that doesn't involve reading and writing? There aren't many. Employers value employees who can read and write well. Employees with these skills can take in and exchange large amounts of information. Your success in a career will depend in part on your reading and writing skills.

Key Reading Skills

It's probably hard to remember the time in your life when you didn't know how to read. You have years of experience by now. You're well on your way to having the strong reading skills you'll need in the workplace.

List some of the reading skills you use in social studies, science, and English classes. You have probably used previewing before. **Previewing** is reading only the parts of a written work that outline or summarize its content. You can find these parts in a book by looking at the table of contents or flipping through the pages. The chapter titles and headings will tell you what's in the book. Previewing saves time when you need a general idea of what the content is.

Skimming is another timesaving reading skill. You are **skimming** when you read through a book or document quickly, picking out main ideas and key points. To skim, look at the first sentence of each paragraph. Also try to identify key words and phrases.

Skimming is very helpful when you're doing research. It's a good way to pinpoint information quickly in references such as encyclopedias and articles on the Internet. At what other times might you skim for information? When wouldn't you use skimming while reading?

When you read for information, you often read quickly. What do you do when you come across an unfamiliar word or phrase? If you stop to look in a dictionary, you lose valuable time. There's another way. Try looking for context clues.

Context clues are hints about the meaning of unfamiliar words or phrases provided by the words surrounding them. You can use context clues to understand the meaning of words you don't know. Context clues can be a real time-saver when you're reading for information. They also come in handy when you're reading just for pleasure.

As you recall, taking notes is a useful listening skill. It is also an extremely important reading skill. As you read, jot down main ideas, useful quotes, new vocabulary, and your own summaries of information. Notes will help you understand and recall what you read.

Reading on the Job

You'll use many of the same skills on the job to gather, evaluate, and interpret information. In the workplace, you'll read directions, letters, bulletins, and reports. You'll need reading skills to do research for projects. Sometimes you'll want to read quickly for general information. At other times, you'll want to read carefully for specific facts. Keep polishing your reading skills. You'll need them just as much in the future as you do now.

Writing Basics

Have you been practicing your speaking skills? If you have, you've got an advantage with writing. Much of the advice for speaking well applies to writing well.

Whether you're speaking or writing, you need to know your purpose, audience, and subject. Writing is a way to communicate. You can communicate better when you know *why* you're writing, to *whom* you're writing, and *what* you're writing about.

TEACHING ACTIVITY. Ask pairs of students to work together to make examples of context clues. Students may use difficult words that they already know or that they come across in reading. Then have the students use the word in a sentence that helps explain its meaning. Let other students figure out the meaning of each difficult word.

CAPTION ANSWER. Students should observe that rewriting in their own words helps them understand the material. They may also comment that they shouldn't copy other people's words without permission or without recording where they got the information.

▼ Follow the same tips for taking notes while reading as you would while listening. Why is taking notes in your own words better than copying someone else's?

TEACHING ACTIVITY. If necessary, go over a basic outline format with the class. You may want to show students an informal outline in which no numerals or letters are used.

Here are some other guidelines for writing:

- *Organize your writing.* Before you begin writing, outline what you have to say. Put your ideas in logical order, such as chronological order or order of importance. Use headings and subheadings to label different parts of your writing.
- *Check your spelling and grammar.* Use a spell checker on a computer. Keep a dictionary close by to check words you are unsure of. Consult a style book for grammar rules.
- *Watch your tone.* Keep your audience in mind. Direct your words to the people who will be reading what you write. Be respectful and polite.
- *Edit your work.* When you think you are finished, go back one more time and read through your work. Make changes in what you have written until your message is clear.
- *Proofread your work.* Carefully check your work for errors.

> ### FIGURE 10-3

COMMON FORMS OF BUSINESS WRITING

At some point in your job, you may need to write a memo, a letter, or a report. What are the similarities and differences between these forms of writing and writing you do now?

A

Memos
Businesspeople use memos to communicate with others in the office. They also send memos to people outside the office who work closely with them. Memos are usually brief and focus on a limited topic. They are often fairly informal in tone.

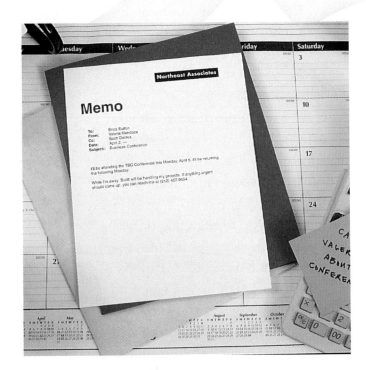

Forms of Business Writing

You've probably written your share of reports for school, and you will write more. You may write every day in a journal. Every few days you may E-mail someone. You have many uses for writing right now.

You'll discover many other uses for writing when you begin working. Some of the common forms of business writing are shown in *Figure 10-3* below.

The basics of writing apply to business writing too. That's all the more reason to keep working on your writing skills. You'll need them in the future.

EXTENDING THE LESSON. Tell students to find an interesting newspaper or magazine article that is fairly long. Have them skim the article, writing down the main ideas and key points. Have them exchange the article with a partner and then compare main ideas and key points.

B
Letters

In general, letters are more formal than memos. They are used to communicate with people outside the office who are customers or who work in other businesses.

C
Reports

The purpose of a report is to address a topic at length. The topic may be a possible new project or the progress of an ongoing project. Reports also often describe the results of research. People both within and outside an office may read reports.

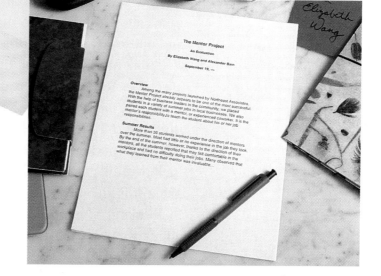

Using Images to Express Ideas

A picture is worth a thousand words. That's what they say. Do you agree? Look around if you need convincing. Look at magazine ads, TV commercials, posters, and billboards. Look at your favorite sites on the Internet. All use **images,** or pictures, as well as words to get their message across. Images include photographs, illustrations, videos, maps, and graphs. A lot of information can be packed into one image.

Images are everywhere you look. They are used to communicate all kinds of information. They grab people's attention and interest them in a subject.

Think of the different kinds of images you've used in work at school. You've probably drawn charts, maps, and graphs for social studies, science, and math projects. Maybe you've illustrated a report or book review. The posters, collages, dioramas, and bulletin board displays you've created have also included images. In each case, images were probably the best or most interesting way to present certain information.

Working with images takes practice. When you are thinking about using an image to convey a message, ask these questions:

- Can this image say something that I couldn't say with words?
- Is the image accurate? Up-to-date? In good taste?
- Is the message of the image clear?
- Is the image interesting? Will it catch people's attention?

The more you work with images, the more creative you'll become. In high school, you may make a video of yourself to include in a college application. One day, you may use words and images to create a brochure advertising your own business.

Images have a huge impact. Be sure to make using images one of your communication skills.

With all the milk I drink, my name might as well be Calcium Ripken, Jr. Really, I'm a huge milk fan. Besides being loaded with calcium, there's nothing like it when it's ice cold. Which is why I drink the recommended 3 glasses a day. And as you'd probably guess, I'm not one to miss a day.

got milk?

The Global Workplace

Time Is a Flexible Concept in Some Cultures

Not all countries start meetings on time. In Latin America, it is normal to arrive from 15 minutes to 2 hours late. Arriving on time is considered rude. In the Middle East, businesspeople are punctual but usually leave far past the predicted meeting end time. In the Far East and in Australia, as in the United States, professional people are usually on time.

Exploration Activity!

Using the Internet or library resources, research the outlook for jobs in Australia. What types of jobs are available there?

▲ People today are very visually oriented. They relate to images. Why might you use images instead of words to communicate something?

CAPTION ANSWER. Images catch people's attention. They can also convey a lot of information in a small space.

TEACHING THE GLOBAL WORK- PLACE. Point out to students that many different types of jobs may be available. Offer students methods for finding out more information about the global job market.

LESSON 10-1 • REVIEW AND ACTIVITIES

LESSON REVIEW AND ACTIVITIES. See the *Teacher's Manual* for answers.

Vocabulary Review

Imagine you're working in your first full-time job. You've volunteered to speak to middle schoolers about how communication skills helped you get your job. Give a talk on the subject to the class. Include the terms below in your talk.

communication
previewing
purpose
skimming
audience
context clues
subject
images
active listening

Check Your Understanding

Choose the correct answer for the following items. Write your answers on a separate sheet of paper.

Connecting to the Workplace

Taking Phone Messages

● Pretend it's part of your job to check your supervisor's phone messages. You are supposed to write a short summary of each message. When you check, there is one call, recorded at 2:10 P.M. on September 24:

"Hi, Andrea. Josh Liu here. I need to know if you want me to book that flight to Los Angeles for next week. If you let me know by the end of the day, I can still get the special rate. I'll be here until six o'clock. You can reach me at 555-6636. Thanks. Talk to you later."

● Using this information, summarize the call in writing for your supervisor.

1. Communication skills include

   _____.

   a. listening, reading, math, and science
   b. speaking, listening, reading, and writing
   c. reading, speaking, math, and listening

2. Three common forms of writing in business are _____.
   a. memos, letters, and reports
   b. notes, letters, and deeds
   c. documents, reports, and trusts

Critical Thinking

On a separate sheet of paper, answer the following questions.

1. What might happen if you do not take time to figure out your purpose before speaking?

2. What kind of image especially grabs your attention: photographs, illustrations, or graphs? Why?

Teamwork

What to Do
● With two other students, choose a career in hospitality or recreation.
● Research the career to find out how communication skills are used in it.
● Use the information you find to create a poster to interest young people in the career. Stress the importance of communication skills in the career. Use words and images to get your message across.

Applying Other Skills

What kinds of tools do you imagine yourself using in the different careers that interest you? None? Don't be fooled. Tools are not just objects like a hammer or a saw. A tool is anything that helps you accomplish something.

Many of the things you are studying now at school are tools for your future. Speaking, listening, reading, and writing are tools that will come in handy in the workplace. Math, science, and computer skills will also follow you out of the classroom. In fact, math, science, and computer skills are among the most important tools people use in careers today.

Math and Science

According to the dictionary, mathematics is the study of numbers, quantities, measurements, and shapes. Science is knowledge about things in nature and the universe. To you, either or both may just be interesting or challenging school subjects. What you are about to read, then, may surprise you.

Discover...
● how to strengthen your math and science skills.
● how to build your computer skills.

Why Is It Important to Build Strong Math, Science, and Computer Skills?
Most careers today call for math, science, and computer skills.

Key Terms...
● mathematics
● science
● spreadsheet
● netiquette
● emoticons

CAPTION ANSWER. Students may name specific or general applications of these basic skills in careers that require training in math, science, or computers.

◀ The math, science, and computer skills you learn in school have many uses outside the classroom. **How do you think you might use these basic skills in a job someday?**

Everyday Skills

The truth is that people—and that includes you—use math and science every day in very ordinary activities. Math helps people understand their paychecks, pay bills, and buy goods and services. People use math and science to weigh, measure, cook, sew, make, and build things. Math and science skills help people play sports, garden, and operate vehicles and machines.

Learning to Think

Is math or science your favorite subject? If so, you may be thinking about careers that require special skills in those areas. Perhaps you see yourself becoming a zoologist, an engineer, or a laboratory technician.

Even if math or science is not a strong interest of yours, you still have something to learn from both. Math and science help you develop good thinking habits. Math teaches you to put things in order and take one step at a time. Science teaches you how to observe things and processes. Both math and science teach you how to solve problems.

Sharpening Your Skills

No matter what your interests or plans for the future, work on your math and science skills. You can't go wrong. Basic skills in math and science will help you in daily activities and in all kinds of careers. Do you need some suggestions for sharpening these skills? Take a look at *Figure 10-4* at right.

Computers

Can you imagine a world not linked by telephone lines and satellite communications? Can you picture schools without computers or offices without fax machines? You probably can't. Computer technology has become a part of our everyday life.

People use computers to get money from automated teller machines (ATMs). At supermarkets and department stores, computers are used to scan bar codes on purchases. At school, you may use computers to do research on the Internet and to write and revise papers. You may use a computer at home to play games or communicate with others by E-mail.

✕ 🧪 = Tips for Building Math and Science Skills

1. Strengthen or expand what you already know.	Look for library books about improving your math or science skills. Check TV listings for public television programs on math skills or science topics.
2. Use a calculator only to check your work.	Do math problems by yourself first. The more you work with numbers, the easier it gets.
3. Play math games.	While you are waiting for the bus, for example, practice your multiplication tables. Think of other ways of testing your math knowledge.
4. Use another interest to help build an interest in math.	If you like horses, for example, make up math problems for yourself based on that. Horses are measured in hands. How long is a hand? If a horse measures 16 hands, how tall is the horse in feet and inches?
5. Organize information in different ways.	Classify things and events. Classify your accessories, for instance. Make a time line of highlights of your vacation or events in the school year. Present research you've done in the form of a table or graph.
6. Develop your observation skills.	Use your senses to observe your surroundings. Note entire objects or situations, and then details. Also practice using thermometers, scales, and other instruments to make observations.
7. Compare and contrast.	Identify likenesses and differences between things to learn more about what you observe.
8. Look for causes and effects.	After something happens, think about *why* it happened. The answer to the question *why* is the event's cause. Also think about *what* happened as a result of an event. Effects of the event will answer the question *what*.
9. Go metric.	Become familiar and handy with the worldwide metric system, known as International System (SI). Learn to convert other measurement units to metric. Practice converting to metric when you cook, sew, and build things.
10. Ask your math or science teacher for special help.	There may be times when you miss a lesson that provides important information or helps you with a particular skill. Get help as soon as you need it so you can keep up and continue to learn.
11. Work with a buddy.	Improve your skills with a friend. Work together. If you are good in English and your friend is good in math or science, trade your knowledge. If you can't find a close friend who is interested, ask someone else to tutor you.

FIGURE 10-4 Working with Charts

Don't let fear of math or science stand between you and your career goals. Try these suggestions for improving your math and science skills. What other methods work for you?

CAPTION ANSWER. Answers will vary; students should share methods of strengthening math and science skills that have worked for them.

Right now, you may not know exactly what you will be doing in the future. There's one thing you can count on, though. No matter where you work, you will use some type of computer technology in your job. Computer skills are as basic to work today as speaking, listening, reading, writing, math, and science.

Building Your Skills

If you haven't spent much time using a computer, it's not too late to start. Begin building your skills now.

Learning to use different kinds of software is one basic computer skill. Software is a computer program or set of instructions for doing a particular kind of work on the computer. Most computer software is "user-friendly." That means it is designed to help you make computers work for you even if you know little about them.

Many people know how to use word-processing software. Do you? With a word-processing program, you can write letters and reports. You can also create many other kinds of documents.

Word-processing software also allows you to edit what you have written quickly and easily. You can add, move, and delete letters, sentences, paragraphs, even a series of pages. All it takes is a couple of keystrokes.

There are other kinds of software you'll want to take the time to learn. Database software can be especially useful in school and, later, on the job. As you recall from Chapter 6, a database is a way of organizing and storing information on a computer. Databases are easy to search. In a database, information is just a click or two away.

▶ With desktop publishing software, you can create professional looking documents. How could you use this kind of software in school? How could you use it in the workplace?

You may already have found some uses for a database at school. Database software also has many uses in business. A store owner might use a database program to track sales or inventory, or items in stock. Many companies also make databases of their customers or of services they use.

You can also use spreadsheets to view and work with information. A spreadsheet is a program that arranges, or "spreads," information, usually numbers, in rows and columns. Spreadsheet software can also display information in graphs and other formats.

Many people and businesses use spreadsheets to keep track of schedules and of money coming in and going out. Perhaps you have a summer job. You want to know how much money you might be able to save over the summer. You could insert information in a spreadsheet about what you will earn and spend each month. Then you could use the spreadsheet program to predict how much money you'll have to put aside for savings.

Becoming a Citizen of Cyberspace

Like most people your age, you probably use the Internet. You may do research, visit favorite sites, E-mail friends, post on bulletin boards. You're a citizen of cyberspace—the huge on-line world.

Cyberspace will seem even bigger when you enter the world of work. Like you, businesspeople use the Internet to find information and communicate by E-mail. They have other reasons to go on-line, too. To save time and money, they E-mail long documents and images instead of faxing or shipping them. They advertise and sell products. They provide information and help to customers. They post job openings and locate job applicants. Some companies even conduct job interviews on the Internet.

Whatever their reasons for going on-line, serious Internet users practice netiquette. **Netiquette** is a term for the accepted rules of conduct used on the Internet. When you use the Internet at work one day, you will need to be especially careful to have good manners. There's no reason why you can't start now, though. Here are some of the basic rules of netiquette:

- When sending a message, always complete the subject line. Readers on the Internet want to be able to identify subjects of messages quickly.
- When responding, state to what you are responding. Never just say yes or no.

CAREER OPPORTUNITIES

Hospitality and Recreation
If you like to learn about faraway places, this might be the job for you.

Critical Thinking
Do you need a college degree to get this job?

Travel Sales Reservations Agent

A travel agency offers an exciting opportunity to join our sales staff. We're looking for motivated people to answer our busy reservation phone lines. Candidates must be outgoing and have sales personalities. You must know how to use a computer and be available for a three-week training class. Experience is helpful but not mandatory.

- Don't type in all capital letters.
- Don't ramble. Internet users appreciate specific, focused messages.
- Use a definite close for your message. Sign your name or write "The End."
- Avoid personal or sensitive issues. Never use obscene language. Do not make insulting remarks about groups of people.
- Use **emoticons,** groups of keyboard symbols designed to show a writer's feelings. See ***Figure 10-5*** for examples.

When you think about it, it makes sense to observe netiquette. Following rules is an important part of being a good citizen—in cyberspace or anywhere else.

RESEARCH. Ask students to choose a career that interests them and research how computer skills are used on the job.

EXTENDING THE LESSON. Have students find out about the work life of someone they know who uses a computer. How much time does this person spend on the computer? What are some advantages and disadvantages?

CAPTION ANSWER. They are a quick, easy, space-saving way to express emotions.

Emoticons

Keyboard Symbol	Meaning or Emotion
:-)	Happiness (smile)
;-)	Just kidding (wink)
:->	Humor (impish grin)
:-(	Sadness, disappointment (frown)
:-o	Emphasis (shout)
=:o	Frustration, confusion (wrinkled brow)

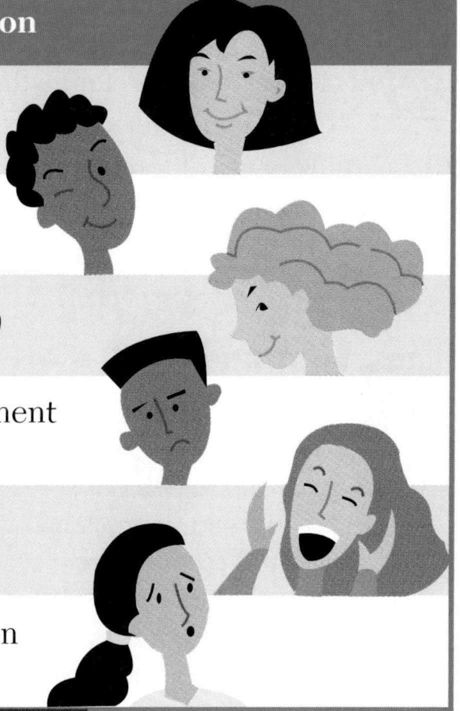

FIGURE 10-5 Working with Charts

Emoticons are also called smileys. Turned sideways, each looks like a face showing an emotion. **Why do you think people on the Internet use emoticons?**

LESSON REVIEW AND ACTIVITIES. See the *Teacher's Manual* for answers.

Vocabulary Review

Write a series of questions and answers that use the following key terms. Write the questions on one side of a sheet of paper and the answers on the other. Trade papers with a partner and answer each other's questions.

mathematics   netiquette

science   emoticons

spreadsheet

Check Your Understanding

On a separate sheet of paper, tell whether each statement is true or false. Rewrite any false statements to make them true.

1. Most careers today call for math, science, and computer skills.
2. Learning to use different kinds of software is one important computer skill.
3. E-mail messages should be typed in all capital letters.
4. Emoticons are used to show a writer's feelings.

Critical Thinking

On a separate sheet of paper, answer the following questions.

1. How might you use thinking skills you learned in math or science in a career that interests you?
2. How would you respond to someone who claims that computer skills are not basic skills?

Community Involvement

What to Do

- The Internet is often described as a virtual community. It's not an actual place on earth. Like a community on earth, however, it brings people with common interests together. Spread the rules of netiquette on the Internet, your virtual community.
- The next time you E-mail someone, follow netiquette.
- Also share the rules with the person to whom you're writing.
- Practice and share other rules you hear about.

Connecting to the Workplace

Working with Computers

- Select one work activity involving computers that appeals to you.
- In a career reference book, find a job related to this area of interest.
- In a paragraph, explain your computer interest and the job you have identified.

Investigating Career Clusters

Hospitality and Recreation

What Is the Hospitality and Recreation Cluster?

Occupations in this cluster involve helping people make travel plans and participate in leisure-time activities. Jobs center around such areas as travel agencies, transportation, and public and private recreation.

Skills Needed

Science skills, communication skills, interpersonal skills, creative skills, organizational skills, and computer skills; good health and physical stamina also required

THE FACTS	Types of Careers in This Cluster	Work Description	Career Outlook	Education
	Travel agent	Help clients make travel arrangements, including flight and hotel reservations	Faster than average	H.S. diploma, Bachelor's
	Reservation ticket agent	Help customers by answering questions, making reservations, and writing and selling tickets	Slower than average	H.S. diploma, Training program
	Hotel clerk	Provide services to hotel, motel, and other lodging establishments	Average	H.S. diploma
	Recreation worker	Plan, organize, and direct activities that help people enjoy their leisure time	Average	H.S. diploma, Bachelor's
	Sports instructor	Teach others to play and enjoy sports	Average	Professional training in sport

Research Activity

The hospitality and recreation industry is a large one that employs many people. Research this occupational cluster and list 15 careers from it. Make a list of a diverse range of jobs from this cluster.

Chapter Highlights

- Communication skills—speaking, listening, reading, writing, and using images—help you get information and share ideas. They'll play a big part in your success both at school and at work.
- Math, science, and computer skills are basic skills for today's workplace.

Recalling Key Concepts

Using complete sentences, answer the following questions on a separate sheet of paper.

1. How does it help to know your purpose, audience, and subject when speaking?
2. What two reading skills would you use if you needed to read a lot of material?

3. What thinking skills do math and science teach you?
4. Why is netiquette important?

Thinking Critically

Using complete sentences, answer the following questions on a separate sheet of paper.

1. Why are speaking, listening, reading, and writing called basic skills?
2. How can you practice active listening on the telephone?
3. What can you learn by solving math problems without a calculator?
4. What do you think is one of the most important business uses of the Internet? Explain your answer.

Building Skills

1. Information—Interprets and Communicates Information

Play telephone with four other classmates. Ask your teacher to whisper some rather complex instructions to one member of your team. That team member should whisper the instructions to a second team member. The second team member should whisper the instructions to the third team member and so on. Have the fifth member write the instructions on the board. Compare the original instructions with the ones written on the board. Then with your team, discuss how you could improve your interpretation and communication skills.

2. Technology—Selects Technology

Work in a team of three people. Create a chart that compares two brands of word-processing, database, or spreadsheet software. Together, research the software. Read magazines, visit computer sites on the Internet, and talk with users and store owners. On a chart, list the strengths and weaknesses of each brand of software.

Applying Academic Skills

1. Social Studies

Ron is a truck driver for a moving company in your state. As his supervisor, you need to give him written directions for his next assignment. Using a state map, plan a route that begins at one point in the state and ends at another point. Using at least three steps, write the directions on a sheet of paper. Then exchange your written directions with another student. Map Ron's route on a road map of your state.

2. Computer Science

With the help of a computer teacher, create a Web page on a science topic of interest to you. Research the topic and collect images that tell about it. Write text for the Web page. Scan images to include on the page. Add links to other Web sites that tell more about your topic.

Discovery Portfolio

Make Reading a Habit

- Create two lists: one of books you'd like to read, the other of books you've read.
- Browse in the library and in bookstores for books you might like. Add titles of any and all books that interest you to your first list. Then read.
- When you finish a book, add the title to your second list. Tell friends and family members about books you enjoyed. Keep both book lists in your portfolio.

Career Exploration: Hospitality and Recreation

- Research a career in the hospitality and recreation career cluster.
- Check the library and the Internet for information about the career.
- If you can arrange it, interview someone with a job in the career.
- Then pretend you work in that career. Write an imaginary letter to someone interested in the career. Include information about the kinds of work, the working conditions, and training and education required. Also include skills needed to do the job.
- Explain the outlook for the career.
- "Send" it to the classmate who sits next to you. Read each other's letters.

Chapter 11

Staying Healthy and Safe

What You'll Learn...

- You will learn how to make healthful choices.

- You will discover how to handle stress.

- You will find out how to stay safe and deal with emergencies.

- **CAREER CLUSTER** You will explore careers in *manufacturing*.

LESSON 11-1
It's Your Health

LESSON 11-2
Make Safety Your Business

LESSON PLAN. See the *Teacher's Manual* for the Chapter 11 lesson plan.

Activity

TRY THIS!

Health is important to people of all ages. Talk with friends and family members about what they do to stay healthy. Ask what they would like to do to be healthier.

APPLY: With a friend or family member, set a simple goal for better health. Work on it individually for one week. Then discuss how you feel. How has work on your health goal affected other parts of your life? Give each other encouragement to continue.

It's Your Health

CAPTION ANSWER. Students can make sure they are making the right choices by eating a variety of healthful foods each day that correspond to the number of servings recommended by the Food Guide Pyramid.

▶ The food choices that you make will affect your health now and for years to come. How can you be sure that you are making the right choices?

Think about those you love most. That might include your brothers and sisters, your parents, other family members, your dog or cat, your best friend. How do you feel when you think about how much they mean to you? Imagine what you would do to keep them healthy and safe.

Now imagine having that same deep feeling of caring for yourself. Think of yourself as your own best friend.

Making Healthful Choices

When you care *about* yourself, you take care *of* yourself. Adult family members do their best to keep you healthy and safe while you are growing up. As you get older, however, you're expected to take responsibility for yourself. Making healthful choices is part of taking care of yourself.

Health is the condition of both your body and your mind. Being healthy is more than being free of pain or illness. When you're healthy, you have the physical and mental energy you need to do things. Where does this energy come from? It comes from eating wisely and getting exercise and rest. Being healthy also involves guarding against sickness and harmful habits or behaviors.

Healthful Eating

Have you ever felt light-headed during gym? Do you forget about eating at lunchtime because you're busy socializing with friends? When you're thirsty, do you reach for your favorite soft drink? Are french fries your idea of a meal?

If you answered yes to any of these questions, it's time to take a close look at your eating habits. Your body may be running on empty.

You may not be eating enough. In addition, what you are eating may not contain enough nutrients. **Nutrients** are the substances in food that the body needs to produce energy and stay healthy. To find out more about nutrients, take a look at **Figure 11-1** below, which shows the Food Guide Pyramid. The U.S. Department of Health and Human Services created

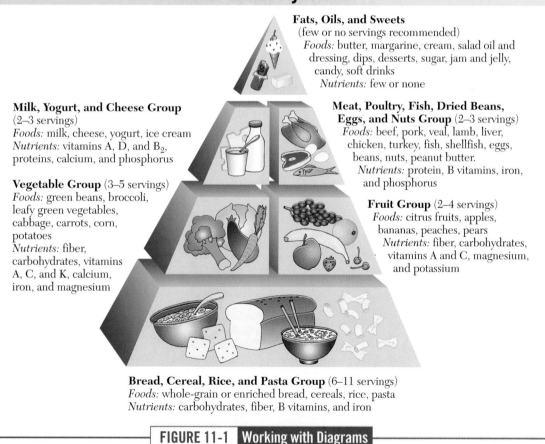

Food Guide Pyramid

Fats, Oils, and Sweets
(few or no servings recommended)
Foods: butter, margarine, cream, salad oil and dressing, dips, desserts, sugar, jam and jelly, candy, soft drinks
Nutrients: few or none

Milk, Yogurt, and Cheese Group
(2–3 servings)
Foods: milk, cheese, yogurt, ice cream
Nutrients: vitamins A, D, and B_2, proteins, calcium, and phosphorus

Meat, Poultry, Fish, Dried Beans, Eggs, and Nuts Group (2–3 servings)
Foods: beef, pork, veal, lamb, liver, chicken, turkey, fish, shellfish, eggs, beans, nuts, peanut butter.
Nutrients: protein, B vitamins, iron, and phosphorus

Vegetable Group (3–5 servings)
Foods: green beans, broccoli, leafy green vegetables, cabbage, carrots, corn, potatoes
Nutrients: fiber, carbohydrates, vitamins A, C, and K, calcium, iron, and magnesium

Fruit Group (2–4 servings)
Foods: citrus fruits, apples, bananas, peaches, pears
Nutrients: fiber, carbohydrates, vitamins A and C, magnesium, and potassium

Bread, Cereal, Rice, and Pasta Group (6–11 servings)
Foods: whole-grain or enriched bread, cereals, rice, pasta
Nutrients: carbohydrates, fiber, B vitamins, and iron

FIGURE 11-1 | Working with Diagrams

Foods are usually grouped according to the nutrients they provide. This pyramid shows you how many daily servings you need from each food group. **Why does the Food Guide Pyramid recommend few or no servings of fats, oils, and sweets?** CAPTION ANSWER. They contain few or no nutrients.

TEACHING ACTIVITY. Remembering the responses in the Discussion Starter activity on energy levels and exercise, take a poll to find out how many students exercise regularly.

CRITICAL THINKING. Ask students if they think they are healthy. Have them list 10 adjectives to describe their own health. Ask them to complete the statement: "I generally feel...," using three of the adjectives they listed.

CAPTION ANSWER. Answers will vary.

the **Food Guide Pyramid** as a guideline for the nutrients you need each day.

Building good eating habits now will help you throughout your life. You can start to eat wisely by getting the number of servings suggested in the Food Guide Pyramid.

Here are some healthful eating suggestions from people your age:

- "Make a breakfast smoothie with milk or yogurt, your favorite fruit, and honey." (Val, age 13)
- "Buy washed and cut veggies and those tiny carrots for snacks." (Josie, age 15)
- "Have milk or juice at mealtimes. Between meals, drink as much water as you can." (Mila, age 12)
- "Volunteer to make dinner once a week. Try new recipes. Have fun putting a meal together." (Pat, age 13)

Exercise for Life

How do you feel when you exercise or play your favorite sport? Your heart races. You breathe harder. When the routine, run, or game is over, you're still raring to go. You're pumped.

Exercise takes energy, but it also gives it back. It helps you feel better physically, mentally, and emotionally. How? Exercise builds strength and endurance. It makes you more alert. It also helps you feel less tense and anxious about things.

▼ Exercise can be a way to have fun with your friends. What activities do you and your friends enjoy?

Employers find that employees who exercise regularly do better work. They don't get sick as often as other employees do. Exercise is especially important if you have a **sedentary** job—one in which you spend much of your time sitting.

People often complain that they don't have time to exercise. The truth is, you don't need that much time. Exercising for 20 minutes three times a week can do wonders for your health.

Finding the time to exercise may not be a problem for you right now. The hard part may be choosing what to do. What do you like? Aerobics? Dancing? Basketball? Running? Whatever form of exercise you choose, make sure it's something you enjoy. Exercise should be fun, not a chore.

One last tip. Make exercise a regular part of your life now. Then you'll always make time for it. Exercise will be a natural part of your day or week, no matter how busy you are.

Time for Sleep

Perhaps your life is already quite busy. Your daily schedule may be something like Oona Hartwell's.

After school twice a week, Oona plays soccer. On the other days, she might go to a friend's house or have a friend over. If not, she talks on the phone with friends. In the evening, Oona feeds and walks her dog. She also helps clean up after dinner. Then there's homework—about two hours a night. If she has any time left over, Oona reads or watches some television.

Oona is usually asleep by eleven o'clock. She is supposed to be up by seven. Frequently, though, she sleeps later than seven. When she leaves for school, she still feels sleepy.

Sleep restores the body and recharges the brain. It is also an important part of the growing process. Most people need at least eight hours of sleep a night. While you're still growing, you may need even more. If you're feeling sleepy like Oona, your body's telling you that you need more sleep.

Without enough sleep, it can be difficult to think and concentrate. You're more likely to make careless errors. When you don't get the sleep you need, your performance can suffer. You

It's a good idea to get up around the same time each day. How much sleep do you get each night on average?

CAPTION ANSWER. Answers will vary; emphasize the importance of getting eight hours of sleep each night; discuss ways students can change their routine to get the sleep they need.

DISCUSSION STARTER. Have students write on a sheet of paper how much sleep they feel people their age should get. Fold the paper and exchange with a partner. Compare answers in class and discuss.

don't want that to happen in the classroom now. You won't want it to happen later on the job.

Give yourself the rest you need to do your best. Try to go to bed about the same time each night. Also avoid foods and drinks that contain caffeine, such as chocolate and some soft drinks. You'll be better rested for your busy day ahead.

Protecting Your Health

Eating a balanced diet and getting the right amounts of exercise and rest are important. There's more to staying healthy, though. You need to protect your health. You can do that in several ways:

- *Practice good hygiene.* **Hygiene** is all the things you do to be clean and healthy. It includes brushing and flossing your teeth and taking regular baths or showers. It also includes washing your hands frequently throughout the day. Washing your hair and wearing clean clothes are other examples of good hygiene.
- *Get regular checkups.* See your doctor once a year. Discuss problems and concerns you have. Ask to have your eyes and ears checked if you've noticed you're having trouble seeing or hearing.
- *Seek help for eating disorders.* An **eating disorder** is a pattern of extreme eating behavior over time. When you have an eating disorder, you may eat too much or too little. You may not like your body. You may have unrealistic ideas

about how you should look. Eating disorders can lead to serious illness or death. If you think you might have an eating problem, get help. Talk to a family member, teacher, school nurse, doctor, or someone else who can help you.

- *Guard against tobacco, alcohol, and drug addiction.* **Addiction** is a physical or psychological need for a substance. Substances that can lead to addiction include tobacco, alcohol, prescription drugs, and illegal substances such as marijuana and cocaine. Addiction to tobacco, alcohol, or drugs can cause depression, heart attack, lung or liver disease, and even death. Addiction affects every part of your life, including your work at school or a job and your relationships with others. If you think you may have a problem with a harmful substance, talk to someone about it. Ask for help. Addiction is a serious health risk, but recovery is possible. Support groups help many people who are recovering from addiction.

Taking risks can be fun and rewarding. Rock climbing is a risk. Trying out for the debate team is a risk. Playing a solo with the jazz band is a risk. Going to college is a risk. Accepting a job is a risk.

Just make sure the risks you take and the choices you make are healthful ones. When you meet a challenge and do your best, you feel great.

CRITICAL THINKING. Ask students to list some of the obstacles to protecting one's own health that are not physical. What do we sometimes do to threaten our own well-being?

CAPTION ANSWER. You can find out what weight is right for you by talking with your doctor.

◀ You can't compare your own best weight with that of your friends. There are differences among people of the same age. How can you find out what weight is right for you?

Some positive situations can be stressful. Would you feel stress in this situation? Why or why not?

Handling Stress

It's test day. You didn't sleep well last night. You couldn't eat much this morning. Your heart's pounding. Your palms feel sweaty. You can't concentrate. What's going on? You are experiencing stress. Stress is the mental or physical tension that is the body's natural response to conflict.

Good Stress, Bad Stress

Stress isn't always a bad thing. Runners may feel stress before a big race. Many musicians feel stress before a concert. Actors often feel it before the curtain rises. You may feel stress the first day of high school or before a job interview.

The kind of stress you feel before or during a big event tells you that what you are doing is important to you. You are excited and focused on what's happening. You want to be and do your best. At such times, stress can actually help you do a good job or get through an event. When the challenge is over, your body returns to normal. The stress goes away.

Sometimes, though, stress stays with you. You may be generally worried or fearful. You may simply feel tired a lot of the time. You may be distracted. You may have headaches or stomachaches. You may not feel like eating, or you may eat a lot. You may not be able to sleep, or you may want to sleep all the time. This kind of stress can wear you out.

You can feel stress anywhere—at home, in the classroom, on the soccer field. Once you enter the work world, you'll feel stress there too. To perform well—wherever you are—you must learn how to handle stress.

Ways to Cope

What can you do about stress, especially bad stress? Here's what health experts recommend. First, try to identify the cause of the stress. Then deal with the problem directly. *Figure 11-2* at right shows some situations or problems that can cause stress. It also offers ideas for dealing with the stress.

Coping with Stress

Causes	Ways to Cope
Major changes, such as marriage, divorce, moving, going to a new school, starting a new job, losing a job, or serious illness or death of a family member	• Be patient. Give yourself plenty of time to adapt to the change. • Try to limit changes in other areas of your life. • Especially in the case of illness or death in the family, let someone at school or work know. Ask for lighter responsibilities (less homework or less demanding assignments at work) for a time. Most people understand and honor such requests. • Gather a support system. Talk about what you are going through with someone. Friends, family members, and other people who care about you can provide insight and encouragement. Seek professional help from a counselor if necessary.
Conflicts or disagreements at home, school, or work	• Talk the problem out with a trusted friend, coworker, or supervisor. • Look for common ground with the other person. Use your conflict resolution skills. • Consider getting someone to mediate—to listen to what both sides have to say.
Too much to do, too little time	• Keep track of how you use your time. What can you change to make your life less stressful? • Set realistic goals. You don't have to be a superhero—someone who does everything. • Review your workload with a teacher, coworker, or supervisor. Get help handling your work. • Set priorities, and then take one step at a time. • Make a schedule. Don't forget to include time for eating, sleeping, exercise, and relaxing. These activities will give you energy to do what you need and want to do.

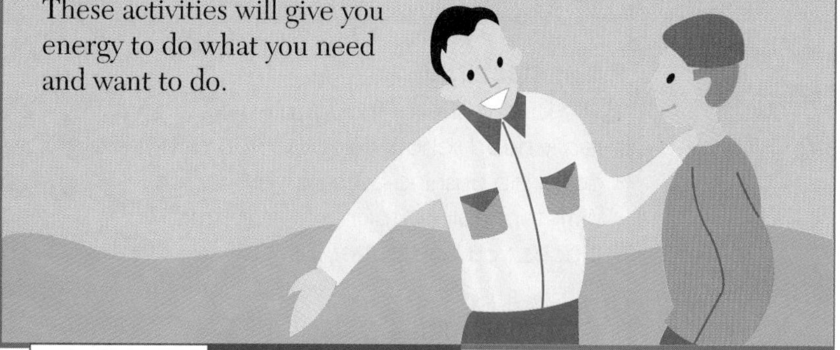

FIGURE 11-2 Working with Charts

Stress is a good alarm system—if you're paying attention. It often tells you that you need to take action or make a change. What do you need to do before you can deal with stress?

CAPTION ANSWER. Students need to figure out what's causing the stress.

EXTENDING THE LESSON. Ask for volunteers to do some reading about the place of fat in nutrition. Generally, fat is not considered helpful to protecting your health. Ask your "experts" if there is such a thing as "good" fat. Have them give a brief report to the class.

Relaxation techniques, or ways of relaxing, are also helpful in stressful situations. Here are several that many people use:

- *Breathe deeply.* Slowly fill your lungs with air. Count to 10 as you do. Hold it. Then slowly release, again to a count of 10. Repeat as needed.
- *Visualize.* Close your eyes. Picture yourself in a peaceful place, away from the stressful situation. The place might be a forest, the beach, a park—wherever you feel calm. What do you feel, smell, and hear there?
- *Take a time-out.* Get away from the stressful situation for a while. Take a walk. Give yourself time to calm down. You may see solutions you didn't see before.
- *Vent.* Share your feelings with a friend, family member, or other person you trust. Ask the person just to listen. Then try brainstorming solutions together.

There's no getting around it. Stress is a natural part of life. Why wait to do something about it? Try out what you've learned about handling stress right now at home and at school. You can use the same techniques later to manage stress on the job and in other parts of your life. Knowing how to manage stress is a life skill. It will help you stay healthy.

TEACHING CAREER OPPORTUNITIES. A machine operator needs to understand the SCANS basic foundation skills and workplace competencies.

CAREER OPPORTUNITIES

CLASSIFIED

THURSDAY, SEP

Manufacturing

Have you ever thought that you don't *really* need school because you can always get a job pushing buttons on a machine? With technology taking over in most workplaces, you had better think twice.

Critical Thinking

What kinds of skills does this machine operator need to know to do his or her job?

Machine Operator

You will weigh incoming rods, maintain role identity, cut to length and finish rod orders, and help with wire drawing equipment. Duties also include hand grinding, swaging, and using power hacksaws and centerless grinders. Requirements: high school diploma and the ability to perform physical work, read micrometers, and handle basic math.

LESSON REVIEW AND ACTIVITIES. See the *Teacher's Manual* for answers.

Vocabulary Review

Imagine you write articles for your company newsletter. Write a short article on tips for healthful living. Include the terms below.

health	hygiene
nutrients	eating disorder
addiction	Food Guide Pyramid
sedentary	stress

Check Your Understanding

Choose the correct answer for each item. Write your answers on a separate sheet of paper.

1. To be healthy, you need to
   _____.
   a. exercise two hours every day
   b. eat wisely and get exercise and rest
   c. skip meals

2. One way to manage stress is to
   _____.
   a. put in more hours at work
   b. eat more often
   c. use relaxation techniques

3. If you exercise regularly now, you
   _____.
   a. won't have to exercise when you're older
   b. will always make time for it
   c. will not get enough rest

Critical Thinking

On a separate sheet of paper, answer the following questions.

1. Which area or areas of your health do you need to improve? What will you do?
2. What methods do you use to deal with stress at school?

Connecting to the Workplace

Wellness Programs

- Many companies offer wellness programs to employees. A wellness program might include exercise classes and classes for managing stress, losing weight, and quitting smoking.
- Do some research on exercise. Identify three forms of exercise employees might do as part of a wellness program at the workplace.

Teamwork

What to Do
- In a small group, make three signs for the school halls or cafeteria that give tips for staying healthy.
- Each sign should offer one tip. Make each tip short and catchy to grab people's attention quickly.
- Post your signs in places where the most people will see them.

Make Safety Your Business

Discover...
- what you can do to stay safe and prevent accidents.
- how the government, employers, and employees make the workplace safe.
- how to respond to an emergency.

Why Take Steps to Stay Safe?

Following safety measures can prevent injuries. That means fewer accidents at home, school, and work, and more time and energy for other activities.

Key Terms...
- Occupational Safety and Health Administration (OSHA)
- workers' compensation
- emergency
- first aid

CAPTION ANSWER. He's wearing the proper safety gear.

Accidents happen. Everyone knows that. What you might not know is that most accidents can be prevented. Accidents don't have to have the serious consequences, or results, that they often do. There are many ways that everyone can help prevent accidents.

Taking and Sharing Responsibility

Play it safe. That's good advice at home, at school, in the workplace—wherever people are active. When you practice safety, you protect yourself and others from harm or danger.

Many people are concerned about your safety and are there when you need help. Family members, teachers, and police are just a few of the people who are looking out for you. That's comforting to know. Even so, you can't always rely on others. It's a good idea to learn to look out for yourself. You need to make safety *your* business.

➤ By following the rules and avoiding unnecessary risks, you can prevent most accidents from happening. **What is this boy doing to stay safe?**

Safety Rules

You probably already take many steps to be safe. Think about the rules of the road that you follow, for example. As a pedestrian, or person traveling on foot, you pay attention to what drivers and others on the road are doing. You always cross at crosswalks or intersections. You look out for vehicles turning right on a red light. When riding in a car, you always wear a seat belt, whether you're seated in the front or back.

It won't be long before you're old enough to have a driver's license. Before you get a license, though, you'll need to learn how to operate a car safely. To do that, you will study a manual and take a class. You will practice on the road with someone who knows how to drive. Then you will take a road test and a written test. These will test your understanding of basic safety rules for the road.

EXPLORE Activity

Can you think of everyday situations in which you follow rules? With a partner, make a chart of rules you follow daily. Write at least five rules in one column. In a second column, write what you believe is the reason for each rule. Which rules listed help keep you safe?

Reducing Risk

Following rules is one part of safety. Avoiding unnecessary risks is another. Many activities involve some chance of harm.

You may enjoy outdoor activities. Do you like swimming or boating? Hiking and camping? Maybe you have a favorite winter sport like skiing or snowboarding. Perhaps you like to skateboard with your friends. There are also many at-home activities, such as cooking, sewing, and making or building things.

These and other activities you may enjoy are supposed to be fun. You don't want to get hurt doing them. Here are three safety secrets for any activity:

- *Respect your limits.* Know how much you are really capable of doing. Pushing yourself beyond your training and ability is taking an unnecessary risk.

The RIGHT Attitude!

Accepting Criticism

Learning new skills sometimes means accepting constructive criticism. If a teacher or supervisor offers constructive criticism, she or he is trying to help you learn. Remember, it's about the work, not about you! Helpful tips can strengthen your skills and teach you how to do your job more effectively.

Apply Your Skills!

Write a journal entry about some comments made about one of your projects. How did you feel about these comments? Were they helpful?

MOTIVATING STUDENTS. Find out if students know of anyone who has been injured at work. What precautions could have been taken in this particular case? Have students volunteer answers.

DISCUSSION STARTER. Ask students who is responsible for safety in the workplace. How is that responsibility divided?

TEACHING ACTIVITY. Have students name some activities they already engage in that carry risks. For each activity, have them list two or three precautions that they normally take.

Remember, to be safe, you need to look out for yourself. What should you do if someone suggests you do something that you know is not safe?

CAPTION ANSWER. Tell them no, walk away from the situation, do what you know is safe.

- *Think before you act.* Ask yourself: Is this situation safe? Are there risks involved? How can I protect myself?
- *Don't give in to pressure from others.* Don't let others push you into doing what you know or sense is not safe.

Working with Others

It is said that there is safety in numbers. In other words, it is often safer to be with others than it is going it alone. That doesn't mean you shouldn't learn how to look out for yourself. It means that when people get together, they can be even safer than they would be individually.

Just think of your own community. You probably already take steps there to protect yourself. For instance, you don't talk to strangers. You always let someone know where you'll be. You keep alert on the streets—especially at night. You also stay away from dangerous and poorly lit areas.

You can also take steps to make your community safe by working with others. You can work with your family and neighbors. Set up a Neighborhood Watch group. Neighborhood Watch members look after one another and one another's homes. They are trained by the police to identify and report suspicious activities. As members of a Neighborhood Watch group, neighbors and families share responsibility for community safety.

Safety on the Job

It's no different in the workplace than it is in your community. In the workplace, the government, employers, and employees team up for safety. They cooperate to create a safe working environment.

The Government's Role

The United States government protects its workers by setting safety standards, or guidelines. It also makes sure accident victims receive care. A special branch of the U.S. Department of Labor, the **Occupational Safety and Health Administration (OSHA),** is in charge of setting safety standards. It also inspects workplaces to make sure that the standards are being followed.

In addition, workers' compensation laws passed by the government protect workers who are hurt on the job. Under **workers' compensation,** injured workers receive financial help to cover both lost wages and medical expenses.

▲ People in different jobs take different kinds of safety precautions. How does this worker protect himself on the job?

The Global Workplace

Religion May Affect the Business of the Day

Religious habits vary from culture to culture. In the Middle East, business leaders take religious matters very seriously. They may stop to pray several times a day. In the Far East, it is considered rude to take photographs of statues of religious figures, like the Buddha. Foreign visitors should learn something about the religious habits and rules of the host country. This will help them adapt to the country's customs.

Exploration Activity!

Research the religions of the Middle East. What are some of the customs of the religions in this area?

Q: What should I do if I don't feel safe at work?

A: The first thing you should do is tell your boss why you don't feel safe. Most bosses appreciate any comments that help make the workplace safer. Write down all the times, places, and reasons you feel unsafe at work. Give the record to your boss or human resources department. Local government agencies and police or fire stations are other resources in your community for advice and help.

CRITICAL THINKING. Ask students if they feel it is right that government plays a major role in making the workplace safer. Do they think that employers should have an equal role? Have students list some of the employer's responsibilities.

Partners for Safety

Of course, employers and employees must do their part for safety. It's up to employers to provide a workplace that is free of health and accident hazards, or dangers. The equipment and materials workers use must be safe. If work conditions are unsafe, employers must tell their employees.

Employers must also take the time to teach workers how to use equipment and materials. "Safety is our number one priority," comments Dick Wentz, president of a plastics manufacturing company in New Jersey.

❝ Training prevents all kinds of accidents. ❞

Wentz knows how costly accidents can be. American businesses spend billions of dollars a year on lost wages, medical expenses, and insurance claims.

When you enter the work world, you will take on new responsibilities. One of those responsibilities will be your own safety on the job. You may operate a piece of heavy equipment or work at a keyboard. Whatever you do, you will have health and safety concerns to consider. You will need to follow safety rules. When you notice unsafe conditions or practices, you will need to report them right away. Safety will continue to be your business, as it is now.

In Case of Emergency

No matter how careful people are, accidents happen. Would you know what to do in case of an emergency?

Is It an Emergency?

An emergency is something serious that happens without warning and calls for quick action. Some emergencies are more obvious than others.

Unusual noises, sights, odors, appearance, or behavior can be signs of an emergency. You might hear crying, moaning, or a call for help, for instance. Alarming sounds such as breaking glass, screeching brakes, or crushing metal can also signal an emergency. You may see sparks, smoke, or fire or find someone lying on the ground. The smell of gasoline, smoke, or some other strong odor can also alert you to an emergency. A person who does not look well or who is breathing or speaking with difficulty may need immediate help.

Once you've identified an emergency, you need to evaluate the scene. Before doing anything, quickly figure out what has already happened. Think about what may happen next. Consider your own safety. It won't do much good to jump in the water to save someone if you can't swim. Other hazards may prevent you from offering to help someone.

◀ Be prepared to handle emergency situations. What should you do even if you aren't sure whether someone is seriously injured?

CAPTION ANSWER. Get help.

What to Do

If someone is injured and you are nearby, stay calm. Then follow these easy-to-remember American Red Cross guidelines. Provide **A-I-D**:

- ***Ask for help.*** If someone is seriously hurt, call 911 or another emergency medical number immediately.
- ***Intervene—step in and offer help.*** If you aren't sure what to do, do nothing. Just comfort the person. Tell him or her that help is on its way.
- ***Do no further harm.*** Do not move a victim unless there is an immediate danger, such as a fire.

The letters of the word *AID* help you remember what to do in an emergency. It also helps to know your ABCs. As ***Figure 11-3*** below shows, the ABCs are another easy way to remember what to do in an emergency.

▶ **FIGURE 11-3**

KNOW YOUR ABCs IN AN EMERGENCY

The American Red Cross ABC guidelines help you remember priorities, or what to do first, in an emergency. Where might you learn more about these first-aid methods?

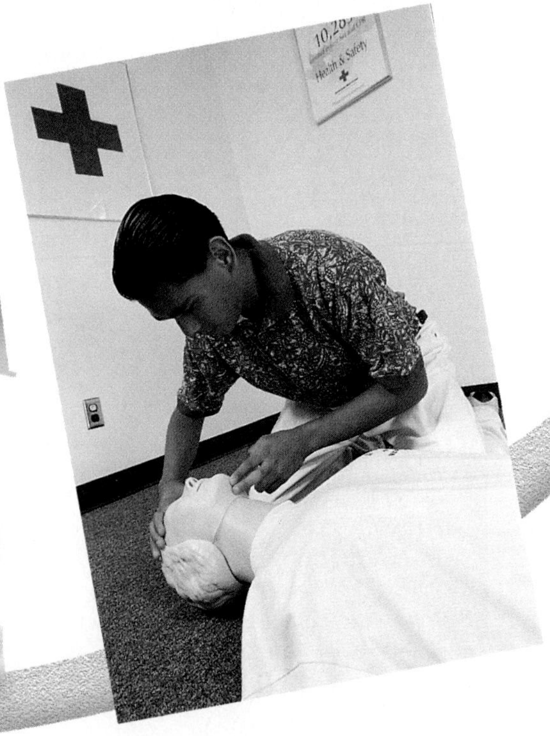

A

Airway

If necessary, clear the victim's airway (the passage that allows the person to breathe). Do this by placing one hand on the person's forehead. At the same time, place two fingers of the other hand under the person's chin. Tilt the head back by pushing on the forehead and lifting the chin.

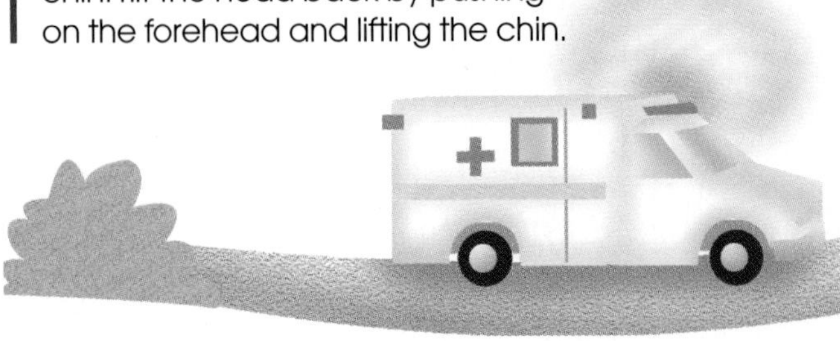

Knowing first aid can often save someone's life. **First aid** is the actions taken in a physical emergency before help arrives.

You never know when you might need to know first aid. Take it from Robby and Carlos. They were just standing at the mall talking when an older man sitting nearby began to have trouble breathing. While Carlos went for help, Robby sat with the man and helped him stay calm. "The emergency team said our quick thinking saved that man's life," Robby explains. "I'm glad we were there and knew what to do."

You may be glad you know what to do someday too. Safety is everybody's business.

EXTENDING THE LESSON. Have students speak with a person who is familiar with CPR or first aid. If there are students who have learned these skills, they could demonstrate some techniques for the class.

C
Circulation
Check to see if the victim has a pulse. Also check to see whether he or she is bleeding severely. If so, press a clean cloth on the wound. Then hold firmly with your palm.

B
Breathing
Check to see if the victim is breathing. Watch for rising or falling of the chest. Also listen and feel for air moving out of the mouth and nose. If the person is not breathing, administer rescue breathing if you know how.

LESSON REVIEW AND ACTIVITIES. See the *Teacher's Manual* for answers.

Vocabulary Review

Your next assignment for the company newsletter is an article about safety on the job. In your article, tell how the government, employers, and employees cooperate to make the workplace safe. Use the terms below.

Occupational Safety and
   Health Administration
   (OSHA)

workers' compensation

emergency

first aid

Check Your Understanding

On a separate sheet of paper, tell whether each statement is true or false. Rewrite any false statements to make them true.

1. When you practice safety, you protect yourself and others from harm or danger.
2. It is the sole responsibility of the employer to create a safe work environment.
3. The first step to take in the event of an emergency is to evaluate the scene, then follow AID and ABC guidelines.

Critical Thinking

On a separate sheet of paper, answer the following questions.

1. What precautions do you take to stay safe at home?
2. Why do you think the government sets safety standards for the workplace?
3. Why is it important to survey the scene of an accident before acting?

Connecting to the Workplace

Handling Emergencies

● Make a chart with four columns, labeled *Jobs*, *Emergencies*, *Safety Precautions*, and *Responses*.
● In the first column, list five part-time jobs open to people your age.
● In the second column, list emergencies that could arise in each job.
● In the third column, describe safety precautions you could take to avoid each kind of emergency.
● In the fourth column, write how you would respond to each emergency. Share your ideas in a class discussion.

Community Involvement

What to Do

● Invite a member of the local chapter of the Red Cross to talk to your class about the organization's activities.
● Prepare questions about the work of the Red Cross.
● Find out what kinds of classes and programs the Red Cross sponsors locally.
● Ask how young people can help the Red Cross.
● Then with others in your class, create a bulletin board display about the Red Cross.

Investigating Career Clusters

Manufacturing

What Is the Manufacturing Cluster?

Occupations in this cluster involve the design and assembly of products ranging from huge earth-moving equipment to the microminiature parts of an electronic instrument. Besides management, jobs center around scientific, engineering, technical, skilled, semiskilled, and unskilled work.

Skills Needed

Science skills, math skills, communication skills, ability to work with your hands, creative skills, technical skills; physical stamina also needed

THE FACTS	Types of Careers in This Cluster	Work Description	Career Outlook	Education
	Chemist	Develop new and improved fibers, paints, adhesives, drugs, electronic components, and other products	Average	Ph.D.
	Industrial engineer	Apply scientific theories to solve practical problems of industrial machinery	Average	Bachelor's
	Science technician	Assist scientists in research	Average	Associate's or Bachelor's
	Textile machine operator	Tend machines that manufacture a wide range of textile products	Slower than average	H.S. diploma, On-the-job training
	Engineering technician	Assist engineers in research, development, inspection, and production	Slower than average	Associate's
	Production manager	Coordinate the activities of personnel in a production department	Slower than average	Bachelor's

Research Activity
Research five manufacturing jobs of interest. Make a chart with three columns. In the first, list the job title; in the second, state the job outlook; in the third, write an explanation for the growth or decline of this occupation.

● Chapter Highlights

- To be healthy, you need to eat wisely and get exercise and rest. You also need to guard against sickness and harmful habits or behaviors.
- Government, employers, and employees share responsibility for creating a safe workplace.

● Recalling Key Concepts

Using complete sentences, answer the following questions on a separate sheet of paper.

1. What are the six groups of food in the Food Guide Pyramid?
2. What are four ways you can protect your health?
3. What is stress?
4. What is OSHA, and how does it help workers?
5. What does *AID* help you remember to do in an emergency?

● Thinking Critically

Using complete sentences, answer the following questions on a separate sheet of paper.

1. What foods would you include in a healthful breakfast?
2. What are two ways you could get more sleep on school nights?
3. What technique do you find most helpful in dealing with stress? Why?
4. Why do you think many young people take risks?
5. How can clear thinking skills help you in an emergency situation?

Building Skills

1. Information—Organizes and Maintains Information

Evaluate your eating habits. For one week, write down what you eat each day. Then categorize your daily food choices according to the groups in the Food Guide Pyramid. In which groups do you need to eat more servings? Fewer servings? Change your daily eating habits to reflect the food groups and servings recommended in the Food Guide Pyramid. Continue to pay attention to what you eat, comparing your daily servings to these guidelines. Make healthful eating a habit.

2. Personal Qualities— Self-Management

Take a personal safety inventory. Think about the safety precautions described in this chapter. Do you follow safety rules and avoid risks in all situations? Prepare two lists. First, list precautions you already take. Then, make a list of ways in which you could act more safely. Practice the items on both lists.

Applying Academic Skills

1. Science

Susan works at a computer all day. Joyce works in a meatpacking plant. Tyrone lifts heavy packages. All three repeat the same motions throughout their workday. As a result, all three have developed repetitive stress injuries, or RSIs. To deal with the problem of RSIs, engineers are working in a new field of science called *ergonomics*. Visit OSHA's Web site, and use library resources to learn about ergonomics. Present your findings in an oral report.

2. Health and Physical Education

With your classmates, design a wellness program for your school. Include choices of exercise, healthful snacks, and stress-beating activities. Schedule time in the school day for each part of the program. Work with teachers, school cafeteria staff, the school nurse, and interested parents to make your wellness program a reality.

Discovery Portfolio

Connecting Careers and Health Issues

- How do the careers that interest you match your outlook on health and fitness? Write a paragraph that describes some of your health and fitness goals.
- List careers you find interesting.
- Explain how each career matches your health and fitness goals.
- Put your summary in your portfolio.

Career Exploration: Manufacturing

Research a career that you find interesting in the manufacturing career cluster.
- Look for information in the library and on the Internet.
- If possible, interview someone with a job in the career you've chosen.
- Create a collage about the career. Include information about the kinds of work, the working conditions, and the training and education required. Also include skills needed to do the job.
- Explain the outlook for the career.

Chapter 12

Moving Toward Your Goals

What You'll Learn...

- You will discover ways to learn and grow in everything you do, including a job.
- You will find out why it is important to reevaluate your goals.
- You will learn about changes you might make in a career plan.
- **CAREER CLUSTER** You will explore careers in **marine science**.

LESSON 12-1
Learning and Growing

LESSON 12-2
Reevaluating Your Goals

LESSON PLAN. See the *Teacher's Manual* for the Chapter 12 lesson plan.

Friends & Family Activity

TRY THIS!

Interview adults you know who love their careers. Ask these questions:
- When did you decide on this career, and why?
- What jobs have you held in your career field?
- How has your career helped you grow?
- Where do you think your career will take you?
- What other career might you choose?

APPLY: Take notes. Present the results of each interview in question-and-answer format.

Learning and Growing

Discover...
- how to get the most out of everything you do, including a job.
- how to get and handle more responsibility on the job.

Why Try to Learn and Grow in All Your Experiences, Including a Job?

Your life is precious. Make the most of everything you do. Your time and energy are investments in your future and your happiness.

Key Terms...
- promotion
- raise

"When are we going to get there?" "Are we there yet?" When you were younger, you probably asked these questions frequently on long trips. As a child, you did not have a clear sense of time. You probably also did not notice the signs and landmarks along the way. Others were in charge of planning the route and getting you to your destination.

Now that you're older, you understand how long two hours, two days, or two years is. That means you can understand and plan for your future. You're able to set goals and achieve them. You're no longer just a passenger. You're in the front seat now, and you've got a good idea of where you're going.

Getting the Most Out of All You Do

Where are you on your journey? You're probably working hard in school. You're looking ahead to high school. You may have some ideas about interesting careers. Maybe you volunteer

CAPTION ANSWER. Answers will vary; students should identify a variety of activities at home, at school, and perhaps in the work world and explain what each has taught them.

➤ There is something to learn from everything you do. What activities are you involved in right now? What have you learned by participating in them?

or have a part-time job. You're probably working toward a variety of goals. Are you getting the most from everything you do?

The Right Attitude

"I'm bored." "I wish I were somewhere else." Sound familiar? Everyone has thoughts like these from time to time. Maybe you were thinking something similar just yesterday at school. Many people have these thoughts at work each day. Thoughts like these can have a negative effect on what you're doing.

Usually it's not your situation—where you are, what you're doing—that triggers this kind of thinking. It's your attitude, or basic outlook on things. A change of attitude can make a huge difference in everything you do. It can make the smallest or least likely activity an important part of your journey.

EXPLORE Activity

See for yourself. The next time you feel bored or wish you were somewhere else, try this. Challenge yourself to find something worthwhile in what you are doing.

Take your least favorite class, for instance. Go into the class with an open mind. Focus on the subject. Practice active listening. Think about what your teacher is saying. Pay attention to what your classmates have to say. Contribute to discussions. Participate in other ways.

For one week, keep a journal. Record what happens in the class. Also record what you discover about the subject of the class, yourself, and your classmates. You may be amazed at what you learn, thanks to your new attitude.

With a positive attitude, you are always ready to learn and grow. You'll find every situation inviting and interesting. Everything you do will have value. Every experience will be a step on the way toward your goals.

Daily Journal

Always Give Your Best

Effort counts as much as attitude. You hear that from everyone—teachers, parents, coaches. Give it your best! Do you?

Giving Criticism

Giving constructive criticism to a classmate or coworker can be just as tricky as receiving criticism. The way in which criticism is given makes all the difference. When offering a critique of someone's work, remember to use a calm voice. Focus on the problem and not on the person, and suggest improvements. Most important, do not make any hurtful remarks. At its best, criticism is a helpful way for people to learn new things.

Apply Your Skills!

Role-play these critiquing situations with a partner.
• You are asked to critique a painting in art class.
• You're captain, and you need to give your teammates some tips for winning a game.
• You're doing an experiment in science, and you need to critique your partner's lab report.

Giving your best is not about being the best. It is giving your hardest effort to something. It means sticking with it and not giving up. What you do may be something you like or don't like. You may succeed or fail. In the end, though, you have the satisfaction of knowing you gave it your all.

Like having a positive attitude, giving your best can bring unexpected rewards. Jules Veanor knows that from experience. He did well in math, but it was not his easiest or favorite subject. Jules's math teacher suggested he take honors math in eighth grade, based on his work in seventh grade. Jules wasn't sure. He was afraid the class would be too hard.

In the end, Jules took his teacher's advice and signed up for the class. "It definitely was a challenge," Jules admits.

> **"** *I gave it everything I had, but I got something back. I learned a lot. I improved my math skills. More than that, though, I feel more confident now about what I am able to do. I won't be afraid of a challenge next time around.* **"**

Growing on the Job

Learning isn't something that happens only in school. Growing isn't something only the young can do. You can learn on a job just as you do in school and in other activities. You continue to grow in different ways throughout your life.

In the workplace, there are opportunities to learn and grow at every level. It will be up to you to look for them and take advantage of them. How will you do that? Again, it's a matter of attitude and effort.

Attitude is Susan James's secret to getting the most out of her volunteer job at a local nursing home. "I look at my job as the most important position at the nursing home," explains Susan. "Of course, there are many other people who have more responsibility than I do. I fill a real need of the residents, though. I offer them companionship and friendship. To me, that's the most important job of all, and I take it seriously."

Extra effort will also help you get the most from a job. You probably know someone who does exactly what's required in class but no more. He or she may get a good grade but not much else. Now imagine two employees in the same job. One always does only what he is told to do. The other does what she is asked and more. She shares new ideas. She volunteers to help out when needed. She is open to suggestions. She is willing to try something new. In other words, she shows initiative. As you recall from Chapter 8, when you show initiative, you do what needs to be done without being told to do it. Which employee do you think learns and grows more on the job?

Whether you're a volunteer or a part- or full-time worker, make your time at work worthwhile. Here are some suggestions for making the most of any job.

- *Do your job as well as you can.* That is, do your assigned work to the best of your ability. Devote equal effort to *all* parts of your job. Finish what you are assigned.
- *Volunteer to do more.* When you've finished your regular duties, ask if there is something else you can do. Be willing to pitch in and lend a hand.
- *Look for opportunities to learn on the job.* Learn to do new tasks that will help you move ahead in your career plan. Learn whatever else you can on the job. You never know how you might use what you've learned.
- *Get more education or training.* Take advantage of every opportunity to further your education. The more education and training you have, the more career choices you will have. Remind yourself of the many options open in education and training by reviewing the chart on page 86 in Chapter 5. When you interview for a job, find out what kind of training the employer offers. Ask if the employer will help pay for classes you take elsewhere. Once you have a job, take courses you need to move up to a better job.
- *Be willing to try new things.* You may have a favorite way of doing something. You feel comfortable with it and see no reason to change. That doesn't mean you shouldn't try new ways to see how they work. You never know—they may work better. They may give you new ideas. If you want to grow, you need to be open to new things.

▲ You learn in many other places besides school or on a job. What skills have you learned at home?

CAPTION ANSWER. Answers will vary but may include cleaning, cooking, painting, carpentry, gardening, shopping, bike maintenance, child care, care of an older person, pet care or training, or sewing.

TEACHING ACTIVITY. Have students close the book. Write on the board the phrase "Giving your best." First discuss how *giving your best* is different from *being the best.* Have students brainstorm the advantages that come from *giving your best* even though a person may fail to *be* the best.

More Responsibility

Growth often leads to more responsibility. Think of the responsibilities and privileges you've begun to enjoy at home now that you're older. At school, you may be a leader in class, on a team, or in a club. You probably became a leader because of your attitude and the skills, knowledge, or experience you have. In high school and beyond, you will have even greater responsibility and independence.

As you grow on a job, you may also find that you are given more responsibility. You may even get a promotion. A **promotion** is a job advancement to a position of greater responsibility and authority. A volunteer, for example, might advance to a paid position. A salesperson might be promoted to supervisor of sales. Promotions offer new challenges. They also usually include a **raise,** or increase in pay.

Who Gets Promoted?

At the end of each school year, your teachers decide whether to promote you—to the next grade. To make their decision, they review your work and grades. They think about whether you can handle work at the next grade level.

Employers take similar steps. They want to make sure that employees they promote can handle additional responsibility and authority. How do they determine this? They review their employees' performances on the job. They also look for certain qualities in employees. Some of these qualities are shown in *Figure 12-1* at right.

Future employers will look for these qualities in you before promoting you. People you may work for right now—the neighbors for whom you house-sit, for example—also have these qualities in mind. They will consider them carefully before adding to your responsibilities or offering you a raise.

Carlos was promoted several times by Shady Grove Day Camp. When he was 13, he was a volunteer camp counselor for a month. He worked with a high school student named Ed who was a full counselor. Together, they were in charge of 12 first- and second-grade campers.

The first week on the job, Carlos carefully observed Ed. He paid attention to how Ed interacted with the campers. By the end of the month, Carlos felt comfortable in his position. He even suggested some new activitites. He volunteered to lead a nature walk, for example—and it was a big success.

Ed recommended Carlos for a paid position as an assistant counselor the following summer. In his new job, Carlos was responsible for leading the afternoon activities. He tried out many new ideas.

The next summer, Carlos returned to Shady Grove as a full counselor. In this position, he earned twice as much as he had

CRITICAL THINKING. Ask students if they would accept a promotion as soon as it was offered in case they "missed out." Would this be fair to yourself or your business?

RESEARCH. Tell students to look up a local business in the Yellow Pages. What are they able to find out about that business's promotion policies? (They might contact the Human Resources department and ask for information and/or written material about company policy.) Have students write a short summary of the policies (average time before promotion, salary increases, and other items).

Checklist of Qualities Employers Look For

- Seniority, or length of time on the job
- Knowledge and ability to perform basic skills
- Willingness to learn
- Initiative
- Perseverance, or ability to finish what you start
- Cooperativeness
- Thinking skills
- Adaptability
- Education and training

FIGURE 12-1 Working with Checklists

These are just some of the qualities employers prize in employees. You can begin to develop many of these qualities right now in school and in other activities. Which are already strong qualities of yours? When do you use or show them?

CAPTION ANSWER. Answers will vary; students should cite specific instances when they have used or shown the qualities they identify.

the summer before. That's because he was experienced and had twice as much responsibility. He even supervised an assistant counselor.

Do You Want More Responsibility?

Each time Shady Grove Day Camp offered him new responsibilities, Carlos thought carefully before accepting. He had to decide whether he wanted more responsibility.

These were easy decisions for Carlos. He liked working at the camp. He was also ready for new challenges. Trying new tasks in familiar surroundings appealed to him.

Can You Handle More Responsibility?

Of course, Carlos also had to ask himself if he could handle the added work. Carlos's first promotion involved more time on the job. Accepting the assistant counselor's job meant that Carlos would spend eight weeks as a camp counselor. This would cut into his summer activities. He would also have less time to spend with family and friends.

Carlos worked out a schedule that allowed time for everything he needed and wanted to do. The schedule took into account his work at Shady Grove during the day.

TEACHING CAREER OPPORTUNITIES. By reviewing and logging data, a fisheries data editor can learn a great deal about marine life. He or she can also learn to recognize those facts that are most important to fisheries. This information, and some courses in marine biology, could lead to a career as a fisheries observer.

CAREER OPPORTUNITIES

CLASSIFIED

THURSDAY, SEPT.

Marine Science

If you are organized, neat, and love sea life, this might be a good entry-level job for you.

Critical Thinking

What kind of knowledge or skills can a fisheries data editor learn to advance on the job?

Fisheries Data Editor

Fishery is looking for somebody to review, edit, and record marine data collected at fisheries. Requirements include a high school diploma and some post-high school courses in marine biology. Experience helping a fisheries observer is a plus. This position requires a high degree of accuracy and attention to detail.

There can be other things to consider when you are offered more responsibility. When Carlos was promoted to full counselor, for instance, he became a supervisor. He was responsible not only for his own work but also for work of an assistant counselor.

When you become a supervisor, your relationships with your coworkers will change. You will be the boss. You will oversee their work and give them direction. You will review their performance. It may be difficult to have close friendships with people you supervise. You will need to ask yourself whether you'll be able to adjust to these changes.

A promotion sometimes requires you to move to a new place. You may have to travel more in your new position. That may mean that you have to live far from family and friends or be away from them for periods of time. Will you be willing to move or travel? Handling more responsibility often involves making personal sacrifices such as these.

Yes or No?

When you're offered a promotion, you must take an honest look at yourself and at your goals. Being offered a promotion is always a good thing. It shows you've earned your employer's trust and appreciation. Not every promotion, however, will be right for you. You may have good reasons for not wanting more responsibility. You may know that you cannot handle what's involved. It's OK to decline, or say no, to a promotion. Just because you are not ready for more responsibility now doesn't mean you won't be ready later. If one promotion is not right, the next one might be.

The important thing is to be honest with yourself and your employer. Leave a door open for the future. Look at all you do in a positive way and keep at it. A positive attitude and your best effort will help you move toward your goals.

▲ When you decline a promotion, talk to your supervisor face to face. Why do you think meeting in person is important?

CAPTION ANSWER. You can explain why you are declining the promotion, clear up any misunderstandings, and leave your supervisor with the impression that you like your work and want to be considered for future promotions.

EXTENDING THE LESSON. Have students research jobs of the future, some of which may not exist yet. Ask students to choose one future career and write a paragraph about the skills they might need for this career.

LESSON 12-1 • REVIEW AND ACTIVITIES

LESSON REVIEW AND ACTIVITIES. See the *Teacher's Manual* for answers.

Vocabulary Review

Imagine you are an employer. Tomorrow you will discuss a promotion and raise with an employee. Write what you plan to say. In your remarks, explain the terms below.

promotion   raise

Check Your Understanding

Choose the correct answer for each item. Write your answers on a separate sheet of paper.

1. A positive _____ and your best effort will help you get the most out of everything you do.
   a. source
   b. company
   c. attitude

2. When you receive a _____ , you receive a position of greater responsibility and authority.
   a. diploma
   b. promotion
   c. raise

Critical Thinking

On a separate sheet of paper, answer the following questions.

1. What experience might you have benefited more from if you had had a positive attitude? Explain your answer.
2. How can a willingness to try new things help you grow? Give an example.
3. What would you do if you were offered more responsibility in your job?

Connecting to the Workplace

Working Toward a Promotion

- With a partner, role-play the following situation. Linette is a bookseller at a bookstore. She has held the job for two years. The position of assistant manager has become available. Linette thinks she is qualified for the promotion. The manager, however, has not offered her the position. Linette feels overlooked and a little angry.
- Role-play a meeting between Linette and the store manager.
- Then discuss with your classmates Linette's handling of the situation.

Teamwork

What to Do

- Some companies give promotions based on the amount of time a worker has been with the company. Other companies give promotions based solely on the worker's ability and performance on the job. Form a team for a debate.
- Which promotion policy do you think is more fair? Why?
- As a team, prepare to support your point of view in a debate.
- Debate with a team that takes the opposite point of view.

Reevaluating Your Goals

Do you ever wish that you could see the future? It would be fun to see yourself 10, 20, or 50 years from now. Just imagine knowing what the future was going to be like. You might do certain things differently in the present.

No one can really know the future, though. There's no way to be sure of exactly what you will be doing 10, 20, or 50 years from now. You can be certain of one thing, however. Some of your goals will change. As your life unfolds into the future, you will need to make adjustments in your plans.

Discover...
- why it is important to check your progress toward your goals.
- why you might make changes in a career plan.

Why Do You Need to Reevaluate Your Goals?

As you grow and change, your goals will change. You'll need to make adjustments in your plans, including perhaps your career plan.

Key Terms...
- notice
- letter of resignation

CAPTION ANSWER. Students should understand that short-term goals are stepping stones on the way to long-term goals.

◄ You should review your career plan on a regular basis. Check to see how well you are moving toward your goals. Which goals would you expect to meet first, long-term goals or short-term goals?

► Continue to explore who you are in high school and beyond. What activities or classes do you look forward to in high school?

CAPTION ANSWER. Answers will vary; students should identify high-school level activities and classes.

MOTIVATING STUDENTS. Ask students if they have learned a new skill in the past year. Was learning something new part of a plan, or did it just "come up"? Discuss students' answers.

DISCUSSION STARTER. What differences can students pinpoint between long-term goals and short-term goals? Which are usually more general, and which are more particular or specific? Have students name some of each.

Reviewing Your Career Plan

Do you get a progress report between report cards at school? A progress report tells you how you're doing in your classes. It may include suggestions for improving your work or raising your grades.

Your progress in school is your focus right now. Although you're exploring careers, you probably haven't launched a real career plan yet. More likely, your main goals are to finish this part of your education and go on to high school. Doing well in school, graduating, and continuing your education are important goals. They are the most important things you can do right now to prepare for any future career.

When you reach high school, you may begin to follow an actual career plan. You may choose classes, activities, and maybe even a part-time job that are related to a particular career. As you work on goals included in your plan, you'll need to review your progress occasionally.

The earlier you develop the habit of reviewing your career plan, the better. That way, your plan will keep pace with your growth. Remember, a career plan isn't set in stone. It should grow and change as you do.

At different points in a career, you'll want to see if you're moving toward the goals you set. You'll also want to make adjustments in your plan to fit the person you have become. You will update your plan throughout your career.

Making Changes

Many things can change your career plan. Just think back over your years in school. How have you changed? In the years ahead, changes will continue to occur.

Changing Direction

In high school and the years beyond, you will just be starting to move toward a career. You will still be learning a great deal about who you are. You will continue to develop your values. Your interests and skills will keep expanding in new directions.

At this early stage in your career plan, you will still be gathering a lot of information. You'll talk to people. You'll do research. You'll work part-time or volunteer your time.

CAREER Q&A

When to Change Jobs

Q: How long should I stay at a job before I move on?

A: As a rule, you should stick to one job for at least a year. Of course there are exceptions. If you feel unsafe or really dislike your job, then you should move on. If you're offered a better job somewhere else, then take it. Otherwise, if you change jobs too often, people will think you're a quitter. Nobody wants to hire a quitter.

DISCUSSION STARTER. Have students consider why an awareness of where one was, where one is, and where one is going is so important? What can happen if a person neglects to consider these questions?

CAPTION ANSWER. You might identify a new career direction by reevaluating your goals.

◀ **You may have several careers in your life-time. How might you identify a new career direction for yourself?**

Changing your career plan may seem frightening at first. In the end however, such a change may open up many new opportunities. What might these opportunities be?

CAPTION ANSWER. A change in your career plan may give you the opportunity to broaden your horizons. You may also learn more about your skills, aptitudes, and interests.

CRITICAL THINKING. Ask students what the relationship is between the ability to plan and the ability to remain flexible. Why are both important?

TEACHING ACTIVITY. Talk to your class about "downsizing" and change in the workplace. Ask students if the employment situation today is different from when their parents were young. What differences can students mention?

A world of possibilities will be open to you. New careers, new choices will emerge. Don't be surprised if you decide to go in an entirely different direction than you had planned. That's what happened to Jocelyn Sanders. Jocelyn had a career plan and knew exactly where she was headed. At least she thought she did.

"I grew up by the ocean, and my dream was to be a marine biologist. When it was time, I chose a college known for its marine biology program. My first years in college, I had to take a broad range of courses to meet various requirements. One way to meet the language requirement was to study abroad for a semester.

"I had studied French and chose to go to France. The experience completely changed my mind about a career. I found living in another culture fascinating. I began to think about careers in the global marketplace. Today, I have a career in international banking. I travel frequently and work out of a major U.S. bank's office in Hong Kong."

You can learn from Jocelyn's experience. Don't be afraid to change your career plan. At this early stage, you'll still be discovering what fits you best. When you find it, go with it. It's OK to change direction.

Changing Jobs

Remember the difference between a job and a career? A job is any work you do for pay. A career is one or more jobs in the same area of interest. During a career, you will hold a series of jobs.

Some of these jobs may be part of your original career plan. Doors to other jobs will open as your career goes forward. Look at *Figure 12-2* on page 260 to see the job changes one person made in the course of a career in biology.

As Gina's experience shows, people change jobs during the course of a career for a variety of reasons. You may feel another job would better fit your skills or personality. You may want new responsibilities or challenges. Maybe the idea of working for a different employer appeals to you.

CRITICAL THINKING. Ask students how people can prepare for a future that may include several careers. (Answers might include good attitude, flexibility, learning new skills, being open to new ideas.)

RESEARCH. Have students find out some good sources for following trends in the workplace, such as the downsizing of large companies and changes in the economy. They may list newspapers, magazines, or electronic sources. Ask them to name one source they had not heard of before.

The Global Workplace

The Work Week May Vary from Country to Country

Work schedules vary around the world. In the Middle East, the work week runs from Saturday to Wednesday or Thursday. Thursday and Friday are the religious days. In Italy, Spain, and Latin American countries, a long break, known as the siesta, often follows lunch. Work stops during this period and resumes later in the afternoon.

Exploration Activity!

Using library resources, research the work schedule and the length of vacations in Europe, the Middle East, and Asia. How much vacation time do workers have in these countries?

TEACHING THE GLOBAL WORKPLACE. Point out to students that many countries have different work routines. Some have longer hours than U.S. workers; others have shorter hours. Offer methods for finding out more information about work schedules.

TEACHING ACTIVITY. Ask an employed adult who has changed careers to speak to the class. Then discuss reasons why people change careers. (Remind students of the distinction between a job and a career.)

Changing jobs is never a snap decision. Whatever your reason, you should always make sure you think the change through carefully. Think about how the change fits your plan.

Bowing Out

You may take a different job in the same company or organization. You may find a new job with a new employer. Once you've accepted a job with a new employer, be sure to give proper notice to your current employer. Notice is an official written statement that you are leaving your job.

▶ FIGURE 12-2

ONE CAREER, MANY JOBS

Gina Cacciotti has held many jobs in her career. She may change jobs several more times. What kinds of jobs might be part of a career that interests you?

1

Gina had always wanted a career in education. As a high school student, she prepared for college by taking a variety of classes. In college, she majored in biology, her favorite subject. She took courses that would help her earn a teaching certificate. She also worked as a student teacher in a middle school.

2

After college graduation, Gina got a job as a middle-school science teacher. She taught seventh-grade science five periods a day. She quickly became a popular teacher. Students loved her science activities and projects.

3

The school principal recommended Gina to a textbook publisher looking for teachers to write science activities. Gina put together activities for a seventh-grade workbook. She later agreed to write a science textbook for seventh graders for the same publisher.

4

Gina continued to teach and do other writing projects for the textbook publisher. When a position as science editor opened up, the publisher offered it to Gina. Gina decided she was ready for a change from classroom teaching. She took the job.

5

After several years as a science editor, Gina was looking for a new challenge. She spotted a job opening for an editor in a different department at her company. The department specialized in educational multimedia products, such as software, videos, and CD-ROMs. Gina applied for and got the job. In her latest project, she is helping create interactive science CD-ROMs for middle school students.

▼ **FIGURE 12-3**
Even if you are leaving a job you don't like, you still must give notice. It's the right thing to do. What does a letter of resignation show your employer?

It is usual to give notice at least two weeks before you are going to leave. Then your current employer has time to find a replacement.

In some places of business, you may need to submit a formal letter of resignation. In a letter of resignation, you explain why and when you are leaving. *Figure 12-3* below shows a letter of resignation.

It doesn't matter what kind of job you have. You may be a newspaper carrier. You may be a manager in a large company.

Letter of Resignation

Ved Risvi
2827 Suncrest Drive
Mason, Illinois 66140

August 1, 19--

Mr. Albert Ziegler
Mason Times
1732 Hedgeview Lane
Mason, Illinois 66138

Dear Mr. Ziegler:

Thank you for giving me the opportunity to work with you at the *Mason Times*. I thoroughly enjoyed working on the paper's staff.

On August 26 I will be returning to Edison High School to begin my senior year. My schedule and responsibilities as a student will not allow me to continue my job as an editorial assistant.

I appreciate all you did to teach me about newspaper editing. I know that my experience at the *Mason Times* will be useful in the career I hope to have someday.

Sincerely,

Ved Risvi
Ved Risvi

It is professional—and courteous—to give notice. Giving notice helps you leave your employer on good terms. As *Figure 12-3* shows, Ved Risvi found out how valuable that can be.

"I worked part-time at a newspaper last summer," explains Ved. "I was going back to school soon, so I knew I couldn't continue working there. I wrote a letter to my boss. I told him that I would be leaving in two weeks to start school. I mentioned how much I had liked my job. I also told him what I had learned. I thanked my boss for hiring me. When I gave the letter to him, he thanked me for writing it. Before I left, he gave me a letter of recommendation. Writing that letter of resignation took just a few minutes of my time. Now, I have a recommendation for that next job in my career plan."

Changing Careers

People today change jobs frequently. As a matter of fact, the average American holds at least seven jobs before he or she reaches age 30. What may be more surprising, though, is that many people have several careers in their lifetime.

People have many reasons for making career changes. Some reach the end of their career plan. Others find their career plan is no longer right for them. Many people change careers to pursue personal interests. A good many choose to run their own businesses, as you'll discover in Chapter 13.

People who've already had one or more careers and are starting another have much in common with you. Like you, they are still getting to know themselves. They are exploring interests and expanding skills.

They know what you will learn. Discovering who you are and what you want to do is a lifelong process. You can learn and grow every step of the way—in new experiences, new jobs, and new careers. Don't forget to stop now and then to check your progress. It's an important part of your journey.

EXTENDING THE LESSON. Ask students to draw a series of cartoons or make a collage of the changes in their own ideas about a future career. Captions can creatively or humorously express the growth that they have achieved.

RESEARCH. Have students check the school or public library for a book of sample letters that includes a formal letter of resignation. Ask students to make a judgment about the letter. Is it adequate, or can improvements be made? Have them rewrite the letter as an informal letter of resignation.

LESSON REVIEW AND ACTIVITIES. See the *Teacher's Manual* for answers.

Vocabulary Review

In a short paragraph for an employee handbook, explain the rules for giving notice. Use and explain the terms below.

notice

letter of resignation

Check Your Understanding

On a separate sheet of paper, tell whether each statement is true or false. Rewrite any false statements to make them true.

1. Your goals will change as you get older. You will need to make changes in your plans.
2. Once you determine a career plan, you shouldn't change it.

3. It is usual to give notice two days before you are going to leave your job.
4. Many people have several careers in their lifetime.

Critical Thinking

On a separate sheet of paper, answer the following questions.

1. Why should you make a habit of reviewing your career plan from time to time?
2. What careers do you think you might have in your lifetime? Give at least three examples.
3. Why is periodically checking your career progress an important part of your lifelong journey?

Connecting to the Workplace

Changing Jobs

- Imagine you have cared for your neighbor's dog for three summers. You walk the dog while your neighbor is at work. You also dog-sit when she goes away on vacation. This summer, however, you have been offered a job as a bike messenger. You've decided you'd like a change.
- Write a letter of resignation to your neighbor that explains why you can't care for her dog as usual this summer. Remember, you want to keep your neighbor's respect and friendship.

Community Involvement

What to Do

- Network with adult friends and family members to identify someone in your neighborhood or community who has changed careers.
- Invite the person to talk to your class about his or her career change.
- With your classmates, prepare a list of questions for your guest before he or she visits.
- Follow up with a thank-you note.

Investigating Career Clusters

Marine Science

What Is the Marine Science Cluster?

Occupations in this cluster involve discovering, developing, improving, and harvesting marine life. Jobs are in areas such as research, fishing and aquaculture, and marine engineering and technology.

Skills Needed

Science skills, math skills, communication skills, and interpersonal skills; physical stamina also needed

THE FACTS	Types of Careers in This Cluster	Work Description	Career Outlook	Education
	Oceanographer	Study the ocean bottom, currents, and chemical composition of the ocean	Good	Ph.D.
	Aquatic biologist	Study the aquatic plants and animals and the conditions that affect them	Good	Master's or Ph.D.
	Fish farmer	Raise fish and shellfish in stock ponds	Good	On-the-job training
	Marine engineering	Design and oversee the construction of marine systems	Good	Bachelor's
	Marine architect	Design and oversee the building and repair of marine craft	Good	Bachelor's
	Scuba diver	Dive to locate and recover wreckage below the water	Good	Voc-Tech, scuba certification

Research Activity

Investigate marine science careers of interest. Make a list of five careers, and research the job duties and working conditions. Pick one, and write one page about that job. Include job duties, working conditions, employment outlook and the reason it interests you.

CHAPTER REVIEW. See the *Teacher's Manual* for answers.

Chapter Highlights

- A positive attitude and your best effort will help you get the most out of everything you do and move toward your goals.
- It is important to reevaluate your goals now and then. As you grow and change, your goals will change. You will need to make changes in your plans.

Recalling Key Concepts

Using complete sentences, answer the following questions on a separate sheet of paper.

1. Why does giving your best make you feel good about yourself?
2. What can you do to increase your career options?
3. What personal sacrifices might be involved in a promotion?
4. Why do people change careers?

Thinking Critically

Using complete sentences, answer the following questions on a separate sheet of paper.

1. What is your attitude toward school? How does it affect your performance at school?
2. How can you tell if you're ready for a promotion?
3. Why might you decline a promotion?
4. When do you think you should review your career plan?
5. What are two advantages of changing careers? Two drawbacks?

Building Skills

1. Thinking—Reasoning

Pretend that you would like a raise in your allowance. First, think about what you could do to earn a raise. For example, perhaps you think you could handle more responsibility around the house. Now, you need to show that you are ready for more responsibility. Helping others and showing initiative are two ways to prove that you're ready. Make a list of at least three ways you can do each at home.

2. Interpersonal—Exercises Leadership

Adam received a promotion and now supervises Paul, a coworker who is also a good friend. Paul has begun coming in to work late and leaving early. He doesn't perform as well on the job as before. When Adam talks with Paul, Paul says: "What's the big deal? I thought you were my friend. You sure have changed since you became boss." What would you say to Paul if you were Adam?

Applying Academic Skills

1. Mathematics

You have worked as a guide at the aquarium for two summers. This summer you have been offered the job again, but with a 4 percent raise. Your salary last summer was $1,875. You work two and half months. How much more will you earn per month this summer than you did the last two summers? What will your earnings be for the entire summer?

2. Language Arts

Pretend you are president of the student council. At the beginning of the school year, it's your responsibility to give a speech to the incoming students. This year's theme is "Giving Your Best." Write a three- to five-minute speech on giving your best at school, on the job, and throughout your life. Practice your speech before an audience of your family members.

Discovery Portfolio

Review Your Career Plan

- Review the career plan you made in Chapter 5.
- Update it if you have any new ideas about goals toward your career path. If you find other careers more interesting now, make plans for them.
- Keep your career plans in your portfolio.

Career Exploration: Marine Science

Select a career that you find interesting in the marine science career cluster.

- Use library resources and the Internet to research the career.
- If possible, also gather information through interviews. Then write a profile of the career. Include information about the kinds of work, the working conditions, and training and education required. Also include skills needed to do the job.
- Explain the outlook for the career.
- Include other interesting information. Trade profiles with a classmate.
- Describe two things you learned about marine science careers by reading your classmate's profile.

Chapter 13

Our Economic System

What You'll Learn...

- You will discover your place in the economy now and in the future.

- You will learn what kind of economic system our country has and how it works.

- You will find out what is involved in starting your own business.

- **CAREER CLUSTER** You will explore careers in *marketing and distribution*.

LESSON 13-1
The Free Enterprise System

LESSON 13-2
Being Your Own Boss

LESSON PLAN. See the *Teacher's Manual* for the Chapter 13 lesson plan.

TRY THIS!

Small businesses—that is, businesses owned and operated by individuals—are everywhere. Ask around to find out if you have adult friends or family members who are their own bosses. Use these questions to learn more about their businesses:

- How and why did you get into your business?
- What do you like about your business?
- What are some problems you face?

APPLY: Share your own ideas for a business with these friends and family members. Ask for their advice about how to launch one of your business ideas.

The Free Enterprise System

Discover...
- the meaning of free enterprise.
- how the free enterprise system works.
- how you fit into our economic system.

Why Learn About the Free Enterprise System?

The more you understand about our economy, the better your chances of reaching your career goals.

Key Terms...
- economics
- economic system
- capitalism
- free enterprise
- regulate
- consumers
- producers
- profit
- supply
- demand

S uppose you had to make a list of everything you spent money on last year. What would be on your list? Magazines, CDs, and clothing might be some of your purchases. Your list might also include movie tickets and haircuts. Would you be able to remember everything you spent money on?

You probably wouldn't be able to remember everything, but your list would still be quite long. As a teen, you are a member of a group with a great deal of spending power. You and others your age buy all kinds of goods and services. Goods, as you recall from Chapter 2, are *items* that you buy, such as in-line skates, jeans, and computer games. Services are *activities* people might do for you for a fee, such as tutoring, bike repair, and teeth cleaning.

► Young people are an important part of the economy. What kinds of goods and services have you purchased in the last month?

Many companies that provide goods and services take the interests of young people very seriously. Some even design products especially for teens. These companies make it their business to know what you and others your age like and want.

What do *you* know about these companies? What do you know about why companies sell goods and services? Have you ever wondered how the prices for goods and services are set? Do you understand why prices rise or fall?

What Is Free Enterprise All About?

You can find the answers to these questions by studying economics. Economics is the study of how people produce, distribute, and use goods and services. *Producing* means creating goods or services. *Distributing* means making goods and services available to the people who need them. Selling is one way of distributing goods and services. Delivering is another means of distribution. *Using* is what people do with goods and services.

How do people produce, distribute, and use goods and services? That depends on their country's economic system. An economic system is a country's way of using resources to provide goods and services that its people need and want.

The economic system of the United States is known as capitalism, or the free enterprise system. Free enterprise means that individuals or businesses may buy and sell and set prices with little government control.

In a free enterprise system, individuals and businesses have a good deal of free choice. The government does not plan what or how many goods or services will be available. It usually does not tell people where to work. It also usually does not tell individuals or businesses what prices to charge.

That doesn't mean, however, that the government has nothing to do with business in a free enterprise system. In fact, the government plays a very important role. As you learned in Chapter 11, it passes laws that set safety standards for the workplace. It also passes laws to regulate, or set rules for, some prices and wages. Laws passed by the government protect everyone who buys and uses goods and services.

MOTIVATING STUDENTS. Have students think about the ways they already fit into the economic system even though they are not yet working. (Do they earn or spend money?)

CAPTION ANSWER. Answers will vary but may include clothing, personal items, jewelry, magazines, CDs, food, computer games, movie and concert tickets, video rentals, haircuts, and manicures.

How Our Economy Works

People like you who buy and use goods and services are **consumers**. Consumers are an important part of the free enterprise system. They're just one part, though. Other parts of the free enterprise system include

- producers
- profits
- prices
- supply
- demand
- competition

Now take a look at how these parts of the free enterprise system work together.

Producers and Consumers

Where do the goods and services consumers buy and use come from? Individuals or companies known as **producers** make or provide them. Producers are another important part of the free enterprise system.

CAPTION ANSWER. Our economic system is called a free enterprise system because individuals and businesses are free to organize and operate, buy and sell, and set prices with little government control.

▼ New businesses are always opening in a free enterprise system. An enterprise is something a person or group of people plans or tries to do. Why do you think our economic system is called the *free* enterprise system?

Many young people are producers. If you design T-shirts, for example, you are a producer of goods. If you baby-sit, you are a producer of a service. Have you ever been a producer? What goods or services did you make or provide?

Once goods and services are produced, people or other businesses consume, or buy and use, them. The people who buy your T-shirts are consumers. The people for whom you baby-sit are also consumers. You become a consumer when you buy lunch, ride the subway, or get your hair cut.

Producers and consumers can't exist without each other. People and business and industry need each other. *Figure 13-1* at right shows how business flows between these groups.

The Pattern of the Economy

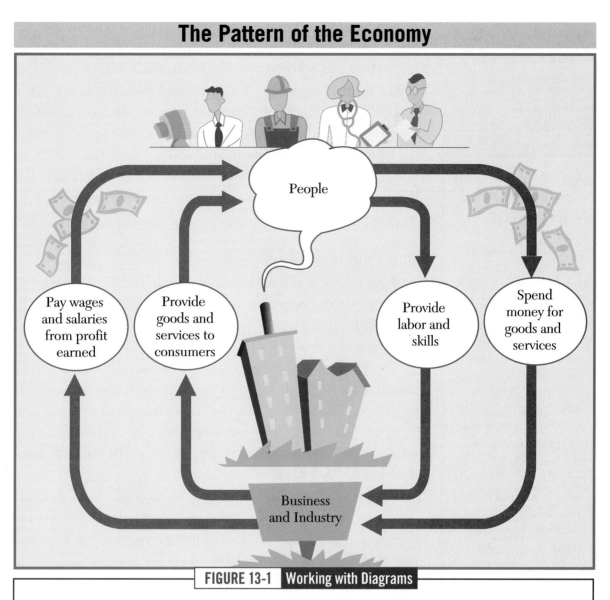

FIGURE 13-1 | **Working with Diagrams**

You play a part in the free enterprise system. You will work to help produce goods and services (if you don't already). You also consume goods and services. The outer part of this diagram shows how the money consumers spend goes into businesses and comes back to you as a worker. The inner part shows how your skills help produce goods and services that consumers like you need and want. **How does the freedom of choice of a free enterprise system affect these processes?**

Making a Profit

Although they can't exist without each other, producers and consumers have very different goals. Producers try to make goods or provide services that consumers will buy. Consumers try to get what they need and want within the limits of how much money they have.

CAPTION ANSWER. Consumers are free to buy what they need and want from the businesses they choose; businesses are free to produce the goods and services they choose; people are free to choose where they'd like to work; business and industry are free to choose people they want and need to work for them.

Why You Should Read the News

Q: Why should I care about economics?

A: Some people believe that if they just ignore economic news, it won't bother them. They're dead wrong. These are the same people who are surprised when they are laid off or when their jobs are computerized. Read the news, and think about how the changes in your community and the world affect your job. Do this and you'll soon figure out why your boss makes the decisions he or she does. You can also use the information to protect yourself and seek new job opportunities.

DISCUSSION STARTER. Ask students, "As a teenager, have you ever been called by a market researcher? What sort of things do those who are researching the market want to know?" (Answers might include what teenagers like and what they buy.)

There are thousands of producers in our economic system. Some are large companies owned by groups of people. Others are individuals who own and operate small businesses. Bike repair shops, hair salons, bakeries, and restaurants are just a few examples of small businesses. Your pet-grooming service and your friend's business selling handmade crafts are two more.

All businesses, both large and small, must earn a profit to keep operating. A **profit** is the amount of money left after the business pays its expenses. The main goal of a producer is to make a profit.

One Producer's Experience

Take a look at Tom Hanshaw's business. Tom grows and sells flowers and vegetables in Peoria, Illinois. His first year in business he made a profit of 100 percent. That year Tom had no expenses.

Tom's parents bought him vegetable seeds and the other supplies he needed. He sold the vegetables he grew to his neighbors. His total sales at the end of the summer were $50. Because Tom had not spent any money to do business, the money he earned was total profit. Tom's profit the first summer was $50—100 percent of his sales.

The second year, Tom used part of his profit from the year before to buy both flower and vegetable seeds. It was an easy decision to grow flowers in addition to vegetables. The first summer, Tom's customers kept asking for flowers.

Tom spent a total of $40 on seeds. He had no other expenses. The garden space was ready to be planted, and he had all the tools he needed. By the end of the summer, Tom had made $253 selling his produce. He made a profit of $213 the second summer.

The third summer, Tom decided to expand his garden. He planned to sell what he grew at a booth at the local farmers' market on Saturdays. What additional expenses do you think Tom faced when he made his garden bigger?

Tom is looking forward to his fourth summer selling what he grows. He expects his profit to continue to grow. What are the secrets to Tom's success as a producer? First, he has few expenses. Like other producers, Tom also tries to provide

goods or services that consumers will buy. He listens to what his customers want. That also helps him make a profit.

Changing Prices

Like any producer, Tom wants to make a profit. Like other consumers, Tom's customers want to get what they need and want for the money they have to spend. You might say a consumer's main goal is to get the most for his or her money.

With that goal in mind, consumers pay a lot of attention to prices. They note changes in prices. They compare prices. Don't you? (You'll learn more about how to be a smart consumer in Chapter 14.)

Think about the last time you had your hair cut. Did it cost more or less than the haircut you had six months before? What kinds of prices have you paid for CDs? Do you always pay the same price for jeans?

There's nothing unusual about changing prices. In a free enterprise system, it's normal for prices to go up and down. Three main factors cause prices to change.

▲ Making a profit is important to both large and small businesses. What kinds of expenses do businesses have?

LOW PRICE GUARANTEE
We'll match any competitor's price...

LOW PRICE GUARANTEE
We'll Match Any Competitor's Current Price On Identical Items

- *Supply and demand.* Supply is the amount of goods and services available for sale. Demand is the amount of goods and services that consumers want to buy. When supply is greater than demand, producers lower their prices. When demand is greater than supply, producers raise their prices.
- *Production costs.* The more it costs to make a good or provide a service, the higher its price. Remember, producers want to make a profit. To do so, they must sell their goods or services for more than it cost to produce them.
- *Competition.* When producers offer similar goods or services for sale, they are in competition. Sometimes competition is great—many producers are offering the same or similar goods or services. When competition is great, prices tend to be lower. When there is little or no competition, prices tend to be higher.

The Global Workplace

Gestures May Have Different Meanings

The common gesture in the United States for good-bye—waving the hand from side to side—has other meanings abroad. In European countries, it means "No!" In Greece, it is an offensive gesture. To wave hello and good-bye in these countries, lift your hand up with your palm facing out. Hold your arm stationary and wave your fingers up and down all together.

Exploration Activity!

Using library resources, research the job outlook in England, Scotland, Wales, and Ireland. Will there be many jobs in these countries?

Looking at the Big Picture

Consumers, producers, profits, prices, supply, demand, competition—each is an important part of our economic system. As you become more involved in it, you will understand these and other parts of the free enterprise system better.

You already have a role in the economy. You are already a consumer because you buy goods and services. If you're not already a producer, you will be one day. In your work life, you will provide goods or services for other consumers. You will also be a voter helping decide what economic policies the government should follow.

How can you prepare to play these different roles in our economic system? Stay informed. You can become informed by doing the following.

- Listen to people who know and understand our economic system.
- Be alert to items in the news about the economy.
- Read newspapers and newsmagazines.
- Ask questions of knowledgeable people when you don't understand something about the economy.

To stay informed, you also need to pay attention to what is going on around the world. Our economy is large and strong, but it is not the only economy in the world. The global economy links the free enterprise system of the United States to all the other economic systems in the world. As you learned in Chapter 2, what is happening in our economy can affect other countries' economies. What is happening in other countries' economies can affect our own economy.

As part of the free enterprise system, you already have a role in the global economy. You will have an even bigger role in the future. Knowing how our economy and the economies of other countries are developing will help you make wise career choices. It will also help you set career goals.

▲ During your lifetime, you will fill many different roles in the economy. How might keeping up with news about the economy help you fill these roles?

CAPTION ANSWER. What you know about the economy will help you make sound decisions both as a consumer and as a producer; it can also help you make wise career decisions.

LESSON REVIEW AND ACTIVITIES. See the *Teacher's Manual* for answers.

Vocabulary Review

Write a series of questions and answers that use the terms below.

economics   consumers
economic system   producers
capitalism   profit
free enterprise   supply
regulate   demand

Check Your Understanding

Choose the correct answer for each item. Write your answers on a separate sheet of paper.

1. In a free enterprise system, individuals and businesses buy and sell _____ .

   a. goods and services
   b. government control
   c. enterprises

2. Someone who buys and uses goods and services is a _____ .

   a. producer
   b. regulator
   c. consumer

Critical Thinking

On a separate sheet of paper, answer the following questions.

1. Why do you think the government regulates some prices and wages in the free enterprise system?
2. Can a consumer also be a producer? Explain your answer.
3. Where might you find people who can teach you about our economic system?
4. What happens to prices when supply is greater than demand? When demand is greater than supply? Exlain why this happens.

Connecting to the Workplace

Making a Profit

- Miguel makes jewelry. He wants to sell his pieces at a craft show.
- He knows that there are already two other jewelry makers signed up for the show. They both sell necklaces and bracelets. Most of their jewelry is in the $12 to $30 range.
- What could Miguel do to compete with the other jewelry makers and still make a profit?

Teamwork

What to Do
- With two other classmates, create an oral presentation for elementary school students about the free enterprise system.
- In simple terms, explain what you have learned about our economic system.
- Design visuals to help younger students understand the basics of free enterprise.
- Arrange to make your presentation to students at a nearby elementary school.

Being Your Own Boss

Dreamer, doer, inventor, organizer—do any of these words describe you? Are you someone who likes to take risks, take action, take responsibility? If so, you may have a future as an entrepreneur. An **entrepreneur** is someone who organizes and runs a business.

If the idea of being your own boss appeals to you, you're not alone. The idea appeals to many people in the free enterprise system. Businesses owned and operated by individuals are an important part of our economy. These small businesses make all kinds of goods and provide all kinds of services. They also put many people to work. More than 95 percent of the people employed in the United States work for small businesses.

Rewards and Challenges

Being an entrepreneur offers many rewards. It also offers many challenges. Ask any entrepreneur how he or she likes running a business. You're likely to hear the same list of advantages and disadvantages.

Discover...
- the rewards and challenges of working for yourself.
- how to start your own business.

Why Learn About Working for Yourself?

In the free enterprise system, many people own and operate their own businesses. One day, you may be one of them.

Key Terms...
- entrepreneur
- business plan
- marketing

CAPTION ANSWER. Answers will vary but may include the following: they can be close to their families; they don't have to spend time commuting to work; they can save money on transportation, clothing, and renting or buying a business location; and the atmosphere may be more relaxed than in another location.

◀ You can gain experience as an entrepreneur by starting a business at home. Why do you think many entrepreneurs like to work at home?

Victor Klepack has been in business for himself since he was 17. He creates logos, or symbols that identify companies. Victor doesn't hesitate when asked about the rewards of being an entrepreneur.

> **❝ I'm in charge. That's the big thing. I'm the one who decides how to operate the business. When I work, how hard I work—it's all up to me. I like having that control over my life. ❞**

> **❝ Every project gives me satisfaction. I make a good income, too. In fact, there's no limit to what I can earn. It's just a matter of deciding how many customers I want to handle. ❞**

Victor is just as open about some of the challenges he faces as an entrepreneur. "I've never had an eight-hour workday," he notes. "When I've got several jobs going, I may be up until midnight or later working. I have to put in long hours because there's a lot of competition out there. I need to deliver quality work. I also need to deliver it on time. If I don't, my customers will find someone else to do the job."

CAREER OPPORTUNITIES

Marketing and Distribution

If you can get people to follow your directions and can keep them happy on the job, this position is worth checking out.

Critical Thinking

Sounds too good to be true? What are some of the challenges of being a car salesperson?

Auto Sales and Leasing Representative

Are you someone who loves success? Are you outgoing and friendly? Do you have a head for numbers? Join the fastest growing car dealership in the West. Some of our reps earn up to $68,000 a year on commission. We will train you and place you in a position. All applicants must have a high school degree.

Long hours and stiff competition are concerns that every entrepreneur shares. That's not all that's on the minds of most entrepreneurs. Running your own business involves financial risk. You can lose the money you've invested, or put into, your business. You may even lose more than you invested. In addition, there are no guarantees of success. Almost two of every three new businesses fail within their first four years.

Would you enjoy the rewards of being an entrepreneur? Would you be able meet the challenges of running your own business? *Figure 13-2* on page 284 shows qualities most entrepreneurs share. What kind of entrepreneur do you think you'd make?

Launching Your Own Business

Is being an entrepreneur for you? You may picture yourself running your own business someday. Maybe you have an idea for a business right now. Whether you launch your business this weekend, next summer, or in the future, you will need a plan.

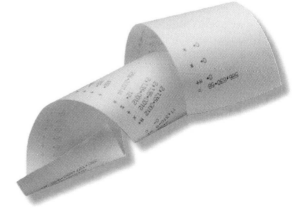

What's Involved

You already know why planning is important. As you learned in Chapter 5, a plan of action helps you reach your goals. To run a successful business, you need a business plan.

A **business plan** gives specific information about your business. It identifies the goods or services you will offer. It tells where your business will be located. It outlines your goals and gives a timetable for meeting them. It may also describe who your customers will be and what kind of marketing you will do. **Marketing** is the process of getting goods and services to consumers. It includes packaging, shipping, advertising, and selling goods and services.

Whatever type of business you launch, you'll probably need some money to get it going. As part of your business plan, you'll

> **FIGURE 13-2**

QUALITIES OF ENTREPRENEURS

Entrepreneurs have many qualities in common. Which qualities do you see in yourself? Which might you have to develop?

A

Motivation
Successful entrepreneurs know what they want to achieve. They believe in their ability to achieve it. They keep themselves motivated by setting short-, medium-, and long-term goals. Then they make and follow a plan for reaching those goals.

B

Sight and Foresight
Entrepreneurs recognize opportunities. They see problems that exist now. They also foresee, or look ahead to, problems that may occur later. They find ways to build success on the problems they identify. They brainstorm solutions and put their ideas into action.

figure out how much it will cost to start and run your business. You will decide how many employees you need, if any, and what you will pay them. You will also predict what your profits will be.

To start a business washing cars or repairing bikes, you may just use money you have saved. If you do not have money of your own to put toward your business, you might borrow some from a family member. Many entrepreneurs borrow money from a commercial lender, such as a bank, to get their business started. Sometime in the future, you may apply for a loan for a business you want to start. When you do, you'll need to have a detailed business plan ready for the lender.

C
Decision Making
Entrepreneurs make business decisions every day. Their decisions must be good ones. The operation and success of their business depend on them.

D
Human Relations
To operate a successful business, entrepreneurs must be able to interact with other people. Entrepreneurs need to build and keep good relations with both employees and customers. They do this by listening to employees and customers and responding to their needs.

Putting an Idea on Paper

Now use your imagination. Use your research and thinking skills. Make a plan for a business you could start and run right now. You don't actually have to start the business. Just dream a little. Then make a plan for how you might make money out of your dream.

EXPLORE Activity

First, you need an idea for a business. Think about your interests and skills.

Nothing comes to mind? Look at the business ideas in *Figure 13-3* at right. You're sure to find at least one idea that matches your interests or skills.

Now develop your business plan. The plan should answer the following questions.

- What will you do? What will you make or provide?
- Where will your business be located?
- What are your goals? What is your timetable for meeting them?
- Who do you expect your customers to be?
- What kind of marketing will you do?
- How much will it cost to start your business? Where will you get the money?
- How much will it cost to run your business? Will others work for you? What will you pay them?
- What do you expect your profit to be?

To answer these questions, you will probably need to do some research. Talk to people who run businesses similar to the one you have in mind. Ask other business-people for advice. Make sure your plan includes all the information listed.

Making a business plan is hard work, but it's also exciting. A business plan is a dream on paper. The next step is to carry out your plan. Running your own business, being your own boss, is an adventure. It's not for everybody. But you never know—it could be for you.

Business Ideas for Young Entrepreneurs

- Baby-sitting
- Tutoring
- Party planning
- House-sitting
- Obedience training
- Videotaping events
- Raising animals for sale
- Catering
- Car washing and cleaning
- Plant-sitting
- Lawn or garden care
- Pet bathing and grooming
- Grocery shopping
- Housekeeping

- Repairing bikes
- Making and selling crafts
- Designing T-shirts
- Animal-sitting
- Delivery or messenger service
- Garage cleaning
- Snow shoveling
- Washing and ironing
- Clothing repair
- Typing service
- Computer tutoring
- Wake-up service
- Growing and selling flowers or vegetables
- Baking services

FIGURE 13-3 | Working with Lists

The list of business possibilities is endless. Have you ever done any of the jobs listed? Which ones? Which ideas would you like to pursue as a business of your own?

CAPTION ANSWER. Answers will vary.

LESSON REVIEW AND ACTIVITIES. See the *Teacher's Manual* for answers.

Vocabulary Review

Write a one-paragraph description of a business you would like to start someday. Use the following key terms in your description.

business plan
entrepreneur
marketing

Check Your Understanding

On a separate sheet of paper, tell whether each statement is true or false. Rewrite any false statements to make them true.

1. Many entrepreneurs are highly motivated.
2. One of every three new businesses fails within its first four years.
3. You need to make a business plan before starting a business.

Critical Thinking

On a separate sheet of paper, answer the following questions.

1. Imagine that you are an entrepreneur. What would you like most? Least?
2. Which would be more important to you if you were an entrepreneur—the rewards or the challenges? Why?
3. Which of the qualities listed in *Figure 13-2* do you think an entrepreneur needs most? Why?
4. What should you consider in choosing a location for a business?
5. What kind of business do you think you would like to own and operate sometime in the future? Why?

Connecting to the Workplace

Promoting Your Business

- Lori loves dogs and wants to start a business as an obedience trainer. She has decided to offer her services to people in her neighborhood first.
- Create a flyer or business card for the business Lori would like to start. Make sure it is visually appealing.

Community Involvement

What to Do

- Select a successful small business in your community.
- If possible, interview the person who owns or runs the business.
- Ask him or her what has made the business succeed.
- Write a brief essay about what you have discovered.

Investigating Career Clusters

Marketing and Distribution

What Is the Marketing and Distribution Cluster?

Occupations in this cluster involve forwarding goods from the manufacturer to the consumer and influencing the consumer to purchase the products. Jobs center around areas such as marketing, purchasing, sales promotion, and selling.

Skills Needed

Interpersonal skills, self-starting skills, creativity skills, communication skills, business skills, and sales skills

THE FACTS	Types of Careers in This Cluster	Work Description	Career Outlook	Education
	Salesperson	Assist customers with choices and purchases in stores	Average	H.S. diploma, Bachelor's
	Sales manager	Direct the sales staff, set sales goals, give advise on promoting sales, analyze results	Average	Associate's, Bachelor's
	Buyer	Purchase merchandise at the best prices	Slower than average	Bachelor's
	Package designer	Design containers, taking into consideration convenience, handling, customer appeal, and cost	Faster than average	Bachelor's
	Market research analyst	Analyze the market conditions for large companies that sell goods	Faster than average	Master's
	Broker	Bring sellers and buyers of merchandise together	Slower than average	Bachelor's

Research Activity

Make a list of five marketing and distribution jobs that interest you. Then, research the particular skills and tasks required of each job. Also, investigate the job outlook and salary range for each particular job. Create a chart that summarizes your findings.

Chapter Highlights

- In a free enterprise system, individuals and businesses buy and sell goods and services and set prices with little government control.
- Organizing and running your own business offers both rewards and challenges.

Recalling Key Concepts

Using complete sentences, answer the following questions on a separate sheet of paper.

1. What are two names for the economic system of the United States?
2. What roles will you play in our economic system?
3. What is an entrepreneur?
4. What kinds of information do you need to include in a business plan?

Thinking Critically

Using complete sentences, answer the following questions on a separate sheet of paper.

1. In what ways do you suppose other economic systems differ from the free enterprise system?
2. Why do prices tend to be lower when there is more competition among producers?
3. Which qualities of entrepreneurs are also important to have when you work for someone else? Why?

Building Skills

1. Thinking—Creative Thinking

Do you, like most entrepreneurs, see problems as opportunities? Think of a need in your school or community that you could fill by starting a business. Write a summary of the need and how your business would fill it. Share your summary with the rest of the class. With your classmates, vote on the most creative business solution.

2. Systems—Understands Systems

Use library or Internet resources to research other kinds of economic systems. Using the information you've gathered, make a chart that describes the economic systems you've discovered. Also compare and contrast these economic systems with the free enterprise system.

Applying Academic Skills

1. Mathematics

Gema sells Popsicles and ice cream at outdoor sports events. She buys Popsicles for 50 cents each and ice cream bars for $75 per hundred. She marks up all the items by 100 percent, selling the Popsicles for $1.00 and the ice cream bars for $1.50. One day, she sold 100 Popsicles and 90 ice cream bars. Her expenses totaled $31.50. What was her profit?

2. Social Studies

With a partner, choose three countries. Find out information about the economic system of each country. Use the Internet and library resources to get the information you need. Then write a report that compares and contrasts these economic systems. Include the advantages and disadvantages of each system.

Discovery Portfolio

Plan for Your Own Business

- Write a journal entry describing how what you've learned about economics affects your view of the world of work.
- Answer the following questions: Would you like to be involved in producing goods or providing services? Why? Are you interested in finding out more about starting your own business? What would you like to know?
- Place the entry in your portfolio.

Career Exploration: Marketing and Distribution

Select a career from the marketing and distribution career cluster.

- Use library resources and the Internet to research the career.
- If possible, also gather information through interviews.
- • Gather information about the kinds of work, the working conditions, and training and education required. Also include skills needed to do the job.
- Explain the outlook for the career
- Write a brief paragraph about how the work someone might do in the career could affect or influence consumers.
- Share your observations with the class.

Chapter 14

Managing Your Money

What You'll Learn...

- You will discover why it is important to manage your money.

- You will learn how to make a plan for spending and saving money.

- You will find out how you can become a smart shopper.

- **CAREER CLUSTER** You will explore careers in *personal services*.

LESSON 14-1
The Money You Earn

LESSON 14-2
You, the Consumer

LESSON PLAN. See the *Teacher's Manual* for the Chapter 14 lesson plan.

Activity

TRY THIS!

List three ways you try to manage your money. Then find out how your friends and family members manage theirs. Ask three friends or family members to list three things they do to manage their money. Compare their lists with yours.

APPLY: In a paragraph, describe new ideas friends and family members have given you for managing your money.

The Money You Earn

Discover...
- what your sources of income are.
- how to make a plan for spending and saving money.

Why Learn How to Manage Your Money?

One day, most of your money will come from the work you do. Then as now, you'll want to make the most of your money. A spending and savings plan will help you make the most of your money now and in the future.

Key Terms...
- income
- gross pay
- net pay
- withhold
- income tax
- Social Security
- F.I.C.A.
- budget
- fixed expenses
- flexible expenses
- interest

Money—most people want more of it. At the same time, many people don't pay much attention to how they spend the money they have. That just doesn't make sense.

You will be earning, spending, and saving money all of your life. You may have only a small amount of money to spend. You may have a large amount. The important thing is to make your money work for you. *What* you have to spend is less important than *how* you spend what you have. That's the key to managing your money.

Your Income

The first step in managing your money is to know your income. Your **income** is the amount of money you receive or earn regularly.

What Are Your Sources of Income?

Where does your money come from? How frequently do you receive money?

► One day, a job will be your main source of income. What are your sources of income right now?

Maybe you get a set amount of money as an allowance once a week or once a month. From time to time, you may receive gifts of money from family members. In addition to these sources of income, you may earn money in a part-time job. You may baby-sit, have a paper route, or do yardwork, for example. An allowance, gifts, and earnings from part-time jobs are the main sources of income for most people your age.

Making Sense of a Paycheck

If you have a part-time job right now, you're probably used to being paid immediately for the work you do. At the end of an evening of baby-sitting, you receive money for the time you spent taking care of the children. Before you go home, your neighbor pays you for the yardwork you did.

At a part-time or full-time job sometime in the future, however, you probably won't be paid as quickly. If you work by the hour, you may receive your pay once a week. If you are on salary, your pay may come every two weeks or once a month.

You will also probably receive your pay in the form of a paycheck. Most paychecks have two parts. One part is the check itself. That's the part you will take to the bank to cash. The other part of a paycheck is the stub. The paycheck stub shows how much you were paid. It also shows the different amounts taken out of your check and why. *Figure 14-1* on page 296 shows an example of a paycheck stub.

Take a close look at Pat Smith's paycheck stub shown in *Figure 14-1*. Compare the payment amounts. Pat's gross pay, or total pay, each week is $206. But Pat doesn't take home all the money she earns. Her net pay—the amount she actually takes home—is $162.79. Like other employers, Pat's employer must withhold, or take out, money from her paycheck to pay various taxes. Net pay is the amount that remains after money is withheld for taxes and other items.

Employers withhold money from their employees' paychecks to pay income tax due on employees' wages. As you might guess, income tax is tax you pay on your income, or the money you make. Income taxes go to the government.

There are three levels of government: federal, state, and local. The federal government runs the country as a whole.

State governments manage the 50 states. Local governments govern counties, cities, and towns. To operate, all three levels need some of the money you make. Tax money also pays for a variety of government services, such as police and fire protection. As Pat's paycheck stub shows, her employer withholds money for both federal and state income taxes.

Employers also withhold money from employees' paychecks for Social Security taxes. **Social Security** is a federal government program that provides benefits for people of all

CAPTION ANSWER. Pat Smith is also identified by name and employee number.

Paycheck Stub

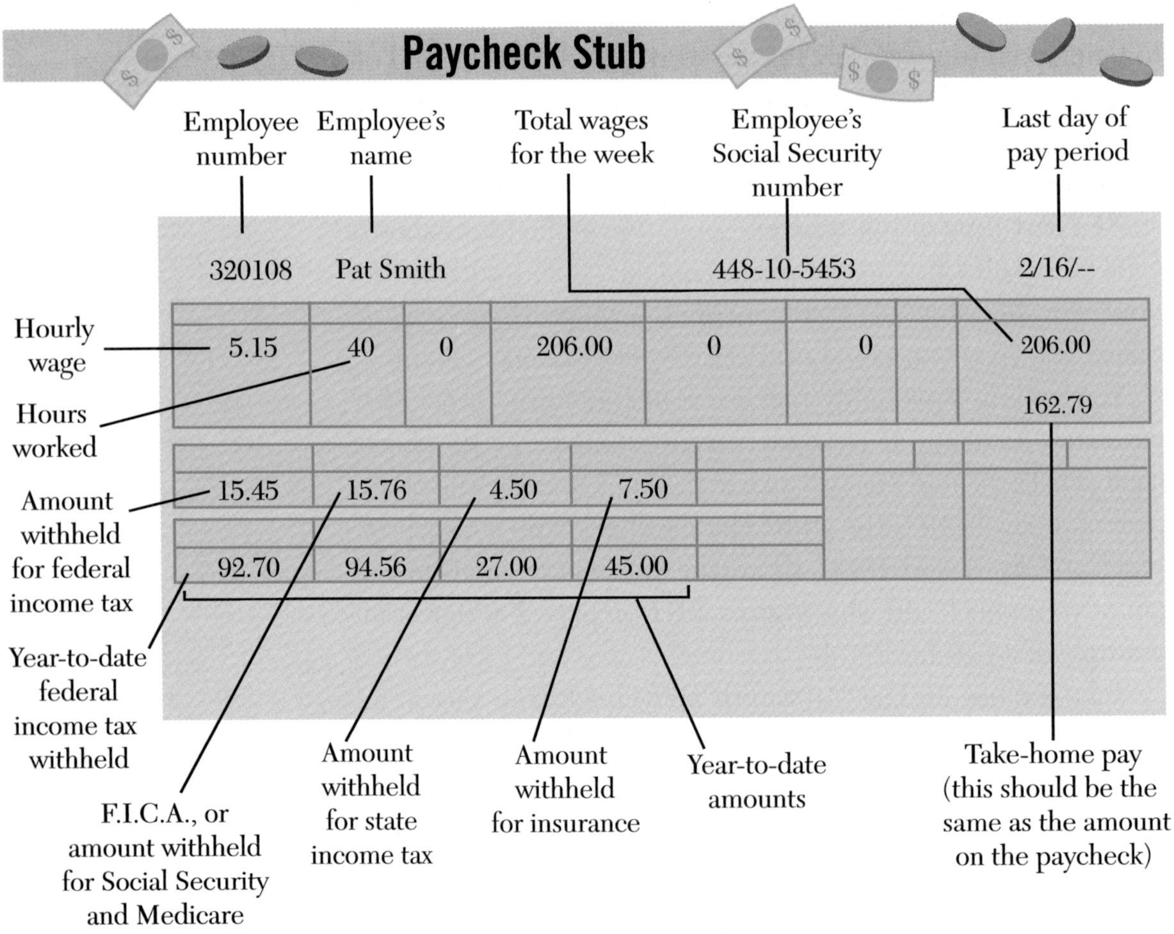

Employee number
Employee's name
Total wages for the week
Employee's Social Security number
Last day of pay period
320108
Pat Smith
448-10-5453
2/16/--
Hourly wage
Hours worked
5.15
40
0
206.00
0
0
206.00
162.79
Amount withheld for federal income tax
15.45
15.76
4.50
7.50
92.70
94.56
27.00
45.00
Year-to-date federal income tax withheld
F.I.C.A., or amount withheld for Social Security and Medicare
Amount withheld for state income tax
Amount withheld for insurance
Year-to-date amounts
Take-home pay (this should be the same as the amount on the paycheck)

FIGURE 14-1 Working with Paycheck Stubs

Pat Smith's Social Security number also appears on her paycheck stub. Do you know your Social Security number? Your parent or guardian probably got one for you when you were younger. A Social Security number is a permanent identification number issued by the government. The government uses it to keep track of your contributions and work history. Your employer will ask you for this number. You will also need to put it on tax forms. **In what other ways is Pat Smith identified on her paycheck stub?**

ages. Workers pay Social Security taxes so they can receive benefits when they retire. The money withheld for Social Security taxes is labeled *F.I.C.A.* on the paycheck stub in *Figure 14-1.* F.I.C.A. stands for Federal Insurance Contribution Act, a law having to do with Social Security taxes.

The money you pay into Social Security gives you benefits from the federal government, such as money for retirement. Money may also be deducted from your paycheck for benefits your employer offers.

As you learned in Chapter 8, health insurance is one benefit many employers offer. Usually the company pays part of the cost of the insurance, and the employees pay part. The employee's part is deducted, or subtracted, from his or her pay. Take another look at Pat Smith's paycheck. As you can see, each pay period, $7.50 for insurance is deducted from Pat's pay.

Making a Budget

Now imagine yourself on payday at your first full-time job. You've just received your first paycheck. What do you do next? Do you spend it all or save some? Do you have bills to pay? If you're smart, you'll have a plan for managing your money.

Right now, you may not have much money to handle, so you may not have a plan for managing your money. When you

DISCUSSION STARTER. Ask students if they are receiving a paycheck, and if so, what should be done with the pay stubs. How should a person organize them?

RESEARCH. Have students obtain sample copies of income tax forms, a W-2 form, and a W-4 form. Discuss in class the information that must be included on these forms.

TEACHING CAREER OPPORTUNITIES. A salon can call a job candidate's former employer or references. If the candidate doesn't have job experience, the salon can check to see if he or she has a certificate from a beauty academy.

CAREER OPPORTUNITIES

CLASSIFIED
THURSDAY, SEP

Personal Services

Do you know exactly what it takes to make somebody look good? Want to change the world by giving people style? Good hairstylists do that and make their clients happy.

Critical Thinking

How do you think a salon can make sure a hairstylist is qualified?

Hairstylist

Busy upscale salon is looking for a hairstylist who has a magic touch with scissors and hair. If you are that person, call us now. We have customers waiting for you.

are working regularly and earning more money, you'll need a budget. A budget is a plan for saving and spending money. It is based on your income—the money you expect to have coming in—and your expenses—the money you will pay out for goods and services.

You may not need to make a budget right now. It can't hurt to give some thought to one, though. You'll be better prepared later when your income and expenses are greater than they are now. You could even try to make and use a budget now. That way, you'll get started on the right foot. Just follow these steps.

Decide on Your Goals

First, get out a pencil and paper or sit down at the computer. List the things you need or want. Do you need money for a new pair of shoes? Do you want to pay for singing lessons so you can try out for parts in school musicals? Are you saving money to buy a birthday present for a friend? Maybe you'd like to put away money for college.

TEACHING THE GLOBAL WORK-PLACE. Point out to students that many jobs may be available. Offer methods for finding out more about the global job market.

The Global Workplace

How Close or Distant to Be

Personal space varies from culture to culture. People from the Middle East stand closer together in business situations than do people from the United States. Men may even touch arms or hold hands. The Japanese, however, stand farther away from each other than we do. Furthermore, they are not inclined toward physical displays of friendship. Mexicans traditionally embrace and stand close together during conversation.

Exploration Activity!

Using the Internet and library resources, research the outlook for jobs in Japan or in the Middle East. What kinds of jobs will be available there?

Divide your goals into short-term and long-term goals. Short-term goals are what you need or want to spend money on now or within the next 12 months. Long-term goals are spending or savings goals that take a year or more to reach.

Write down the amount of money each goal will cost. You may have to look in stores or at newspaper ads to get an idea of what things cost. You can also get this information by calling businesses and talking to people.

 Paying for part of your education is an excellent goal. Why is it important to set and work toward such a goal now?

CAPTION ANSWER. Students may observe that higher education is expensive, and the earlier you begin saving, the more money you will have available when you are ready to further your education.

Make Choices

Now look at your lists. You'll probably have more items listed than you have money for. That's why prioritizing is the next step. As you know, when you prioritize, you put items in order. You order them from first to last or from most to least important. What you need to do now is put your goals in order of importance.

Think about which goals are most important to you. Your most important goal will be number 1 on your list. The next most important goal will be number 2, and so on.

Prioritizing will help you see clearly which goals are wants and which are needs. It will help you make choices. You may have to give up or put off reaching some of your goals in order to meet others. You may need a bike to get to your summer job, for example. To get the bike, you may have to give up the new clothes or CD player you want.

Figure Out Your Income and Expenses

The next step is to figure out your income and expenses for each month. First, write down how much money you expect to have coming in. Include all your sources of income: allowance, gifts, earnings, and possibly tips, from a job.

Q: My parents are always getting credit card offers in the mail. How many credit cards should a person have?

A: Some people think that having lots of cards makes them important. They apply for every credit card offer that comes their way. This makes as much sense as going to the super-market and buying all 20 brands of cereal available. Like all businesses, banks are trying to get more customers or cardholders. Be a smart customer. Figure out which credit cards best suit your needs and apply for one or two of them.

Then write down your expenses for each month. You'll have two kinds of expenses: fixed expenses and flexible expenses. **Fixed expenses** are expenses you have already agreed to pay and that must be paid by a particular date. They are usually the same each month. To have your own telephone line, for example, you may pay your parents a set amount each month. You may pay bus or subway fare to get to school each day. Someday you may have a car payment due each month. Rent is another fixed expense.

Flexible expenses are expenses that come irregularly or that you can adjust more easily. These expenses may be different each month. Entertainment costs, such as concert tickets, are flexible expenses. Clothing and medical costs are others.

Set Up Your Budget

Now you're ready to set up your budget. A written plan for spending and saving is best. The form shown in *Figure 14-2* on the right is a good place to start.

First, fill in the information about your income and expenses. Your income should be equal to or more than your total expenses. If it isn't, you may have to make some changes.

If you need to make changes, take a look at your flexible expenses. They are usually easier to change than fixed expenses. You may pack your lunch every day instead of buying it, for example. You may decide to buy new clothes next month instead of this month. Another way to approach the problem is to increase your income. You may decide to get a part-time job or work more hours, for instance. You may consider getting a job that pays more.

Are you finished filling in income and expenses? Don't forget savings. Remember, a budget is a spending *and* savings plan. A savings plan helps you put aside money for long-term goals and unexpected needs. You may save for holiday activities or a trip. Some teens begin saving for a car or a college education.

All you have to do is set aside part of your income each month. You may save 10 percent of your monthly income, for example. Jesse Reeves knows how quickly savings can add up. Jesse's monthly allowance is $40. He also makes $90 a week repairing bikes and skateboards at a shop in town. Jesse saves 10 percent of his monthly income. How much money will he save in one year? [$480]

Jesse keeps his savings in a savings account at a local bank. You should keep your money in a bank, too. You can make more money that way. The bank will pay you money known as **interest** to use the money in your savings account. The interest is added to the money in your savings account. It's another source of income for you!

DISCUSSION STARTER. What are some benefits students can think of for having a budget? After they brainstorm, tell students to write a short paragraph summarizing their views about the value of budget planning.

MOTIVATING STUDENTS. Give students some examples of goals and costs, such as the down payment on a new car ($3,000) or the purchase of a computer and printer ($2,500). Have them choose different savings rates, such as $50 or $100 per month, and work through the time it would take to achieve the goal.

A Budget Form

	Budgeted Monthly Expenses	Actual Monthly Expenses
Savings		
Fixed Expenses		
Flexible Expenses		
Total Spent		
	Expected Monthly Income	Actual Monthly Income
Total Income		

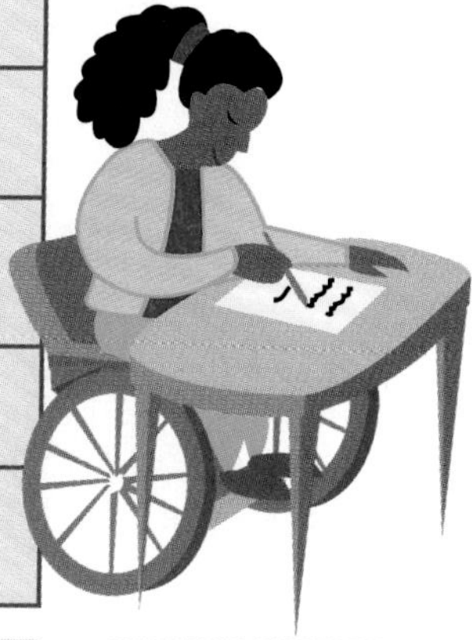

FIGURE 14-2 Working with Charts

Many people use a form like this for their budget. **How would you use the column at the far right?**

CAPTION ANSWER. You would use it to keep track of how much you actually spent or took in during a particular month; you might refer to it if you needed to adjust your budget.

Staying Within Your Budget

You prepare a budget and begin to follow it. Your job isn't over, though. Like any other plan, your budget should be adjusted to fit your needs and wants. Check your budget at the end of every month. How are you doing? Does your income cover your expenses? Do you have money for savings? Do you need to adjust some of your flexible expenses? Do you need to increase your income?

You'll find other tips for staying within your budget in *Figure 14-3* below. These spending rules will also help you be a smart and responsible consumer. You'll learn more about that in the next lesson.

Staying Within Your Budget

- *Keep track of your spending.* Carry a small notebook with you. Make a note of every penny you spend. You'll never have to ask yourself where your money went.

- *Don't carry around a large amount of cash.* You'll be too tempted to spend it on impulse. Just take what you think you'll need for your trip.

- *Shop smart.* Always think before you spend. Compare prices. Shop at discount stores whenever you can.

- *Whenever possible, pay with cash.* Credit cards can be dangerous. They make overspending too easy.

FIGURE 14-3   Working with Lists

You can stick to your budget if you follow a few simple spending rules. Which suggestion do you find most helpful? Why? Which suggestions do you already practice?

LESSON REVIEW AND ACTIVITIES. See the *Teacher's Manual* for answers.

Vocabulary Review

Write a paragraph about managing your money. Include the terms below in your paragraph.

income

gross pay

net pay

withhold

income tax

Social Security

F.I.C.A.

budget

fixed expenses

flexible expenses

interest

Check Your Understanding

Choose the correct answer for each of the following items. Write your answers on a separate sheet of paper.

1. Money that you earn regularly is your _____.

    a. flexible expenses
    b. F.I.C.A.
    c. income

2. Employers take out, or _____, money from employees' pay for various taxes.

    a. itemize
    b. withhold
    c. budget

Critical Thinking

On a separate sheet of paper, answer the following questions.

1. What do you think is the main source of income for people your age? Support your answer.

2. Why is it important to be flexible about your budget? What problems might arise if you are too flexible about your budget?

3. What would you do if you needed to increase your income right now?

Connecting to the Workplace

Understanding Savings

- Imagine that you earn $40 a week from tutoring, delivering newspapers, and an allowance.
- How much money should you put in a savings account each month?
- How much money would you have saved after a year? After two years?
- How would you use your savings?

Teamwork

What to Do

- Working in a group, create a fictitious teen. Make up facts about the teen's finances, including goals, income, and expenses.
- Trade information with another group.
- Have the other group create a budget and work out money-management problems for the teen you invented.
- Have members of your group do the same for the teen the other group invented.

You, the Consumer

Discover...
- how you can get the most for your money.
- ways that people pay for purchases.

Why Become a Smart Shopper?

Thinking before you spend pays off. When you do some research and comparison shop, you get more for your money.

Key Terms...
- impulse buying
- warranty
- exchange
- refund

You save for months to buy something you want. Maybe you have your eye on a new pair of athletic shoes, some skis, or a CD player. Finally you have enough money set aside to make your purchase. You go to the store, hand the salesperson your money, and the item is yours.

A few days later, you pass a different store. In the window, you see a similar item for less money. In fact, it not only costs less. It also has more features or is of higher quality. How could that be?

You took the time to save, and you reached your goal. Between saving for your purchase and actually making it, however, you forgot something. You skipped several important steps. Smart shoppers can tell you what those steps are.

CAPTION ANSWER. Answers will vary; students should cite one or more of the factors named and should identify different types of stores (department stores, specialty stores, chain stores, factory outlets, discount stores) that provide what is important to them.

▶ Price, selection, and services may vary widely among different types of stores. What factors are most important to you? What types of stores provide these for you?

Becoming a Smart Shopper

Smart shoppers get the best value for their money. They get great satisfaction from the purchases they make. They also save a lot of money over time. What can you do to become a smart shopper? It's simple, really. You need to gather information, compare quality and price, and read the fine print.

Gather Information

Smart shoppers gather information before making a purchase. They find out as much as they can about the item they want or need. This kind of research helps them make an informed choice when they decide to buy something.

When you get in the habit of gathering information about products, you also can avoid impulse buying. **Impulse buying** is making a sudden, unplanned decision to buy. Everybody is prone to it from time to time. Just think of the last time you decided to buy candy or a magazine while waiting in a checkout line. The problem with impulse buying is that you often purchase things you don't need. You may also purchase items that are not worth the money you spend. More often than not, these items are not part of your budget.

Those are three good reasons to get information about products in advance. How do you get information? Believe it or not, it's possible to find out quite a bit without even walking into a store.

Newspapers are one source of information. Check out newspaper ads for products you wish to purchase. Use the ads to find out which stores in your area carry the products you want. You may also find product prices in newspaper ads. You can use this information to comparison shop without leaving home.

▲ Consumer magazines can help you decide which brand of product to purchase. You can also ask friends and family members for recommendations. What questions might you ask them about product brands?

Smart shoppers often do research on products in magazines. *Consumer Reports* is just one magazine that helps consumers make choices. It compares prices, quality, and features of several brands of the same product. It also reports on how easy different brands are to use and how often they need to be repaired.

Many smart shoppers also depend on word of mouth. In other words, they get information about products by talking with friends and family members. Are they satisfied with a product? What do they like or dislike about it? Would they buy the product again? Think of people whose opinions and judgment you trust. Wouldn't you find their answers to these questions valuable?

Compare Quality and Price

You've got some information. Now you're ready to go to the store. It's time to do some comparison shopping.

Always compare both the quality and the price of an item you want to buy. You may be surprised. A more expensive product isn't always the better product, for example. Jerome Ticknor found that out the hard way.

❝ *If one item was more expensive than another, I just assumed it was higher quality. That's not always true. I bought a high-priced jacket with a designer label. The first time I washed it, it fell apart. I saved three months for that jacket. I didn't even think of checking how well it was made.* **❞**

▶ Items you want to buy for a reduced price may be marked "As Is" or "All Sales Final." Be sure to check them carefully for defects. Try them on if appropriate. Why is it important to do this before purchasing such items?

Items on sale can also fool you. They may be less expensive than regular-priced items. At the same time, they may not be of the same quality. Remember quality when you shop at a sale. Before making a purchase, make sure the goods on sale are real bargains. A good-quality item at a low price is a bargain.

There may be times, on the other hand, when you are willing to pay a high price. A higher-priced item may very well be good quality. Stop and think about whether it is right for you, though. Higher-price items may have more features than you need. For instance, having 10 speeds on your bike may not be a feature you want or need. If so, it won't be worth the extra money to you.

Read the Fine Print

Smart shoppers don't stop there. To get further information about a product, they always read the labels on the item. Labels tell about the features of a product. Labels describe use and care. They also give information required by law on products such as clothing and food.

▲ If an item you purchased breaks or does not work as it should, check the warranty. **What have you purchased that included a warranty?**

EXPLORE Activity

A clothing label must contain the following:
- name of manufacturer, or maker
- country of origin
- fiber content
- instructions for care
  Food labels must provide this information:
- name of product
- name and address of manufacturer
- weight of contents
- ingredients, with the greatest quantity first
- nutrients contained

Find this information on labels on both a piece of clothing and a food package. Record what you find for each. Then next to each, explain in writing why you think the information is included on the label. Share your ideas in a class discussion.

In addition to labels, many items come with a warranty. A **warranty** is a guarantee that a product meets certain standards of quality. Sometimes a product does not work as claimed in the warranty. When that happens, the manufacturer must either repair or replace it.

A warranty protects you after your purchase. If you're a smart shopper, though, you'll find out what the warranty covers before you purchase the item. Then you'll know what the manufacturer promises. Some warranties apply only to certain parts of the product or to specific conditions. Some expire, or end, after a certain period of time. Be aware of what you're getting into. Read the fine print in both labels and warranties.

Making a Purchase

You've done your homework as a shopper. You've gathered information. You've compared quality and prices. You've read labels and checked the warranty. What's next? You're ready to make a purchase. How are you going to pay?

► Comparing quality and price helps you get the best value for your money. **Have you ever done any comparison shopping? Describe your experience.**

Ways to Pay

Most teens just use cash when they make a purchase. That's not the only way to pay, however. *Figure 14-4* on page 310 shows some of the different methods people use to pay for their purchases.

Be responsible about your purchases. Think carefully before you make your selection. Choose a way of paying that is both convenient and practical for you. All your purchases should fit your budget.

Refunds and Exchanges

Have you ever been unhappy with a product you purchased? Your new audiocassette player may not have worked properly. Maybe the jeans you bought turned out to be the wrong color or size. What did you do?

When purchases don't work out for one reason or another, you usually have two options. You can ask for either an exchange or a refund. An **exchange** is a trade of one item for another. You might ask to trade a pair of jeans that don't fit for a different size, for example. A **refund** is the return of your money in exchange for the item you purchased. If you decide you just don't like the style of jeans, you might ask for your money back.

When you're unhappy with something you purchased, follow these rules. If you do, you'll be more likely to get an exchange or refund.

- *Know the store's policy.* Every store sets its own rules for exchanges and returns. These are usually posted where you pay. Read the rules. If you don't understand them, ask the salesperson before paying for your purchase. Never assume you can return an item.
- *Keep proof of your purchase.* The sales receipt is proof of the price, date of purchase, and store where you bought the item. At most stores, you will have to show your receipt to make an exchange or receive a refund.
- *Make sure an exchange or refund is possible.* Damaged or sale items may be marked "As Is" or "All Sales Final." In these cases, you cannot return the item.

The RIGHT Attitude!

Relax

Ready—set—relax! Those are good starting instructions for a job interview, a major test, or any other potentially stressful situation. Take the time to prepare yourself in advance. Shortly before the interview or test, review carefully. Then relax! Feeling calm and confident will help you do your best.

Apply Your Skills!

Break into groups of four or five. Brainstorm a list of relaxation techniques. List some you've tried and some you have read or heard about. Try one of the techniques. Present your list to the class.

CRITICAL THINKING. Ask students to explain why a purchase on a credit card can end up costing them much more than the price of an item.

TEACHING ACTIVITY. Ask students to review the important things to remember when making an exchange or asking for a refund. Have students explain the rules about returns listed in the text in their own words. Emphasize that they should find out store policies about exchanges and refunds when buying the article.

• *Be prompt and prepared.* If you have a problem with a purchase, don't waste time. Take the item, the sales receipt, and warranty (if any) to the store. Be ready to describe the problem. You may have to fill out a form that includes your reason for returning the item.

Alma Perez of Buena Park, California, found out about these rules the hard way. "My favorite clothing store was having an incredible sale. Some things were marked down 75%! I got a little carried away. I bought a huge bag of clothes, many of which I didn't even bother to try on. Two of the sweaters and one pair of jeans didn't fit me. When I tried to return them, the manager explained that these items fell under the 'All Sales Final' rule. I was out $60. I'll never make that mistake again!"

Becoming a smart shopper takes some time and some practice. It pays off, though. The next time you're thinking about buying something, put what you've learned to work. See for yourself how your money can work for you.

▶ FIGURE 14-4

WAYS TO PAY FOR PURCHASES

Cash is not the only way to pay for a purchase. Compare and contrast the different methods of payment consumers can choose. When might you use each?

A

Check

Checks are an especially convenient way to pay bills. A check is a written document that permits the transfer of money from a bank account to a person or business. To pay by check, you must open a checking account with a bank or credit union. You deposit, or put, money into the account. Then you can write checks up to the amount of money in your account.

B

Debit Card

Many people use debit cards to pay for purchases. When you use a debit card, money is withdrawn directly from your account. You might use a debit card to pay for groceries rather than carry a large amount of cash to the store.

C

Layaway

When you do not have enough cash to buy something, you might use a layaway plan. A layaway plan is a scheduled payment plan for a purchase. You pay a small amount of money down on the item you want. Then you make regular payments until you have paid the full amount for the item. When you have paid in full, the item is yours to take home.

D

Credit

Many consumers use credit to purchase items that cost more money than they have on hand. Credit is a sum of money a person can use before having to pay back the credit lender. Credit allows you to receive a good or service now and pay for it later. People often use credit to buy expensive items such as furniture, appliances, and cars.

Credit cards are the most common type of credit. You receive a monthly bill for your credit card purchases. If you cannot pay the bill in full, you must still pay a minimum amount.

LESSON REVIEW AND ACTIVITIES. See the *Teacher's Manual* for answers.

Vocabulary Review

Write a dialogue between two friends talking about how to be a smart shopper. In the dialogue, include the terms below. Then, with a friend, perform the dialogue for the class.

impulse buying   exchange

warranty   refund

Check Your Understanding

On a separate piece of paper, tell whether each statement is true or false. Rewrite any false statements to make them true.

1. Smart shoppers compare quality and price before they purchase any product.
2. A higher-priced item is always a better product than a lower-priced item.
3. One way to pay for a purchase is through F.I.C.A.

Critical Thinking

On a separate sheet of paper, answer the following questions.

1. Why might it be important for people to read about the use and care of a product before they decide to purchase it?
2. What is the relationship between price and quality? What should you consider when you are comparing price and quality?
3. Why do you think so many people prefer to buy items on credit? What are some of the risks involved in buying on credit?

Connecting to the Workplace

Developing a Purchase Plan

- You have an idea for a business of your own. You would like to offer computer services, such as typing, to people in your community.
- Your family has a computer, but you'd like a computer of your own for your business.
- You have savings you could use to purchase a computer.
- Make a checklist of the steps you would take to get the most computer for your money.

Community Involvement

What to Do

- Make a directory of the best places in your community for teens to shop for goods and services.
- List the name and address of each store. Then write a short description of the kinds of goods or services each offers.
- Include some "insider" comments of your own about bargains or special items or services at the place listed.
- Circulate your directory among your classmates.

Investigating Career Clusters

Personal Services

What Is the Personal Services Cluster?

Occupations in this cluster involve providing services that help people care for themselves and their possessions. Jobs center around areas such as domestic services, lodging services, barbering and cosmetology, dry cleaning and laundry services, and food and beverage preparation and service.

Skills Needed

Communication skills, people skills, creative skills, organizational skills, strong sense of taste and smell, cooking skills, hospitality skills

THE FACTS	Types of Careers in This Cluster	Work Description	Career Outlook	Education
	Gardener	Take care of lawns and flower gardens in private homes and public places	Average	On-the-job training
	Assistant hotel manager	Manage the front desk, housekeeping, food service, sales, and security	Faster than average	Associate's, Bachelor's
	Cosmetologist	Give manicures, scalp treatments, facials, and makeup treatments	Average	Voc-Tech, certification
	Dry cleaning worker	Operate dry cleaning equipment and pressing machines	Faster than average	On-the-job training
	Chef	Prepare food, direct others in food preparation	Faster than average	Two-year culinary, On-the-job training
	Food server	Take orders, serve food and beverages, make out check for meals	Faster than average	On-the-job training

Research Activity

Choose five personal services occupations. Research the job outlook for these services. Make a chart listing the occupations, job outlook, and salary ranges. Are these jobs growing or declining in number? Research the reasons for the growth or decline; explain your findings in a few sentences.

CHAPTER REVIEW. See the *Teacher's Manual* for answers.

▶ Chapter Highlights

- The money you receive or earn regularly is your income. Sources of income include allowance, gifts, and earnings from a job. Making a budget is a smart way to manage the money you earn.
- Smart shoppers gather information about a product before purchasing it. They compare quality and price. They also pay close attention to labels and warranties.

▶ Recalling Key Concepts

Using complete sentences, answer the following questions on a separate sheet of paper.

1. What is income?
2. What three things must you do before you can set up a budget for yourself?
3. What does every good budget include?
4. What do you need in order to pay for a purchase by check or debit card?

▶ Thinking Critically

Using complete sentences, answer the following questions on a separate sheet of paper.

1. Why is it important to be honest with yourself about income and expenses when making a budget?
2. Why do you need to be careful when you gather information about products from ads in the newspaper?
3. What advice would you give someone who has just started to use a credit card?

Building Skills

1. **Information—Organizes and Maintains Information**

   Develop a filing system that organizes sales receipts, warranties, and special instructions for products. Set up the system in your home. Encourage family members to use the files. Describe your filing system to a friend.

2. **Systems—Monitors and Corrects Performance**

   Make a simple budget you can use to manage your money for one month. Use the form for a budget on page 301. At the end of each week, check to see how well you are staying within your budget. Make changes as needed, such as adjusting your flexible expenses. At the end of the month, make a new budget that will span several months. Draw on your experience with the one-month budget to create a new budget that will work for you.

Applying Academic Skills

1. Social Studies

Most people are used to paying money for goods and services. Another way to get the items you need is by bartering. When you barter, you trade goods and services without the use of money. If you've ever swapped comic books or baseball cards, you've done some bartering. Arrange to barter services with a friend or family member. Write a paragraph about your experience.

2. Mathematics

Imagine that you spend $5 a week on soft drinks, candy bars, and potato chips. Did you know that in five years your snack habit could cost you more than $1,300? Instead of buying junk food, why not open a savings account? Find out what happens when you put $5 a week in a savings account that pays 6 percent interest. How much would you have after one year?

Discovery Portfolio

Researching Consumer Purchases

- Think of a major purchase you'd like to make, such as a stereo or a computer. Gather information about the product, and look for the best place to buy it.

- Start saving money for your purchase. If you don't have enough income, think of ways you could earn extra money.
- Put a photo or drawing of the desired item in your portfolio to remind you of your goal.

Career Exploration: Personal Services

Select a career from the personal services career cluster.
- Use library resources and the Internet to research the career.
- If possible, also gather information through interviews.
- Find information about the kinds of work, the working conditions, and training and education required.

Also include skills needed to do the job.
- Explain the outlook for the career.
- Use your findings to write a classified ad for a job in the career field.
- With your classmates, create a bulletin board display for jobs in this career cluster.

Living a Balanced *Life*

What You'll Learn...

- You will discover how to balance work responsibilities and personal responsibilities.
- You will learn how to manage your time and how to make your time count.
- You will find out what is involved in being a good citizen.
- **CAREER CLUSTER** You will explore careers in **public service**.

LESSON 15-1
Work Isn't Everything!

LESSON 15-2
Giving Something Back

LESSON PLAN. See the *Teacher's Manual* for the Chapter 15 lesson plan.

Friends & Family Activity

TRY THIS!

As an adult, you will juggle different responsibilities at home, at work, and in the community. Identify two adult friends or family members who have various responsibilities. Ask them to describe the challenges and rewards of their busy lives. Look for answers to these questions:

- How do you handle all your responsibilities?
- What would you do differently if you could?
- What advice about juggling responsibilities do you have for young people?

APPLY: Write a profile of each person, based on your discussion.

317

Work Isn't Everything!

Discover...

- why it is important to balance the different parts of your life.
- how to make time for school, work, family, and friends.

Why Make Time in Your Life for Other Things Besides Work?

Life is more than work. Friends, family members, and activities other than work bring meaning to life. They may also give meaning to the work you do.

Key Terms...

- balance
- leisure
- time management

All work and no play—just imagine what that would be like. Wouldn't it be dull if one part of life took over all the others?

You may find it difficult to imagine a life of all work and no play. You do work at school and at home. You may also volunteer your time or have a part-time job. Your life, however, probably includes other kinds of activities.

In other words, your life probably has balance. There is balance when opposite sides or parts of something have the same weight, amount, or force. You probably spend an equal amount of time and energy on all the parts of your life. You pay attention to your responsibilities at school, at home, and on the job if you have one. You also have leisure, or time to do what you like.

CAPTION ANSWER. Answers will vary but may include the following: soccer, volleyball, basketball, biking, dancing, skateboarding, and in-line skating.

► To be mentally and physically healthy, people must have time to play. What physical activities do you enjoy in your free time?

In the future, work is likely to take up a great deal more of your time and energy than it does now. Like many other people, you may begin to feel a pull between work and other parts of your life. Finding a balance and keeping it may become a challenge. Will you be up to the challenge?

The Need for Balance

Julie Myers is a flight attendant with a major U.S. carrier. She has been a flight attendant for 15 years. Here's Julie's advice:

> **❝ Just keep this in mind. No matter what happens at work, don't forget what you're working for. ❞**

Balancing Work and Personal Life

"Take it from me," Julie goes on. "When I first started out, my work was my life. I put in huge blocks of time on the job. I loved what I did, and I couldn't get enough of it. I was always ready to fill in when others were sick or had time off.

"My schedule was crazy, but I didn't really notice. I was used to it, I guess. It caught up with me, though. I'll never forget the morning seven years ago when I woke up in a hotel in Los Angeles. I was on the crew for the early flight east. I felt tired and empty. I was working all the time, but I had no idea what I was working for. I sat up in bed and thought, 'What's going on here? Is this what life is all about?'"

These days, Julie is in the air only three days most weeks. She usually spends just two nights away from home. Then she has a block of time off, which she spends with her husband and two boys at their home in Pittsburgh.

"After that 'wake-up call' in Los Angeles," explains Julie, "I took a close look at what is important to me. My family is at the top of my list. Then there's running, gardening—well, the list

CAREER Q&A

Expect Change. That's Life!

Q: I never feel like my life is balanced. Does that mean I'm a loser?

A: Few people feel their lives are balanced all the time. Life is always changing, and balancing those changes is a lifelong task. The week before a big test, you'll probably have to study and not meet with friends. But if a friend's going through a breakup, you might spend more time talking to him or her than on your homework. It's normal that your priorities will always be changing. If they stop changing, you might be in trouble! Change is the essence of life.

TEACHING ACTIVITY. Have students make an entry in their Discovery Portfolio, using the following sentences: "At this time, I believe my most important reason for working will be . . . This reason will bring balance to my life."

goes on. I've got a lighter schedule now, and my life is more balanced. I feel much happier."

What's Your Life About?

As Julie realized that morning in Los Angeles, life is about much more than work. Work is an important part of life and has many rewards. It isn't all that gives meaning to life, however. Your personal goals, your interests, and the activities you spend time on outside of work are valuable. The people you care about and who care about you bring meaning to your life, too.

Whatever your career someday, remember that you have a responsibility to yourself as well as to your job. Try to balance the different parts of your life—your work and your commitments to yourself and others.

The right balance will make you happier and healthier. It will make you more satisfied with everything you do.

EXPLORE Activity

Give yourself a wake-up call today. Take some time to think about what your life is about. Who is important to you? What is important to you? Make a list of people and activities that make your life meaningful. Keep your list in your portfolio.

Do you think that your list will change as time goes on? How?

Making Your Time Count

Identifying what is important to you is the first step in the balancing act of life. The next step is to figure out *how* to balance the different parts of your life.

Finding Time

How well do you manage your time? Do you usually stay up late to finish your homework? Do you run out of time when you're working on a big project? Are you often late for school? Does your family complain that they never see you? If you have any of these problems, you need to learn and practice time management. **Time management** involves choosing how to spend your time and creating a schedule for your choices.

Time management skills will help you in all areas of your life. You will have more time for special activities, such as sports and hobbies. You won't constantly be late or forget to do important tasks. You will also have more time for yourself and others.

You can begin to develop time management skills now. Soon time management will become a habit. It will serve you your entire life.

Try some of the tools and techniques shown in *Figure 15-1* on page 322. They'll help you make time for everything that's important to you.

Being Present

Time management skills help you make time for all kinds of things. If you manage your time well, you may even feel as though hours have been added to your day.

The Global Workplace

Gift Giving in an Appropriate Manner Is a Good Thing

When visiting a foreign country, it's customary to bring a gift for the host to show one's gratitude for hospitality. In Japan, gift giving and receiving are formal processes. Wrap the gift, give it with both hands, and make sure the gift respects the closeness or distance of the relationship. In Eastern European countries and Russia, Western products are highly valued. Gifts that show a sensitivity for the host's tastes are greatly appreciated in Latin America.

Exploration Activity!

Using the Internet or library resources, research the outlook for jobs in Eastern Europe or in Latin America. What kinds of jobs will be available there?

CRITICAL THINKING. Ask students how spending time creating a schedule will end up saving them time. Have they ever known someone with a really busy schedule? How did this person manage his or her time?

RESEARCH. Have students find an example of a time line from a school, company, or other source. Have them explain how it shows "the big picture."

TEACHING THE GLOBAL WORKPLACE. Point out to students that many jobs may be available. Offer methods for finding out more about the global job market.

Having time for everything that is important to you isn't all there is to it, though. You want the time you spend to count. Making your time count is all about being present. When you are present, you are fully alive and alert to whatever you're doing.

You may be working on a homework assignment, a task around the house, or a project on the job, for example. How can you be present? How can you pay close attention to what you are doing? Here are a few suggestions:

- *Avoid interruptions.* If a friend calls while you are doing your homework, for instance, tell him or her that you will call back when you are finished.
- *Stay on task.* Stick with what you're doing until it is done. Don't stop to read that magazine you find while cleaning your room. Save it for later. Later will arrive sooner when you focus on what you are doing.
- *Don't try to do too many things at once.* Concentrate on one task or activity. Give it your best. You'll complete tasks more quickly, and you'll do a better job.

> **FIGURE 15-1**

TIME MANAGEMENT TOOLS AND TECHNIQUES

Think of time management as making choices. You can spend your time doing this or that. If you have just a few choices, finding the time may be easy. If you have lots of choices, you may need help organizing your time. Many people find these tools and techniques helpful. Which have you used before?

A Make a "To-Do List"

Some people use a list as a reminder of tasks to complete. Once a day or once a week, make a "To-Do List" for the next day or week. As you complete each task, cross it off the list. You'll get a boost from each task you complete.

To Do

Pack lunch
Feed cats and clean litterbox
Begin research for social studies report
Read two chapters of book for English
Do math homework
Go to yearbook staff meeting
Call Josie
Shop for Mom's birthday present
Put air in bike tires

B

Prioritize

If you have a long list of tasks, you may not know where to begin. Try ranking the tasks in order of importance. Label top-priority activities with an A. They need to be done first. Mark the activities you need to complete next with a B. Activities marked with a C are the least important. If you don't get to them, they can wait until tomorrow or next week.

C

Break Big Projects into Small Steps

Large or long-term projects are often the most difficult to manage. It's easy to focus on what has to be done today and tomorrow. When you do, however, you may overlook things that are farther off. Try breaking big projects into manageable steps. Then treat each step as a separate task.

D

Set Up a Schedule

Once you know what tasks you have to do, you need a schedule for doing them. A schedule is a list or chart showing when tasks must be completed. Many people use a calendar or day planner for scheduling. You can enter tasks on your schedule as soon as you know about them. Then you always know what's coming up.

E

Make a Time Line

For big projects, you may want to create a time line. This kind of chart shows the order of events in time. A time line can help you see the stages in a complicated or long-term project. You will be able to see where you are in a project at a glance. You will also see what you need to do now.

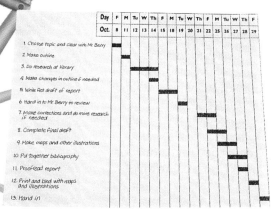

Exercise

Exercise is great for your physical health, but its benefits go beyond fitness. Regular exercise can improve your attitude. So, when the stresses of school or work make you feel pessimistic and exhausted, set aside a half hour during the day for exercise. Not only will this do wonders for you physically, but it will help you mentally, too.

Apply Your Skills!

Make a list of 10 benefits of exercise. Share your list with the class.

Being present at work means being focused on what you are doing. Being present in your activities with others also involves focus. When you focus on others, you show them love, care, and attention. Here are some ideas for making your time with others count.

- *Communicate.* Make talking and listening to friends and family members a priority. Share your thoughts and feelings. Listen to what others have to say, what problems they're facing, what interests them. Practice active listening.
- *Be considerate.* Pay attention to the little things that make life more pleasant for everyone. Do things without being told. Surprise others with small favors.
- *Offer praise and encouragement.* Remember how good it feels to hear an encouraging word. Show your appreciation for the efforts of others. Give others support.
- *Keep promises.* If you say you'll be somewhere or do something, stick to your word. Be dependable.

Time at work is valuable. Time with others is precious. Use your time wisely at work. Find time for talking, listening, and just being together with friends and family. Be present wherever you are, whatever you are doing. That's the best way to make your time count.

CAPTION ANSWER. When working parents can leave their young children at day-care centers, they can concentrate on their responsibilities at work. In their spare time, working parents can enjoy activities with their children.

▶ There are no easy rules for balancing work and family responsibilities. Everyone's situation is different. How do day-care centers help some parents fulfill their work responsibilities? What can working parents do to focus on family in their spare time?

LESSON REVIEW AND ACTIVITIES. See the *Teacher's Manual* for answers.

Vocabulary Review

Create a diagram that shows the connections between balance, leisure, and time management. Include the terms below in your diagram.

balance

leisure

time management

Check Your Understanding

Choose the correct answer for each item. Write your answers on a separate sheet of paper.

1. It is important to balance your work time and your _____ time.
    a. business
    b. life
    c. personal

2. To help you make time for what is important to you, use _____.
    a. time management tools and techniques
    b. other people's time
    c. free time

Critical Thinking

On a separate sheet of paper, answer the following questions.

1. When a job takes up a good deal of your time, why is it especially important to set aside time with family and friends?

2. Which time management tool or technique would help you set aside time to do your homework? Which would help you manage a long-term project?

3. Give an example of a task you're working on now in which you're not making your time count. Which suggestions from the text could you use to help you be "present" on this task?

Connecting to the Workplace

The Importance of Time Management

- Imagine that you run a housecleaning business in your neighborhood on weekends. A friend works with you. She does excellent work but does not manage her time well. She has trouble arriving at work on time. She sometimes forgets tasks she was supposed to do. She is always in a rush by the end of the day.
- What time management suggestions would you give your coworker?

Teamwork

What to Do
- Identify a long-term group project in which you are involved in one of your classes. If you are not involved in such a project, think of a long-term project you'd like to do with others.
- Make a time line to track the stages of the project.
- Use the time line to explain the different stages of the project to the class.

Giving Something Back

Discover...
- your responsibilities to your community.
- how you can contribute to the life of your community.

Why Is It Important to Get Involved in Your Community?

Taking an active part in your community is not only a responsibility. It is also a way to enrich your life. When you get involved, you meet people and learn new skills. You also make your community a better place to live.

Key Terms...
- register

With whom do you spend your time? Do you have a special group of friends? What other groups do you belong to?

Start small and work up. You may have a circle of friends. You and the other students in your favorite class form a group. Are you part of an athletic team? Do you belong to a club? You may not think much about it, but you are also a member of your school.

Your family is a group. Then there's your neighborhood. You and your neighbors make up a group. Beyond your neighborhood is your community and all the people in it.

What Being a Citizen Means

Members of a community, such as a town, city, state, or country, are called citizens. You are a citizen, just like others in your community. As a citizen, you enjoy certain rights. You also have certain responsibilities.

CAPTION ANSWER. Answers will vary; students may mention clean-up, recycling, and fund-raising projects.

➤ When members of a community work together, they make life better for everyone. What kinds of community projects have you participated in?

Respecting Others

Remember the key to getting along with others? You learned all about it in Chapter 9. The key is respect, or consideration, for others.

When you show respect for others, you make a good member of any group. Showing respect for others is a responsibility of every citizen. Show respect for other members of your community by treating them as you—and they—would like to be treated. Wait your turn, for example, instead of trying to get to the front of a line.

Speak respectfully to adults, such as older citizens, teachers, and police officers. Greeting adults and calling them "Mr.," "Ms.," or "Mrs." is another way to show your respect.

Remember to show respect to everyone, not just people you know or like or who are like you. If someone holds different values or beliefs from yours, be open and accepting. If you disagree with someone, give that person a fair chance to explain his or her opinion.

Caring for What You Share

As a citizen, you also have a responsibility to take good care of the property you share with others in your community. Be as careful with library books or playground equipment, for example, as you would be with your own possessions. Then the next person will be able to use and enjoy them too.

Do the same with other community property, such as recreation areas, the school building, and streets and sidewalks. Take a moment to pick up litter and discard it in the proper place, for instance.

Staying Informed

Knowing what goes on in your community is also your responsibility as a citizen. You need to stay informed about issues and events.

Does your community have a newspaper? Read it. Listen to local radio and television reports for news about goings-on in your community. Talk to your family members and neighbors to learn what they think about issues. Share information you have.

Making Your Voice Heard

Staying informed is one way of preparing for one of your most important responsibilities as a citizen. That responsibility is making your voice heard.

Voting is one way responsible citizens express their points of view. The votes of citizens help decide who our leaders will be and what laws we will live by. When you choose not to vote, you let other people make these decisions for you. You disregard an important responsibility.

You must be at least 18 years old to vote. You must also **register**, or officially sign up as a qualified voter. Once you're registered, you'll want to cast an informed vote when elections take place. To do that, you need to learn about the candidates, or people up for election, and the issues.

Methods for registering to vote vary from place to place. Find out how registering is done in your area. Call the League of Women Voters, your county election commission, or the county registrar's office. Ask how, when, and where citizens can register to vote. Also ask what documents they need to bring along.

Using the information you've gathered, put together a pamphlet about how to register to vote. Ask your teacher to make photocopies of the pamphlet. Hand out copies to other students at your school.

CRITICAL THINKING. Suggest to students that it won't be long before they start to vote. Do they think their vote will really make a difference? (It can make a bigger difference than they realize.)

TEACHING ACTIVITY. Remind students that they will need to register to be able to vote. Explain briefly to them how this is generally done.

RESEARCH. Have students find out who represents them. Have them make a chart showing their elected officials: local, state, and federal representatives.

Doing Your Part

Your responsibilities as a citizen will grow as you get older. They will grow as you move into the work world and get your own place to live. One day, you'll be a taxpayer and a voter.

That's not to say that your responsibilities as a citizen right now are not important. In fact, you may already be playing a very important role in the life of your community. You may be donating your time and energy to others by serving as a volunteer.

TEACHING CAREER OPPORTUNITIES. Safety is of the greatest importance. A journeyman lineman must not operate any machine that he or she has not been trained to use. Taking chances can put the entire work crew at risk. First Aid and CPR are essential skills in the event of an emergency.

CAREER OPPORTUNITIES

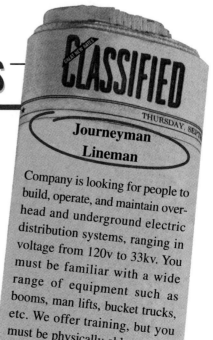

Public Service
People who bring water and electricity into a neighborhood are providing a public service that is often overlooked.

Critical Thinking
A journeyman lineman's job can be dangerous. What are some skills that might keep him or her out of danger?

CLASSIFIED

THURSDAY, SEP

Journeyman Lineman

Company is looking for people to build, operate, and maintain overhead and underground electric distribution systems, ranging in voltage from 120v to 33kv. You must be familiar with a wide range of equipment such as booms, man lifts, bucket trucks, etc. We offer training, but you must be physically able to operate the machinery.

Ways to Lend a Hand

Aaron picks up groceries for his elderly neighbor once a week. Casey helps out at the local community recycling center on Saturdays. Davon reads to young children at the public library after school. Yoko helps paint houses with her Habitat for Humanity group. Don takes part in events such as walkathons to raise money for different causes.

Young volunteers are active in every community. Do you and your friends volunteer your talents and skills to your community? What do you do? What would you like to do? How can you make a difference?

EXPLORE Activity

There are many ways you can help others in your community. You might collect used clothing for the needy or hand out magazines and newspapers to people in a hospital or nursing home. You might volunteer at your local library. Teaching computer skills, tutoring, or giving piano lessons are other ways you can volunteer.

Think of three ways you could volunteer in your community. Write a paragraph about each. In each paragraph, explain what you could contribute, or give, to your community as that kind of volunteer. Also describe what you think *you* would receive from the experience.

The Rewards of Good Citizenship

There are many rewards to being a volunteer. One of the most important is that you feel good about yourself. When you help someone else, you see how valuable your time and energy can be to others. That gives you a sense of self-worth. You have the sense of accomplishment that comes from a job well done. When you volunteer, you also gain valuable work experience.

Here's what Alberto Fuentes of Falls Church, Virginia, has to say about giving back to his community: "I've been tutoring

TEACHING ACTIVITY. Name some volunteer activities for students and explain where to look for them. (Hospitals, senior citizen centers, libraries, and museums are some examples.) Point out that even though students may not be paid for their work, they will receive valuable experience for choosing (or not choosing) a career.

EXTENDING THE LESSON. Have a class discussion about the importance of voting. Ask students to imagine they are talking to a "devil's advocate" who doesn't think it's important to vote.

English for the past six months. I'm from Peru, so we speak mostly Spanish at home. Last summer a boy from Puerto Rico moved in across the street. He's my age and ended up being in my class. I noticed that he was having trouble in English and science. I remembered what it was like when I first came to the United States. Sometimes I didn't even understand the instructions on a test. I asked him if he'd like some help. We meet twice a week for about an hour, and he's doing much better now. He called me last night to tell me he got a B+ on his last English paper. I can't tell you how good that made me feel. I think I was even happier than he was! When you help someone else, it's an awesome feeling. And the experience you get can help you, too. Maybe I'll be a teacher someday!"

▲ There may be a volunteer opportunity for you as close as next door or just around the corner. What skills or interests could you contribute to your community?

CAPTION ANSWER. Answers will vary; students should identify specific skills or interests of their own that might be used to benefit their community.

There's no doubt about it. Being a good citizen helps you in many ways. It gives you a sense of belonging and a feeling of pride. You are able to share community spaces, such as libraries, parks, and museums, with others. You are also able to share your ideas, interests, and skills. Along the way, you develop skills that will be useful to you throughout your life. Some may even lead to a career one day.

You get so much from your community. It's your responsibility to give something back.

LESSON REVIEW AND ACTIVITIES. See the *Teacher's Manual* for answers.

Vocabulary Review

Create a poster that encourages people to register to vote. On your poster, emphasize and explain why voting is such an important responsibility. Make sure the term below is prominently featured on your poster.

register

Check Your Understanding

On a separate sheet of paper, tell whether each statement is true or false. Rewrite any false statements to make them true.

1. Members of a community are called citizens.
2. Citizens have responsibilities not rights.
3. The key to getting along with others is showing responsibility.
4. Two responsibilities of citizens are voting and volunteering.

Critical Thinking

On a separate sheet of paper, answer the following questions.

1. What are two ways you show respect to others in your daily life?
2. Why do you need to be well informed to fulfill your responsibility as a voter?
3. How will your responsibilities as a citizen grow as you get older? Give two examples of responsibilities you imagine yourself having when you're an adult.
4. What activities or services in your community would be impossible without volunteers?
5. Do you know of any volunteers who are working to make life better for the people in your community? Briefly describe their contributions to your community.

Connecting to the Workplace

Applying Citizenship Skills

- You can apply your citizenship skills on the job. Write a two-page essay about how the citizenship skills described on pages 328–331 might be useful in the workplace.
- Read your paper to the class.

Community Involvement

What to Do

- Suppose you have a lawn-and-garden or baby-sitting service. Your business is good, and you have many customers. You'd like to offer the same services in your community from time to time as a volunteer.
- How could you serve your community doing yardwork or baby-sitting as a volunteer? Name two ways.

Investigating Career Clusters

Public Service

What Is the Public Service Cluster?

Occupations in this cluster involve supplying services, many of which are supported by tax money, to the public. Jobs center around such areas as city and town services, protective services, the armed services, postal services, public utilities, education, and social services.

Skills Needed

Interpersonal skills, strong oral and written communication skills, physical stamina, creative skills, judgment skills, math skills, mechanical skills

THE FACTS	Types of Careers in This Cluster	Work Description	Career Outlook	Education
	Detective	Gather facts and collect evidence for criminal cases, participate in arrests	Faster than average	H.S. diploma, On-the-job training
	Water treatment plant operator	Regulate the motors, pumps, and valves that purify drinking water	Good	Voc-Tech, On-the-job training
	Schoolteacher	Prepare lessons, grade papers, attend meetings, serve on committees, supervise school activities	Faster than average	Bachelor's, Teacher training program
	School counselor	Help people handle personal, social, educational, and career problems	Faster than average	Master's
	Social worker	Help people affected by poverty, alcoholism, drug abuse, behavior problems, or illness	Faster than average	Bachelor's or Master's
	Power distributor	Control the flow of electricity throughout an area	Slower than average	H.S. diploma, On-the-job training

Research Activity

Research 10 public service occupations. Make a chart showing the projected job growth for these careers. Are public service occupations expected to grow or decline? Write a sentence that explains the rate of change for each job.

Chapter 15 Review

Chapter Highlights

- It is important to balance your work time and your personal time.
- Citizens have rights and responsibilities. Voting and volunteering are two important responsibilities of citizens.

Recalling Key Concepts

Using complete sentences, answer the following questions on a separate sheet of paper.

1. Why should you try to balance the different parts of your life?
2. What does time management involve?
3. What are five tools or techniques of time management?
4. What are the requirements for voting?

5. How does volunteering help you feel good about yourself?

Thinking Critically

Using complete sentences, answer the following questions on a separate sheet of paper.

1. Does your life have balance? Explain your answer.
2. How do you practice being focused when you are with others?
3. Which citizenship skills do you need to work on?
4. What are some ways you can make your voice heard until you are old enough to vote?

Building Skills

1. Resources—Allocates Material and Facility Resources

Zach collects and trades comic books. He would like to buy and sell them for a profit, giving the money he makes to a local homeless shelter. A comic book fair is coming to town. For $25, Zach could reserve a place in the fair hall. For $5 more, he could reserve a display table. Zach knows a place where he could rent a table for $3. He could buy a used folding table for $10. What should Zach do? Why?

2. Resources—Allocates Human Resources

Balancing job and family responsibilities is not easy. Flextime and on-site day care are two "family-friendly" benefits employers offer. Use the Internet and library resources to find out about one of these benefits. In an oral report, explain how the benefit helps reduce stress and helps employees be more productive.

Applying Academic Skills

1. Social Studies

U.S. citizens have many rights and responsibilities. Some responsibilities, such as paying taxes, are required by law. Some, such as caring for shared property, are not. In a small group, identify a problem in your community. Find out what, if anything, is being done about it. If something's being done, join the effort. If not, plan a way to solve the problem and carry out your plan. Write an account of your group's effort for a local newspaper.

2. Language Arts

Write a self-evaluation of how you manage your time. Do you procrastinate? Do you meet deadlines? Are you always on time? Read your self-evaluation. What would you like to change? How would you go about changing?

Discovery Portfolio

Using Time Management Skills

- Think about a project or job you've had. It may have been a project at school or at home. It may have been a volunteer or for-pay job. How well did you use your time?
- List the ways you used time well. List the ways you could have improved your use of time. Keep your lists in your portfolio as references for your next project or job.
- After you complete the new project, analyze it in the same way. Are your time management skills any stronger?

Career Exploration: Public Service

Research one career that you find interesting in the public service career cluster.

- Use library resources and the Internet to research the career. If possible, also gather information through interviews.
- Include information about the kinds of work, the working conditions, and training and education required. Also include skills needed to do the job.
- Explain the outlook for the career.
- Create a poster to encourage people to pursue the career you've selected.

Looking Beyond *Today*

What You'll Learn...

- You will learn about life changes you may experience.

- You will explore ways to handle challenging personal and job-related changes.

- You will discover how to think about, plan for, and move toward your future.

- **CAREER CLUSTER** You will explore careers in *transportation*.

LESSON 16-1
Dealing with Change

LESSON 16-2
The Future Is Coming

LESSON PLAN. See the *Teacher's Manual* for the Chapter 16 lesson plan.

Activity

TRY THIS!

List two major changes that you have experienced so far in your life. Then interview three adult friends or family members. Ask them if they have experienced the same or similar changes. Find out how they handled them. Take notes.

APPLY: Compare your findings with those of your classmates. What changes did people have in common? What helped them deal with these changes? Make a list of their tips for future use.

Dealing with Change

Discover...
- how to deal with personal changes beyond your control.
- kinds of personal changes you might choose in the future.
- how to handle job and career changes.
- ways of looking at and preparing for change.

Why Think About Changes That Might Happen Sometime in the Future?

You'll have some idea of what to expect. You'll know how you might feel and what you can do. You'll feel confident about dealing with the changes that come your way in life.

Key Terms...
- stepparent
- blended family

O ne thing you can count on in life is change. You may know this already from your own experience.

Some changes are expected. Others are not. Even when we know to expect change, it can still take us by surprise. Change is also hard to predict. The idea of it makes many of us nervous or uneasy. In some situations, change is beyond our control. We have no choice but to accept it.

Personal Changes Beyond Your Control

You've probably already experienced many changes in your life—some pleasant, some not. You can be sure that more change will come your way. You may even look forward to some changes. You were probably eager to become a teenager. Maybe you can't wait to get a driver's license. You may be looking ahead to the day when you graduate from high school. Moving into your own place may be something else you see yourself doing one day. As you get older, you will continue to experience all kinds of personal changes.

➤ Life is full of changes. What big changes have you already experienced? What changes are you looking forward to?

Many changes are predictable. You can plan for them. You know that you will soon be entering high school, for example. Other changes happen to you. Many are not changes you would choose. They can be difficult to handle.

Divorce, remarriage, moving, illness, and death are all unexpected changes. Like a sudden storm, changes such as these can catch you by surprise. They can even upset and uproot you.

Family Changes

Many families have to deal with the changes that divorce brings. Divorce can be very difficult for children of all ages. If your parents divorce, you may feel as though your world has been turned upside down. You may worry about who will take care of you or where you will live. You may wonder how or if you will continue to see both your parents.

The remarriage of one divorced parent is also a big change. It means there is a new adult in the house. This **stepparent**—the spouse of your mother or father—may also have children. They become your stepbrothers and stepsisters. The family that forms when two single parents with children marry is called a **blended family.** As you might expect, it can take time for everyone in a blended family to feel like a family.

Everyone adjusts to the changes after divorce or remarriage in his or her own way. You need to be patient. It is also helpful to have some support. Cassidy Turner tells how she dealt with the changes in her family.

"I wasn't prepared at all when my parents divorced," Cassidy recalls. "I was 10 at the time. My mom and I moved in with my grandmother in a different town. I missed my school and my friends, and I really missed my dad. We only saw each other a few times a month. It was such a hard time. Almost everything in my life changed."

▲ Family changes often bring about new roles and responsibilities for family members. What roles and responsibilities do you have in your family?

CAPTION ANSWER. Answers will vary; students may identify various household chores and responsibility for younger siblings.

MOTIVATING STUDENTS. Ask students if their own generation is more used to change than earlier generations. Can they think of reasons why this might be so? Discuss and share reasons.

CAPTION ANSWER. Answers will vary. Changes students have experienced may include becoming a teenager, moving, the illness of a family member, divorce, the birth of a sibling. Students may be looking forward to graduating from high school, getting a driver's license, getting a job, and moving into their own place.

CRITICAL THINKING. Write the words *blended family* on the board. "Blended" is not being used literally here. What is the literal meaning? Do students think it is a good image of what happens in these sorts of families?

DISCUSSION STARTER. Ask how many students' families have relocated in the past two years. What are some usual causes of relocation?

"I wasn't sure how to handle all the changes. I really needed help, but I didn't know where to turn. My mom and dad were going through a lot of changes themselves. My grandmother was around, though. I started talking to her. I told her what I was feeling. I talked about everything on my mind.

❝ I guess if I had one word of advice for others going through what I did, it would be this. Don't be afraid to ask for help. Find someone to talk to. Oh, and there's something else I can say from my own experience. Things do get better. ❞

Changing Places

In addition to adjusting to the changes that divorce brought, Cassidy had to deal with moving to a new place. Families move to different places for many reasons. Most children and young adults don't choose to move. Adult family members usually make the decision. The rest of the family may not have much choice in the matter.

If you've ever moved to a new place, you know how hard it can be. You often have to change schools. You may leave friends, neighbors, and even family members behind. Feeling comfortable in your new environment takes time.

Illness and Death

The serious illness or death of a friend or family member is another change beyond your control. You may feel scared, worried, nervous, helpless, sad, or down. Friends and family members may have their own fears and concerns. They may not notice what you are going through.

People deal with illness and death differently. Remember, there is no "right" way to react or grieve. It does help to talk through your thoughts and feelings with someone. That person may be a close friend, a family member, or a counselor. The support of others can help you adjust to the difficult changes that come with illness or death.

◀ Changes beyond your control can be difficult to handle alone. Who would you go to for help if you were going through a difficult change?

CAPTION ANSWER. Answers will vary but may include a relative, neighbor, teacher, friend, school counselor, coach, clergy member, or other trusted adult.

TEACHING ACTIVITY. Have students record in their Discovery Portfolios their most important changes in the last two years. Have them write about whether it was a pleasant or unpleasant change.

TEACHING ACTIVITY. Be sure students understand that if a major change occurs, such as serious illness or the death of a family member or friend, the best thing to do is to ask for help. Ask students to review what kinds of help are available. List sources of help on a sheet of paper that students may keep.

Dealing with What You Can't Control

Don't underestimate changes you can't control. These changes can affect your relationships with others, your work at school or on the job, and your health.

What can you do? Focus on the things you *can* control. Talk about your feelings. Ask a relative, neighbor, teacher, counselor, or clergy member for advice. Listen to and respect the feelings of other family members.

Above all, be patient with yourself. You can't control everything that happens. You can, however, learn to be flexible.

Choosing Change

Can you think of changes you might choose—now or in the future? When you are older, you will move into your own place. You will choose where and how you will live. You may also choose to marry and have children someday.

The changes you choose—and the timing of your choices—will have an effect on other parts of your life. How will you choose wisely?

CRITICAL THINKING. Have students imagine they are 10 years older. What big changes might they have gone through by then? Ask students to think about whether they expect the changes to be more external or internal.

You may listen to the advice of people close to you. You may read books on the subject. You may make a list of the pros and cons of the change you have in mind. You may search your heart to discover what's right for you. You may think about how the change will fit or affect your personal and career goals.

You may find it helpful to review the seven basic steps of decision making in Chapter 4. You may already be practicing these steps. If so, you'll be prepared when you need to make a major life decision. The process should come naturally to you by then.

Even when you choose to make a change, you won't know exactly what will happen. What you can be sure of is that it will affect every aspect of your life. You should also know that you will make mistakes. Don't panic. You can learn from your mistakes. You can get help if you need it.

Changing Jobs or Careers

Personal changes are one kind of change you will experience throughout your life. You will also face changes at work. In the years to come, you'll continue to discover more about yourself. You'll grow and change. Your experiences, interests, and previous jobs may lead to new job and career choices.

You may decide to change jobs or careers. Some work-related changes you experience, however, may be the result of decisions made by others. What are these unwanted changes, and how can you deal with them?

Losing a Job

Have you ever lost a school election? Been passed over by the swim team? Been replaced by someone else at a job such as baby-sitting, newspaper delivery, or yardwork? How did you feel? In general, no one of any age likes to lose.

People do lose jobs, though. *Figure 16-1* at right describes some of the reasons why.

Reasons for Losing a Job

You are fired.	If you are fired, it's important to find out why. It usually means that your employer wasn't happy with you or your work. That information will be helpful in your job search and next jobs.
Your company is downsizing.	When a company goes through downsizing, it gets rid of jobs. Jobs are cut to make the company more efficient or to cut costs.
You refuse a transfer.	Your employer may want to send you to work in another location. The job might be in another office, city, state, or even in another country. If you are unwilling to go, you may lose your job.
You are laid off.	Some companies lay off workers when business becomes slow. If you are laid off for a long time, you may have to look for other work.
The company is sold.	You may lose your job if your company is sold to another company. The new company is now in charge. It may decide that it doesn't need all the people in your company.

CAPTION ANSWER. Answers will vary.

FIGURE 16-1 | **Working with Charts**

People lose jobs for many reasons. Has anyone you know lost a job for one of these reasons? Which reasons are new to you?

There's a good chance that you'll lose a job at least once during your working career. If you do, you'll probably feel angry, afraid, depressed, or discouraged.

Don't be ashamed of feeling such strong emotions. It's only natural. Don't let these feelings take over, though. Keep your chin up. Remember that losses always present opportunities. You have a chance to make a fresh start. Things may be even better this time around.

Rethinking the Future

If you lose a part-time job, you'll probably find another one. When you're an adult, however, finding a new job won't always be easy. In the end, you may even decide to pursue a new career.

There was a time when most people worked at one job their entire lives. That's no longer true. Many people today change jobs or careers to suit their changing skills and interests. In

The Global Workplace

Coming to the United States Can Be Complicated, Too

Adjusting to customs and routines in the United States can be tricky for the foreign visitor. To make a visitor's stay easier, remember to enunciate clearly and slowly. Use visual aids, and write out numbers and addresses. Learn a few common words or phrases from the visitor's language to make him or her feel more comfortable. Simple steps such as these will make a foreigner's visit much easier and more enjoyable.

Exploration Activity!

Many U.S. companies have offices in foreign countries where they do business. Using the Internet and library resources, research U.S. multinational companies. What are some international companies?

◄ Losing a job is hard. Why might the loss of a job be an opportunity?

CAPTION ANSWER. You get a chance to make a fresh start, which could lead to an even better job.

RESEARCH. Ask students to find a recent magazine article on changes in the workplace due to rapidly changing technology and down-sizing. Have them summarize any suggestions for adapting to change that they can find.

addition, you can no longer count on having the same job or career for your whole life. Jobs and careers are changing rapidly as technology, people's needs, and the world's resources change. Just think about this. Not so long ago, no one had even heard of many of the technology-related jobs we know today. These jobs include Web master and multimedia developer.

Losing a job or being forced to change careers can be a shock. It's a blow to your self-esteem. You may worry about the future or be afraid to try again. Give yourself some time to adjust. Then get ready to rethink your future and revise your career plan! A positive attitude will help you succeed.

Looking for a New Job or Career

The sooner you start, the sooner you'll be working again. To get started, ask yourself these questions:

- What do I want to do next? What new interests might lead me toward a new job or career?
- What skills and abilities do I already have?
- How can I get the education or training I need for a new job or career?
- What new short- and long-term goals will I set for myself?

EXTENDING THE LESSON. Ask students to research the job outlook (in the most recent Bureau of Labor Statistics, for example) for an industry that interests them. Is employment expected to hold steady or to decline? Have students give a short report.

Changes at work happen. You can count on it. Just be prepared and keep an open mind. That can make all the difference when you're faced with job or career changes you did not choose.

Ready for Change?

How can you prepare for change? Think of yourself as a quick change artist! *Figure 16-2* below offers some tips for adjusting to change.

> **FIGURE 16-2**

ADJUSTING TO CHANGE

No matter what changes occur in your life, you will have to adjust to them. Here are some positive tips for adjusting to change. How can you use each tip in your life right now?

A

Plan Ahead

If you know about a change in advance, prepare for it even if you do not want it to happen. It will be easier to adjust to the change. Perhaps you know you'll be transferring to a new school. Find out about the school before your first day. Visit if you can. Talk with people there. You'll feel more comfortable when the first day of school arrives.

B

Share Your Feelings

Use your support group. Talk to friends, family members, or other trusted people. If needed, find someone who's trained to help people with their problems. Teachers, school counselors, coaches, and religious leaders can help you handle change.

Family

C

Find Something Positive About the Change

Looking for something positive can be challenging at times but very rewarding and often surprising. Remember that changes are part of life. They help you grow. Even the most painful changes can be the source of something positive. It does not help to keep thinking about what is wrong or different. What can you learn from the experience?

Friends

D

Learn to Be Supportive

Pay attention to family members, friends, and coworkers. Notice when they are having a hard time. Figure out how you can help. You want people to be there for you. Learn to do the same for them. Reaching out to others will remind you that you're not alone.

Be a Lifelong Learner

Get ready for change by becoming a lifelong learner. You started learning the day you were born. You will continue to learn your entire life—if you are willing. How can you be open to learning? Always be on the lookout for opportunities to learn new things. Know how and where to find the latest information and resources.

Even now, as a student, you can take advantage of learning opportunities outside of school. Look for workshops, special training courses, volunteer opportunities, and other apprenticeships. You'll be amazed at the new things you discover about yourself, work, and other life experiences. The Internet is another rich source of information for people looking for jobs or switching careers.

EXPLORE Activity

Did you know that you are already a lifelong learner? How can you tell? Keep track of how you learn. Do you take classes outside of school? What do you learn from people in your family? Do you read books or the newspaper? What do you watch on television? Every day for a week, record every place or situation in which you learn something. Write down what you've learned in each.

Share your list of learning environments with a few classmates. What learning environments do you have in common? Find one environment on a classmate's list that you never thought of. Think about how you might add it to your list.

Get Support

Another way to prepare for change is to build a support network. Friends, family members, teachers, and counselors can be a great source of support in times of change. You can go to them for advice. They will listen and offer encouragement. They will remind you that you are worthwhile. They will also often tell you the truth as they see it. Other people can be a good resource when you need reassurance or ideas.

While you're at it, think about how you can support other people in your life. It's not a one-way street, you know.

EXPLORE Activity

Who is always there for you? Whom could you go to for support? Start a list on a sheet of paper. Write down the names of people you could turn to. Include their telephone numbers. Jot down why you've listed each person.

Then take this second step if you wish. Talk to or contact each person on your list. Ask if he or she is willing to be part of your support network. Keep your list in your portfolio. Add or subtract names from your list as desired.

CAPTION ANSWER. Answers will vary but may include workshops, special training courses, and volunteer opportunities.

Life is an adventure, filled with surprises. Along the way, you will experience all kinds of changes. Some will make you happy. Others will make you sad. No matter what changes are in store for you, you will have to deal with them. There's no getting around it. Change is part of life. Make the best of it.

▼ It's always worthwhile keeping your skills up-to-date. What learning opportunities do you take advantage of outside of school?

LESSON REVIEW AND ACTIVITIES. See the *Teacher's Manual* for answers.

Vocabulary Review

Imagine you're a counselor. Tomorrow you are scheduled to discuss life changes with a group of teenagers. Write down what you plan to say. Include the terms below in your talk.

stepparent
blended family

Check Your Understanding

Choose the correct answer for each item. Write your answers on a separate sheet of paper.

1. Personal changes beyond a person's control include _____.
   a. death
   b. graduation
   c. school

2. Many changes are _____. You can plan for them.
   a. unexpected
   b. predictable
   c. random

Critical Thinking

On a separate sheet of paper, answer the following questions.

1. What personal changes do you see yourself choosing someday? How might you prepare for them?
2. Painful changes can be the source of something positive. Think of an unwanted change in your life that led to something positive. How did it help you grow?
3. How does being a lifelong learner help you prepare for change?

Connecting to the Workplace

Handling Stress

- John's mother is seriously ill. He is very worried about her. He finds it hard to sleep. He is falling behind at work because he can't concentrate.
- No one at work knows about John's situation at home. His boss is concerned that he is not doing his work. His coworkers are concerned about his health.
- Should John share with others what he is going through? Explain.

Teamwork

What to Do
- Work with one or two classmates—and a school counselor if possible.
- Create a guide for students who are going through difficult personal changes. Your guide should begin with a list of changes young people experience.
- It should provide suggestions for how you can help yourself in each situation.
- It should also give tips for how friends and family members can help.
- Include a list of school and community resources in your guide.

The Future Is Coming

To be in charge of your life, you need to plan for the future. Your plan can start in your head. It works better, though, if you write down your plan. Keep your plan in a safe place, in your portfolio or in a file on your computer. That way, you can refresh your memory by referring to it. You can see how well you're doing. You can also make changes in your plan when you want to.

Make Plans Now

Some people don't like to make plans. Maybe it's because they're afraid that things won't turn out the way they thought. That's not a very positive way to look at life! In fact, the opposite is true. People who plan and set goals for themselves see things happen!

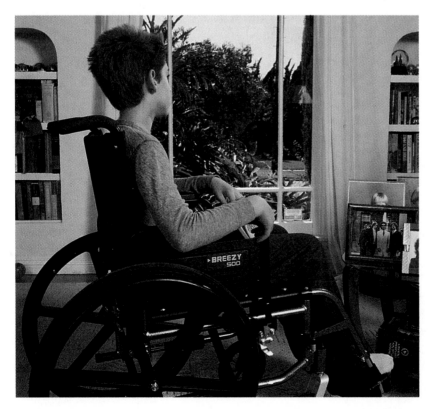

Discover...
- why you should plan for the future.
- the power of positive thinking.
- how you can start to move toward the future.

Why Is It Important to Think About the Future?

The future is coming—whether you're ready or not! If you don't bother to think about the future, it will simply arrive. If you think about it, you can create the kind of life you want.

Key Terms...
- accomplishments
- fulfilling

CAPTION ANSWER. Answers will vary but may include the following: a good education, specific skills, flexibility, a positive attitude.

◀ Thinking about the future? It helps to have a plan and a positive attitude. What else do you need to move toward the future you imagine for yourself?

Have you got a plan? What are you waiting for? Chapter 5 gives you some hints about how to begin. Your plan now may include getting good grades or working part-time during the summer. It may also include graduating from high school or saving money for college. Try to include a career goal in your plan.

A reasonable career goal right now might be to explore several careers that interest you. Talk to people who work in those careers. Do research at the library and on the Internet.

Your ideas about your future may change as you explore careers and other things that interest you. Don't be afraid to change your goals and your plan as you need or want to. That's how it should be. After all, it's your plan!

▲ You can tell this employee really enjoys his work. Why do employers value a positive attitude?

CAPTION ANSWER. Answers will vary but may include the following: because people enjoy being around positive people; a positive attitude can be contagious; a positive attitude makes positive things happen.

MOTIVATING STUDENTS. Ask students if they know someone who seems to be in charge of his or her life. What qualities does this person have? Does this person seem to have a plan for life?

DISCUSSION STARTER. Ask students whether not having a plan for the future means you are spontaneous or irresponsible. Why might people not want to plan? Do students think a plan in the head is the same as a plan written down on paper? Discuss.

Be Positive!

Planning isn't the only way to think about the future. A positive attitude makes the future bright. It increases your chances of reaching any goal you set.

Let's face it. There is always something to complain about. It's raining. You wish you could drive. Your friend is mad at you for no reason. You left your lunch at home. You didn't do well on your last math test. You're tired of your hair. The list goes on and on.

Trade In Your Negative Thoughts

Have you ever thought about trading in your negative thoughts? When you find yourself saying or thinking negative things about yourself or anything else, stop! Replace those negative thoughts with positive ones.

Can you think of someone who has a great attitude? He or she is probably fun to be around. Such people have bad days like anyone else. In general, though, they're upbeat. They try to stay positive.

Most people like to be around positive people. Employers are no exception. Parents look for baby-sitters who like children. Restaurants want to hire people who are friendly to customers. Businesses prefer employees who can stay positive—even under pressure.

EXPLORE Activity

Divide a sheet of paper into two columns. In the left-hand column, write down both positive and negative thoughts you have about yourself. In the right-hand column, list evidence that disproves each negative thought you've listed.

For instance, perhaps you've written "I'm lazy" in the left-hand column. In the right-hand column, list every example you can think of to prove you're *not* lazy. Perhaps you take care of your little brother. Maybe you do chores, play soccer, take piano lessons.

As you list the evidence against each negative thought, think about where the thought comes from. Do you think you're lazy because you don't always finish your homework? That could be a time management problem. Review Chapter 15, and find a way to use your time better.

As you disprove each negative thought, cross it off in the left-hand column of your list. When you've run through the list, read the positive thoughts that remain in both columns. Feel good about yourself!

The RIGHT Attitude!

Winning Gracefully

It's tough enough to be a good loser. But what about a good winner? In school and work, there will be many times when you win something through your good effort. Although you may feel like celebrating, remember to be considerate toward the people around you. Avoid bragging about your good luck or your success at work.

Apply Your Skills!

Role-play with a partner these "winning" situations:
- you land the starring role in a play
- you are elected class president
- you get an "A" on your science project

Making Things Happen

A positive attitude is not only more fun—it makes things happen. Forming positive images helps you take action toward your goals.

Begin by developing positive attitude toward yourself. Take time to notice all your **accomplishments**—everything you do well.

CAPTION ANSWER. Positive thinking helps you take action toward your goals.

◀ Have you heard of the expression "the power of positive thinking"? What does this expression mean to you? Why is it important to be positive?

EXPLORE Activity

Each day for several weeks, write down five of your accomplishments. They may be big or small. At the end of one week, you'll have 35 accomplishments on your list. In three weeks, you'll have 105! Try it. You'll like what you see. You'll also like how you feel.

Count up your accomplishments. Add to them. Remind yourself of them. They will contribute to your positive attitude. They will also help you move forward, into what you see for yourself in the future.

Move Toward Your Vision

In this book, you've taken a look at your interests, your values, your skills, your aptitudes, and your personality. You've started to explore careers. You've taken a peek inside the world of work. You've learned about making decisions and making plans. You've practiced setting both short- and long-term goals.

You can use the information in this book now. You can also turn to it later when you look for a full-time job and plan your career.

CAREER OPPORTUNITIES

Transportation
Did you ever wonder how food gets to the supermarket? What about the clothes at a department store? Usually, a truck driver brings such items to the appropriate store.

Critical Thinking
Make a list of a truck driver's responsibilities. How does safety rank in the list?

Truck Driver

Distributor of industrial plastics needs experienced driver for 20-foot straight truck. Must be over 21 years of age and have a valid driver's license and an excellent driving record. Class C required. Because of safety concerns, we conduct preemployment drug screening.

There's No Time Like the Present

The present is the perfect place to start thinking about the future. It's where you begin to take steps toward your goals. It's where you can really make a difference.

Many people worry so much about the future that they can't act in the present. You learned about the importance of goal-setting in Chapters 5 and 12. Goals help you act. They also help you stay in the present, because each step begins there.

As you set your personal and career goals, remember the importance of small steps. If you move too fast toward a goal, it's easy to skip important steps. It's like trying to run a marathon when you've never run a mile.

Each small step toward a personal goal or a career goal is a small victory. That feeling of success encourages you to take another small step. Before you know it, you've arrived!

Exploring Possibilities

The world isn't discovered only by famous explorers. You're an important explorer too. You explore your own personal world as well as the world you share with other people.

Step by step, you're exploring the world around you. You may discover a career that no one else has ever imagined. You may invent something or do something that changes people's lives.

Right now you're exploring a world of possibilities, including many possible careers. Expect the best as you go forward. Expect your life to be happy. Expect to have loving relationships. Expect to succeed in school. Expect to find **fulfilling,** or satisfying, work in a job you love. Last but not least, expect that you have something special to offer the world, because you do.

▼ You've just begun to explore the world of possibilities before you. What tools or techniques can you use to explore careers?

LESSON REVIEW AND ACTIVITIES. See the *Teacher's Manual* for answers.

Vocabulary Review

In a two-page essay, describe what makes your life fulfilling now. Also imagine yourself 20 years from now. Explain what you want your accomplishments to include. Use the terms below in your essay.

accomplishments   fulfilling

Check Your Understanding

Choose the correct answer for each item. Write your answers on a separate sheet of paper.

1. People who plan and set _____ for themselves see things happen.
   a. goals
   b. dreams
   c. traps

2. A _____ can make things happen.
   a. negative attitude
   b. positive attitude
   c. responsible person

3. You should start thinking about your future _____.
   a. when you're an adult
   b. now
   c. after you graduate

4. As you set your personal and career goals, it's important to remember to _____.
   a. take large steps
   b. skip important steps
   c. take small steps

Critical Thinking

On a separate sheet of paper, answer the following questions.

1. What are you doing now to plan for the future?
2. How does a positive attitude help you reach goals?
3. Why is it important to focus on what you can do in the present?

Connecting to the Workplace

Developing a Positive Attitude

- Think of a job that interests you. With a partner, role-play how a person with a positive attitude would act in the job you've chosen.
- Then role-play a person with a negative attitude in the same job.

Community Involvement

What to Do

- What might a positive attitude do for your community? Promote having a positive attitude by making posters, buttons, or flyers to spread around your community.
- Think of catchy slogans to feature in the format you choose.

Investigating Career Clusters

Transportation

What Is the Transportation Cluster?

Occupations in this cluster involve the movement of people and goods from one place to another. Jobs center around areas such as highway, airborne, and rail transportation.

Skills Needed

Attention to rules and procedures, coordination skills, good vision, mechanical skills, and physical skills

THE FACTS	Types of Careers in This Cluster	Work Description	Career Outlook	Education
	Truck driver	Pick up goods from factories and deliver them to warehouses, terminals, or stores	Average	CDL*, On-the-job training
	Pilot	Transport passengers, cargo and mail; spray crops; test aircraft; take aerial photographs	Slower than average	Bachelor's, Commercial pilot's license
	Air traffic controller	Keep track of the planes flying in the air, regulate air traffic in and out of airports	Slower than average	Bachelor's, Training program
	Locomotive engineer	Operate machinery, interpret signals, be responsible for the safety of the train	Slower than average	H.S. diploma, On-the-job training
	Bus driver	Collect fares, issue transfers, and drive route	Good	CDL*, On-the-job training
	Subway operator	Operate subways transporting people throughout the city and suburbs	Faster than average	H.S. diploma, On-the-job training

---

Research Activity

Investigate transportation careers of interest. Make a list of five, and research the job duties and necessary skills for those jobs. Report your findings on a chart. Do you see any patterns in work skills? Write a few sentences about what skills are necessary for all transportation occupations.

---

*Commercial driver's license

CHAPTER REVIEW. See the *Teacher's Manual* for answers.

▶ Chapter Highlights

- Personal changes beyond your control, such as divorce or death, can be difficult to deal with. It is important to seek help for difficult personal changes when needed.
- Planning is a good way to create a bright future for yourself. Your plan may include both personal and career goals.

▶ Recalling Key Concepts

Using complete sentences, answer the following questions on a separate sheet of paper.

1. What are some personal changes you might choose?
2. Why might you lose a job?
3. Who besides friends and family members can help you adjust to change?
4. What do you need to do to be in charge of your life?
5. When can you make things happen—in the present or the future? Explain.

▶ Thinking Critically

1. Why do you think change makes people nervous and uneasy?
2. When could you have helped yourself adjust to change by planning ahead?
3. How can you create a fulfilling life for yourself?
4. Would you call yourself a positive person? Why or why not?
5. What do you imagine you will be doing in the future?

Building Skills

1. Thinking Skills—Seeing Things in the Mind's Eye

Think about how you could make your community a better place. Come up with a plan that includes all the details. Break down your plan into small, manageable parts. List the small tasks needed to accomplish your goal.

2. Basic—Writing

Read a book about someone who made a difference in the world, such as Mother Teresa, Gandhi, or Dr. Martin Luther King, Jr. What goals did they have? What steps did they take to achieve their goals? Write a book review that answers these questions.

3. Interpersonal— Teaches Others

Create or locate a picture book for younger students about life changes they may experience. Such changes may include divorce, remarriage, moving, illness, and death. Share your book with elementary school students.

Applying Academic Skills

1. Language Arts

Write a rap or poem that talks positively about your future. Include details about the kind of work you'll be doing. You might also include your accomplishments. Tape record it to keep and play back some years from now.

2. The Arts

Choose a medium for celebrating your accomplishments. When you complete your art project, share it with a friend or family member. Then display it in your bedroom so you can be reminded of your accomplishments.

Discovery Portfolio

Focus on Change
- Make a list of the changes that you might face in the future.
- Determine which changes are predictable and which may be unplanned.
- Discuss how you will handle each of these changes when they occur.
- Keep your list in your portfolio for future use.

Career Exploration: Transportation

Select a career you find interesting from the transportation career cluster.
- Use library resources and the Internet to find out about the career.
- If possible, also gather information through interviews.
- Then write a description of the career. Include information about the kinds of work, the working conditions, and training and education required. Also, include skills needed to do the job.
- Explain the outlook for the career.
- Include other interesting information in your description.
- Give an oral report on the career.

Glossary

A

accomplishments   Everything a person does well. (p. 353)

active listening   Listening and responding with full attention to what's being said. (p. 201)

addiction   A physical or psychological need for a substance. (p. 229)

annual report   A summary of a company's business for the year. (p. 118)

aptitude   A person's ability to learn something. (p. 9)

assess   To judge. (p. 189)

attitude   A person's basic outlook on life. (p. 68)

audience   Anyone who receives information. (p. 199)

B

balance   The situation when opposite sides or parts of something have the same weight, amount, or force. (p. 318)

benefits   The "extras" an employer provides in addition to pay. (p. 155)

blended family   The family that forms when two single parents with children marry. (p. 339)

body language   The gestures, posture, and eye contact people use to express themselves. (p. 140)

budget   A plan for saving and spending money. (p. 298)

business plan   A document that gives specific information about a business, including its goals, the goods or services it will offer, and a description of its customers. (p. 284)

C

capitalism   The free enterprise system. (p. 273)

career   One or more jobs in the same area of interest. (p. 26)

career clusters   Groups of careers that have similar job characteristics. (p. 43)

career interest areas   General kinds of activities people do in many different careers. (p. 45)

chronological order   Time order, or the order in which events happen. (p. 96)

classifieds   Newspaper advertisements organized in classes, or groups. (p. 110)

commission   Earnings based on how much a worker sells. (p. 155)

communication   The exchange of information between senders and receivers. (p. 198)

compromise   To give up something to settle a disagreement. (p 179)

conflict   A strong disagreement. (p. 177)

conflict resolution   A step-by-step process used to settle disagreements. (p. 179)

consumers   People who buy and use goods and services. (p. 274)

contact list   A list of people one knows and will contact to build a network. (p. 107)

context clues   Hints about the meaning of unfamiliar words or phrases provided by the words surrounding them. (p. 205)

cooperate   To work with others on the job to reach a common goal. (p. 161)

cover letter   A one-page letter a job seeker sends along with a résumé telling who he or she is and why he or she is sending a résumé. (p. 131)

coworkers   People who work together in the workplace. (p. 151)

D

database   A software program that stores data, or information, in different ways for easy searching, sorting, and organizing. (p. 114)

decision   A choice one makes about what action to take. (p. 62)

decision-making process   A series of steps used to identify and evaluate choices to arrive at a decision. (p. 70)

demand   The amount of goods and services that consumers want to buy. (p. 278)

disability   A condition such as blindness, a visual or hearing impairment, or paralysis. (p. 158)

discriminate   To treat someone unfairly because of race, age, gender, religious beliefs, nationality, physical appearance, or disability. (p. 158)

E

eating disorder   A pattern of extreme eating behavior over time. (p. 228)

economics   The study of how people produce, distribute, and use goods and services. (p. 273)

economic system   A country's way of using resources to provide goods and services that its people need and want. (p. 273)

economy   The ways people make, buy, and sell goods and services. (p. 32)

emergency   A serious event that happens without warning and calls for quick action. (p. 238)

emoticons   Groups of keyboard symbols designed to show a writer's feelings. (p. 217)

empathize   To see things from another person's point of view and to understand his or her situation. (p. 176)

employee   Someone who works for a person or business for pay. (p. 150)

employer   A person or business that pays a person or group of people to work. (p. 115)

entrepreneur   A person who organizes and runs a business. (p. 281)

entry-level   Lower-level. (p. 154)

ethics   The rules of behavior that govern a group or society. (p. 163)

exchange   A trade of one item for another. (p. 309)

exploratory interview   A short, informal talk with someone in a career that one finds interesting. (p. 54)

F

F.I.C.A.   The Federal Insurance Contribution Act, a law having to do with Social Security taxes. (p. 297)

Glossary

first aid The actions taken in a physical emergency before help arrives. (p. 241)

fixed expenses Expenses that people have already agreed to pay and that must be paid by a particular date. (p. 300)

flexible expenses Expenses that come irregularly or that people can adjust more easily than fixed expenses. (p. 300)

Food Guide Pyramid A guideline for the nutrients a person needs each day. (p. 226)

format The arrangement of something, such as a document. (p. 129)

free enterprise A type of economic system in which individuals or businesses may buy and sell and set prices with little government control. (p. 273)

fulfilling Satisfying. (p. 355)

full-time At least 40 hours a week. (p. 27)

G

global economy All the world's economies and how they are linked. (p. 32)

goods Items that people buy. (p. 32)

gross pay Total pay. (p. 295)

H

health The condition of one's body and mind. (p. 224)

hygiene All the things people do to be clean and healthy. (p. 228)

I

images Pictures. (p. 208)

impulse buying Making a sudden, unplanned decision to buy. (p. 305)

income The amount of money a person receives or earns regularly. (p. 294)

income tax Tax paid on income. (p. 295)

initiative The willingness to do what needs to be done without being told to do it. (p. 162)

interest The money banks pay depositors for the use of their money. (p. 301)

interest inventory A checklist that points to one's strongest interests. (p. 4)

interests Favorite activities. (p. 2)

internship A formally defined temporary, position, usually unpaid, that requires a greater commitment of time than volunteering. (p. 88)

interview A formal meeting between a job seeker and an employer about a possible job. (p. 135)

J

job Work that a person does for pay. (p. 26)

job application A form that asks questions about a job seeker's skills, work experience, education, and interests. (p. 133)

job lead Information about a job opening. (p. 105)

job market The need for workers and the kinds of work available to them. (p. 32)

job shadowing Following a person on the job for a few days to learn about a particular career. (p. 55)

L

learning styles   The different ways that people naturally think and learn. (p. 14)

leisure   Time to do what one likes. (p. 318)

letter of resignation   A formal letter that explains why and when an employee is leaving his or her job. (p. 264)

lifestyle   The way a person uses his or her time, energy, and other resources. (p. 27)

long-term goal   A goal that takes a long time to reach. (p. 93)

M

marketing   The process of getting goods and services to consumers, including packaging, shipping, advertising, and selling goods and services. (p. 284)

mathematics   The study of numbers, quantities, measurements, and shapes. (p. 211)

mediator   Someone who helps two opposing people or groups compromise or reach an agreement. (p. 179)

medium-term goal   A goal that is more challenging and takes longer to achieve than a short-term goal. (p. 93)

minimum wage   The lowest hourly wage an employer can legally pay for a worker's services. (p. 156)

N

netiquette   The accepted rules of conduct when using the Internet. (p. 216)

net pay   Take-home pay. (p. 295)

networking   Communicating with people you know or can get to know to share information and advice. (p. 105)

notice   An official written statement that one is leaving one's job. (p. 262)

nutrients   The substances in food that the body needs to produce energy and stay healthy. (p. 225)

O

obstacle   Something that stands in the way of a decision or action. (p. 63)

Occupational Safety and Health Administration (OSHA)   A special branch of the U.S. Department of Labor in charge of setting safety standards and inspecting places of work to see that the standards are being followed. (p. 237)

orientation   A program that introduces new employees to their new company and its policies and procedures, or ways of doing things. (p. 151)

outcome   The result or effect of a decision or action. (p. 68)

overtime   Extra pay for each hour worked beyond 40 hours a week. (p. 154)

P

part-time job   A job in which a person works up to 30 hours a week. (p. 88)

performance reviews   Meetings between an employee and his or her supervisor to evaluate how well the employee is doing his or her job. (p. 166)

personality The combination of an individual's attitudes, behaviors, and characteristics. (p. 13)

prejudice A negative attitude toward a person or group that is not based on facts or reason. (p. 178)

previewing Reading only the parts of a written work that outline or summarize its content. (p. 204)

prioritize To put in order from first to last or from most important to least important. (p. 84)

procrastinate To put off deciding or acting. (p. 84)

producers Individuals or companies that make or provide goods and services. (p. 274)

profit The amount of money left after a business pays its expenses. (p. 276)

promotion A job advancement to a position of greater responsibility and authority. (p. 252)

purpose Overall goal or reason. (p. 199)

R

raise An increase in pay. (p. 252)

references People who will recommend a job seeker to an employer. (p. 133)

referral Someone to whom one has been referred, or directed, who may have information about a job or job opening. (p. 108)

refund The return of money in exchange for a purchased item. (p. 309)

register To officially sign up as a qualified voter. (p. 328)

regulate Set rules for. (p. 273)

relationships A person's connections or dealings with other people. (p. 174)

research Investigating a subject and gathering information about it. (p. 50)

respect Consideration. (p. 174)

résumé A summary of a job seeker's personal information, describing education, skills, work experience, activities, and interests. (p. 127)

S

salary A fixed amount of pay for a certain period of time. (p. 155)

school-to-work program A program that brings schools and businesses together so that students can gain work experience and training. (p. 111)

science Knowledge about things in nature and the universe. (p. 211)

sedentary Spending much time sitting. (p. 227)

self-esteem Recognition and regard for oneself and one's abilities. (p. 177)

services Activities people do for others for a fee. (p. 32)

short-term goal A goal to start working on right away. (p. 93)

skill The ability a person develops to do something he or she has learned. (p. 9)

skimming Reading through a book or document quickly, picking out main ideas and key points. (p. 204)

Social Security A federal government program that provides benefits for people of all ages. (p. 296)

spreadsheet A software program that arranges information, usually numbers, in rows and columns or displays information in graphs and other formats. (p. 215)

stepparent The spouse of one's mother or father following her or his remarriage. (p. 339)

stress The mental or physical tension that is the body's natural response to conflict. (p. 230)

subject Main topic or key idea. (p. 200)

supervisor The person who checks and evaluates the work of an employee. (p. 152)

supply The amount of goods and services available for sale. (p. 278)

T

team planning A process that involves setting goals, assigning tasks, and communicating regularly with others on a team. (p. 186)

technology The use of ideas, methods, tools, and materials to get things done. (p. 3)

temporary job A part-time or full-time job that lasts only a short while, such as for a couple of weeks or months. (p. 89)

time management Choosing how to spend one's time and creating a schedule for one's choices. (p. 321)

V

values The ideas a person lives by and the beliefs that are important to that person. (p. 6)

volunteering Working without pay. (p. 55)

W

wages A fixed amount of money paid for each hour worked. (p. 153)

warranty A guarantee that a product meets certain standards of quality. (p. 308)

withhold To take out. (p. 295)

workers' compensation A state-run program that gives injured workers financial help to cover lost wages and medical expenses. (p. 237)

work permit A document needed by workers under 16 and sometimes by those under 18, showing that the young person knows the limits on the number of hours young people can work and on the kinds of jobs they can hold. (p. 104)

workplace Another name for the work world; any place where work is done. (p. 33)

Page numbers given in *italics* refer to charts or illustrations.

Index

Index

Index

Index

Index

Index B

Page numbers given in *italics* refer to charts or illustrations.

School-to-Work Applications and Connections

Photos

Lori Adamski Peek/Tony Stone Images 222–223;
Bill Aron/PhotoEdit 116, 351;
Bruce Ayres/Tony Stone Images 156, 341;
Davis Barber/PhotoEdit 131;
Daniel Bosler/Tony Stone Images 313(B);
Bozell Worldwide 209;
Michelle Bridwell/PhotoEdit 193(B), 331;
Robert Burke/Tony Stone Images 80–81;
B. Busco/The Image Bank 47;
Gary Buss/FPG International 42;
Peter D. Byron/PhotoEdit 121(T);
Jose Carrillo/PhotoEdit 308, 319;
Frank Cezus/Tony Stone Images 270–271;
Stewart Cohen/Tony Stone Images 24, 333(B), 349;
Gary A. Conner/PhotoEdit 279;
David K. Crow/PhotoEdit 174;
Jim Cummins/FPG International 219(B);
Robert E. Daemmrich/Tony Stone Images 152, 176;
Mary Kate Denny/PhotoEdit 62, 82, 185, 229, 283;
Digital Stock 127, 133, 146, 147, 252;
Myrleen Ferguson/PhotoEdit 92, 162, 175;
David Frazier/Tony Stone Images 357;
Tony Freeman/PhotoEdit 186, 189, 278, 327, 328;
Stephen Frink/Tony Stone Images 267(B);
Tim Fuller Photography 26–27;
Mark Gamba/Stock Market 236;
Glencoe Stock 21, 39, 59, 79, 101, 123, 147, 171, 195, 221, 245, 269, 291, 315, 335, 359;
Spencer Grant/PhotoEdit 9, 239, 251, 260, 307, 339;
Jeff Greenberg/PhotoEdit 2, 219(T), 243(T);
Jeff Greenberg/Visuals Unlimited 77(T);
Howard Grey/Tony Stone Images 106, 289(B);
Charles Gupton/Tony Stone Images 47, 57(B);
Chris Hamilton/Stock Market 316–317;
Bob Handelman/Tony Stone Images 124–125;
Mark Harmel/FPG International 30;
John Henley/Stock Market 121(B);
C. P. Hickman/Visuals Unlimited 143(T);
Walter Hodges/Tony Stone Images 277, 357;
Willie Holdman/International Stock 157;
Billy Hustace/Tony Stone Images 57(T);
Richard Hutchings/PhotoEdit 178, 304;
David Joel/Tony Stone Images 193(T);
Kaluzny/Thatcher/Tony Stone Images 299;
Bonnie Kamin/PhotoEdit 22–23, 169(T), 169(B), 338;
Hal Kern/International Stock 157;
Mitch Kezar/Tony Stone Images 237;
Michael Krasowitz/FPG International 135;
Dick Luria/FPG International 259;
David Madison/Tony Stone Images 234;
Felicia Martinez/PhotoEdit 70;
Tom McCarthy/PhotoEdit 84;
Patti McConville/The Image Bank 47;
Lawrence Migdale/Tony Stone Images 37(T);

David E. Myers/Tony Stone Images 32;
Michael Newman/PhotoEdit 18(B), 50, 52, 54, 111, 142, 158, 160, 177, 252, 255, 257, 267(T), 274;
Jonathan Nourok/PhotoEdit 71;
Novastock/PhotoEdit 224;
Objectgear 20, 38, 39, 97, 100, 195, 221, 227, 265, 314;
Dominic Oldeshaw 4–5, 94–95, 116–117, 240–241;
José L. Palaez/Stock Market 47, 77(B);
Greg Pease/Tony Stone Images 99(B);
Steven Peters/Tony Stone Images 157;
Photodisc 14, 21, 34, 43, 53, 58, 59, 68, 75, 78, 79, 89, 90, 96, 97, 101, 115, 122, 123, 163, 170, 171, 187, 188, 194, 200, 202, 214, 215, 220, 235, 244, 245, 249, 250, 254, 260, 268, 269, 283, 290, 291, 295, 306, 308, 315, 321, 330, 331, 334, 335, 340–342, 353, 358, 359;
Rick Poley/Visuals Unlimited 143(B);
Larry Prosor/SuperStock International 336–337;
A. Ramey/PhotoEdit 184;
Patrick Ramsey/International Stock 46;
Mark Richards/PhotoEdit 154, 183, 248, 333(T);
Jon Riley/Tony Stone Images 99(T), 102–103;
Elena Rooraid/PhotoEdit 345;
James Shaffer/PhotoEdit 55;
Ian Shaw/Tony Stone Images 205, 208;
Frank Siteman/PhotoEdit 28;
Frank Siteman/Tony Stone Images 48;
Don Smetzer/Tony Stone Images 148–149, 352;
Jeff Smith/PhotoSmith 140–141, 180–181, 206-207, 284–285, 310–311, 322–323;
Inga Spence/Visuals Unlimited 37(B);
Don Spiro/Tony Stone Images 289(T);
Bruce Stoddard/FPG International 313(T);
SuperStock International 167;
Telegraph Colour Library/FPG International 1, 13, 40–41;
Arthur Tilley/FPG International, 226, 281;
Steve Torregrossa 64–65, 262–263, 346–347;
Robert Torrez/Tony Stone Images 126;
Penny Tweedie/Tony Stone Images 198;
Dana White/PhotoEdit 292–293;
Keith Wood/Tony Stone Images 243(B);
Ted Wood/Tony Stone Images 172–173;
David Young-Wolff/PhotoEdit 9, 11, 46, 72, 108, 113, 136, 138, 150, 196–197, 204, 211, 228, 230, 258, 272, 294, 305, 306, 318, 324, 326, 355;
David Young-Wolff/Tony Stone Images 18(T), 60–61, 104, 157, 246–247

Illustrations

Morgan-Cain Associates 3, 4–5, 6, 10, 15, 25, 26–27, 34, 35, 44, 46–47, 64–65, 67, 74, 86, 87, 94–95, 97, 107, 109, 114, 116–117, 128, 129, 132, 140–141, 156–157, 164, 180–181, 191, 201, 203, 206–207, 213, 217, 225, 231, 240–241, 253, 262–263, 264, 275, 284–285, 287, 296, 301, 302, 310–311, 322–323, 343, 346–347